Acclaim for James Reston, Jr.'s

DOGS OF GOD

"Colorful and readable. . . . Reston paints a vivid picture of a myriad of Christian, Jewish and Muslim characters playing out the dramas of fifteenth-century Spain."   —*Jerusalem Post*

"Engaging, richly-detailed and well-researched. . . . An important book. . . . The apocalyptic, blood-soaked Spain of the fifteenth century—the most powerful nation in the world at that time—is not merely the past, but a warning for us about where our own choices may be leading us."   —*Albany Times Union*

"A vividly told narrative history."   —*The Guardian* (London)

"Isabella, Columbus and the Moorish leaders are presented in a manner that makes them more than simply icons on a page—their strengths, weaknesses, desires and goals are portrayed as a literary character's would be, making their stories far more interesting. . . . Perhaps the most universally approachable work on the subject and a fascinating read."   —*Edge* (Boston)

"Riveting. . . . Rarely has medieval history seemed so urgent."
                    —*Kirkus Reviews*

"Reston portrays a vivid sequence of events set in Spain, Portugal and Italy, teeming with detail and color."   —*Scotland on Sunday*

"A highly entertaining, thoughtful and complex narrative that both introduces and analyzes a greatly misunderstood era." —*Publishers Weekly*

"Speaks volumes about the importance of the separation of church and state, the evils of religious terrorism and the power of fear. . . . As readable and captivating as a good novel."   —*The Flint Journal*

JAMES RESTON, JR.

DOGS of GOD

James Reston, Jr., is the author of thirteen books, including *Warriors of God*, *The Last Apocalypse*, and *Galileo: A Life*. He has written articles for *The New Yorker*, *Esquire*, *Vanity Fair*, *Time*, *Rolling Stone*, and many other publications; three plays; and the scripts for three *Frontline* documentaries. He lives in Chevy Chase, Maryland.

DOGS OF GOD

COLUMBUS, THE INQUISITION, AND THE DEFEAT OF THE MOORS

JAMES RESTON, JR.

ANCHOR BOOKS
A Division of Random House, Inc.
New York

FIRST ANCHOR BOOKS EDITION, OCTOBER 2006

Copyright © 2005 by James Reston, Jr.

All rights reserved. Published in the United States by Anchor Books, a division
of Random House, Inc., New York, and in Canada by Random House
of Canada Limited, Toronto. Originally published in hardcover in the United States
by Doubleday, a division of Random House, Inc., New York, in 2005.

Anchor Books and colophon are registered trademarks of Random House, Inc.

The Library of Congress has cataloged the Doubleday edition as follows:
Reston, James, 1941–
Dogs of God : Columbus, the Inquisition, and the defeat
of the Moors / by James Reston, Jr.—1st ed.
Includes bibliographical references and index.
1. Inquisition—Spain.   2. Muslims—Spain—To 1500.   3. Spain—History—
Ferdinand and Isabella, 1479–1516.   4. Columbus, Christopher.   I. Title.
BX1735.R46 2005
946'.03—dc22   2005045461

Anchor ISBN-10: 1-4000-3191-5
Anchor ISBN-13: 978-1-4000-3191-7

Author photograph © Alan Hart
Book design by Deborah Kerner
Maps designed by David Cain

www.anchorbooks.com

R.F.R.

and

T.B.R.

with love

CONTENTS

❖

PRINCIPAL CHARACTERS

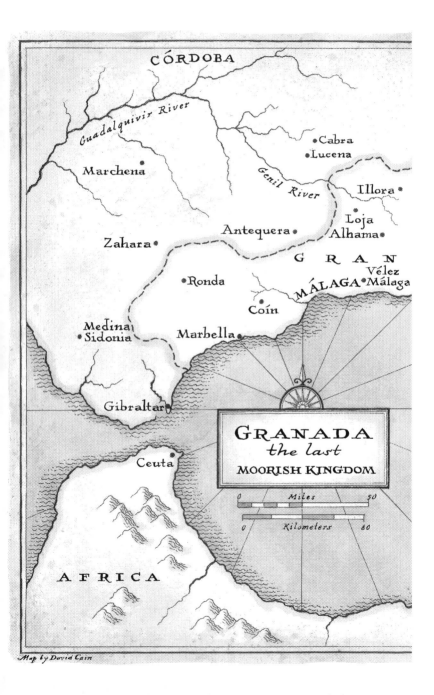

Map by David Cain

JAÉN

Vélez
Blanco

Baza

Moclín

Darro River

Guadix

Andarax River

Granada

SIERRA NEVADA

ALPUJARRAS

A D A

ALMERÍA

Salobreña
Motril

Adra

Almuñécar

Santiago de
Compostela

ASTURIAS

León

NAVARRE

Pamplona

Baiona

Astorga

Burgos

ARAGON

Bragança

Valladolid

Zaragoza

Zamora
Salamanca

Segovia

Tarragona

Barcelona

CATALONIA

Tortosa

CASTILE

Madrid

Teruel

PORTUGAL

EXTREMADURA

Plasencia
Toledo

Guadalupe

La Guardia

Valencia

ROCK OF
SINTRA

Lisbon
Évora

S P A I N

Córdoba

Murcia

ALGARVE
Lagos

Huelva

ANDALUCÍA

Seville

Guadix

POINT
OF SAGRES

Palos

Antequera

Granada

Cádiz

Ronda

GRANADA

Almería

Málaga

Gibraltar

SPAIN
in 1492

0   Miles   100

0   Kilometers 200

DOGS OF GOD

GRANADA, SPAIN

 From my terrace in the ancient Arabic barrio of Albaicín, I look across the Darro River to the great red palace of the Alhambra and then down the narrow gorge to the rotund Gothic Royal Chapel, shaped to suggest a crown, where King Ferdinand and Queen Isabella are buried. On the side of the chapel these days a banner hangs to commemorate the 500th anniversary of Queen Isabella's death, and there is talk again of her beatification as a saint of the Roman Catholic Church.

No banners hang on the Alhambra to commemorate the final defeat in 1492 of the glorious, lost culture that was the Caliphate of the Moors. There are, however, other reminders. The memory of the gruesome train bombings in Madrid this year is still fresh and raw. Just as the perpetrators of the crimes of September 11 invoked the Christian Crusades of the eleventh and twelfth centuries, the Islamic perpetrators of the Madrid atrocity sought to justify their mass murder partly by invoking the defeat of the ancient Moors. The crime was supposed to be a long-overdue act of historical revenge for the attack on Muslims in Al Andalus (as the Moorish Caliphate was known).

"You know the Spanish crusade against Muslims and the expulsions from Al Andalus are not so long ago," the Al Qaeda spokesman said, in taking responsibility.

Far-fetched, hollow, and sinister as this rationale sounds to Westerners, it is important to appreciate that historical resentments are deeply and sincerely felt in the Islamic world. The conflict between the Catholic monarchs of fifteenth-century Spain and the Moorish caliphs of Granada was a holy war between Christianity and Islam. Its ferocity and passion were no less than that of the Crusades or, for that matter, of the conflict that has been allowed to develop in the Middle East today between the West and the Arab world, between Christianity and Islam. Undeniably, in the fertile imagination of some Arab activists, the recapture of Al Andalus for Islam is coupled with the termination of the state of Israel and the end of the American occupation of Iraq. Given the splendor of Moorish culture, this fantasy can have broad emotional appeal.

The Alhambra and the Royal Chapel are the physical monuments to the epic events that happened here in the extraordinary, seminal year of 1492. In the Tower of the Comares across the way, in the exquisite, ethereal Hall of the Ambassadors, it is said that Columbus received his final instructions for his adventure across the Ocean Sea. No artistic bricks or statuary exist to praise or mourn the two-hundred Jewish families who lived in Granada and who were expelled from Spain a few months before Columbus received his royal authority. But when Columbus made his way from Granada to Seville and then on to Palos, from whence he departed for the New World, the roads must have been clogged with Jews departing Spain, scattering across sea and border in response to the Edict of Expulsion of Ferdinand and Isabella and their Inquisition. Columbus sailed on the day after the date set by the Inquisition as the final deadline for the departure from Spanish soil of all Spanish Jews, the fabled Sephardim. The betrayal and suffering of Sephardic Jews comes down to us today as both catastrophe and prologue.

In fact, it is little appreciated, especially by Americans, how intimately the discovery of the New World is bound up with the victory of Christianity over Islam in the so-called Spanish Reconquest, with the expulsion of Spanish Jews, with the terrible Spanish Inquisition, and with the papacy of a Borgia pope. In this book I have tried to make those links. It is one of the enduring ironies of this period that the barbaric, medieval institution of the Spanish Inquisition contributed greatly to the founding of the first modern "nation-state."

The inclination to ignore or downplay these connections continues today. In the years before the millennium of 2000, the Vatican promised to "purify its history" by looking into the dark corners of its past, such as the inquisitional trial and imprisonment of Galileo in the seventeenth century. Despite this, in June 2004, the Holy See announced that the Spanish Inquisition was really not as bad as it has been portrayed. Fewer witches were burned at the stake, its pronouncement read, and fewer heretics were tortured into conversion than had been previously thought. "Vatican Downsizes the Inquisition" was the headline in the *New York Times*. Purifying in 1998 turned to sanitizing in 2004.

It has been suggested that the three most important years in American history are 1492, 1776, and 1865. Of these, 1492 goes far beyond American history. It is pivotal as well in Spanish history, in Jewish and Arab history, in World and Church history. Indeed, it is difficult to imagine another single year in the past millennium when so many significant strands of history came together and so changed the world in one swoop: the completion of the 500-year movement to conquer the Moors, the end of the 800-year reign of the glorious culture of Islamic Spain, the consolidation of the modern Spanish state, the sinister explosion of the Spanish Inquisition, the Spanish renaissance in art and literature, the expulsion of the Jews, the discovery of the New World, and the subsequent division of the world between Spanish and Portuguese spheres of influence.

Fourteen hundred ninety-two is a year that can aptly be called apocalyptic both in the original meaning of the word, as revelation or disclosure, and in its more modern usage of colossal calamity. That so many important forces of history converged at one time inevitably begs the question whether the hand of God was at work in the confluence. To the Christians, the Arabs, and the Jews of the late fifteenth century alike, there was no doubt. Such great and terrible things do not happen simultaneously at random. Providence had to be involved, and the major players were merely God's instruments, either for glory or for disaster.

I have woven here a tapestry of the years leading up to 1492 and of the forces that came together in that apocalyptic year. This is not history in the traditional sense; I have not included every fact and date. It is the converging strands that concern me. The story begins with the courtship and fortuitous marriage of Ferdinand and Isabella. Their union unites the principal provinces of Spain, Castile, and Aragon. The story proceeds with the challenge of Portugal's pretenders to the succession of the Spanish throne.

This epic is spun from the elements of event and character. The major players are giants. Beside the monarchs there is Christopher Columbus; Tomás de Torquemada, the incarnation of the Spanish Inquisition; Boabdil the Unfortunate, the last king of the Moors; João II of Portugal, who missed his chance to sponsor Columbus; the court rabbis Don Isaac Abravanel and Don Abraham Senior; Enrique IV, Isabella's predecessor and fay half brother; and Cardinal Rodrigo Borgia, later Pope Alexander VI. The lesser players are no less interesting. They include El Zagal the Valiant One, the great Moorish warrior; the marquis of Cádiz, who was the very paragon of medieval chivalry; the Florentine firebrand, Girolamo Savonarola; and the Cardinal of Spain, Pedro González de Mendoza, who was called "the third king of Spain."

The human qualities of these characters—piety, greed, bravery, weakness, bigotry, obsession, forbearance, persistence, cruelty, blindness, artistry, and decadence—had an immense influence on how the history unfolded. By no means does Columbus dominate this story, as his voyages have sometimes been allowed to do in American education. I have tried to bring to life this marble man, to put him in his proper context in the events of late fifteenth-century Spain. His shortcomings make his accomplishment no less heroic. For him to have emerged triumphant from this cauldron is truly extraordinary.

Across the way and down the gorge of history, the bells of the Royal Chapel ring out the hours sonorously. In this dry season the wind comes off the plain, across the ocher, tiled roofs of the town, and up my narrow valley. In the distance dogs bark, and the sound echoes off the medieval wall above me, and back down the abyss. And in the evening, the Alhambra is luminous.

JAMES RESTON, JR.

AUGUST 2004

· PART I ·

CONFLUENCE

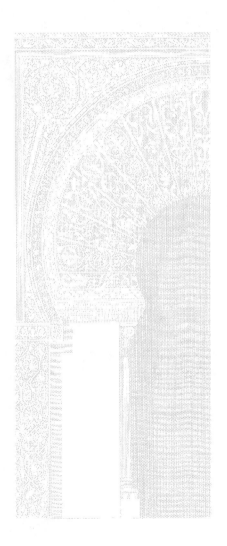

The Land of the Infidel

IBERIA

Castile, that flat expanse of tableland in central Spain, some 300 miles across, derives its lovely, lilting name from the Spanish word *castillos*, or castles, for so many of these daunting crenellated bastions dot its windswept steppe. From the tenth century onward, they had been built one by one as a protection against the ferocious Moors to the south.

With its principal towns of Ávila, Burgos, Segovia, and Valladolid, the territory of Old Castile was first to be liberated from the Mohammedan horde that had swept north into the Iberian peninsula in the eighth century. In pushing the infidels back, Ferdinand I established his kingdom in A.D. 1037. Not many years later, the province of León to the north was joined to it, and the Kingdom of Castile and León made its capital at Burgos. In the decades after Ferdinand I's death in 1065, the kingdom was expanded south. Toledo was captured in 1085, and Ciudad Real, Cuenca, Guadalajara, and Madrid were taken soon after. By the beginning of the twelfth century, the forces of Christianity were making steady progress in taking back from the Moors land claimed by the Church. The process became known as the Spanish Reconquest.

The Reconquest was a crusade, every bit as intense as the storied crusades of Godfrey of Bouillon and Richard the Lionheart in Palestine. From the days of Charlemagne in the ninth century, the dream of driving the Arab heathens from the Iberian peninsula had been the sacred calling of every Christian king in the north. Ferdinand I had thrust as far south as Seville before retreating, but it was the recapture of Toledo in 1085 that shocked the Islamic world to its core. For several hundred years, as the Berber dynasty of the Almorávidas in Granada gave way to the fanatical Almohádes, and eventually to the brilliant Nasrids, and as the great Alhambra was constructed above the bowl of the Andalusian *vega*, there was thrust and counterthrust between Christians and Muslims. Yet, a kind of stasis was established.

But such detente was not to last. In A.D. 1236, Córdoba, the seat of Moorish culture since the eighth century, fell to the Christians, followed by Valencia in 1238, and Seville in 1248. In an elegiac lament, the Moorish poet Al-Rundi wrote of the devastation Moorish Spain felt at its defeat by the infidel.

> *Mosques have become churches*
> *in which only bells and crosses are found . . .*
>
> *O who will redress the humiliation*
> *of a people who were once powerful?*
> *Yesterday they were kings in their own homes.*
> *But today they are slaves in the land of the Infidel.*

By the year 1265 the Mohammedan empire, the glorious Al Andalus, had been reduced to the province of Granada and a line of ports around Cádiz.

Despite this upheaval, the 150 years from the mid-thirteenth century to the end of the fourteenth century would be a period of relative tranquility. It was to become the golden age of diversity in medieval Spain. The Christians comprised half the population of the peninsula, the rest being Jews and Moors. The Jewish population, numbering about 120,000, maintained good relations with the Christian kings of Castile. Under the rulers of the Almohádes, the Jews had been repressed, and they responded by helping the Castilian kings in their perpetual struggle against the Moors. When the Christians seized more and more Moorish territory, they returned the favor, and Jews soon held numerous important posts in the royal court. Meanwhile, Arabs living under Christian rule (called Mozarabs) were tolerated and nurtured. Through them the wisdom of the Arab world, from its science to its arts, was translated from the Arabic into Latin. This trove of learning was then sent north into the largely illiterate principalities of Central Europe.

The reign of the Castilian king Alfonso X (1252–84) represented the high point of this cross-fertilization. Schooled in Arabic and known as *El Sabio*, the Learned One, Alfonso was responsible for great cultural and social works. Even as he gave lip service to the traditional obligation of Christian kings to confront and conquer the Moors, he set out to create a Christian culture in the north of Spain that was equal in glory to Moorish culture in the south. He ordered both the Koran and the Talmud to be translated into Latin. And he promoted valuable translations from Arabic astronomy that came to be known as the Alfonsine Tables and that would guide the study of astronomy for the next two hundred years until the revolutionary work of Nicolaus Copernicus changed everything.

These tables were produced by a collaborative effort of fifty astronomers in 1252, including a clutch of Arabic astronomers and an important Jewish astronomer named Yehuda ben Moses Cohen. They sought to plot the path of the planets as a series of intricate and interrelated epicycles and to describe the constellations beyond the planets. In the Alfonsine Tables, the Arabic names for certain stars like Altar, Betelgeuse, Rigel, and Vega were used. Later, Alfonso was said to have remarked, apocryphally no doubt, that if he had been present at creation, he could have given the Good Lord some hints.

Under the Learned One other technical fields were also enriched through the translation of Arabic science. Arabic chemical words came into European languages: alkali, alcohol, camphor, elixir, syrup, talc, and tartar. Mathematical terms like azimuth, zero, sine, root, algebra, nadir, and zenith came from the Arabic, as did botanical names like ginger, lilac, jasmine, myrrh, saffron, sesame, lemon, rhubarb, and coffee. Modern Spanish contains approximately eight thousand words derived from Arabic.

The humanities and arts also found their patron in Alfonso. Under this remarkable king a seminal collection of medieval poetry and music was compiled, as well as an illustrated book of games, *Libro de los Juegos*, about dice and chess played on boards of different sizes. Historical memory was important to him as well. He encouraged the writing of a history called *Crónica General*, insisting that it be written in the language of the common man. By this simple act, Castilian became the standard for written and spoken Spanish. Alfonso also initiated the formation of a comprehensive legal code, *Las Siete Partidas*, which among other things removed his kingdom from papal influence. This remarkable achievement had one glaring deficit, however. It associated all Jews with the Antichrist, declaring them to be helpmates of the Devil, and the prime villains in the last days of the coming apocalypse.

Alfonso's cultural influence was to last well beyond his death. Much original literary work, including the prose of Infante Don Juan Manuel and the poetry of the archpriest of Hita, was created in what became known as the School of Alfonso. Better as a man of letters than a leader of men, he nevertheless added the port of Cádiz to the Kingdom of Castile, in an arrangement with his vassal, the Moorish king of Granada.

❖

After the fall of Córdoba to the Christian side in 1236, the center of Islamic Al Andalus shifted to Granada. Its natural circumstance protected the province of Granada better than Córdoba. Its capital city, also called Granada, was built on the slopes of the massive Sierra Nevada, the highest mountains in all of Spain. These daunting and gorgeous peaks, rising over 11,000 feet, separated Granada from its seaport of Málaga to the south. Their highest peak, the Mulhacén, is named for the father of the last Moorish king. Between the Sierra Nevada and the coast, only fifty miles south, lie the Alpujarras Mountains with their rich and fertile bottomlands. Málaga was then the richest seaport in

Spain. It was a bustling hub of trade with North Africa and Venice, Constantinople and Alexandria.

After the Moorish conquest of Spain in the eighth century, the emir of Al Andalus had been a vassal of the caliphs of Damascus and Baghdad. But this western outpost of Islam was the first of the Muslim provinces to break free of its Oriental masters. When the Mongols destroyed the caliphate in Baghdad in 1258, the independence of Al Andalus was solidified, and the Spanish Moors began to relate more to Europe than the Middle East. In arts and agriculture, learning and tolerance, Al Andalus was a beacon of enlightenment to the rest of Europe. In the fertile valleys of the Guadalquivir and the Guadiana rivers, as well as the terraced slopes of the Alpujarras, agriculture surpassed anything elsewhere on the continent. Moorish filigree silver- and leatherwork became famous throughout the Mediterranean. In engineering, the skill of the Spanish Moors had no parallel, and the splendor of their architecture was manifest in the glorious mosque of Córdoba, the Giralda and Alcazar of Seville, and the Alhambra of Granada. Its excellence in art and literature, mathematics and science, history and philosophy defined this brilliant civilization.

Among its finest achievements was its tolerance. Jews and Christians were welcomed, if not as equals, then as full-fledged citizens. They were permitted to practice their faith and their rituals without interference. This tolerance was in keeping with the principles of the Koran, which taught that Jews and Christians were to be respected as "peoples of the Book" or believers in the word of God. Jews and Christians were assimilated into Islamic culture, and occasionally, Moorish leaders helped to build Christian houses of worship.

In 1248, work began on the colossal Alhambra in Granada. With its thirteen towers and fortified walls above the ravine of the Darro River, the river of gold, the red palace took shape over the next hundred years. The extraordinary rooms of its interior—the Courtyard of the Lions, the Hall of the Two Sisters, the Court of the Myrtles—were finished at the end of the long process under the reign of Yusef I in the mid-fourteenth century. With their arabesque moldings and gold ornament and vegetal carvings, these rooms became the wonder of the world. Most stunning of all was the Courtyard of the Lions, whose Oriental feel was more reminiscent of Japan than the Middle East and whose vision was to replicate the Garden of Paradise.

For all its might and intelligence, creativity and tolerance, the kingdom of the Moors had been steadily shrinking since the beginning of the second millennium of Christ. The Reconquest of Spain by the Christians had pushed south slowly but relentlessly. At the beginning of the fifteenth century, the Moorish state was in its twilight, reduced to the humiliation of vassalage, enduring only at the sufferance of the Castilian kings, whose might increased year by year.

The question was only who would finish the job . . . and when. The answer was the Catholic sovereigns, Ferdinand and Isabella, in their triumph over the Moors in the apocalypse of 1492.

❖

If the thirteenth century in Spain represents the apogee of tolerance and cross-fertilization between the three great religions of Christianity, Judaism, and Islam, the seeds of later trouble were sown during the same period. For it was early in that century that the institution of the Inquisition was established in earnest.

The problem of wayward belief had bedeviled the Christian Church since its earliest days. And yet, very early on, the attitude toward heretical views was one of forgiveness, tolerance, and exhortation. Christ himself had set the tone in an interchange with the apostle Peter, when Peter asked his Saviour (as recounted in Matthew 18:21) how many times he should forgive one who sinned against him.

"I say not unto thee until seven times," Jesus replied, "but Until seventy times seven."

And later St. Paul addressed the question of heresy in his instructions to Titus, the bishop of Crete (the Epistle of Paul to Titus, 1:10). "Vain talkers and deceivers" polluted the company of true believers, Paul wrote, and the purveyors of "Jewish fables" were among them.

"Reject the man who is a heretic after the first and second admonition, Knowing that he who is so subverted and sinneth condemns himself" (3:11). There was no mention of punishment.

This stance of suasion, admonition, and reconciliation lasted until the fourth century, when the doctrine of the early Church faced its first major challenge with the Manichean heresy. To Manicheans, the world was essentially evil, but through effort and discipline, the individual could achieve perfection. They believed in Christ but denied the Holy Sacraments. They rejected the authority of the pope and replaced him with their own high priest.

To deal with this departure from official doctrine, the Church moved from persuasion to excommunication to confiscation of property and, finally, to corporeal punishment for the heretic. The administration of physical pain, however, was turned over to secular authority. In A.D. 382, the emperor Theodosius decreed that Manichean heretics should be put to death, and their property seized. In the seventh century in Spain, the concept of heresy was extended to Jews when a Spanish Visigoth king ordered that Jewish "heretics" should be threatened with fear into returning to the Church, and if they did not buckle under, their children should be seized. In the eleventh century, Manichean heretics were burned in France.

But it was during the early part of the thirteenth century, with the arrival of St. Dominic, that the treatment of heresy reached a new level of vigilance. Domingo de Guzmán hailed from minor Spanish nobility, distantly related to the great House of Guzmán in central Castile. Educated at the University of Palencia, he took his religious calling seriously, twice attempting to sell himself into slavery to pay for the liberation of Christian captives in Moorish hands. In 1202, as a deputy to the bishop of Osma, Dominic was sent on a diplomatic mission to Toulouse, where, to his horror, he witnessed the perversions of the Albigensian heresy.

In part, the Albigenses were reacting to the depravity and extravagance of the Catholic priesthood in southern France. Called neo-Manichean, the Albigenses, like their predecessors from the fourth century, saw the world as gripped in an eternal struggle between the forces of good and of evil. They rejected the authority of Rome and railed against the corruption of Catholic priests. They rejected the Old Testament and scrapped the sacraments of baptism for the believers and marriage for their leaders, who were known as the *perfecti*. The mass of believers, in contrast to their pure leaders, were granted wide moral licence and freed from religious obligations.

From this experience in Toulouse, Dominic conceived the idea of a religious order devoted solely to the goal of combating heresy and propagating the true Catholic faith. As the idea advanced, the pope, Innocent III, declared a crusade against the Albigenses and set the nobility of northern France against that of the south in a bloody civil war that was to last for twenty years. Early in this crusade the papal legate to southern France was said to have uttered the words:

"Slay all. God will know his own."

In the wake of mortal combat, Dominic and his cohorts followed the battle by engaging heretics in debate and seeking to reconcile them to the true faith. In 1215, his followers held their first gathering as an Order of Preachers; they were the first inquisitors. Three years later, they received formal Vatican sanction as an order and established monasteries in Segovia and Madrid. Initially, they were known as the Militia of Christ, and only later, after Dominic's death in 1221 and his beatification as a saint, as the Dominicans. Only much later still did they become known familiarly as the "hounds of God."

Twelve years after St. Dominic's death, his dogs and their Inquisition were formally entrusted with the job of eliminating the vestiges of the Albigensian heresy. It would take them another sixty years. In this union of military action and inquisition lay the model for the future.

Over the next hundred years Dominican monasteries proliferated throughout Spain. In the eastern Iberian kingdom of Aragon, a formal office of the Inquisition was firmly established. In the year 1314 several heretics were banished, and several more were burned at the stake, though most suspects were "reconciled" to the faith. Fourteen years later, in 1325, the burning of a heretic was made into a spectacle as King James II of Aragon, his sons, and two bishops attended the festivities. In the 1330s, in Aragon, Dominican inquisitors prosecuted the first cases of witchcraft and Devil worship.

Twenty years later, during the horror of the Black Death, one Nicolás Eymeric was made a cardinal and appointed Grand Inquisitor of Aragon. In 1376 he would publish his famous *Guide to Inquisitors (Directorium inquisitorum)*, which was to become the standard manual for the next several centuries. In it Eymeric codified explicit instructions to his inquisitors for proceeding against suspect worshipers. The heretic, Eymeric wrote, was one who thought he could pick the parts of Christian doctrine he liked and discard the parts he disliked. His masterwork contained three parts. The first defined the fundamental tenets of the faith which the Christian was obligated to believe. The second was a catalogue of errors such as denying the Holy Trinity or engaging in Devil worship or the conjuring of devils through magic. And finally, he defined some sixty-nine separate heresies, a number of which were Manichean in nature.

The inquisitor, wrote the cardinal, must be "modest in his bearing, circumspect in prudence, firm in his constancy, eminently learned in the sacred teaching of the Faith, and abounding in virtues." Because his work was dangerous, and because, like Eymeric himself, the religious policeman was likely to be the most hated of priests, his love of God must transcend his fear of men. His power derived from the pope, and it included the authority to prosecute bishops and priests and to maintain his own prisons. For those who were denounced, there was a presumption of guilt. Eymeric enumerated the tricks that a wily culprit was likely to use in an examination and offered strategies to unmask such deceptions. When a confession began, it was likely to be a gushing torrent, and it should be allowed to continue to its end, lest the heretic "return to his vomit." Should torture be needed to confirm guilt, only a bishop could order its administration, and it should be employed only as a last resort. Euphemistically, torture was called putting the suspect "to the question," but Eymeric warned inquisitors not to rely too heavily upon it.

"Some are so soft-hearted and foolish that they will admit everything, even though it be false, under light torture, while others are so obstinate that no matter how much they are tormented, the truth is not to be had from them. In putting men to the question, the greatest prudence is to be exercised." Still, on the administration of torture, Cardinal Eymeric was responsible for one major procedural change: before him, the rules forbade the repeat of torture a second time. But in the parsing of the *Directorium inquisitorum,* torture could be "suspended" and then "continued" but not repeated.

Despite the hair-splitting definitions of Eymeric's manual, the hunt for heretics was not a widespread preoccupation in medieval Spain until well into the fifteenth century; public displays of inquisitional ire were rare and scattershot. Until the arrival of Ferdinand and Isabella, the prosecution of the wayward was known as the "Old Inquisition," and it was reasonably benign and toothless, at least compared to what would follow. Partly due to the achievement of Alfonso the Learned in the thirteenth century, it did not exist at all in Castile, for he had put his realm beyond the reach of the Vatican.

It would be left to Ferdinand and Isabella to institute the new, entirely more virulent Inquisition, and to make it into a uniquely Spanish institution. In that new endeavor, the successor to Nicolás Eymeric as Grand Inquisitor for all of Spain would cast a far broader and darker shadow.

His name was Tomás de Torquemada.

❖

In the centuries before 1468, the Reconquest of Spain for Christianity went hand-in-hand with efforts toward unifying the northern Spanish realms. To the west of Castile lay Spain's nemesis, Portugal. Originally part of León, the Portuguese kingdom was established as an independent state in A.D. 1095. It too had been overrun by the Moors. Yet once the Moors were thrown out of Portugal—Lisbon was recaptured in 1147 and the southwest of the country at the end of the same century—Portugal aggressively defended its independence. At the dawn of a new era, one man did more than any other to launch the golden age of Portuguese exploration, Prince Henry the Navigator.

Before this visionary prince, the conventional view of the world was derived largely from the speculations of Ptolemy in the second century and from ancient Greek geography. Under these precepts, only three continents, Europe, Asia, and Africa, were believed to exist. The Indian Ocean was presumed an inland sea, Africa an island, whose vast central part was desert, "a land uninhabitable from the heat." As the fifteenth century began, the furthest point on the African coast known to Europe was Cape Bojador (in what is today southern Morocco). Common lore suggested that any white man who ventured beyond the Rio de Oro in Cape Bojador would be changed into a black man, as God's punishment for impious prying. The concept of the heavens was bound up with theories about the twelve pillars of the zodiac and the twenty-eight mansions of the Moon. The world itself was shaped like a pear, upon whose protruding stem lay the Garden of Paradise. To the west was "the green sea of Darkness," where any adventurer foolish enough to hazard was sure to be swallowed up by terrible, oceanic whirlpools.

Between the second and the fifteenth centuries, only the voyages of the Vikings in the far north, the explorations of Arab mariners down the east coast of Africa, and the overland journeys of Marco Polo had expanded the ancient knowledge of the world. The results of these voyages were melded with romances of discovery from such dubious sources as the *Arabian Nights* and the wanderings of Sinbad the Sailor.

But the superstitions of his time did not daunt the Portuguese prince, Henry the Navigator. Indeed, he set out to test and challenge those superstitions. If he was driven by his scientific curiosities and the certainty of the greater power and glory that Portugal would derive from new discoveries, he was also a crusader, determined to extend the rule of Christ on earth. The flags of Portugal and of Christ flew together from his ships in a noble quest for knowledge, for empire, and for souls that without their enterprise would be lost forever. In presenting his plans to his people over thirty years, he combined his motives in the phrase "Crusade of Discovery."

His caravels were the best in Europe. They sailed under the flag of the Order of Christ, whose sailors and marines were the successors of the fabled Knights Templar and of which Henry the Navigator himself was a grand master. As his evangelicals were known for their ferocity, so his sea captains were famous for their seamanship. To support them, the prince harnessed the talents of his Jewish and Moorish mathematicians and astronomers to the art of mapmaking. In 1445, his courageous mariners passed Cape Bojador, maintained their skin color, and discovered Cape Verde and Senegal. A year later, they pressed southward to Guinea.

Their dream was to find a way around Africa to India. Though this would not happen for another fifty years, when Bartholomew Dias rounded the Cape of Good Hope in 1488 and Vasco da Gama reached India in 1498, Portuguese sailors discovered and colonized the island of Madeira, where the first children born on that outpost were christened Adam and Eve. From Madeira they proceeded to the Canaries and the Azores, and Henry began to flirt with the thought that sailing due west could eventually bring the mariner to India.

With Henry's voyages down the coast of Africa and the establishment of Western outposts, the European slave trade began in earnest. At first the prince promoted this vigorous trade as a tool of Christian conversion. It was seen as an act of charity, guided by the will of God, even as the Africans violently resisted the brutality of their purported saviours. Even after the Navigator died in 1460, the impulse toward further discovery (and further slavery) continued undiminished. Portugal reigned as the great seapower of Europe.

As fate would have it, a young Genoese sailor worked on the crew of one of these Portuguese voyages to Guinea. His name was Cristoforo Colombo. We know him today as Christopher Columbus.

❖

To the east of Castile lay the Kingdom of Aragon and the small, feisty, Kingdom of Navarre. Aragon comprised the principalities of Valencia, Catalonia, Majorca, and the other Balearic Islands, as well as Aragon itself. The kings of Aragon also held sway over Sicily and Naples, and thus, Aragonese medieval history had long been bound up with that of

Italy. The King of Aragon ruled his kingdom tenuously, however. For there was a long tradition of local liberty called the *fuero* or jurisdiction, which accorded local barons the power over their villages and lands and forbade the king from stationing "foreign" troops on their soil. This generally produced a weakened monarchy that was in an unsteady state of conflict with its princes.

At the opening of the fifteenth century, two brothers held the thrones of Castile and Aragon. Tranquility but not union came from this relationship. King Juan II of Castile was married to Isabel of Portugal, who was the grand-niece of Henry the Navigator. From this union issued two children, Isabella, born in 1451, and Alfonso, two years later. Aragon also sported a king named Juan II, and he was married to a Castilian woman of royal, and significantly, Jewish blood, named Juana Enriquez. From this union came one son, Ferdinand.

Ferdinand of Aragon was born one year after Isabella of Castile, in the year 1452. Forty years later, they would be proclaimed "the Catholic monarchs." Together, they would become the champions of the Spanish Reconquest, patrons of the New World, the unifiers of the Spanish Empire, and the purifiers of the Catholic faith.

2

Sowers of Discord

 The childhood of Isabella of Castile was not a happy one. In the years 1454–64, until Isabella was thirteen years old, she and her brother, Alfonso, resided in the royal retreat southwest of Segovia called Arevalo. Its castle was small but well fortified, notable for an expansive keep beneath its rounded, crenellated walls, and well staffed with a strong component of monks and nuns to mind the royal upbringing. Their father, King Juan II, died in 1454, when Isabella was only three, and their mother, Isabel of Portugal, had fallen into a depression after each of her confinements. After her husband's death, she receded completely into a permanent melancholy, withdrawing into the silence of her chambers.

Juan II had had a long and decidedly undistinguished reign of nearly fifty years, from 1406 to 1454. Weak, amiable, and dependent, fond of pomp and ceremony, jousting tournaments, and literary colloquies, with no taste for conflict or statecraft, he had fallen under the sway of a clever court manipulator named Alvaro de Luna. Though de Luna was illegitimate, he issued from a noble house in Aragon, and he had learned well the diversions and the charms of court life. Dashingly handsome and irresistible to women, he wrote poetry and loved music. In becoming the king's favorite, he garnered great wealth. Juan conferred upon him the titles of Grand Master of St. James and Constable of Castile, and with such titles and power, de Luna became the shadow king, quietly building his private bureaucracy within the realm. So

close were king and consort, wrote a chronicler, that "lascivious" relations were suspected. "For thirty-five years [the king] lived happy at [de
Luna]'s side and submissive to his will."

By Maria of Aragon, his first queen, King Juan had one son, Enrique.
In Enrique's youth, de Luna introduced the boy to homosexuality, to
make him compliant and easy to control, and this would have grave im-
plications for the future. De Luna managed the king's sex life well into
adulthood. "The greatest marvel," wrote a chronicler, "had been that
even in the natural acts [the king] followed the orders of the Constable,
and though young and of good constitution, and having a young and
beautiful queen, if the Constable said not to, he would not go to her
room, nor dally with other women, although naturally enough inclined
to them." This marriage was shortlived. Maria of Aragon died in 1447.
For his new wife, Juan II took Isabel of Portugal, by whom Juan, despite
his queen's moodiness, was totally captivated.

In 1449, in an event that doomed Juan's reign and had immense im-
plications for Spanish history, the crown demanded of Toledo the sum
of 1 million maravedis to support the army. De Luna became the king's
hammer, and the consort put this unpleasant responsibility of collecting the surtax in the hands of his most accomplished associates, the
group known famously as the *conversos* or "the converted."

The conversos were persons of Jewish heritage who either themselves or through their forbears had converted from Judaism to Christianity. In the dreadful year 1391, a wide-scale massacre of Jews swept
across Spain. Four thousand were killed in Seville alone, and the
killings spread to most of the major towns of the country through the
summer of that year. The demand was made that Jews either convert or
die. Nearly a third of Spanish Jews acquiesced to the rite of Christian
baptism. Such persecution continued into the early years of Juan II's
reign.

As baptized Christians, the former Jews were entitled, technically, to
the rights and privileges of all Christians. They intermarried freely with
Christians of "pure blood" and began to integrate socially, politically,
and culturally into the wider society. After a time, it was hard to find a

prominent family that did not have a converso as a relative. That included the forbears of tiny Isabella of Castile, whose paternal grandmother was the daughter of a conversa. The conversos continued in their role as the king's tax collectors and became the backbone of the professional and commercial gentry. As such, resentment, jealousy, and even hatred toward them was rife.

In January 1449, as Alvaro de Luna arrived in Toledo to oversee the collection of the surtax, a rebellion broke out, its ire focused on de Luna and the conversos. The insurgents took over the city and for nine months the rebellion raged. From it came three documents which were to alter the course of Spanish history. In May, as Juan II approached the city with his army, the rebels presented their king with a petition later called the Toledan Petition. It placed the blame for the rebellion on the excesses of Alvaro de Luna and his converso tools. De Luna had "granted the offices of the Castilian government to infidels and heretics, enemies of our sacred faith, our king, our persons and our estates." The conversos were enemies per se of the Spanish people. Worse, they were all secret Jews, whose conversion was fraudulent and insincere, and who clandestinely still followed Jewish rites and beliefs. Jews, ancient or modern, were a race, the petition argued, and it was their race rather than their overt or covert beliefs that made them evil servants of the Devil and cohorts of the Antichrist. The conversos were, therefore, traitors and heretics to country and to faith.

To prove the point, Castile's first inquisitional tribunal was convened. The good Christians of Toledo were invited to offer secret evidence of heresy against their neighbors. This was the seed of a process that was to grow with the unification of the Iberian peninsula under one rule and with the final demise of the Islamic south. It was a process that would take on a distinctly Spanish character until the Spanish Inquisition became synonymous with the extreme of Christian intolerance and violence.

Three weeks later Toledo's rebels issued a second pronouncement called the *Sentencia-Estatuto*, or Judgment and Statute. Jews, it proclaimed, were the central evil of Castilian society. Conversion to Christianity could not mask their perfidy. The conspiracy of the conversos aimed to kill "all the Old Christians in the city and transfer the city into the hands of its enemies." Among other inflammatory provisions, all conversos were henceforth barred from public office and denied the right to give testimony in court. The prohibitions applied not just to the living but to their future offspring. To underscore their seriousness, the rebels hanged the bodies of several conversos in the public square, including the town's leading converso.

With the situation wildly out of control, the Vatican finally entered the fray. In September 1449 a papal bull against the rebels was issued, and their leader was excommunicated. In the light of future history, the champion of the Vatican's forceful anti-rebel position was ironic indeed. He was the cardinal of San Sisto, Juan de Torquemada. Cardinal Torquemada was himself a converso, and thus Jewish blood ran in his veins, and thence on to his nephew, the future Grand Inquisitor of the Spanish Inquisition, Tomás de Torquemada. In 1449, Cardinal Juan de Torquemada, the Vatican's preeminent theologian, was the voice of reason and enlightenment. He compared the persecution of Toledo to "a scorching wind which damages the flowers in the garden." He was astonished "that Christians could inflict such pain on other Christians," branding the rebels as racists and cowards who spewed their hate from dark corners. To this elder Torquemada, a Christian, once baptized, was a Christian without qualification, for baptism was a gift of God. It was permanent, and it could not be withdrawn. He identified with the pain of the conversos, because he was one himself. But as one who held such titles in Rome as Master of the Palace and Defender of the Faith, he was also a great advocate for papal power.

"If ever it was incumbent on Catholic doctors, as soldiers of Christ, to protect the Church with powerful weapons, lest man, led astray by simplicity or error or craft or deception, should forsake her fold, that duty devolves upon them now. For in these troubled times, some pestilent men, puffed up with ambition, have arisen. With diabolical craft and deceit they have striven to disseminate false doctrines regarding spiritual as well as temporal power. They have assaulted the whole church, inflicting grievous wounds upon her, and proceeding to rend her unity, to tarnish the splendor of her glory. Shamefully to obscure her beauty, they have undertaken to crush the primacy of the Apostolic See. . . ."

The last word was left, however, to a fire-eating priest named Marcos García de Mora. He was to supply the passion and the vitriol to the rebellion. In November 1449 he put forward his *Memorial*, the third important document of this period. Addressed not only to the pope and the king but to all good kings and queens in Christendom, it was as powerful and influential a piece of religious demagoguery as Church history has ever seen. He cast Alvaro de Luna as a tyrant, but merely a tool of a wider conspiracy. It was the conversos as a group and a race who exploited de Luna, who held Toledo in their sinister grip, and for that matter, all of Castile. The baptism of this "collection of beasts" was insincere and fraudulent by definition, for Jews were not capable of sincere conversion. They could not be altered or improved by Christian ritual.

Conversos were an "abhorred, damned, and detested group, species and class of baptised Jews and those who came from their lineage." The *Memorial* revived the concept of "Judaizing," in which the conversos as secret Jews were forever conspiring to undermine true believers and true Christianity. Conversos were "adulterous sons of infidels, fathers of all greed, sowers of all discord, rich in every malice and perversity, always ungrateful to God, opposed to his orders, and deviating from his ways." If Jews were constitutionally evil, one had to look no further than the Bible to know it. He invoked or misinvoked Psalm 95:10–11.

"It is a people that do err in their heart, and they have not known My ways/Unto whom I swore in my wrath that they should not enter into my rest."

García's *Memorial* was a wild, scurrilous harangue. Not long after it was issued, its author was taken out and hanged as a traitor. But its arguments were broadcast widely, and they succeeded in altering the terms of the debate over race and religion in Spain. For a popular audience which resented the power and influence of the conversos, the *Memorial* found favor.

Throughout these disastrous events, Juan II's wife, Isabel of Portugal, inveighed against Alvaro de Luna to her husband. In 1451 during her pregnancy with Isabella, and more pointedly afterward, it was de Luna who managed her medicines. Suspicions arose that de Luna was poisoning his detractor, which was probably true. In 1453, despite her infirmities, the queen finally won out. De Luna was seized, charged with high treason, and beheaded. A year later, Juan II died, and his foppish son by his first marriage succeeded to the throne as Enrique IV.

If Enrique was more clever than his father, he was also, if anything, a greater abomination. It was said that he was an enemy of Christians and worshiped in a heathen manner. In his court he promoted criminals and country bumpkins. And he soon found himself in open warfare with his prominent *caballeros*, especially after they accused him of ordering a priest, in the aftermath of a violent storm in Seville, to preach that the devastation was "divine punishment for public depravity" and, as such, "the pure effect of natural laws."

That the king should appeal to natural laws struck his nobles as ironic. It was written that he found pleasant odors repulsive "and prefers the stink of severed horse hoofs and burnt leather." This shocker suggested witchcraft, for horn and hoof were associated with the Devil, and burnt horn or leather was used by witches in their spells (although the nauseating smoke of burnt hoof was also the remedy of the day for epileptics).

That the king was also a practicing homosexual was widely known. "The king is so effeminate," wrote the court scribe, "that he even goes in the middle of the night to the house of his new favorite, in order to entertain him when he is ill, by singing and playing the sitar." His queen of twelve years was the long-suffering Blanche of Navarre. No children issued from this marriage, for it was never consummated. For a congenital weakness, Enrique was dubbed *"El Impotente."*

"The impotence of the king to procreate was notorious," wrote a scribe. But it was left to a visiting German doctor to say why. Enrique's "member" was, in size and length, *debile e parvum*, "crippled and small," and he could not achieve an erection. His doctors gathered to scratch their heads and finally decided upon the remedy: a medieval version of artificial insemination. In the Latin of their medical diagnosis, his member was *mulgere*, milked. A golden tube was inserted in the queen's womb, into which the king's manhood was poured; but alas the infusion did not work. The king's semen was *aquosum et sterile*, "watery and sterile."

As the medieval world turned, the blame was placed not on Enrique but upon his queen. Ritualistically, the Spanish crown appealed to the pope to annul the marriage of twelve years. The rationale given to the Holy Father was unusual. Compliant, and no doubt well-paid, prostitutes were brought forward to give evidence to the Vatican that Enrique, suddenly *"El Potente,"* had copulated with them. The examiners at the Vatican must have heard this testimony with muffled snickering, but they pronounced the marriage ended due to a demonic spell cast over it. Blanche of Navarre was banished. In May 1455, Enrique took a new queen, Juana of Portugal, the sister of the Portuguese king. She was a lusty wench, and she promptly presented the crown with a different problem.

In 1462, when Enrique's half sister Isabella was eleven years old, Juana gave birth to a daughter. It was clear to all that Enrique's majordomo, Beltrán de la Cueva, was the father. So clear was it that the child, named Juana after her mother, was dubbed *"La Beltraneja."*

❖

In 1464, matters took a serious turn when Isabella and her younger brother, Alfonso, were called to the court in Segovia. By this time the court of their half brother had become a swamp of corruption and intrigue. The person most affected was Alfonso, who, though only eleven years old, was the sole male in the immediate line of succession, and whose role in life, it seemed, was to be a pawn. Enrique IV made him a virtual prisoner. "Alfonso, wrenched from his mother's arms, existed as though buried, exposed to perversity, and in danger of cruel death," wrote a chronicler. Upon their arrival, Enrique announced that he was passing over Isabella and Alfonso as his heirs, and making his "own" daughter the next in line to succeed him. An oath of allegiance to La Beltraneja was drawn up. To strengthen the case, the nose of the baby was broken to make her look more like the horse-faced king.

Whatever Isabella at age thirteen and Alfonso at age eleven may have thought about this slight, the court nobles revolted. Enrique was already in deep trouble with his aristocracy. Through his self-indulgence and love of luxury, he had squandered the rich surplus that his father's favorite tax collector, Alvaro de Luna, had amassed in the royal treasury. Wags and poets made fun of his court as being populated by sodomites and whores. One poet had encouraged the king toward greatness: "You were made king of the earth, by He of the Heavens, so that you and those you command [could] turn His wrath against the Moors." But the king's appetite for the Reconquest had been feeble. Enrique was no warrior.

Further charges abounded. The king was coddling conversos and Jews, it was claimed, and one Franciscan agitator tried to shock the royal court into action by claiming that he could produce one hundred foreskins from the sons of conversos in high places. The king had also alienated the Catholic bishops by calling them ridiculous goatskins and treating their pronouncements with contempt. "Instead of pursuing a war against the Moors," one detractor wrote, "he wars on his own vassals, on good manners, and on ancient laws."

In September 1464, a group of rebel nobles circulated a counter-petition throughout the land, declaring Enrique to be an unfit ruler. Not only was the king a perverse homosexual, the petition charged, but he was making a mockery of the Reconquest. Not only was he was under the thumb of Beltrán de la Cueva, but the infanta was not even the king's own child. Later, in Ávila, a ceremonial dethronement of Enrique took place in a square near the cathedral. A mannequin dressed as the king in mourning clothes was propped upon a mock throne, a scepter in one hand and a sword in the other. Solemnly, the archbishop of Toledo, Alfonso Carrillo de Acuña, boomed out a litany of grievances, whereupon, stagily, first the scepter, the king's symbol of justice, and then the sword, his symbol of the kingdom's defense, was removed, and finally the royal raiments until the naked effigy was kicked to the ground. In his place, the nobles proclaimed the eleven-year-old Alfonso to be the true King of Castile.

This would later be remembered as the Farce of Ávila. In the famous contemporaneous poem known as the *Coplas de Mingo Revulgo*, the prophecy was delivered that Enrique IV "will either be punished or God will provide another good king."

Knights and priests chose up sides, and Castile slipped into civil war. Once again Jews and conversos were drawn into the fray, for Enrique, like his father, was regarded as soft on heresy. The rebels called for a stiff Inquisition, with a full range of harsh penalties for insincere Christians.

Again, the hotspot was Toledo. There, sixteen hundred dwellings were burned, and a sizable number of conversos massacred, including the two leaders of the conversos in the city. Their naked bodies were strung up in the central square where the crowd gawked at their lower extremities to see if they were circumcised, sure evidence of secret Jewishness.

The chaos finally came to a climax on August 20, 1467, at the Battle of Olmedo. The outcome was indecisive, but it led to a division of lands between Enrique IV and the forces of the young prince Alfonso. This accommodation lasted less than a year, for in July 1468, Alfonso fell suspiciously ill. The plague was first thought to be the cause, but as the prince declined, it became clear that he had been poisoned. King Enrique's current court favorite, Juan Pacheco, marquis of Villena, was implicated in the foul deed, for previously he had tried, without success, to lure the prince into homosexuality the better to control the boy. But the prince had complained about these pornographic solicitations. Pacheco stood to lose the riches and estates he had amassed through his court conspiracies if Alfonso prevailed.

Alfonso lingered for three days before he died. His corpse was taken to Arevalo for burial. If in life he was surrounded by minders who tried to corrupt, to exploit, and to disorient him, in death he was beatified. He was the "holy child" whose soul was "immaculate" and whose brief and contested shadow reign had given his people great hope. Archbishops and princes and other notables briefly suspended their hostility toward one another to gather and mourn the boy king.

Isabella was genuinely grief-stricken at the death of her younger brother and withdrew to a convent in Ávila to mourn. As she prayed, the shattered rebel forces fell into a fever of plotting. Deprived of their male pawn, they were desperate and endangered; their hope was Isabella. In Burgos they met to craft another brickbat to the king. He was, they charged again, in the grip of "infidels," referring partly to his beloved Moorish guards, and of "enemies of the Catholic religion." They scoffed once more at his plans to name his infant daughter as his successor, when it was a mockery to "call her Princess which she is not." And then they converged in haste on Ávila.

But the time was inauspicious, for Ávila was suffering with an outbreak of the plague. Its narrow streets, close quarters, and high walls were the perfect incubator for pestilence. Enrique dared not enter it, and Isabella dared not leave. There, her chief adviser was the most powerful churchman in Spain, the archbishop of Toledo, Alfonso Carrillo de Acuña. The archbishop was a severe and intimidating presence, and he was determined to turn aside any accommodation with Enrique. The prelate fell to his knees before Isabella. She was now, he proclaimed, the true Queen of Castile. He urged her to replace Alfonso as the symbol of the rebellion against Enrique.

In the midst of this tornado of countervailing winds stood an impressive seventeen-year-old infanta. Isabella had blossomed into a tall, chestnut-haired, blue-eyed beauty, with a clear complexion and a steady gaze. From her pious upbringing in the company of stern, devout monks, from the absence of a father and the presence of a mother gone mad, from the grief of a murdered brother and imprecations of scheming nobles, she had developed a quiet strength and inner serenity. To the plea of Archbishop Carrillo, she said neither yes nor no, but withdrew to a wooded place called Cebreros to ponder the question.

When she emerged from her retreat, Isabella demurred. So long as her half brother was still king, she would honor him and seek a reconciliation. More civil strife must be avoided. The authority of the king and the integrity of succession must be respected. She would wait for her throne, rightfully acquired. It was her first significant act of statesmanship, and it showed the promise of the future.

By mid-September, the pressure and the humiliation became too great for Enrique. He still held enough power to repulse the efforts to dethrone him, but not enough power to execute his plan for succession. Genuinely fond of Isabella, he was moved and relieved by her decision not to replace her late brother as a pretender to the throne. Emissaries sped back and forth between the camps to fashion the outlines of an agreement. When the terms were finalized, and the royal signatures affixed, the king called for his half sister to meet him in a council of peace.

A site for the conference south of the town was chosen. Isabella rode to it on a humble mule, with her venerable Archbishop Carrillo walking painfully by her side, in a gesture of obedience and fealty. An entourage of sprightlier nobles accompanied them in a colorful procession. Not to be outdone, Enrique arrived with his nobles from Palencia, Benavente, and Miranda de Ebro, among them the suave and treacherous Juan Pacheco, marquis of Villena. He alternately had performed the roles of favorite and traitor to the king. The murderer of Alfonso was now acting as peacemaker between the parties. The king's retinue also came with its own rival curia. It included the archbishop of Seville, who for a pretty price of valuable lands and precious jewels had become the guardian of the king's infant daughter. At his instructions the baby was being carted around the countryside in a basket while the cauldron of succession boiled. Also along was the bishop of León, who came as the Vatican's legate, armed with papal authority to bless any agreement.

The royals finally gathered in a salubrious field outside a place called Toros de Guisando. Near the ancient stone carvings of bulls, said to have been fashioned in the time of Hercules, the ceremonials were magnificent. While the archbishop of Toledo, scowling in disapproval, held the reins of her mule, Isabella removed her wide-brimmed hat, kissed the hand of the king, and embraced him warmly. Then their treaty was ratified as the entire assemblage swore allegiance to King Enrique as "their king and natural lord." The pontifical legate "dissolved and untied" whatever oaths of allegiance they might have signed before to any other. Isabella, in turn, was to be Princess of the Asturias and Enrique's rightful heir. In addition, she was given the Castilian towns of Ávila, Medina del Campo, Úbeda, Huete, Escalona, Alcaraz, and Molina as her own. To her as well, the gathering three times swore their allegiance.

The claim of the child, La Beltraneja, was negated. In the months earlier, her lusty mother had paved the way. For Juana had become pregnant with the child of yet another court gigolo, and despite the efforts of her maids to construct a painful bodice to mask her condition, her dalliance had been discovered. "The queen, Juana of Portugal, has not used her person cleanly, as comports with her duty as servant to the king," it was now declared. As the papal legate nodded approvingly, the king "was not and is not legitimately married to her." Juana had already fled to the castle of the father of her first child, Beltrán de la Cueva. He had turned her away, laughing heartily to his drinking buddies that "he had never cared much, anyway, for her skinny legs."

Solemnly, the papal legate declared that the previous oath of allegiance to Juana of Portugal that Enrique had forced upon his nobles was now null and void.

In return, the king received one major concession. He was to have a say in whom Isabella would marry. The concession was conditional. She in turn insisted that he had no right to force a husband upon her against her will.

The way was paved for a very serious misunderstanding.

3

He and No Other!

❖

SARAGOSSA AND VALLADOLID

As the princess and the king rode off together, past the ancient bulls of Hercules and into the afternoon calm of Toros de Guisando, the question of whom Isabella would marry hung weightily in the air. In Enrique's mind, geopolitical considerations came first. He felt confident that he had secured the right to choose a husband for his half sister and now heir. The king's immediate problem was to repair the damage with Portugal that the fiasco over La Beltraneja had caused, but his tilt to the west was not new. For more than four years Enrique had had his eye on Alfonso, King of Portugal, as husband for Isabella.

Apart from the embarrassments of the past months, the Portuguese king was an interesting prospect. A widower, thirty-six years old and with an estimable reputation as a warrior, and not incidentally, Isabella's cousin, he was known as O *Africano* for his capture of the Alcazar-Seguer in Africa and his siege of Tangiers. He already had a son, and so from Isabella's standpoint and no doubt to her relief, the pressure on her fertility would not be overbearing. And she would become the Queen of Portugal. From Enrique's viewpoint, this had the advantage of putting her at safe remove from the Castilian rebels who still sought to use her against him.

At first, Isabella was not averse. Her mother's roots had given her a natural and sentimental bent toward Portugal. When as a girl she had first met Alfonso, he was more than twice her age and seemed very grand indeed as the conqueror of distant, exotic lands. But when she became of marriageable age, the aging Alfonso did not look so grand, and she raised objections. Complications and tensions had developed between the Portuguese and Castilian courts—Isabella would later write that the meeting of the two royal representatives had been a "complete disaster"—and the match had been put off.

Enrique was furious and threatened to imprison the infanta in the Alcazar of Madrid for her part in undercutting his plan. It was a threat only, for Enrique appreciated the dire consequences of breaking with her completely. But his fury did succeed in extracting a promise from Isabella, soon broken, not to engage in any marriage negotiations on her own while Enrique went south to Andalusia.

By 1468, other interesting marital possibilities had arisen. At first, Don Carlos, the eldest son of Juan II of Aragon, the Prince of Viana, and the heir to the Kingdom of Navarre, seemed like the front-runner. But mysteriously and suspiciously, before this possibility could go anywhere, the vigorous Carlos died. The focus shifted to Pedro Giron, master of Calatrava, a member of the powerful Pacheco family whom Enrique sought to win over by marriage. But Isabella rejected this match out of hand.

Other foreign prospects captured Enrique's attention. The King of France, Louis XI, had designs on Catalonia, the rich province just south of the Pyrenees which was rebelling against Aragonese rule. A match between Castile and France would cement French control over Catalonia and surround Aragon, to the mutual benefit of both Castile and France. Louis XI proposed to unite Isabella with his brother and heir apparent, Charles, duke of Berry and Guienne. Overtures also came from England, powerful and wealthy still after the draining misadventures of the Crusades. The duke of Gloucester, the future Richard III, was casting about for a suitable mate. He was only a year younger than Isabella.

Enrique IV forged breezily ahead. Preliminary arrangements for an English match were made and then broken in favor of the French.

Given Richard III's subsequent reputation for wickedness and brutality, dramatized later by William Shakespeare, as well as his exile and probable assassination, perhaps it was just as well for Isabella. The French prospect turned out to be even less appetizing. With more than geopolitics on her teenage mind, she had dispatched a friar to France on a pretext to scout the duke of Berry. His report was depressing. The effeminate duke had foppish French manners, bandy little legs, and could scarcely mount a horse without help.

But there was another option. He was Ferdinand of Aragon, the late Carlos's younger brother and Isabella's second cousin, who like the future Richard III of England was a year her junior. Her chaplain's secret report bristled with sex appeal. Unlike the wimpy Charles of Berry, this *caballero* had no difficulty in mounting a horse, for he had been raised in a military camp. At the age of seventeen he already had considerable battlefield experience, having commanded his father's forces in a victorious battle against the Catalans.

"He has so singular a grace," Isabella's spy reported, "that everyone who talks to him wants to serve him."

Of medium build, well proportioned and muscular, Ferdinand was an excellent rider and avid sportsman. If his sparse education limited his knowledge and wisdom, it advanced his cunning and taught him to be a good listener. Nor did his limited schooling crimp his eloquence, for he was an inveterate talker. His eyes sparkled with curiosity, his lips were sensuous, his chin prominent and determined. Already he showed promise as an outstanding leader of men.

Ferdinand and Isabella had one other thing in common: their Jewish heritage. He derived his through his mother, Juana Enriquez.

Yet, Ferdinand had another quality that might be hard to control. He loved women—indeed, so much so that as his negotiations with Isabella proceeded and before their agreements were consummated, Ferdinand would father two children by different women.

With a stubbornness that would become a mixed blessing later, Isabella knew she had found her man. Ferdinand's star rose further when his father sweetened his prospects by making him king of the

Aragonese colony of Sicily. To her adviser, the archbishop of Toledo, Isabella remarked that "it must be he and no other." The archbishop agreed. That they were second cousins and therefore subject to the ban on unions within the third tier of consanguinity was a problem, but not an insurmountable one. A papal dispensation would fix that. Yet they needed to be careful. It was certain that Enrique would object to this match.

Through the fall of 1468, as clandestine contacts between the camps intensified, Isabella reached out to nobles and prelates across the realm, speaking privately with those who had reservations and writing a collective letter to those who were on her side. In the collective response, the amenable nobles acknowledged that the proposed marriage would probably give the king indigestion, but that the proposed match was a good and "convenient" idea. As a virtual orphan who stood to inherit everything from her late father, and whose mother was ill and indisposed, Isabella was within her right to choose as she saw fit. Because her brother, the king, had married foolishly, it was imperative that she marry wisely. Of her choices, Ferdinand, the King of Sicily and heir to the Kingdom of Aragon, was clearly the best and most virile of the lot.

Before matters could go any further, however, the intermediaries of the two sides, operating still in high secrecy, had to agree on the fundamentals of power. Of the two kingdoms, Castile and Aragon, Castile was the larger, stronger, and richer; Aragon's treasury had been exhausted by the persistent troubles with the Catalonian rebels and warfare with France. And so if Ferdinand was to be favored with Isabella's hand, he must forego the customary authority of a feudal king. Only through her would he derive his power. She and Castile must remain the dominant partner.

At the tiny Aragonese town of Cervera west of Barcelona, a medieval version of a prenuptial marriage contract known as the "Capitulations of Cervera" was drawn up. This historic document ran counter to feudal tradition where the male always took the reins of power. In the Capitulations of Cervera it was Ferdinand who did the capitulating. He swore to defer to Isabella in matters of state, to obey Enrique, the king, while Enrique lived, and to respect Castilian law. He must live in Castile and appoint only Castilians to high office. And he must accept the holy obligation of all Spanish Catholic kings to attack, and conquer if possible, the infidel Moorish state of Al Andalus. To demonstrate his earnestness, Ferdinand agreed to seal the pact with 40,000 gold florins.

Predictably, it would not be many weeks before word of Isabella's engagement reached Enrique in the south. Just as predictably, he exploded in fury. His half sister had broken her pledge to him at Toros de Guisando. Her treachery undercut their solemn agreement that she would marry no one without his consent. She responded with equal passion. It was he, not she, who had scuttled their pact by pressing the case of the old king of Portugal, that Africano, on her, or that of the effete, bandy-legged prince in faraway France. She resented the presence of his agents and minders in her court, for they were browbeating her. One of them had promised a Portuguese invasion if she did not agree to marry the Portuguese king. If this was not enough to undercut any romantic feelings in her, these bullies made her feel like a prisoner. She did not mention that her own mother, Isabel of Portugal, had emerged from the darkness of her depression to try to dissuade Isabella from this match.

"I am alone and deprived of my just and proper liberty and the exercise of free will that marital decisions, after the grace of God, require," she wrote indignantly to Enrique. "I consulted with the grandees, prelates and *caballeros* about the matter. They responded that marrying the king of Portugal in no manner redounded to the benefit of your kingdoms . . . but all praised and approved the marriage with the Prince of Aragon, King of Sicily."

Meanwhile, the word of the engagement raced through the streets. Children began to chant a jingle about the "flowers of Aragon" sprouting in Castile, as they waved tiny flags of Aragon. Romance was in the air. The fantasy of a handsome young king and beautiful queen uniting Spain in a true confederation sent quivers of excitement through the streets. Among the aristocracy, however, old divisions reemerged; sides were chosen up, and once again, civil war loomed.

The court of the princess moved west to the safety of Valladolid, a town whose Moorish name belied the fact that it had been recovered from the infidels in the tenth century and become the traditional residence of past Castilian monarchs. From there, Isabel's chief adviser, the archbishop of Toledo, dispatched several envoys to Saragossa with orders to return with the strapping bridegroom as soon as possible, before Enrique could get back to Old Castile.

Meanwhile, far to the east, Ferdinand had been scrambling to raise his earnest money. This was no easy task, for his father, the present King of Aragon, was engaged in a fierce war in Catalonia—indeed, he lost the town of Gerona, north of Barcelona, to the French just as Ferdinand came asking for his marriage gold. Forty thousand florins was not inconsequential, and a number of the nobles of the Aragonese court opposed the match. Eventually, though, Ferdinand's father focused and relented. He sent his son to Valencia, where Ferdinand enjoyed heroic status from past military accomplishments and which was now the chief port of the kingdom since Barcelona was in the grip of rebellion. There, the prince finally raised his surety in kind. Able to raise only half the money in gold, he accepted the gift of a gorgeous ruby and pearl necklace from the town councilors. He would argue that the regal necklace was worth the remaining 20,000 florins.

When Isabella's envoys arrived to collect him, they settled upon a plan to make the dangerous journey west to his wedding in disguise, dressed as wealthy merchants and their servants. They would have to pass through Aragonese villages controlled by thieves and Castilian villages controlled by Enrique. They did not underestimate the king's capacity for mischief. Everyone understood that assassination was not beneath the unpredictable king.

Ferdinand gamely took the role of a lowly servant. Humbly, he served meals to the Castilian envoys and groomed their mules. Along the way the prince's food was roasted and boiled and tasted by others. When the party finally reached the frontier of Aragon and Castile, it was met in the tiny village of Burgo de Osma by an armed squadron of two hundred soldiers, sent by the archbishop of Toledo. The Prince of

Aragon and King of Sicily could at last reclaim his royal dignity. Traveling at night, they moved through the hostile territory along the upper valley of the Duero River without incident. Eight days later, on October 9, he arrived safely in Duenas, only a few miles from Valladolid.

With Ferdinand safe in Duenas, Isabella sat down and wrote an elegant, conciliatory, and touching letter to Enrique. "Very high and very distinguished Prince King my Lord," she began. Once again she announced her intention to marry, "a very reasonable thing to do at my age." In making her choice, she had consulted the princes of his kingdom, who had approved. From this union of prince and princess would emerge a more powerful union of Castile and Aragon. She noted that Enrique had attempted to "impede the entrance of the prince and king" into her presence, but she wished to inform the king that her espoused was nearby and had no intention to "create scandals and other bad things in your kingdoms nor to disturb your nobles, as your highness has suggested." Rather, Ferdinand was of good intentions, and he offered his services to the king.

"May the Holy Trinity protect your highness and make you prosper in these good times."

A day later, under cover of darkness, the prince was secretly taken to meet his fiancée for the first time. As matchmaker, the archbishop of Toledo was the host for the assignation, and it was he who conducted Ferdinand into the presence of Isabella. She sat demurely, the picture of humility, piety, and beauty. At first glimpse, Ferdinand was so stunned by her beauty and presence that he blurted out a few disjointed and embarrassing words. But their priest-facilitator smoothed the situation calmly, and the two teenagers fell eventually into animated conversation.

"The presence of the Archbishop stifled the romantic impulses of the two whose hearts strengthened in their mutual contemplation," wrote the effusive chronicler. "It was not long after that they experienced the legal joys of matrimony."

There was but one sour note. At the end of their encounter, Ferdinand approached his bride-to-be and kissed her hand, an act at which she recoiled, for it made him seem like just another flatterer. Later, in commenting on this, the archbishop of Toledo waved it aside as trivial. Even if Ferdinand was somewhat below Isabella in stately power, she had given her hand to him, and for that, she owed him total obedience.

On October 18, the feast day of St. Luke, Ferdinand formally and officially entered the city with great ceremony. Crowds lined the streets as the procession of nobles and prelates rode grandly by in their exquisite, jeweled robes, their horses caparisoned with equally exquisite embroidered harnesses and stirrups. The day was filled with lively jousts and tournaments and sword-and-staff competitions with canes. The rejoicing would continue for seven days.

On October 19, in a formal ceremony, the Capitulations of Ferdinand and the Aragonese throne to Isabella and the throne of Castile were read formally before the royal assembly, as well as a papal bull waiving the prohibition against a royal marriage within the third ring of consanguinity. And then, in the palace of a local grandee named Juan de Vivero, the archbishop of Toledo, assisted by the Cardinal of Spain, Rodrigo Borgia, married the couple. The ceremony was solemn, it was said. A number of disapproving nobles were present solely to protect their interests. They sat on their hands, scowling sullenly as the archbishop blessed the couple and their union.

That night, the marriage was consummated. By longstanding tradition, courtiers were posted at the door to the royal bedchamber. When the appropriate time had elapsed, they burst into the bedchamber to strip the bed of its sheet. This trophy they brought to the eager crowd below, displaying its stains as if the relic were a triumphal battle flag. To ensure no fraud, more witnesses were sent in to double-check the bed itself.

"And then," the chronicler wrote, "trumpets blared, kettledrums sounded, and minstrels sang."

The long reign of Ferdinand and Isabella had begun on a most satisfactory and auspicious note.

4

As Much as the One Is Worth

Eleven and a half months later, in Duenas, Isabella gave birth to a daughter. The unrelenting hostility of King Enrique, who remained furious about her uncertified marriage, tempered the joy of motherhood, however. A month after the birth, on November 20, 1470, the king reversed formally the agreement of Toros de Guisando. Juana, the notorious "La Beltraneja," now nine years old, was in attendance, as her prior acknowledged illegitimacy was voided, and she was once again proclaimed to be the legitimate heir. The King of Portugal threw his weight behind this newest effort. A new papal bull now declared the previous bull null and void. In the winter of 1470–71, Enrique took the next step by disinheriting Isabella, though how a half brother disinherits a half sister is not exactly clear. A pronouncement proclaimed her to be a dissolute woman, who had acted shamefully and stubbornly against the king's counsel, and therefore had disdained the laws of Castile.

Had it not been for the armed conflict that the latest reversals occasioned, and the intertwining of Portuguese ambitions, the situation would have been a court farce. But once again nobles and notables of all stripe chose sides and, no doubt with a sigh, strapped on their armor once again. Civil war would continue, it seemed, until El Impotente died. By 1473, towns and villages were lining up on Isabella's side. Even the king's favorite city of Segovia, with its lions, Flemish altarpieces, Moorish Alcazar, Roman aqueduct, and tiled patios, had deserted to Isabella's side. It finally dawned on Enrique that reconciliation was his most sensible course.

Facilitating this reconciliation was a surprising figure. Abraham Senior, the court rabbi, was a fifty-seven-year-old Jew who was something of a financial genius and who had been a quiet influence behind the scenes in arranging the marriage between Ferdinand and Isabella. Born in Segovia, he worked in the one area that remained officially open to Jews, tax collection. By enriching the coffers of the crown's treasury through skillful administration, he had gained enormous influence in the royal court, capturing the admiration of the aristocracy, as well as the affection of Isabella. With this clout, he had become the de facto leader of the 120,000 Spanish Jews, as well as the queen's chief adviser for secular matters. His intelligence, wit, and bearing had made him a favorite if unconventional presence in the court. In gratitude for his services, Isabella was to grant him a lifetime pension of 100,000 maravedis. As a bonus, he was able to escape some of the harsh restrictions that were required of his brethren.

❖

In December 1473, half brother and half sister finally met in Segovia. Arm-in-arm, they danced and sang and paraded before their subjects joyously, as if nothing awkward or untoward had passed between them for the previous five years. They were joined by Ferdinand, who had been away in Aragon most of the year fighting the French. A whole new set of proclamations and bulls were drafted, as Isabella was reinstated as princess and heir. Amid all this apparent amity, it was incumbent upon the heirs to the crown of Castile to guard their backs, for scoundrels and assassins lurked in the shadows.

In the years 1469–73, if the relentless strife between petty nobles seemed like business as usual in the Spanish heartland, there were several events on the ecclesiastical front worth noting, portents of more worrisome events to come. In 1471, a new pope acceded to the throne of the Holy See. He was Sixtus IV, an Italian Franciscan priest of humble origins, and a confirmed nepotist, who was addicted to great luxury and who loved art and architecture. (The building of the Sistine Chapel and the establishment of the Vatican Library were among his lasting achievements.) Sixtus had propagated two sons, whom he immediately installed in important ecclesiastical posts, just as his nephew was made a cardinal. The new pope became quickly embroiled in Italian politics, forcing Rome and the Church into a desperate struggle with Florence and Lorenzo de Medici. As a consequence, this pope was both pliant and distracted from Spanish affairs during this critical period.

Sixtus owed his election partly to a rising star in the Roman Curia, a Spanish cardinal named Rodrigo Borgia to whom the pope delegated the responsibility for Spanish affairs. For his efforts, Borgia had become the vice chancellor of the Vatican. In the summer of 1472, Cardinal Borgia was dispatched to his homeland, ostensibly to mediate for peace in the civil war, to restrain Alfonso of Portugal in his ambitions for Spain, to advocate for a crusade against the infidels in the south, and to deliver the papal blessing for the marriage of Ferdinand and Isabella.

For this diplomatic and military mission, Borgia's extensive party arrived, with great ceremony, at Tarragona. The papal legate promptly alienated both his countrymen and the Portuguese with his arrogance and extravagance and "other unbraked passions." He entertained at lavish banquets and insisted on grand processions, complete with several hundred soldiers and musicians, for his arrivals. Cardinal Borgia would stay for a year, spending months in Ferdinand and Isabella's court, while he devoted most of his energies to enriching the House of Borgia with wealthy bishoprics. In Portugal, he carried on scandalously with the ladies of the court. The cardinal of Pavia remarked that Borgia's sole purpose seemed to be to dazzle his countrymen with wealth and spectacle.

With the pliant Sixtus as her pope and the dissolute Rodrigo Borgia as her cardinal, Isabella had as her confessor quite a different character. His name was Tomás de Torquemada, the Dominican prior of the Monastery of Santa Cruz in Segovia. Torquemada had grown up in Valladolid and was the nephew of the great Cardinal Juan de Torquemada, who had been such a noble defender of the conversos during the troubles of 1449. Tomás de Torquemada was tall and pale, with thick eyebrows. His flattened boxer's nose was the most prominent feature of his face, and its lumpy folds seemed all the more prominent because of the ring of hair and bald top that distinguished the tonsure of a Dominican friar. Known for his privations, he walked barefoot, slept on planks, and wore the hair shirt beneath the wool of the white and black cowl of his order. For his efficient administrative skills he had risen rapidly in the ranks of the Dominicans.

Torquemada burned with a vivid hatred of heresy and of any Christian of whatever background who might conceivably be guilty of it. His grandmother had been a Jew, and this dirty little secret seemed to drive his passion against Jews and Christians of Jewish heritage into a determined and permanent rage. He longed for the "pure blood" of an old Castilian Christian, and believed that Jewish blood was darker in hue as it contaminated the body. In the absence of any prosecution of heretics at all in Castile, the "Old" Inquisition was not good enough for this bloodless fanatic. As he received Isabella's confessions during this period, he sought to extract a promise from her:

"If you ever come to the throne, you must devote yourself to the liquidation of heresy, for the glory of God and the exaltation of the Catholic Church."

The last of Isabella's quartet of holy men was Alfonso Carrillo de Acuña, archbishop of Toledo and primate of Spain. In 1473 at the Council of Aranda, Carrillo made an effort to upgrade the standards of Spanish priesthood, for the ignorance and corruption of country friars had become an embarrassment and led to violent clashes with Jews and conversos. Henceforth, examinations for the priesthood would be required, and priests were obligated to read and write Latin, which was the lingua franca of the Church and the foundation of all religious instruction. Holy men were forbidden to wear silk or colorful decoration, which undermined and distracted their focus from their spiritual call-

ing. They must abstain from gambling, and they were required to celebrate mass at least four times a year.

Laudable as these measures were, they did little to restrain radicals
who in the name and the garb of holy orders continued to agitate
against the House of David. In 1473, another wave of pogroms swept
Spain, starting in the reconquered towns of Andalusia and spreading
north to such cities as Valladolid and Segovia. During Lent that year
when a group called the *Cofradia del Caridad*, the Brotherhood of Charity, were marching through the streets of Córdoba, a young conversa
girl emptied water on the parade from an upper story. As drops fell on
the statue of the Virgin Mary they were carrying, pandemonium
erupted, and the brothers of charity chanted: "Death to the conversos,"
with terrible consequences.

Isabella's reconciliation with the king coincided with her break with
her archbishop. For the archbishop of Toledo himself was not incor-
ruptible. He had come under the sway of an itinerant huckster named
Fernando de Alarcon, who by all accounts had married many times in
many places and, so one chronicler wrote, had corrupted clerics from
Cyprus to Sicily and brought them to "incests and all sorts of obsceni-
ties." Alarcon professed knowledge in the magical properties of herbs
and minerals; among his talents, he told the primate of Spain, was his
ability to change stone into gold. His secret lay in phosphorous, which
contained the light of the sun, he claimed, and which had miraculous
powers. Since the archbishop's interest in gold was extravagant, the al-
chemist was brought into the archbishop's court and given a laboratory
to ply his wondrous techniques. Only the archbishop was blind to this
fraud, apparently. Strife and dissension reigned in the court as a result
of this bizarre friendship.

Eventually, when the charlatan ran short of money, Isabella was
asked to contribute to his support. Caught between her gratitude to her
archbishop and her certain knowledge of Alarcon's schemes, she played
along for a time. But she was instinctively contemptuous of superstition
and sorcery, and eventually had the faker ejected from the palace and
beheaded. The archbishop, in a pique, switched his loyalty to Enrique

the Impotent and to the aspirations of the nine-year-old Portuguese pretender called La Beltraneja.

✦

In 1465, four years before Isabella married Ferdinand, the last Moorish Caliphate of Spain endured as a mere shadow of past glory. At its height, the realm of Al Andalus covered most of Spain. It had eighty cities, including Córdoba with a population of over a million, and twelve thousand villages on the banks of the Guadalquivir River alone. Since the mid-thirteenth century its expanse had shrunk to the mountainous province of Granada, nestled amid the stately peaks of the Sierra Nevada and the Alpujarras foothills, and extending south to its ports of Málaga and Almería on the Costa del Sol. Isolated from its spiritual roots in the east, and attacked continuously from the north, Granada was a fading jewel, an enclave of learning and culture, and a model of religious tolerance. So long as all citizens recognized the caliph as their ruler, Jews, Christians, and Mohammedans lived peaceably together as "people of the Book." The city of Granada itself comprised some 70,000 houses and had a population of 400,000. Distinctive walled gardens bloomed with pomegranates, date trees, and jasmine. The air was perfumed with orange blossoms. The vistas to the snowy peaks in the distance were magnificent. The Moors imagined that the paradise of the Prophet was situated in that part of heaven above Granada.

The heart of the caliphate was the magnificent Alhambra. The jewel and the symbol of the 800-year rule of Islam in Spain, this red palace had awed and inspired the common man and the composer and the poet alike for centuries. "Give him alms, woman, for nothing in life is worse than being blind in Granada," a modern poet would write. And a fourteenth-century poet, Ibn Zamrak, the vizier to Muhammad V (1362–91), wrote of the Alhambra:

The Sabika hill sits like a garland on Granada's brow
In which the stars would be entwined

And the Alhambra (Allah preserve it)
Is the ruby set above that garland.

It was as much a royal village as it was a palace, as much a set of luxuriant gardens as fortress. Within the walls of the complex, it was said that forty thousand soldiers could be garrisoned. From its lofty terrace the colossus towered above the city and looked out to the *vega*, or plain, which stretched some thirty miles to distant hills.

As the last bastion of Islam in the West, the caliphate had survived partly through its deference to the warrior kings of Castile. For centuries the Christian kings had taken their oaths of office with the pledge to destroy the infidel kingdom of the south. In urging on Isabella's weak father to greater glory, a poet of the time wrote to him pointedly: "You were made king of the earth by He of the Heavens,/ So that you and those you command/Turn His Wrath against the Moors." It was the king's duty to his God and his faith and his subjects. For decades there had been periodic thrusts on both sides of the frontier, but for much of the fifteenth century a truce had been in effect. In these intermittent periods of truce, the price of peace was a tribute to be paid in the city of Córdoba every year by the Moorish kings to the emissaries of the Christian kings.

But in 1465, a fiery and resentful prince, Muley Aben Hassan, succeeded his father, Ishmael, as the emir of Al Andalus and abruptly terminated the tribute. Witnessing his father kowtowing to the Christian envoys over the years, he had developed a passionate distaste for the groveling. The mere mention of the practice sent him into a fit of rage.

In his youth, Muley Aben Hassan had married a strong, energetic, and determined woman. Her name was Ayxa, and for her fortitude and rectitude she was known as "the Chaste." By her the caliph was presented with a son, Abu Abdullah Muhammad, who would become better known as Boabdil. Legend has it that upon his birth the court astrologers had been summoned to foretell his future. But when they marked the positions of the planets on his birthday and regarded the signs of zodiac in his horoscope, they recoiled in fear and horror: Although it was written in the book of fate, they whispered, that the boy would one day sit on the throne, it was also written that during his reign the great caliphate of Al Andalus would fall to conquest and collapse. This curse of astrology turned the father against his son and his wife. Both were rejected and ostracized. In the court of the Alcazar, the son became known as "Boabdil the Unfortunate."

After Ayxa the Chaste, the sultan took a very different wife. She was a Christian slave, whose father had been captured in combat, and who had been brought to Granada as an infant where she was raised as a Muslim. She was given the name first of Fatima and then, due to her stunning beauty, the name of Zoraya or Morning Star. As assertive as she was beautiful, she was taken into the sultan's harem and quickly became his favorite. Bearing the sultan two sons, she pressed them forward as an alternative to Boabdil as heirs to the throne.

Within the furtive court a faction formed behind Zoraya's ambitions, and the harem became a hotbed of intrigue and dissension. Totally captivated by his sultana, and yet driven to distraction by the machinations of his court, the sultan took the extreme measure of putting several of his sons to death in the Alhambra's Courtyard of the Lions. At Zoraya's urging, he also imprisoned his son Boabdil in the Tower of the Comares, with the intention of executing him as well and thus expunging the curse of Boabdil's horoscope. Shaking his fist at the stars, Muley Hassan reportedly declared: "The sword of the executioner shall prove the fallacy of those lying horoscopes, and shall silence the ambition of Boabdil."

But as the legend goes, Ayxa the Chaste snuck into Boabdil's prison with her maids, tied scarves together, and lowered Boabdil to the ledges above the Darro River, where her confederates were waiting to spirit the prince away to the city of Guadix.

❖

In Segovia, the festival of reconciliation between Enrique IV and Isabella lasted through the Christmas season of 1473 and into the new year. On Epiphany a sumptuous banquet was laid out, with song and dancing and endless courses, and the monarchs ate through most of the day, until in the evening, Enrique, suddenly looking pale and wan, drooped and collapsed. He was carried to his chamber, where he waved his doctors away, for he had always been suspicious of them and their poisons. Perhaps he had good reason, for it came to be widely believed that the king was poisoned by his Jewish physician, a man named Se-maya. If it was poison, it was very slow-acting. The episode began a slow, gradual decline in his health, marked by vomit and blood and inattention over many months, until on December 11, 1474, in Madrid, El Impotente died.

Isabella learned of her half brother's death in Segovia and repaired to the Church of San Miguel for a mass of mourning. Outside the church, a platform was hastily constructed for her exaltation to the throne. Soon after the mass, she appeared radiant before a large gathering of nobles and the papal legate. She cut a dazzling figure, richly attired in a brocaded gown and bejeweled in gold and precious stone.

At the edge of the crowd stood the ghostly figure of her confessor, Tomás de Torquemada.

The cry went up that the king was dead. One by one the nobles came forward to swear their allegiance to their new monarch, and as something of an afterthought, to her husband, Ferdinand, who was not present. After the ceremony, she mounted a magnificent steed, richly caparisoned with fabrics embroidered with intricate designs, and the parade began through the streets. Heading it was a single knight, who held aloft a naked sword to symbolize the power of the throne, and, after the Spanish fashion, to warn all evildoers of the queen's power to punish. The standard-bearer followed, dressed in a costume of bluish velvet silk bordered with green—blue for loyalty, green for hope. After him, the nobles walked on foot dressed hastily in their finest velvet, and behind them, the queen. A great and jubilant crowd of well-wishers trailed.

The chant became "Castile, Castile, for the very high and powerful lady, our lady the Queen Doña Isabel," repeated three times, and followed by "Castile, Castile, for the very high and powerful lord, the King Don Ferdinand, her legitimate husband." From the start, homage to

Ferdinand was to be secondary. A few traditionalists grumbled that the queen had appropriated the reins of power which rightfully belonged to the male and the king. But this dissent was drowned out by those who pointed to the accession as hers alone while the king's was derivative.

During these heady days of transition, Ferdinand had remained in Aragon presiding over a conclave of his unruly nobles. Within a few days of Enrique's death, he received word of Isabella's hasty coronation. He recoiled at hearing that she had paraded through the streets of Segovia behind the masculine sword of justice. Why had she gone forward without him? Was some sinister plot at work? Hastening to her side, Ferdinand rode through Castilian towns with great ceremony, showing the flag and scepter of his new role as King of Castile. He did not take seriously the prenuptial concessions he had made. His first priority was to set straight who was in charge in this marriage. Transcending mere "Capitulations" was the obligation of every good and pious Christian woman, even a queen, to honor and obey her husband. He was entitled to this deference. He expected and demanded it. He was in for a surprise.

On January 2, 1475, Ferdinand arrived in Segovia, where Isabella received him warmly. It would not be many hours before their respective delegates got right to the business of power sharing. The Capitulations were read once again. Ferdinand's councilors emphasized the lack of historical precedent for a royal wife holding power superior to her husband's. It had never happened in Aragon, and in Castile such an arrangement had not existed for several hundred years. Especially bitter for Ferdinand to swallow was the provision that, should Isabella die, power would pass not to Ferdinand but to their children. Ferdinand, and Aragon, would be marginalized. Isabella stood firm, an iron will beneath her warmth and feminine charm, and her husband had no choice but to acquiesce.

The court scribe tried to put the best face on the sharp disagreement between them with the blandishment: "The love of his wife calmed the king's ire and obeying his feelings, he assented with good grace to his wife's entreaties." Whatever the disparity in their real power, they presented henceforth a united face to their subjects. Their motto became, somewhat disingenuously: *"Tanto monta, monta tanto—Isabel como Fernando—*As much as the one is worth so much is the other worth—Isabella as Ferdinand."

Ferdinand and Isabella scarcely had time to catch their breath before a new disaster loomed. The Portuguese king, the estimable, jilted O Africano, Alfonso V, announced his intention to wed the issue of dubious pedigree, La Beltraneja, and signaled his intention to march on Castile to put his lady on her rightful throne. His army was formidable: nine thousand foot soldiers, nearly four thousand cavalry, along with heavy artillery and a contingent of Lombardian engineers. The War of Succession was under way again. In late May, this force entered Spain through Albuquerque and turned north. A week later, Isabella, distraught at the Portuguese invasion, miscarried a male heir to the throne while she was traveling to Ávila.

Through the summer of 1475 the Portuguese army made its way north into the Castilian *meseta,* occupying the royal town of Arevalo before it moved deeper into Castile, reaching the vicinity of Salamanca and Zamora. Along the way an anti-coronation was held for the young La Beltraneja, and now there were two queens of Castile. After the city of Zamora defected to the Portuguese, the enemy took charge of the strategic town of Toro and laid siege to its fortress, high on an outcropping of rock above.

With this first military engagement of their reign, both Ferdinand and Isabella wallowed in the glory and tragedy and the bathos of war. Before strapping on his armor and heading west, Ferdinand made out his will, providing for the fortunes of his children, granting considerable charitable donations to prisoners of the Moors and for the dowries of impecunious girls. And he expressed his desire to be buried with Isabella, wherever she wished to find her final resting place. "We were united by marriage and by a unique love in life. Let us not be parted in death." Before he rode off, he dispatched another love message that bore the stamp of every young man on his way to combat: "God knows that it weighs on me not to see your ladyship tomorrow, for I swear by your life and mine that I have never loved you more."

Meanwhile, in the finest tradition of chivalry, he challenged Alfonso the African to a duel to the death in single combat.

Isabella, in turn, felt deeply her role as the defender of Castile and empress of the armies. Like Joan of Arc or Eleanor of Aquitaine, she wished to ride in glory at the head of her forces, for she was ashamed at the Portuguese presence in Castile and longed for revenge. Now twenty-four years old, she watched wistfully as the troops departed on their mission to lift the siege of Toro's alcazar and recover the town itself. For the moment she would resist the temptation to go to the front lines.

When only days later that same army returned in retreat, having failed to lure Alfonso into single combat, or to engage the well-entrenched Portuguese defenders, her wistfulness turned to anger. To her husband and her commanders she spoke through clenched teeth. "If you say that women, since they do not face dangers of war, ought not to speak of them, I respond, who risks more than I do? I risked my King and Lord, whom I love above all else in the world, and I risked many noble lords," she said. "I would wish unknown danger rather than certain shame. Of my feminine fury and your masculine patience, I marvel. By daring to vent my anger I have quieted the passion that naturally grows in the hearts of women. I bare my soul because I do not have the power to lessen the pain nor to drive it out. The best release for a sufferer is to vent her distress to those who may commiserate with her."

It was left to Ferdinand to meet this fury. He spoke of their challenge in Toro. The fortress was perched on high ground, above steep cliffs, and his army did not have the artillery to reach the lofty battlements. The enemy had refused battle. In fact, the African had accepted Ferdinand's invitation to single combat, provided that Isabella and Beltraneja be kept as hostages and prizes. Such an absurd proviso Ferdinand could not honorably accept. What he did not say was that his forces were disorganized and lacked a central command, as individual lords of the realm controlled their own soldiers.

Gently but firmly, he berated his queen for her lack of patience and want of encouragement. "I had believed that in returning in despair I would hear from you consoling and encouraging words. Women are always dissatisfied, and you in particular, my Lady, since the man who could satisfy you is yet to be born." They were not ashamed, nor was this the final battle. "No one is as obliged to please women or to benefit the world as the man is to satisfy his own honor."

After the shame of the first non-battle of Toro, the determined queen took a more active role in military affairs. She met with commanders, deployed troops, dispensed orders, and conferred with Ferdinand on military strategy. Through the fall of 1475 the African spread his troops between various fortresses in western Castile. Through the winter, Ferdinand challenged his adversary at Zamora and Burgos. Late in the winter, both bastions fell. Isabella personally rode to Burgos to accept its surrender. The tide seemed to be turning.

Then on March 1, 1476, at a place called Peleagonzalo outside Toro, Ferdinand caught Alfonso's army in the open. The battle was pivotal. Though the Portuguese force, which had the edge in numbers, fell smartly into battle formation, the Castilians seemed to have the greater motivation. The natives were commanded by a cardinal in full battle gear, who led a ferocious cavalry charge that sliced through Portuguese lines. His name was Pedro González de Mendoza; when he was not leading cavalry charges, he had replaced Archbishop Carrillo as Isabella's most important religious adviser and confessor. The second Battle of Toro lasted three hours. While its outcome was inconclusive, the Castilians ruled the field at the end of the day.

The Battle of Toro virtually ended this long struggle over succession. Rebellious towns in the west of Castile, in the Extremadura and León, seeing that the momentum had shifted to the Spanish monarchs, came over to Isabella's side quickly afterward. It would be another three years before the Treaty of Alcáçovas formally ended the War of Succession in 1479. In that agreement, Portugal recognized Isabella as the rightful

Queen of Spain, with sovereignty over a vast and expanding kingdom from the Pyrenees to Andalusia, only the Moorish emirate at Granada yet to be pacified. Spain's right to the Canary Islands was also conceded, and the islands would soon become a critical way station in the explorations across the ocean. Castile conceded Portugal's right to the Portuguese discoveries along the coast of Africa, while Spain claimed dominion over any lands that might be discovered to the west of the Canaries.

And finally, the Treaty of Alcácovas also ended the long-running melodrama of La Beltraneja. Instead of marrying Alfonso, she entered the Convent of Santa Clara in Portugal and dropped from the pages of history.

With the evaporation of the foreign threat in 1476, Ferdinand and Isabella turned their gaze to pacifying their own vast domain and subduing defiant, rambunctious nobles . . . by any means necessary.

5

The Lady
and Her Brotherhood

 With their victory at the Battle of Toro complete, Ferdinand and Isabella, the glamorous young monarchs of a new Spain, surveyed their vast dominion and wondered how in the name of God it could be governed. For three quarters of a century the land had been torn asunder by dissension, rebellion, weak and corrupt kings, foreign invaders, dishonest prelates, independent fiefdoms, ambitious and greedy nobles, and wanton criminals. Its roads were unsafe. Murder was rampant. Thieves and robber barons had plunged the land into anarchy. Poverty was everywhere. Plague and disease were horrific. But with Portugal defeated, France, for the moment, at bay, the Moorish Caliphate in the south weak and shrinking, and the issue of succession settled, security and consolidation were the watchwords of the day.

How might they take advantage of the victory over Portugal? How could they exert greater control over an empire that had almost doubled in size? They turned, in 1476, to an ancient tradition known as the *hermandad,* a religious brotherhood of vigilantes. The first instance of such militants was recorded in the twelfth century when some effort had to be made to protect the stream of pilgrims who walked over the Pyrenees and across northern Spain to Santiago de Compostela in Galicia. This first *hermandad* patrolled the route of the pilgrims, much as the Templars patrolled and protected pilgrims who traveled to Jerusalem in the Holy Land. In succeeding centuries, these vigilante bands spread arbitrarily across Spain, as contiguous cities and towns sought to protect the roads for travel and commerce between them from thieves and killers. The vigilantes were given broad powers, including summary execution. In a curious turnabout, executions took place first, and trials were held afterwards. Execution, medieval style, was by bow and arrow. A target was pinned to the condemned man's heart. The firing squad lined up, and each individual bowman was rewarded or fined for the accuracy (or inaccuracy) of his shot.

In April 1476, only a month after the Battle of Toro, the monarchs convened a Cortes, or national congress, at Isabella's birthplace of Madrigal de las Altas Torres to consider the security of the patrimony. There, the delegates petitioned the monarchs to create a national constabulary, and to control it from the top.

"The order must come from on high," they petitioned; "then it will have the greater vigor and force."

It was determined that the *hermandades* would be expanded and institutionalized into a national police force. Every municipality in the realm was ordered to establish a *hermandad* within a month; for every one hundred citizens, there should be one *hermandad* policeman. By recruiting the force mainly from the ranks of the peasantry, the *hermandad* was by definition a check on independent feudal lords, great and small, who were exploiting and oppressing and robbing the poor, and worse, challenging the authority of the crown. Since this royal constabulary was beholden to national rather than local control, its justices of the peace had the power to override local judges and grandees. It quickly became apparent that the new royal militia could be very useful in collecting taxes as well.

The blessing of the Church was also conferred upon the *hermandades*. At Madrigal, they were given the name *Santa Hermandad*, the Holy Brotherhood. In case of resistance by nobles opposed to the creation of an armed police force with powers superseding their own authority, the Cortes put forward the timeworn rationale of needing the national police as a protection against foreign invasion. This pretext was convenient. The effect was, of course, to centralize power and to spread fear through the land, especially among dissidents against the crown. At Madrigal the nobles had accepted the reconstitution of the national force as a temporary expediency. But the sovereigns quickly perceived its usefulness, and it would last for another twenty-two years.

The *hermandad* was the main focus of the Cortes of Madrigal, and its consequences were far-reaching. It could be argued that only through the rigorous enforcement of the law by a vigilant police could Spain be truly united and be transformed from a feudal into a modern state. But the national police was not the only measure considered. Bowing to a pressure that never seemed to disappear, the Cortes returned to the state of Jews and Moors in the kingdom. On this matter, it turned the clock back once again ominously. The Cortes vacated a law that forbade the jailing of Jews and Muslims for debts owed to Christians. More insidious, the body passed a regulation requiring Jews and Muslims to wear an insignia of their persuasion on their clothing. Henceforth, Jews and Muslims were barred from holding office in local communities. The joining of a national police with repressive religious persecution pointed the way to disaster.

Apologists for the monarchs argued emptily that these measures protected Jews from the arbitrary persecutions and abuses of radicals by standardizing the regulations for the whole kingdom. Each repressive and racist measure built upon a century of persecutions in Spain and moved the kingdom closer to its odious final solution. In their complicity Ferdinand and Isabella bear the major blame.

In 1476 in Old Castile, there were fifteen grand families and fifty second-rank noble families, as well as an entire cast of minor, threadbare nobles. In fact, Spain had a higher proportion of nobles relative to the general population than any other country in Europe (10 percent as opposed to 1 percent in France). The principal nobles sported various titles such as duke, marquis, count, and viscount; lesser nobles, in shades of Cervantes, often had trouble affording horse and sword. To a large extent, the stature of the powerful houses had been attained through successful commercial ventures over the generations. The archbishop of Toledo, Alfonso Carrillo de Acuña, for example, was the scion of the Acuña family, which had dominated the powerful guild of sheepherders. Valladolid had long been the domain of the hereditary admirals of Castile. The *hermandad* was meant to break the power and independence of these families and guilds.

The new constabulary challenged the historic autonomy of the nobility, which for centuries had been codified in a concept called the *fuero viejo*, or old jurisdiction. The *fuero viejo* defined the balance of power between the crown and the noble families. Traditionally, the crown could arbitrate questions of justice, could declare war, and dispense royal honors and positions. Beyond that, the nobles ruled their roosts as mini-kings. Outside Castile, in other parts of the far-flung kingdom, and in Ferdinand's kingdom of Aragon especially, the *fuero* was even stronger than in Castile.

But a new age of centralized authority was beginning.

✦

In her mid-twenties, with several years as queen behind her, Isabella was developing into a formidable woman and leader. She could be soft and feminine, flighty and overindulgent in her dress, owning roomfuls of elaborate gowns and closets packed with jewels and gold ornament. She could be merciful and tender, promotional of the arts and literature. She went out of her way to bolster the authority of her insecure husband. Yet Isabella had another, fiercer quality: she possessed great personal courage. In 1476, the year after her coronation, hearing of an insurrection against her local authority, she hastened from Tordesillas to Segovia. Upon reaching the city, she found it under siege by a raging mob that was on the verge of stringing up her chosen mayor. Rejecting the advice of her terrified councilors to shore up the castle gates against the rabble, she instead threw them open and then strode confidently into the mob.

"Tell me what your grievances are, and I will do all in my power to redress them," she called out to the startled protesters. They wanted the marquis sacked and replaced with someone more progressive.

"It is done," she replied, "and you have my authority to turn out any of his officers who are still in the castle." Before long the mob was chanting, "Long live the Queen!"

While she was independent and self-reliant, she was, of course, exceedingly devout, pursuing her daily and even hourly prayers with the vigor of a nun. Her watchword came from St. John the Evangelist, the author of the book of Revelation: "Make me passionately virtuous in your image and zealous for the faith." That very piety led her to appoint the most bloodless and rigid of the clergy as her closest advisers.

It was this unshakable, rigid faith that gave her character its hard, unforgiving side. She could be narrow-minded and stubborn and uncompromising, especially where religious principle was involved. Her confessor, the Dominican priest Tomás de Torquemada, narrowed and hardened her character further. In 1477, the queen became a tertiary sister of the Dominican Order. Yet it was in this very faith that she derived her strength and moral courage. Everywhere, she confronted the contempt and disrespect toward her sex. A woman as leader? Even as the nobles addressed her as "most powerful Queen and Lady," they murmured that her skill and forcefulness in the affairs of state made her masculine. This common slur merely underscored the fact that she was a woman of great forcefulness.

In the year after the Cortes of Madrigal, largely due to the institution of the *hermandad,* most of Old Castile had fallen into line, and through the efforts of Ferdinand, Navarre was pacified. Isabella felt that she could turn her attention to the more unruly territories of the Extremadura and Andalusia. The Extremadura, that windswept, sparsely populated arid region along the Portuguese frontier, had welcomed the Portuguese invasion during the War of Succession and remained sympathetic to the claims of Isabella's rival, La Beltraneja. This rolling, empty expanse of wheat fields and holm oak possessed some of the greatest estates of Spain, which were held by the powerful families of Ponce de León, Guzmán, and Villena. These lords were accustomed to operating without interference from mere kings. Now the queen swept through their country with her entourage, establishing a regional *hermandad*, presiding over symbolic legal proceedings, demanding deference to the crown, subjugating resistant castles, and restoring peace and order. In the face of formidable opposition, and not inconsiderable personal danger, she was defiant and unafraid.

"I have come to this land, and I do not intend to leave it, nor to flee danger nor to shirk my duty," she said. "Nor will I give comfort to my enemies who cause such pain to my subjects."

On this campaign south she tarried memorably at the remote village of Guadalupe, where she prayed before the dark carving of the Virgin Mary, said to have been fashioned by St. Luke himself. Like the many pilgrims who had preceded her, and the mariners, like Christopher Columbus who was to come there later, she was transported by the holy shrine. It was her paradise.

Seville was then the southernmost town of Castile and the kingdom's most populous metropolis, with 45,000 residents. The traditional capital of Andalusia, a city divided by the Guadalquivir River, it was the principal inland port of Isabella's kingdom. Twenty leagues from the sea, it was the embarkation point for Spanish explorations to the south and west and teemed with sailors, teamsters, beggars, urchins, thieves, and tradesmen—"the people of the river," Cervantes called them later. Its impressive wooden pontoon bridge, supported by seventeen barges, was clogged with traffic that crossed over from the city's center to the commercial barrio of Triana. After Christian forces had reconquered the city in A.D. 1248, among the first acts of the new rulers was to reconstitute the Almohad mosque as a Christian cathedral, dedicating it to the Virgin Mary. The mosque itself had been demolished in 1402, and upon its ruins, plans were made to erect the largest cathedral in the world, an epic task that would take a hundred years. But relics of Seville's Moorish past outshone the gigantic, prosaic Christian shrine. Rising above the gargantuan cathedral was the magnificent twelfth-century Moorish belltower, the Giralda, and across the plaza, the Moorish fortress, the Alcazar, within whose walls were rooms and patios and salons of such exquisite artistry that they were rivaled in that time only by the striated mosque at Córdoba and the salons of Granada's Alhambra. Amid this splendor of lost elegance, Isabella took up residence above the Patio of the Dolls.

But Seville had its dark side. In the magical thinking of 1477, with its nightmares of the apocalypse and its dream of a second coming, and with the "Jewish heresy" perceived to be more rampant there than anywhere else in Spain, it was believed that the Antichrist would make his appearance in Seville before the final battle between good and evil. This emissary of the Devil would take power there, before the messianic king, called "the Hidden One" or "the Bat," could arrive to confront and defeat him. The Bat would then move on to conquer Granada, and free Spain at last of its infidels. Once Spain was secured for Christ, the Hidden One would complete the triumphal vision of Christian conquest by traveling to the Holy Land and securing Jerusalem. It would not be long before Ferdinand began to see himself as the Bat, while Isabella was put forward, perhaps even in her own mind, as the reincarnation of the Virgin Mary.

The past century added to Seville's reputation for terror. In the terrible year of 1391, Seville was the site of the first large-scale slaughter of Jews. The tirades of a rabble-rousing, Jew-hating priest and agent provocateur, Ferrón Martínez, had sparked the killing and stealing. The Jewish quarter was attacked, and four thousand of Seville's Jews were murdered. Their property was plundered as greed merged with hatred. Martínez's mobs rampaged through the narrow streets of the ghetto. Seville's outbreak became the catalyst for similar pogroms across Castile and into Aragon. This purge was quickly dubbed the *"guerra santa contra los Judios*—holy war against the Jews." Some of the great houses of Jews in Seville were donated to favorites of the Castilian king.

And it was in the Seville of the late fourteenth century that the insidious choice of death or baptism was first advanced. The pressure to convert had continued unabated for another twenty-five years, until by 1412 nearly twenty thousand Jews had forcibly "converted" to Christianity. Once Jews converted, they were free to reclaim their old jobs.

For the previous decade, before Isabella's arrival in Seville in 1477, two of the most prominent, wealthy, and independent lords of southern Spain had competed and occasionally warred against each other for ascendancy. The balance was currently tipped in favor of Don Enrique de Guzmán, the count of Medina-Sidonia, over Don Rodrigo Ponce de León, the marquis of Cádiz.

But matters were by no means settled. The marquis of Cádiz was blithely levying taxes on wine, bread, and fish without royal authorization, to support his private armada, while the count of Medina-Sidonia was mobilizing the conversos of Seville to resist the royal imposition of a *hermandad* in his city. As Isabella approached the city, the duke lobbied his converso supporters, stressing that the founding of the *hermandad* would be a disaster for them. With their support, Guzmán stationed four hundred conversos in the city's fortress to resist the queen's interference. Isabella knew she must tread lightly. If she needed to pacify the powerful lords, she also needed their support, for Andalusia was a strategic borderland with the hostile forces of Portugal on one side and the infidel Caliphate of Granada on the other.

The queen entered Seville to a tumultuous welcome. In the cheers of her subjects, the resistance of the count of Medina-Sidonia quickly melted away. Isabella made it clear that she had come to Seville and to Andalusia to quell lawlessness and to stamp out tyranny in the region, for there was strife between powerful nobles in Córdoba and Jerez as well. Toward that end, she held a weekly public audience in the Grand Hall of the Alcazar, in which she sat upon a golden throne and personally arbitrated and adjudicated local disputes, listening patiently to long-winded pleas for mercy, and even ordering an occasional execution, all in the service of God and for the peace and security of the state, of course. The count of Medina-Sidonia found it difficult to compete with this exercise of royal power, but he continued to urge the conversos in his camp to resist. He would come to regret it. In due course, both the duke and the marquis prostrated themselves before her. The marquis of Cádiz handed over fortresses in Jerez and the Alcalá de Guadaira, which he had fortified against her.

During her weekly audiences an impressive array of prelates and *caballeros* stood at Isabella's side, in a display of religious and secular solidarity. In the antechambers of the Alcazar the clergy began to argue that a *hermandad* in Andalusia would be inadequate to pacify these influential lords permanently. A strong civil guard, answerable only to the crown, would be markedly strengthened, they again whispered, with a vigorous Inquisition, for the strongest supporters of local hegemony were conversos in high places, and these influential men were all secret Jews. In the city with the largest Jewish population in Spain, heresy was rampant, especially in high places, they whispered, and it needed to be rooted out. The plague of heresy had spread from local grandees to the general public. Especially forceful in making the argument for an inquisition was Alfonso de Ojeda, head of the Dominican monastery of San Pablo, who seemed to be equally gifted in his rabble-rousing from the pulpit and his whisperings to the queen in the fragrant gardens of the Alcazar.

On so grave a matter as the convening of an Inquisition, Isabella wished to consult with her husband. In September 1477, Ferdinand arrived from Aragon and was greeted warmly by his queen. His stay was short, but significant. After his departure, the chronicler wrote matter-of-factly, "The king stayed some days in which the queen became pregnant." No doubt the matter of an Inquisition was discussed, but nothing definite was decided.

On June 30, 1478, Isabella gave birth to a son, to the great relief and joy of the court. That the crown now had a male heir was cause for great celebration. A covey of courtiers and prelates were present in the birthing chamber. They were there to certify, as tradition demanded, that indeed the prince was the offspring of the king and queen.

Three days of festivities marked the blessed birth of the baby, Juan. A few days after that, the infant's baptism into the Christian faith was accomplished with great and triumphant fanfare in a chapel draped with silk and satin. The Cardinal of Spain and archbishop of Seville, Pedro González de Mendoza, officiated, while a host of dignitaries, including two godparents—the papal nuncio, Niccolò Franco, and the duchess of Medina-Sidonia—looked on proudly. In the feel of the ceremony was a hint of reference to the birth of Christ with the kings of Orient in attendance.

"Clearly we see ourselves given a very special gift by God," a chronicler wrote, "for at the end of such a long wait, He has desired to give him to us. The queen has paid to this kingdom the debt of virile succession that she is obligated to do. It is clear that this queen is moved to do things by divine Inspiration. . . . God has chosen the tribe of Isabella which he prefers."

Within a few weeks, Isabella's confinement was over. In late July, she put her mind to the next traditional ceremony for her son and heir, his presentation to God. Days before this service, which would take place on August 9, 1478, an upsetting omen appeared in the heavens and sent fear through the land. On July 29, a sudden and unexpected eclipse of the sun plunged Spain into darkness during the day, a darkness so intense that stars were visible in the heavens. Terrified about what this meant for the land and for the Catholic monarchs and for tiny Don Juan, people rushed to their churches for solace.

Meanwhile, the momentous question of an Inquisition hung in the air, until the queen was back on her feet. It was not as if the idea was something new. The institution had existed, in name only, for 250 years in Aragon. This was the "Old" Inquisition, in which the victims were few and randomly chosen as examples of heresy. In 1474, Ferdinand had revived a quiet Inquisition in Sicily, a move that elicited no particular interest in Spain. But in 1477 the monarchs received a visit from the inquisitor of Sicily, which brought the question to the forefront. The inquisitor came to Seville to reconfirm his right to possess one third of all properties confiscated from convicted heretics.

That great riches might be obtained by an Inquisition captured Ferdinand's immediate interest, but there might be a more profound benefit in consolidating royal authority over the vast empire. Isabella resisted. She could not approve of harsh measures, especially against a group like the conversos who had faithfully served the crown, measures which seemed so inconsistent with the teachings of Jesus Christ. The

Sicilian inquisitor met her resistance with colorful tales about the fear that the Inquisition induced in his flock. The Inquisition was a powerful instrument of social control, he said. It could be used with equal effectiveness across the social spectrum, from the nobility to the common people alike. Seville was an especially good place to start a vigorous Inquisition. The towns of Toledo and Burgos might have just as many Jews and conversos, but in unruly Seville, conversos held the highest positions of power, from the mayoralty down, and they were supported by the duke of Medina-Sidonia, who must be laid low. Seville could serve as an object lesson for the rest of the kingdom.

Meanwhile, Ferdinand, seconded by Friar Ojeda and the papal nuncio to the Spanish court, appealed to the queen's conscience. They trotted out the old arguments that the conversos, along with unbaptized Jews, insulted Christian relics and icons, and even engaged in the ritual murder of Christian children as a mockery of Christ's death on the Cross. In the face of this passionate invective, Isabella's opposition faded.

A report containing the slurs against the New Christians was widely circulated, as Isabella reluctantly instructed the Castilian ambassador in Rome to solicit from the pope, in her name, a papal bull authorizing the establishment of an Inquisition for Castile.

On November 1, 1478, Pope Sixtus IV issued his bull *Exigit sincere devotionis*. It authorized the Catholic kings to appoint inquisitors in Castile for the purpose of expunging heresy that was rampant throughout the land. It specifically pointed to a deviation by certain Christians, who "after having been duly baptized" had reverted to the Jewish "superstition" and who were secretly engaging in the ceremonies, rites, and customs of Jews. By vesting the power of appointment in the hands of Spanish royalty rather than the Vatican, it was assured that from the outset, the Spanish Inquisition was in the control of royal secular authority, not a foreign entity, even if that foreign entity was the Vicar of Christ. Of particular interest to Ferdinand was the provision in the pope's bull which authorized the crown to fine the culprits and confiscate their holdings, and to deposit the sizable proceeds into the hard-pressed royal treasury.

With this papal authority in hand, Isabella was still hesitant. Instead of appointing inquisitors, she appointed a commission to investigate the scope of heresy in Seville, and actively to encourage any lapsed Christians to renew their faith. This was a stopgap measure that would block a true Inquisition from getting started for two years. But the pieces were in place. Sitting on Isabella's Commission of Inquiry was Archbishop Mendoza and the most vociferous advocate of a crackdown, Friar Ojeda.

Thus, the strands of future Spanish history were coming together in the years 1478 and 1479. The *hermandad* would soon be joined with an Inquisition and, together, employed as an instrument of terror and obedience. The ever-strengthening persecution of Jews was a harbinger of a final solution.

6

Leathery Turtles
and Ravening Wolves

TOLEDO

Toledo, navel of Spain, founded by Hercules, Roman city, imperial capital of the Visigoths, was the most important city of the Iberian peninsula. Citadel of the Moors, refuge and hellhole for Jews, triumph and stain for Christians, City of Three Cultures, in Toledo all of past Spanish religious history was compressed. The Visigoths had lost it to the invading Moors in A.D. 712 after its rough king, Rodrigo, had seen an Arab beauty named Florinda bathing naked in the Tagus and raped her. This outrage brought the African hordes north across the Strait of Gibraltar in a fury of vengeance. The Jews of the city, who had long suffered persecution under the Goths, had opened the city's gates for the invaders and were rewarded for their heroics by the Moors. After his defeat, a woebegone Rodrigo had lamented, in self-pity and self-absolution, that "I've given away my kingdom for a *cava*." *Cava* in Arabic means "whore."

In the nearly four hundred years that the Moors ruled the city, Toledo became a haven and a lure for persecuted Jews across the wide expanse of Mediterranean lands. The Jewish population of the city was among the largest in the peninsula, along with Seville, Málaga, Córdoba, and Granada. Toledo's reputation for openness, as a haven of tolerance, and as a center of learning, especially of translation, spread far and wide. Since the eastern Jews from as far away as Baghdad were fluent in Arabic as well as the tongue of the street called Romance (a hodgepodge of garbled Latin and the precursor of modern Spanish and

French), they graced the ateliers of translation and worked beside Arabized Christians, called Mozarabs, to transfer the Romance of the Jewish translators into formal Latin.

Thus dawned the golden age of Spanish Jewry, often dated to the years 900–1300. In this period, brilliant figures emerged. They included Avicebron (1022–1070), also known as Solomon ben Gabirol, who was born in Málaga and who became an important figure in the Hebrew School of philosophy and poetry. His work was to have a profound influence on the Christian Scholastics later, and he was to serve the Jewish vizier in the Berber kingdom of Granada as a physician and chronicler. A hundred years later came the great Maimonides (1135–1204), also known as Moses ben Maimon, who was born in Córdoba, whose book of Jewish law was a monumental achievement, and whose works in religion, philosophy, and medicine earned him an everlasting reputation for range and brilliance.

Alongside these great Jewish scholars were other notable figures who flocked to Toledo for its vibrant intellectual atmosphere and for this cross-fertilization of civilizations. These included Averroës, who was born in Córdoba and later became the chief judge there, as he served as the personal physician to two Moorish caliphs. He became famous for his integration of Islamic thought with Greek classics, especially Aristotle and Plato. There was Adelard of Bath, who came to Spain to learn Arabic, became an interpreter of Arabic scientific knowledge, and translated Euclid's *Elements* from the Arabic into Latin. And there was perhaps the greatest translator of all, Gerard of Cremona, an Italian who lived most of his life in the twelfth century in Toledo and to whom over eighty translations of medicine, science, and philosophy are attributed, including Ptolemy's *Almagest*.

When, in 1085, Alfonso VI defeated the Moors and recaptured Toledo for the Christians, it was said that his horse went down on its knees before the Bab-al-Mardum mosque, and that later, a cross of Jesus Christ was found squirreled away and bricked up in a remote corner of the mosque, where it was bathed in the light of a lamp that had miraculously stayed lit since the time of the Visigoths. The mosque was promptly renamed Cristo de la Luz. Alfonso proclaimed himself to be the "Emperor of Toledo," and he appointed the heroic El Cid as its first mayor. In the distant hills, the defeated general of the Moors, Abdul Walid, swore not to leave until he reconquered his beloved city. He too fell to his knees, praying to Allah to allow him to continue to gaze at his city until he had accomplished his goal. And in granting the Moor's wish, legend has it, Allah turned the sad warrior to stone. The figure of his noble, turbaned head can be seen high above the city to this day.

Like Rome, the city rested upon seven hills. The Tagus River curled around the city's Alcazar, affording an approach by land on only one side. Within its warren of narrow streets and lanes, Jews and Christians and Arabs had lived side by side alternately in rancor and in harmony, over the centuries. The flowering of cultural splendor and religious tolerance had come in the thirteenth century, during the reign of Alfonso X the Learned. During his splendid reign, from 1252–1284, the three religions coexisted peacefully in harmony. Toledo's principal synagogue, whose ceiling was supported by cedars of Lebanon, whose distinctive arches were Moorish, and whose capitals were Gothic, had been built in the ninth century. But early in the fifteenth century it had been stormed by a mob, led by a Christian rabble-rouser named Vincent Ferrer, and converted into a church, renamed Santa Maria la Blanca.

In the horror of 1391, when the orgy of killing and plunder was visited on Jews across Spain, Toledo's war against the Jews was fierce. The mass conversions under duress took place here as elsewhere, under the watchful eye of demagogues and murderers. Friar Vincent Ferrer was the most effective of these. A Dominican of Valencia, he was later sainted upon the argument that he had miraculously converted no less than 35,000 Jews. The most ferocious recruiters, it seemed, were conversos themselves, who displayed the most passionate anti-Semitism and tried to justify themselves with the harshest acts. The converso issue refused to die, as a new wave of anti-converso violence broke out in 1467 in Toledo and again during the War of Succession (1475–79).

Thus, as Ferdinand and Isabella took up residence in Toledo and looked toward convening a historic Cortes in early 1480, the air was rife with hate and racist passion, directed against Jews and converted Jews alike. In the streets, children chanted songs about Jews as "brutal animals," "bloodthirsty devils," and in the unkindest cut of all, "leathery turtles." Priests invoked Matthew 7:15, "Beware of false prophets, which come to you in sheep's clothing, but inwardly they are ravening wolves." The official chronicler of the new sovereigns, Andrés Bernáldez, the Curate of the Palace, set the tone for convening of the Cortes when he wrote of the Jews:

"This accursed race is either unwilling to bring their children to be baptized, or if they do, they wash away the stain on returning home. They dress their stews and other dishes with oil, instead of lard. They abstain from pork, keep the Passover, eat meat in Lent and send oil to replenish the lamps of their synagogues. With many other abominable ceremonies of their religion, they entertain no respect for monastic life, and frequently profane the sanctity of religious houses in violation or seduction of their names. They are an exceedingly politic and ambitious people, capturing the most lucrative municipal offices and preferring to gain their livelihood by traffic in which they make exorbitant gains, rather than by manual labor or mechanical arts. By their wicked contrivances they have amassed great wealth, and thus are often able to ally themselves by marriage with noble Christian families."

The ravings of anti-Semites and provocateurs was one thing, but the society of nobles was now moving toward a broad consensus that an Inquisition was needed and would be highly useful.

❖

On January 2, 1480, the delegates to the Cortes gathered in Toledo for their important session. They came from the fourteen major towns of Castile: Burgos, León, Ávila, Segovia, Zamora, Toro, Salamanca, Soria, Murcia, Cuenca, Toledo, Seville, Córdoba, and Jaén. Three lesser towns—Valladolid, Madrid, and Guadalajara—were also represented. Various prelates and *caballeros* represented King Ferdinand, and of course, in attendance also were Isabella's two principal ecclesiastical advisers, Friar Hernando de Talavera and Cardinal Pedro González de Mendoza.

Talavera was a scholarly and humble Hieronymite monk; significantly, he was Torquemada's successor as the queen's confessor. His connection to Toledo was deep, for he had been born in that city fifty years before of a mother who was a converted Christian. His Order of St. Jerome, founded in Toledo a hundred years earlier, emphasized the study of Scripture and active work in the Church, as well as an intensely personal bond with the Almighty. He was currently the prior of the Monastery of Santa María del Prado near Valladolid. At her first confession, the queen had knelt for the session, and waited for her confessor to join her. But Talavera remained bolted to his chair.

"Is it not customary for both parties to kneel?" the queen asked quizzically.

"No, Your Majesty," the monk replied, "this is God's tribunal. I act here as His minister. It is fitting that I should keep my seat, while Your Highness kneels before me."

In relating this story to the king, she gushed enthusiastically, "This is the confessor I wanted!" Promptly, the king had retained his services as well, and the prelate rose rapidly in influence and responsibility. For the queen he would set a high standard of moral example. "Regard the level to which you were born, Your Majesty, and why you were placed at the peak of honors," he said. "You must aspire to perfection in your position. If you are Queen, you ought to be a model and an inspiration to your subjects in the service of God."

The second of the queen's chief prelates was Cardinal Pedro González de Mendoza. This powerhouse hailed from the famous Mendoza clan of Guadalajara, a family that, since the eleventh century, had ruled a string of strategic castles in their vast domain from Guadalajara to Almarzon. So intimidating was the Mendoza tribe at this point in history that they were known grandly as "the Mendoza." González de Mendoza had been an important figure in the royal court since Isabella's childhood. In his early career as bishop of Calahorra, when rebels had challenged the competence of Enrique IV, he had given a powerful and influential speech on the virtues of obedience, even when the king was hopelessly ineffective.

"The Holy Scriptures expressly forbid rebellion and order obedience to kings," he declared, "even if the king is unlearned in kingship. Because the destructions suffered by divided kingdoms are incomparably greater than those suffered because of an incompetent king. . . ." From the see of Calahorra, González de Mendoza had been promoted through the ranks of the Church to the bishoprics of Osma and Siguenza, to the archbishopric of Seville, as he took part in the intrigues of the court.

He was a very different sort than the pious, ascetic Talavera. He was prolific both as a writer and a lover, having sired three sons, two of whom issued from the queen's lady-in-waiting. He also had a taste for grand ceremony. When Cardinal Rodrigo Borgia came to Spain in the summer of 1472, González de Mendoza had ridden a humble mule in the welcoming procession, but he was preceded by drummers and trumpeters, flanked by thirty knights, and followed by two hundred light infantrymen. During that visit, González de Mendoza negotiated a cardinal's hat for himself.

Over time, due to his power and influence as a statesman more than a priest, he became known first as the "Great Cardinal" and later as "the third king of Spain." Along with the rest of the Mendoza clan, the cardinal had been active in the War of Succession, seemingly on both sides, for the Mendoza initially opposed the marriage of Ferdinand to Isabella and had put their castles on alert to block the groom from reaching his marriage site in Valladolid. But when it counted, González de Mendoza swung over to the winning side. He stood firmly now on the side of the young sovereigns . . . indeed, he stood with Ferdinand at the Battle of Toro in 1476 in full battle gear and in command of the cavalry.

For the past two years, González de Mendoza and Talavera had worked as a team. To Talavera, the cardinal had delegated the task of evangelizing the insincere and recalcitrant conversos. His sermons addressed doctrinal questions deftly. The first convert was Jesus Christ himself, and the city of Israel had become the city of Christ, he argued. All the prophecies of the Old Testament had been realized in the life of Jesus, and there was no longer any place in the land for the Old Law. "Think not that I come to destroy the law, or the prophets," the friar quoted Matthew 5:17. "I am not come to destroy, but to fulfill. / For verily I say unto you, Till heaven and earth pass, one jot or one tittle shall in no wise pass from the law, till all be fulfilled."

But if Talavera's sermons did not sway the insincere Christian of Jewish blood, stiffer measures dictating proper religious practice were given biblical sanction. "And into whatsoever city or town ye shall enter, enquire who in it is worthy," the friar quoted Matthew 10:11. ". . . and if the house be worthy, let your peace come upon it; but if it be not worthy, let your peace return to you." The Church announced practical measures for the city by which a Christian might demonstrate his worthiness and any Christian engaged in secret Judaic practices might be flushed out. Henceforth, every Christian household was required to display an image of the Cross or a picture of the Virgin Mary. Henceforth, washing the dead in hot water, and swaddling the corpse in a new shroud, and most especially, putting a piece of money in its mouth in the Hebrew custom was prohibited. Henceforth, cooking in the kosher style was forbidden. Upon the pain of arrest, a mother was not to plunge her newborn child into a basin of water, gold, silver, seed-pearl, wheat, and barley in the Hebrew fashion. And the Church would be vigilant in monitoring how New Christians buried their dead, for the Jewish custom of burying their dead outside the city was well known.

Cardinal González de Mendoza gave his blessing to these ordinances. An announcement of them was nailed to the doors of churches. Their purpose, the Great Cardinal said, was "to nurture the Christian life so that Christianity might thrive in this noble city and this monarchy." Any who disobeyed them would suffer the most severe penalties. Talavera added darkly that "in some cases offenders would have to die."

There was another member of this team. He was Alfonso de Ojeda, the most rabid promoter of a fierce Inquisition. His sermons were so incendiary that people were reminded of the notorious Friar Vincent Ferrer, the guiding force behind the forced conversion of Jews in the early part of the fifteenth century. A Dominican at the Monastery of San Pablo, Ojeda was dubbed "Friar Vicente the Second." Privately, to the monarchs he had been whispering shocking stories of Jewish and converso perfidy and blasphemy for several years. When the monarchs were in Córdoba in 1478, for example, Ojeda arrived at the court with news of six conversos in Seville who had blasphemed the Catholic faith on Holy Thursday, and had the town in an uproar.

More publicly, Ojeda's sermons were riveting. Apocalyptic foreboding spiced them throughout, engendering widespread panic. The Spanish land was moving into the Last Days, Ojeda preached, a time when all good Christians should expect the Day of Judgment on earth. In preparation, the Holy Mother Church and all of Spain needed to be purified. All Jews would be swept from the land. For good measure, the conversos too, who were neither Christian nor Jew, would also disappear in the Final Battle.

This triumvirate—the Great Cardinal, the cerebral theologian, and the firebrand—formed the core of the Commission of Inquiry that Queen Isabella had set up two years before to look into the practicalities of a possible Inquisition. The firebrand, Friar Ojeda, was the commission's leader. Now, they came to the Cortes armed with their findings.

This trinity would soon enough be joined by a fourth prelate, the prior of the Monastery of the Holy Cross in Segovia: Tomás de Torquemada.

❖

The first order of business for the Cortes was financial. Due to the ineptitude and corruption of their predecessor, Enrique El Impotente, Ferdinand and Isabella had inherited a royal treasury that was virtually empty. Desperate measures had been quickly adopted to sustain the royal forces during the expensive, four-year War of Succession. Now it was essential for Ferdinand and Isabella to take control of the towns of Castile, but also the nobles, especially the fifteen most powerful families such as the Mendoza, Ponce de León, Medina-Sidonia, Pacheco, and Albuquerque clans. From the beginning of their reign the young monarchs had pursued a determined policy to undermine the power of the great families, which had grown to an intolerable and disruptive level under the weak monarchs of the past and whose extraordinary power made the land unruly and chaotic.

The great families sustained themselves through taxes on commerce and agriculture within their domains. Predictably, the royal treasury often did not receive its fair share. The process of emasculating the nobility needed to begin by reviewing (and eventually eliminating) the extravagant grants that had traditionally been accorded these families by the crown, and also to remove the historic exemptions from taxation that they had enjoyed in the past. Toward this purpose, the tax collection system needed a complete overhaul, for it was characterized by inadequate accounting and reporting and downright corruption.

Since conversos were the most skilled tax collectors, they were both pressured by the crown to make their sporadic collection more regular and efficient and resented by the objects of their efforts. At the Cortes, the monarchs initiated a sweeping reform. Its effect was to centralize the entire process of tax collection under the control of the monarchy. Of particular notice was the medieval system called the *merced*, which dealt with liens on royal revenue purchased by the noble families and held for life or in perpetuity. After much wrangling in the Cortes of Toledo, the royal confessor, Hernando de Talavera, was put in charge of investigating the validity of past *mercedes* and tightening the controls on the issuance of new privileges.

Reforms in other important areas of administration were also set in motion at the Toledo Cortes. These too would speed the centralization of power in the hands of the monarchs. The ragged, uneven, and unequal system of justice was reviewed, as the most prominent lawyer of the land, Díaz de Montalvo, was ordered to standardize Castile's jurisprudence. This massive job eventually became known as "the Edicts of Montalvo."

The Cortes of Toledo in 1480 became a turning point. With the national police, *Santa Hermandad,* in place, the tax collection and justice systems restructured and centralized, and the military orders subjected to central command and control, the path to an absolute monarchy was begun.

Left hanging only was the question of an Inquisition. And not an Inquisition like the one of old, but a modern, ferocious, awe-inspiring Inquisition that would be taken very seriously indeed.

❖

After the Cortes had been meeting in Toledo for several months, it finally turned to the Jewish question. It was quickly agreed that the harsh laws of 1412, known as the Laws of Valladolid, had never been enforced. These laws of separation were the fulfillment of the anti-Jewish campaign that had begun with the massacre of Jews in 1391, and the conversion of tens of thousands of Jews to Christianity. At their core, the laws were a bludgeon for conversion, for to remain a Jew afterward was to be isolated and impoverished, humiliated and degraded. Their intent was to separate the remaining Jews from the rest of the population. Jews were to be confined to a ghetto, forced to wear red badges identifying their lineage, to wear their beards long and uncut, to be barred from holding important governmental positions, from having their own markets and from selling the food Christians ate and the clothes they wore, to cease to minister to Christians as physicians or apothecaries.

Now, the Cortes decided, with the connivance of Ferdinand and Isabella, these laws were to be dusted off and rigorously enforced. The delegates granted a period of two years for the ghettos to be built. After that, a Jew would be given eight days to move. If he did not, he was subject to the whip and to the loss of all his property. Jews were to wear the badges on their shoulders in the daytime. They were not to be seen on the streets after dark.

With the Jews thus well separated in what a nineteenth-century historian called an "iron ring," the crown could deal cleanly and efficiently with the heresy of the hollow Christian. But that would be a matter not for the Cortes but for the commission that Isabella had set up two years earlier.

In these apocalyptic days, the time had arrived to join the battle with the Antichrist and his master, the Devil. For, it was said, the Devil speaks with a Toledan accent.

7

A Glimpse of Hell

SEVILLE

 On September 17, 1480, Friar Alfonso de Ojeda presented the report of his two-year commission to Isabella and Ferdinand. On the same day, with royal blessing, Cardinal Mendoza and Tomás de Torquemada appointed two Dominican friars as the first inquisitors of the revitalized Holy Office. They were ordered to depart at once for Seville and take up their duties in the city regarded by the purifiers of the faith as the hotbed of heresy in Spain. Ironically, as the inquisitors were making their way to Seville to root out insincere Christians, the council of that city appointed twenty-three conversos to collect the taxes for the region. Thus, prominent members of the suspect class were being rewarded for their skill and their value to the kingdom at the same time as they were being investigated for heresy.

Ten days later, Isabella and Ferdinand issued a sweeping proclamation which set the stage for the first inquisitional trials. "In our kingdoms there are some bad Christians, both men and women, who are apostates and heretics," the document read. "Although they have been baptised in the True Faith they bear only the name and appearance of Christians, for they daily return to the superstitions and perfidious sect of the Jews. Scornful of the Holy Mother Church, they have allowed themselves to incur the sentence of censure and excommunication, together with other penalties established by the Apostolic laws and constitutions. Not only have they persisted in their blind and obstinate heresy, but their children and descendants do likewise. Those who treat with them also are stained by that same infidelity and heresy."

By mid-October, after its solemn processions through the streets on the Sabbath were met with glowering hostility, the Inquisition became operational in Ojeda's Monastery of San Pablo. At first, the inquisitors met such resistance that the crown felt compelled to issue an order to all the governors of the realm to assist and facilitate the work of the Holy Office, or else.

Its presence in Seville caused an immediate panic in the city. More than eight thousand people fled south into the province of Cádiz, and west into the Extremadura, where they hoped for protection from the powerful magnates of the provinces, Rodrigo Ponce de León and the count of Medina-Sidonia. Yet the inquisitors would not be trifled with. On January 2, 1481, in a proclamation that bore the royal imprimatur, they demanded of the marquis of Cádiz and the count of Medina-Sidonia that all refugee conversos be seized and returned to Seville within fifteen days. Any defiance would be greeted with excommunication and the loss of property. This was stiff language, and the magnates minded it. The refugees were dutifully returned and placed in the custody of the Inquisition. Their very act of fleeing placed them under grave suspicion of heresy. Flight was itself an admission of guilt. Their property was sequestered.

Thus, within the first several months of its existence, the Inquisition was provided with an immense pool of suspects, ripe for interrogation. So great was their number that the Inquisition felt compelled to shift its headquarters from the Monastery of San Pablo, across the wooden pontoon bridge over the Guadalquivir River, to the expansive Castle of Triana, where the dungeon capacity was greater.

Shortly after their demand for extradition, the inquisitors issued their second proclamation. Called the Edict of Grace, this insidious proclamation stipulated a period of thirty to forty days to allow all persons who knew or suspected that they might be guilty of any heresy or apostasy, of practicing or observing Jewish rites or ceremonies, to turn themselves in to the Inquisition. At that time they should confess their errors in full and graphic detail. And then they must demonstrate a sincere and complete repentance. In a written confession, they must express the understanding that their heresy was a sin against Jesus Christ himself, and that through sincere repentance they would be escaping their "just due."

The test of true repentance upon which their life depended would be their sincerity. The best way to prove sincerity was to name other Christian converts whom they knew to be secret Jews. As this edict was later refined, children who turned in their own parents would be rewarded with lesser punishment. The matter was then turned upside down, as it was decreed that the children of any convicted heretic would suffer disgrace and impoverishment for the sins of their fathers. If the heretic did not turn himself in within the grace period, and this was found out later, the matter would go especially badly for him.

The inquisitors would do all in their power to help the relapsed and the benighted to recover their faith through repentance. Judgment would be swift; its severity, financial or corporal, left to the discretion of the inquisitors. If the inquisitors failed in their manifold effort to show the heretic the error of his ways and to bring him to the glory of full repentance, the accused would, in sadness, be turned over to the secular arm. Of such hopeless recalcitrants the earth must be purified, and that unpleasant task was reserved for the layman. For a priest was forbidden to shed blood. His lay accomplice must accomplish the execution bloodlessly, by burning. As the crime was heresy, and heresy was evil incarnate, the punishment must mimic the fires of Hell.

While many conversos had fled Seville at the Inquisition's pronouncements, braver souls had remained in the city to plan a stiffer resistance. Their ringleader was one of the most prominent and wealthy conversos of Seville, Diego de Susan, who was also the *regidor*, or alderman, of the city. He convened a secret meeting of judges, lawyers, and other influential figures in the parish of San Salvador and gave a rousing call to arms.

"How do these Inquisitors dare come against us? Are we not the leading citizens of this city? Are we not well liked by the people? Let us gather our men. You and you and you," he said, pointing to his eminent friends, "have many of your men ready. Let's divide the arms, people and money among our leaders, and anything else that is necessary for our purpose. And if they come to seize us, let's cause a brawl. We shall kill them all, and avenge ourselves of our enemies."

This was bold talk. And in the gathering such assertions were rare. "Having men ready appears to be a good idea," said a nervous old man on the fringe. "But how? Where are the bravehearts?" Where indeed? The plot faced the power of both Crown and Church.

In the days that followed, the resistance sought to mobilize its forces. But it could not think of everything. Diego de Susan had a sensuous and flirtatious daughter, so beautiful that she was known as *hermosa hembra*, "beautiful female." And she was carrying on a secret liaison with a Christian cavalier. In an unguarded moment, she revealed her father's secret to her lover, who immediately passed the word to the inquisitors.

Diego de Susan was seized instantly, as was the caretaker of Seville, in whose house a cache of weapons for one hundred men was discovered. The two men were packed across the river to the dungeons of Triana. There, the firebrand of the Inquisition, Alfonso de Ojeda, the prior of the Dominican monastery of San Pablo, took personal charge of the case. De Susan's considerable estate was marked for confiscation, but he would not have long to grieve over its loss. (Nor would *hermosa hembra*, for her indiscretion redounded to extreme prejudice against her father. In disgrace she entered a convent, where her beauty quickly faded. And at her death, so the story goes, she requested that her skull be mounted over the door of the house of her indiscretions and betrayal near the Alcazar of Seville, with the inscription: "Where I lived badly, as an example and punishment of my sins.")

As the religious police fanned out in Seville, the uncovering of the nascent resistance increased the terror in an already terrorized city. Upon the representations of Friar Talavera, the most prominent, wealthy, and learned of the city's converso community were rounded up, and further resistance evaporated. In the dungeons of the Triana Castle and the crypt of the Monastery of San Pablo, the hasty trials went forward with little or no evidence, unless it had been extracted by torture. In one case, Friar Ojeda accomplished the miracle of providing testimony against a suspect from a witness who had been in the grave for twelve years. To the critics of their process, the Dominicans repeated the cry of the Crusaders: *"!Dios la Quiere!*—God wants it!"

While Friar Ojeda supplied the passion, and Cardinal González de Mendoza contributed the political muscle, Friar Talavera became the Inquisition's early theologian. Prodded by Queen Isabella, Talavera wrote an apologia for the Holy Office in 1481. In it he declared his scorn for Jews and all things Jewish, for they were aberrations and anachronisms of history. The true Israel belonged to the passionate and evangelizing Christian. The Law of Moses was obsolete, and any who adhered to it served Satan.

❖

On February 6, 1481, the first executions took place. Their grisly spectacle was dubbed an *auto-da-fe,* or Act of Faith. To the faithful, it was an occasion of both joy and hate, ratifying one's own faith as it eliminated one who had betrayed baptism, the gift of God. From the beginning, the *auto-da-fe* was organized as a theatrical extravaganza of major interest. On this first occasion the condemned were seven influential conversos of Seville, six men and a woman, who had been secretly denounced and swiftly tried.

At the Cathedral of Seville, the procession gathered. At its head was a company of Dominicans, in their rough woolen black and white cowls, walking barefooted, and holding aloft the banner of the Inquisition. Its centerpiece was a green cross of knotted wood, flanked by an olive branch signifying forgiveness and reconciliation, and a sword signifying eternal justice. Encircling the knotted cross was the phrase *"Exurge Domine et Judica causam tuam*—Rise up, Master, and Pursue Your Cause!"* Psalm 73:27 about the destruction of the wicked was the watchword: "For lo, they that are far from Thee shall perish: Thou hast destroyed all them that go a whoring from Thee."

Leading these dogs of God was the head dog, Friar Alfonso de Ojeda, radiant in the realization of his life's passion. Behind the Dominicans came local magistrates, followed by soldiers carrying the wood for the fires. After them came the heretics, nooses around their necks, holding devotional candles, and dressed in yellow gowns of shame. Flanking the condemned were halberdiers, carrying their ax lances, vigilant lest any of the apostates should bolt and run. And behind them came other hooded friars, chanting admonitions to repentance and invocations to salvation. And finally came the drummers, beating a slow beat of impending death on their kettledrums.

From the cathedral this grim procession snaked through the narrow streets, so that all could see and taunt. A frenzied mob quickly gathered, eager for blood and the smell of burning flesh. In due course, the procession passed through a city gate and came into an open field outside the walls. This was appropriately called the *Tablada*, or stage, although later it would be better known as the *quemadero*, or burning place. For this first Act of Faith, there were merely wooden posts for the victims. Later, as a conservation measure, the wooden posts would be transformed into an expansive stone scaffold, with reusable stone pillars. The place was delineated on its four sides by plaster statues of four prophets. One chronicler of the time gave the impression that the statues of the prophets were actually hollow, and the heretics were enclosed inside for their slower burning, in the manner of Phalaris, the Sicilian tyrant of the fourth century B.C. He had encased his victims in a brass bull for roasting, so their screams would mimic a braying bull. Of this place, the chronicler of the monarchs would write that it was "where heretics are burnt and ought to be burnt as long as any can be found."

Once the mob gathered at the *quemadero*, Alfonso de Ojeda stepped forward to deliver a lengthy, passionate sermon. This was the culmination of his long and frustrating campaign of public advocacy and of private prodding of the royals. The process of purification had begun in the hellfire of Seville. The evildoers who defiled and polluted the world were to be liquidated. Ojeda was jubilant, radiant with his love of God and hate for the traitors of his faith.

His florid, apocalyptic oratory rolled over the mob. His text was: "The jealousy of the faith of Jesus Christ has inspired this Inquisition." In Revelation (20:12–15) the books from the Day of Judgment were kept, listing the judgments for all. The prophet St. John of the Apocalypse "saw the dead, the great and the small, standing before the throne, and the books were opened; and another book was opened, which is the book of life; and the dead were judged from the things which were written in the book according to their deeds. . . . And whosoever was not found written in the book of life was cast into the lake of fire."

More frightening still were the uses of the apocryphal preaching of St. Peter (generally agreed by scholars to have been written for the Apocrypha in the second century): "Some were hanging by their tongues and these were they that blasphemed the way of righteousness, and under them was laid fire flaming and tormenting. . . . And there were also others, women, hanged by their hair above that mire which boiled up; and these had adorned themselves for adultery. . . . And in another place were gravel stones sharper than swords or any spit, heated with fire, and men and women clad in filthy rags rolled upon them in torment."

When Friar Ojeda finished his oratory, a notary read out the details of the crimes of each. Of a heretic, the details were almost boilerplate: he had engaged in Jewish rituals; he had eaten unleavened bread and kosher meat; he had removed leg tendons from lamb in accordance with the scriptural passage in Genesis 32:32 after Jacob wrestles with the Lord: "Therefore the children of Israel eat not of the sinew which shrank, which is upon the hollow of the thigh, unto this day; because he touched the hollow of Jacob's thigh in the sinew that shrank"; he had attended secret services in the house of Jews; he disbelieved the concept of a Christian Paradise and scoffed at the Host as the body and blood of Christ; he had profaned the sacred rites of true Christians.

A bombastic accusation concluded this recitation. The confession of the apostate, however it was extracted, was read out. Then the sentence was pronounced. The penitents were given one last chance for a full admission of guilt and to repent sins and misdeeds before they met their maker. For a conversion on the scaffold, the accused had the privilege of being strangled before he was burned. Most, kneeling before the expressionless inquisitors, did so.

The true faith was satisfied. Repentance constituted the final victory of the Church. When the climactic moment came, ardent parishioners lit the pyre in the certain knowledge that they would be rewarded with indulgences for their pious deed. As the flames leapt upward, the Dominicans could be certain that no blood was being shed. The purity of their oath to their order had been respected. In Ojeda's mind, they were acting out the earthly version of Judgment Day as the Gospel of St. Matthew (25:31–32) had described it: "When the Son of man shall come in his glory, and all the angels with him, then shall he sit on the throne of his glory; and before him shall be gathered all the nations and he shall separate them one from another, as a shepherd divideth his sheep from the goats."

As the flames licked heavenward, the crowd gasped at the horrible spectacle. Women wept and rejoiced, screamed in horror and fell to their knees in prayer and pity, fear and thanksgiving. All were experiencing the uncertainty between salvation and damnation on the Day of Judgment.

The fires of the *Tablada* were meant to be a glimpse into the mouth of Hell.

❧

A week hence, the second *auto-da-fe* took place at the *Tablada*. This featured Diego de Susan, the leader of the brief Seville resistance, who had been personally tried and tortured into a confession by Alfonso de Ojeda. But de Susan was tough, and he maintained both his defiance and even his good humor to the end. With the noose dangling from his neck and dressed in his yellow gown, he turned to one of his executioners on the scaffold and suggested that they exchange togas as an act of friendship, as if this was some sort of sporting event. The reports of his demise varied. One said, "it seems that he died as a Christian," while another announced wistfully, "he was a great rabbi."

At de Susan's Act of Faith, there was one notable absence: Friar Alfonso de Ojeda. To many in the crowd, this must have appeared strange, for de Susan's fate was the personal triumph of the Dominican. He had dealt with the converso personally in the interrogation chamber, in the dungeon of Triana, and in the torture chamber.

But after his rousing sermon on February 6, Ojeda had fallen ill. It is not clear whether his affliction was pneumonic or bubonic, whether he had become infected by the ubiquitous rat flea or by some airborne bacteria. It is not recorded whether his symptoms were spitting blood through the mouth and nose, accompanied by horrible fevers, or whether he had developed bubos, the size of apples, in the groin or armpit. If his plague was pneumonic, he died within seventy-two hours. If it was bubonic, he might have lasted a day or two longer. In either case, his death was gruesome.

For one so attentive to the wrath of God, he would surely have lashed out at some wicked force. For so rabid an anti-Semite, he could well have blamed the Jews, as so many other Christians had done in the previous 150 years, since the first medieval plague had leapt across the Straits of Gilbraltar and entered Iberia from the Moorish lands of North Africa in 1348. Perhaps he embraced the popular supposition that the pestilence was cosmic, a diabolical conjunction of Jupiter and Saturn, or the theory that with a terrestrial earthquake, a fissure had been opened in the ground, from which the gas of pestilence gushed. Perhaps he saw the epidemic as yet another sign of the coming apocalypse. It is not likely that he blamed his own sinfulness for his disease, for Ojeda admitted of no moral faults. Perhaps in his last hours of life, he tried some of the remedies of the time: lancing the boils or drinking strong spirits or holding a bouquet of various aromatic spices to his nose or applying a plaster of pigeon dung or pig fat. Whatever he did, whatever the form of his pathogen, his Black Death was horrible.

Ojeda was not alone. Rather, he was a forerunner. In Seville's dreadful visitation, the first cases of the plague had appeared in the city the previous fall. During the cold months of 1481, the incidence was small. But as the weather grew warmer that year, the number of victims soared, for warmth and humidity nurtured the contagion. Decaying animals and human bodies piled up in the streets, emitting a terrible stench. Few volunteered to bury them.

Civil order broke down. Once again, old Italian rumors were revived about the source of the pestilence: an invasion of eight-legged worms that killed you by their stink or black smoke that melted mountains. In the panic, citizens raced to quack measures for prevention: smelling aromatic wood and spice like juniper and rosemary, washing hands and feet with vinegar and rosewater, ingesting figs and nuts before breakfast, pepper and saffron later in the day, along with plenty of onions and garlic, but not too much to make the humors of the body hot, so that the pores of the skin might open. Sinful desserts were a bad idea, as were meat and fish that might spoil.

One recipe for plague medicine went as follows:

Take five cups of rue (woody herb with bitter leaves) and if it be a woman, leave out the rue, for rue is restorative to a man and wasting to a woman; and then take thereto five crops of tansey (bouquet of composite herbs) and five little blades of columbine, and a great quantity of marigold flowers full of small chives from the crops that are like saffron chives. . . . Then take a quantity of good treacle, and bray all these herbs therein with good ale, but do not strain them. And then make the sick drink it for three evenings and three mornings. If they hold it, they shall have life.

Holding it was the problem.

In the end, since the root cause of the pestilence was the wrath of God, prayer was the best medicine of all. Families disintegrated, as wives fled from husbands, sisters fled from brothers. The pestilence spread, as Boccaccio described it a century earlier, like "a fire racing through dry or oily substances."

What Boccaccio had written about Florence in 1348 was true of Seville in 1481. "How many gallant gentlemen, fair ladies, and sprightly youths, who would have been judged hale and hearty by Galen and Hippocrates, having breakfasted in the morning with their kinsfolk, acquaintances and friends, supped that same evening with their ancestors in the next world!"

Before the plague spent itself a year later, fifteen thousand would die in Seville, more than a third of the population of that port city.

Like a two-headed dragon, Plague and Inquisition were joined in what seemed like a wider diabolical plan. The important signs of the End Times were manifest: wars and rumors of war, pestilence, chaos, hate, poverty, famine, sacrilege, and heresy. Blame was heaped on familiar culprits: the pestilence had come from the south, from the flea-ridden, rat-infested ships that came from the heathen lands of the east to the last Moorish state . . . or from the Jews, fouling the water supplies. The vials of God's wrath were full. The Temple was filled with the smoke from the glory of God. Who shall not fear Thee, O God? Seville was the Lord's threshing floor, where in His harvest the wheat was separated from the chaff. Pestilence and Inquisition were His instruments. It was as if vultures perched on the gargoyles of the cathedral of the stricken city.

There seemed to be no discrimination. The just as well as the iniquitous were slain. Even the pure of heart and the pure of blood were not spared.

8

Woe Is Me, Alhama

 In the fall of 1479 Ferdinand rejoined his queen, arriving in Toledo like Hannibal, riding an elephant that had been the gift from an ambassador from Cyprus. Days before, Isabella had given birth to a daughter, Juana.

Ferdinand was now rightly an emperor. Earlier that year, his father, Juan II of Aragon, had died in Barcelona at the ripe age of eighty-three. With that death, the principal domains of Spain, Castile and Aragon were united at last for the first time in four hundred years, and the foundation of the Spanish Empire from the Pyrenees to Gibraltar, from Sicily to the Balearic Islands to Valencia to the Portuguese frontier, was formally laid. The horizons south to Al Andalus, east to the Holy Land, and eventually west across the unknown beckoned, and the possibilities seemed endless.

With this historic realization, the notion of divine guidance grew in the popular imagination. The first providential step had arrived with the unification of the peninsula under one crown. Next was the purification of the populace from heresy and unbelief and rebelliousness; and after that, the completion of the Christian Reconquest by eliminating Gog and Magog, the last vestige of Islam in the Spanish land. That would be the fulfillment of a 500-year-long process. Lastly, toward the end of the century and the advent of the Jubilee year of 1500, the Antichrist, with his army of Jews and Muslims, would be confronted and defeated. The triumphal crusade would end with the reconquest of

Jerusalem for Christianity, and in the apocalypse, the offering of a pure Christian paradise to God.

God's plan was clear. The instruments for this divine glory were this fertile and pious queen and her diligent, cunning, and brave husband. Through them the prophecy of St. John the Evangelist, her patron saint, and of the book of Revelation would be realized. Spain, as beacon to the world, was entering the countdown to the last days. Isabella would reign as history's counter to the submissive, sinful, weak-minded Eve, as the reincarnation of the Virgin Mary, and as the Apocalyptic Woman of the Bible. She stood, clothed in the sun, standing upon the half moon, adorned with a crown of twelve stars, holding her boy-child and heir, Juan, as the Apocalyptic Woman held Jesus. With her feet she would trample the evil serpent, and with her double-edged sword, slay this Devil-Beast with its seven heads and ten horns.

This perfect queen, together with her husband, the Hidden One, would bring about the New Spain, the New World, the New Jerusalem.

Early in the new decade of the 1480s, the war over succession was complete. Portugal had ceased to be a threat. The royal police had been established. The crown had pacified the upstart nobles. The Inquisition was getting under way, and the fiscal system was overhauled. And so the internal controls were in place. Ferdinand and Isabella could at last begin to think about their grander vision for the Jubilee and perhaps for the apocalypse: their oft-postponed crusade against the Moors and the final demise of the infidel kingdom on the Spanish peninsula.

❖

Before the accession of the fiery Muley Aben Hassan to the throne of Granada in 1462, the price of peace between the Christian domain in the north and the Islamic province of Granada in the south was 1,000 pistoles of gold, and sixteen hundred Christian captives. If there were no captives to hand over, Granada was required to deliver to Córdoba an equal number of Moors as slaves. With Muley Aben Hassan, the payment ceased.

Ferdinand was now ready to press the issue. He sent his ambassadors to Granada to demand a resumption of the tribute as the condition of peace. The result was a rude rebuff. King Ferdinand was to be told that the mint that once was used to produce coins for Christians was now producing scimitars and axes for Moors. Ferdinand could not have been displeased, for the insult was the pretext for the next step in God's plan. "I will pick out the seeds of this pomegranate one by one," he had said ominously. (*Granada* is the Spanish word for "pomegranate," and the pomegranate was the symbol for the Moorish Caliphate.)

"Christian Spain does not thirst for rapine and revenge," a scribe wrote, "but for that pure and holy indignation which every Spanish knight entertains at beholding this beautiful dominion of his ancestors defiled by the footsteps of Infidel usurpers. It is impossible to contemplate this delicious country, and not long to see it restored to the dominion of the true faith, and the sway of the Christian monarchs." Only the timing for the final war against the Moors was in doubt.

Muley Aben Hassan proceeded to make the decision for war even easier for the Castilian monarchs. The Moor was greedy, bellicose, and impetuous. His Christian enemies, he knew, would invade his land sooner or later. Why not then a preemptive strike? And so he cast his eye on the various Christian fortresses near his border, and focused on the castle of Zahara, northwest of Ronda and just a few miles into Christian Andalusia.

Zahara was an imposing fortress, built on a rock outcropping on a mountain peak between Ronda and Medina-Sidonia. The dwellings within its walls were hewn out of rock, and it had but one fiercely guarded entrance. So impregnable was this gate thought to be that ladies of unapproachable virtue across Spain were given a variation of its name, *Zahareña*. Muley's spies were telling him that after years of peace, Zahara's defenses were soft and sloppy. He determined to test them.

A few days after Christmas in 1481, the sultan marched out of the Alhambra leading his forces to the western frontier under the cover of a ferocious storm. In howling winds and driving rain, his scaling ladders were quietly placed against the castle's walls, and the Moors surprised the sleeping garrison. The battle was brief and decisive. With the defenders either dead or in chains, the sultan left the place in the care of his men-at-arms and returned home.

Days later, he buoyantly prepared a lavish celebration for his victory over the Christians, as the bedraggled survivors were marched into Granada. But instead of rejoicing, the common people of Granada were seized with anxiety over the consequences of the reckless attack, for it broke the truce that had given the Moorish state a measure of tranquility. Their anguish increased with the sudden appearance in the Alhambra of a grotesque anchorite named Alfaqui. This ancient hermit, with flaming eyes and piercing voice, lived in a cave in the Sacromonte on a slope north of the Alhambra and rarely ventured out in public. Now, waving a bony finger at the crowd, he shouted,

"Woe unto Granada. Its hour of desolation approaches. The ruins of Zahara will recoil upon our heads. The end of the empire is at hand."

In the Courtyard of the Myrtles in the Alhambra, these warnings were dismissed as the ravings of a crackpot. He was "one of those fanatic infidels possessed by the devil," wrote one chronicler, "who are sometimes permitted to predict the truth to their followers, but with the proviso that their predictions shall be of no avail." But outside the palace, his warnings were taken more seriously as people recoiled in horror. The prophet was not finished. With a throng building behind him, he wandered down the hill into the city to continue his diatribe.

"The peace is broken! The war of extermination has begun. Woe! Woe! to Granada. Its fall is at hand! Desolation shall dwell in its palaces; its strong men shall fall beneath the sword. Its children and maidens shall be led into captivity."

When the news of Zahara reached Ferdinand, he feigned shock and indignation and injury. This was the spark he needed to mobilize his Andalusian subjects. The time had come at last to launch his righteous crusade. He knew it and welcomed it. His first order was to put all the Christian fortresses along the border with the Moorish kingdom on high alert.

The man most affected by these events was Rodrigo Ponce de León, the marquis of Cádiz, for his holdings in Andalusia were vast and included the borderlands with the Moorish kingdom. Zahara had been one of his prize fortresses. Importantly, he was eager to reaffirm and demonstrate his loyalty to the crown, after the embarrassment of having been ordered to return the converso refugees from the Inquisition, and in the hope that the crown would cease its efforts to undermine his independent base.

In his service the marquis had a considerable corps of spies. Many of them were Moors who had converted to Christianity and who could easily mingle with their Islamic brothers. In January 1482, he dispatched them into the borderlands to watch for further enemy expeditions, but also to gauge the readiness of the Moorish strongholds. Within days, he received an interesting report from one of his most reliable agents that the city of Alhama was ripe for the picking.

Alhama was deep within the Moors' kingdom, no more than twenty miles southwest of the city of Granada itself. Significantly, it lay astride the vital strategic road between Granada and Málaga. If that road were cut, it would isolate Granada from its major port and source for reinforcements in North Africa. The town itself was large and prosperous, known since Roman times for its salubrious hot springs and for its commanding fortress, which hovered over the town from a high perch on a rock ledge overlooking a deep gorge. Behind that palisade rose a high sierra. The Alhama River nearly encircled the town.

Without seeking Ferdinand's approval, the marquis of Cádiz assembled an impressive force of Andalusians at Marchena, some three thousand light cavalry, four thousand foot soldiers, and a company of engineers. Without informing his soldiers of their exact mission, the marquis led them east through Antequera, the first of the Andalusian towns to fall to the Christian forces seventy years earlier, and then into the slopes around Alhama. On the night of February 5, they reached the environs of the town and moved silently to the rock ledge beneath the walls. As the town slept, a single sentinel patrolled the battlements.

A squadron of three hundred handpicked commandos now crept silently to the walls, carrying scaling ladders. Soon enough they were over the parapets and into the town. If the town slept initially, it awoke quickly to the alarm, and hand-to-hand combat raged in the streets. It was said that the Moors, sensualists as they were, were weakened by the pleasures of their hot baths, and by their sense of false security. But they outnumbered the Christians, and they fought valiantly for their homes. While the fighting raged, engineers went to work on breaching the walls of the fortress. When the breach was accomplished, the battle was drawn; by dusk, Ponce de León held the town. From the dungeons of the fortress, a number of prisoners from Zahara were liberated.

It was later written that the chivalrous Rodrigo Ponce de León had suffered the pleas of his commanders to evacuate the place, so deep was it within enemy territory, because it could not be defended.

"God has given the citadel into Christian hands," he had replied stoutly. "He will no doubt strengthen them to maintain it. We have gained the place with difficulty and bloodshed. It would be a stain upon our honor to abandon it for imagined dangers."

Alhama was entrusted to the care of Iñigo López de Mendoza, the second count of Tendilla, a distinguished and highly cultured member of the Mendoza family—a brave, frugal, and pious warrior, and the brother of the Grand Cardinal of Spain. The count was the very model of medieval chivalry and learning, and he sought to instill in his defenders the highest principles of honor, duty, and piety. "A just war is often rendered wicked and disastrous by the manner in which it is conducted," he is said to have told his soldiers. "The righteousness of our cause is not sufficient to justify corrupt means. A lack of order and obedience among troops may bring ruin and disgrace upon the best-laid plans."

In the succeeding months, Muley Aben Hassan came twice to the citadel to try to reclaim it, but twice he was turned away. In Granada, his people turned on him for this disaster. "Accursed be the day that you lit the flame of war in our land!" wailed one protester. "May the holy Prophet bear witness before Allah that we and our children are innocent of this act! Upon your head, and upon the heads of your children until the end of the world will rest the sin of Zahara!" Ay di mi

Alhama became the wail in the street. "Woe is me, Alhama." And this lamentation would be put into Moorish verse. Centuries later, Lord Byron translated it into English.

> *Letters to the monarch tell*
> *How Alhama's city fell;*
> *In the fire the scroll he threw*
> *And the messenger he slew*
> *Woe is me, Alhama . . .*

And once again the hoary figure of the prophetic old anchorite named Alfaqui figures in the epic poem.

> *Out then spake an aged Moor*
> *In these words the king before:*
> *"Wherefore call on us, oh King?*
> *What may mean this gathering?"*
> *Woe is me, Alhama!*
>
> *"Friends! Ye have, alas! To know*
> *Of a most disastrous blow,*
> *That Christians, stern and bold,*
> *Have obtain'd Alahama's hold."*
> *Woe is me, Alhama!*
>
> *Out then spake old Alfaqui*
> *With his beard so white to see*
> *"Good King, thou are justly served,*
> *Good King, this thou hast deserved."*
> *Woe is me, Alhama!*

The last Spanish crusade had begun.

✧

In the spring of 1483, Pope Sixtus IV made the crusade official. He issued a papal bull sanctioning and sanctifying the resumption of the War of Spanish Reconquest. Presented to Ferdinand and Isabella by the papal nuncio at the Monastery of Santo Domingo al Real de Madrid, with the Cardinal of Spain and other dignitaries in attendance, the bull levied a financial obligation on the hierarchy of the Church and of the military to finance the endeavor and promised sweeping indulgences to those who participated. Taking up the crusade was made a religious duty, even if one's effort was merely to raise money for the expensive war ahead. The call to crusade was published and distributed widely throughout the realm, a task made much easier and much quicker now since the printing process had been invented in Germany a few years before.

Meanwhile, in the province of Granada, the last enclave of Islam in Western Europe, the internal strains were great. Dissension against the tyrannical and brutal sultan, Muley Aben Hassan, had boiled to the surface. That he had put his kingdom at great risk by his strike against Zahara was broadly deplored. The loss of Alhama was devastating. The prophetic words of the aged anchorite hung in the air. As the sultan returned empty-handed from his unsuccessful attempts to recapture Alhama, the disenchantment increased, and a conspiracy against the Moorish king was organized within the Alhambra.

When Muley retreated to his country palace at Alixares, the rebels seized the Alhambra and the neighborhood on the hill across from it called Albaicín. Upon the sultan's return from the country, the gates of the fortress were shut tight against him. From the parapets, the rebels shouted down that the king was deposed, and his son, Abdullah Muhammad, known as Boabdil, was installed in Muley's place.

"Alihu Akbar!" the king is said to have exclaimed. "It is pointless to combat what is written in the book of fate. It is predicted that my son should sit upon the throne of Granada. God forbid that the rest of the prediction come true." With that, Muley retreated north to the city of Baza to organize his supporters. "This rash flame will burn itself out," he proclaimed confidently. "In time the situation will cool off and the people will listen to reason."

But the people of Granada showed no signs of returning their allegiance to him. In desperation, Muley staged a disastrous raid on the Alhambra. Five hundred of his best soldiers succeeded in scaling the walls and entering the fortress, and a terrible fight through the streets of the Alhambra and the gardens of the Generalife ensued. After much bloodshed, Muley's men were eventually turned back, and the old tyrant retreated south to Málaga, where his younger brother, Muley Abdullah, known as *"El Zagal*—the Valiant," reigned.

And so as the Christian crusade marshaled its forces for an organized campaign against the last Moorish state, the Moors themselves were divided into two warring camps, father against son, Granada against Málaga.

Flushed with the success at Alhama, King Ferdinand called a council of war in Córdoba to ponder his next move. Throughout the land, spurred by the papal bull making the crusade a pious obligation, provisions of foodstuffs and wine were requisitioned. From the *Santa Hermandad* thousands more cavalry and foot soldiers were pressed into duty for the growing army of invasion. Lest the Moors receive substantial reinforcements from the Muslim lands of North Africa, Ferdinand strengthened his armada in the Straits of Gibraltar, a task made easier by the fact that the Rock itself had passed into Christian hands twenty years earlier, in 1462. Before the king's councilors lay the question of what to do about the prize of Alhama, exposed and deep within the enemy territory as it was. Among the seasoned warriors sentiment was strong to level the place, so that the Moors might not recapture a strategic stronghold. Against this faction Queen Isabella spoke out forcefully.

"Shall we destroy the first fruits of our victories?" she demanded to know. "Shall we abandon the first place we wrest from the Moors? Perish the thought. It would give succor to the enemy, and cast our councils as feeble. You speak of the toil and expense of maintaining Alhama.

Did any doubt, on undertaking this war, that it would involve infinite cost, labor, and bloodshed? Shall we shrink from the cost, in this moment of gaining our first glorious trophy?"

Grumbles were heard around the room, but the queen dismissed the naysayers curtly. "Let us hear no more about the destruction of Alhama," she said with finality. "Its walls are sacred. It is a stronghold granted to us by Heaven, in the center of this land of infidels. Let us only concern ourselves with how to extend our conquest and capture more cities."

With that, orders to reinforce the fortress were issued.

Casting his eye over the map, King Ferdinand now focused on the stronghold of Loja, a prosperous town a few leagues northwest of Alhama, astride the main east-west road of the caliphate, and defended by an alcazar that dated back to the ninth century. If the Christian Holy War could wrest it from the Moors, the gateway to the rich plain around Granada itself would be thrown open.

Ferdinand was eager to get started, since he had missed out on the glorious triumph of Alhama, for which the marquis of Cádiz was being lionized. But the marquis now urged caution; until the army could be provisioned, and more reinforcements of the Holy Brotherhood brought in from the north, they should wait. To attack now would be foolhardy. The royal army consisted of a mere five thousand cavalry and eight thousand foot soldiers, scarcely enough to capture and hold well-defended castles or to defeat the fierce army of the Moors. Moreover, the Moors were strengthening their forces.

Despite the objections of his commanders, Ferdinand, full of zeal and itching for glory, ordered his army to march. Within a few days, in late winter of 1483, he stood before Loja. Its circumstance was not advantageous to the attackers. The town was situated where the Genil River narrows into a deep gorge and passes between two large, rocky hills. Olive groves covered the broken hills, which were scored and striated by a series of deep ravines. The landscape provided no natural place for the whole army to camp, nor for the artillery to be effectively positioned, nor for the cavalry to gather. Across the gorge, the fortress was well defended, and under the command of a stalwart fighter, Ali Atar. This fierce Moor was the father-in-law of Boabdil. Despite his ninety years of age, he was described as "fiery in his passion, sinewy and powerful in his frame," and he had terrorized the Christian border towns for decades. Now, he would prove himself to be a formidable foe. As he watched the disjointed movements of the Christian army across the river from the crenellated walls of his fortress, the canny old Moor remarked, "With the help of Allah, I will give those strutting *caballeros* a good stirring up."

Across the Genil River was a single bridge, and above it to the north was the imposing, steep massif known as the Albohacen. Since the terrain was unsuited to cavalry action, the king ordered the marquis of Cádiz to seize the high ground, which he did. Once Albohacen was in Christian hands, however, it was hard to know what to do with it. Ali Atar knew, however. Under cover of darkness, his troops stole across the bridge and set an ambush. The following morning, the old warrior and his men raced across the bridge, flags flying and scimitars raised, shouting the praises of Allah in an apparent attack on the hill. The Christians, thinking they had an easy prey, raced down the hill to engage the enemy. Ali Atar then wheeled his soldiers around in an apparent retreat and rout, and the Christians galloped heroically into the trap. It was an old trick of Muslim battle tactics, and the result was mayhem on Albohacen, with important knights lost on the Christian side.

King Ferdinand fared little better the following day. It was gradually dawning on him that his destiny as the liberator of Andalusia might be more difficult than he imagined. To make things worse for Ferdinand, word came that Moorish reinforcements, led by the king of the Moors, Muley Aben Hassan himself, were coming from the south. Realizing that the marquis of Cádiz had been right about the insufficiency of his forces, Ferdinand ordered a retreat. When he saw the Christians strike their tents and the Christian soldiers move out, Ali Atar sallied forth once again, disrupting the Christian lines and throwing the retreat into chaos. At one point, King Ferdinand found himself surrounded. He was saved only by the quick thinking of the marquis of Cádiz, who charged in with seventy cavalrymen to beat back the Muslims.

Leaving its heavy baggage behind, the Christian army fled seven leagues to the west until it reached an outcropping known as the Rock of the Lovers. All along the way, Ali Atar harassed this disorganized retreat mercilessly. At the Río Frio, the old Moor watched the Christian army scatter and bid it good riddance. Muley Aben Hassan arrived a short time later with his army. Upon his arrival, too late to finish the job, Muley lamented the lost opportunity. "They have come and gone like a summer cloud," he is supposed to have remarked. "All their boasting has been mere empty thunder." Not content to leave the matter there, the Moorish king marched to Alhama once again. But there he found the bastion defended by an even stronger garrison.

The month of March 1483 saw the conflict become a game of thrust and parry, with booty rather than religious conquest its main purpose. The Moors got the best of it. Muley Aben Hassan launched a raid, by way of Gibraltar, deep into the lands of Rodrigo Ponce de León and of the count of Medina-Sidonia, and returned to Málaga laden with Christian spoil. In retaliation, the Christian lords attacked the hamlets and villages in the rugged terrain of the Axarquia west of Málaga which they thought would be easy picking. But the combined forces of Muley Aben Hassan and his brother, El Zagal the Valiant, fell upon the exposed Christian army in an open valley and crushed it. The remnants fled into the low hills, where another Moorish contingent waited in hiding. In this total rout the cream of Andalusian nobility was decimated. Eight hundred knights were killed, and fifteen hundred were taken captive. The site of the battle would forever be known as *la Cuesta de la Matanza*—the Hill of the Massacre.

For this brief period, the land of Spanish Islam seemed safe, even transcendent. Bedraggled Christian captives were paraded in Málaga, while the bloodied survivors of the rout in the Axarquia, including the marquis of Cádiz, trickled into the Christian border towns. "A great affliction has overwhelmed all Andalusia," a Christian chronicler wrote.

"There was no drying the eyes which wept for her." Other scribes drew broader, sharper lessons. "Our Lord consented to it because most of those people went with robbery in their hearts rather than to serve God," said the historian of the royal court. Of the Christian disaster west of Málaga, another wrote:

"It was intended as a lesson to their overconfidence and vain-glory. They overrated their own prowess, and thought that so chosen a band of chivalry had but to appear in the land of the enemy and conquer. It was to teach them that the race is not to the swift, nor the battle to the strong, but that God alone giveth the victory."

When, in the night sky over Al Andalus, a brilliant crescent moon, symbol of Islam, rose, it seemed to many to be the smile of the Prophet.

❖

With the rousing success of Muley Aben Hassan and his brother, El Zagal, their stock rose rapidly among the people throughout the land of the Moors. The standing of Muley's eldest son, Boabdil *El Chico* (The Small), dropped proportionately, as stories of his sloth, his love of luxury, his preoccupation with trivial games and festivals made the rounds of Granada's streets. Now in his twenties, Boabdil had never been tested in battle. If he was to retain the respect of his people and the crown of his father, he needed to sally forth. His father-in-law was the indomitable Ali Atar, the lord and hero of Loja, and this fierce old warrior pressed the point with his son-in-law.

Seemingly forever, Ali Atar had run free through the borderlands of Christian Andalusia, foraging and harrowing and ravaging at will. His parties struck terror in the border towns, and his spies were constantly on the alert for new opportunities. They told him now that the Christian town of Lucena, on the road to Córdoba, was weakly defended and easily taken. When the old Moor put the idea to Boabdil, it appealed; and he soon mustered a force of nine thousand foot soldiers and eight hundred cavalry.

The day of Boabdil's departure from the Alhambra, April 20, 1483, was exactly a month after his father's victory over the Christians west of Málaga. It would later go into lore that his wife, Morayama, hung upon the young king's neck weeping and pleading with him not to go. To this shameful display, Boabdil's mother, Ayxa the Chaste, gave a sharp rebuke. "Why dost thou weep, daughter of Ali Atar? These tears do not become the daughter of a warrior, much less the wife of a king. More danger lurks within the walls of this palace than the curtains of a war tent. By prowess upon the battlefield, your husband must purchase the security of his throne."

Out of the Alhambra El Chico rode magnificently, astride a massive white charger richly and colorfully caparisoned, armed with shining lance and scimitar. As he passed through the Arch of Elvira, he playfully struck his lance against the arch stone, and broke its blade. At this bad omen, his commanders blanched, but Boabdil rode on undeterred. Their worries deepened a day later when a fox raced wildly through the ranks, even close to the monarch himself, and eluded all the arrows and darts of the king's soldiers. It was a second portent. A vizier suggested that they turn back, but El Chico waved the man aside.

At Loja, Ali Atar joined his son-in-law, and the colorful column moved eagerly across the bridge and past Albohacen, the scene of so recent a Moorish triumph. The procession moved over the frontier at night toward Lucena, hoping to avoid detection. But alarm fires soon blazed across the hilltops, and the Moors knew that there would be no surprise. The first to receive the news of the enemy incursion was the count of Cabra, whose strong fortress lay only a few leagues north of Lucena. More than 1,000 well-trained fighters and 250 experienced and battle-hardened *caballeros* were under the command of the count. Unfurling his family's standard, whose symbol was a goat, the count and his contingent moved out with dispatch to reinforce the weak garrison of Lucena.

At daybreak, fog covering the hills and ravines around Lucena, El Chico sent a demand to the town to surrender. As they waited for a reply, the Moors fanned out in the countryside to gather up herds of cattle and casks of the famous Montilla wine. While they foraged, the Christian spies observed their movements carefully. In the early morning it was reported to the count that the main force of the Moors was then in a nearby arroyo.

With the mist covering the valleys and hills, the count of Cabra decided that he should not wait for further reinforcements. He must seize this opportunity. To his soldiers he invoked the spirit of Santiago, St. James the Moorslayer, who in the sacred ninth-century Battle of Clavijo had come out of the heavens to aid the Christians and had personally slain ten thousand Moors. This legend had great currency with the Christian forces now. They were to march, confident of divine inspiration, secure in their belief that the benevolence of the Virgin Mary would enfold and protect them.

"Santiago!" was the battle cry, and it would soon be mixed in the din of war with *"Allah Akbar!*—God is Great," as the Christian force came upon the Moors resting in the deep valley. As the Christian army fell upon the Moors, mass confusion reigned. Ali Atar spied the Christian banner through the mist and mistook Cabra's goat for a dog, which was the symbol of the strong Christian bastions of Baeza and Úbeda. "All Andalusia is in movement against you," Ali Atar shouted in alarm to El Chico. "I advise you to retire." And then the old warrior heard a trumpet, sounded by the single Italian in the Christian ranks. Ali Atar knew that sound well as the signature of the much-feared soldiers of Lombardy. "The whole world is against you!" Ali Atar screamed at his king.

Through the drizzle the one unmistakable figure was El Chico himself, conspicuous on his great white stallion and embroidered apron. As the foot soldiers attempted to scramble across a swollen stream called Mingozales, the king's defenses seemed to melt away. Nearly deserted by the streambed, Boabdil realized immediately that he made a tempting target. And so he dismounted and hid among the bushes and willows. But a Christian cavalier came upon him moments later, and soon two more arrived. Seeing that his situation was hopeless, and puffing himself up with his full dignity, he demanded to surrender honorably to the senior knight, as befitted his station. He was taken way to Lucena to be imprisoned for a day in the Torre del Moral.

The disaster of Lucena did not end with the capture of the Moorish king. Ali Atar too was cornered later in the day. His surrender was demanded as well, but his reaction was different. "Never to a Christian dog!" he hissed defiantly and moments later his skull was split. The battle had turned into a rout.

Twenty-two Muslim battle flags fell into Christian hands on that day. They were taken to a church in the village of Baena. In the years that followed, they would be brought into the streets on the feast day of St. George, the dragon slayer, to mark the turning point in the last war against the Moors.

9

The Inquisitor's Martyrdom

❖

 In the year that followed the first, smoldering *auto-da-fe* of the new Spanish Inquisition in Seville, the Holy Office worked steadily and diligently at the enormous, nationwide dragnet it had conceived for itself. The inquisitors were about the business of God's vengeance, and His judgments could be cruel. In the words of an apologist, they were cutting away "a rotten limb" from the body politic. "Once the evil men are liquidated, God will bring His mercy."

The challenge was not so much to deal with the prominent conversos and heretics like Diego de Susan—their cases were easily dispatched—but to manage the thousands upon thousands of cases involving ordinary people that awaited disposition. In this budding reign of terror, the Church encouraged accusations of heresy; because a mere accusation presumed guilt, and because it was so easy to accuse a neighbor or friend, even in an effort to save oneself, the caseload mounted exponentially. The task was organizational as much as legal or ecclesiastical or purgative: to discriminate between the recalcitrant and the compliant, to distinguish between those who were beyond the help of the Church and must therefore be turned over to the "secular arm" for punishment, and those who might be "reconciled" with the Christian faith. There was as well the financial side, the aspect of the business that most interested Ferdinand: how to manage and dispose of the vast amount of confiscated land and property that devolved to the hands of the Inquisition, and how to translate this property into a fund to finance the War Against the Moors.

In Seville, the first three inquisitors were overwhelmed. Inevitably, they sought to lighten their workload by summary judgment, or a quick resort to torture to secure a confession. In the first year of its life, the local Holy Office cut many corners. Abuses were common. In due course, the reports of this abuse reached the Vatican, carried to Rome by influential conversos who were themselves in danger.

On January 29, 1482, Pope Sixtus IV issued a stern warning both to the Spanish monarchs and to the inquisitors about the excesses of the Spanish Inquisition. The inquisitors were disregarding judicial procedures, the pope charged in his Brief. Individuals were being accused in violation of justice and "punished by severe tortures." The crime of heresy was being alleged indiscriminately without foundation. The pope demanded that the procedures of the Inquisition be brought into concert with common law. If the abuses continued, he would fire the current inquisitors and replace them with more responsible prelates.

Stern as his rebuke sounded, Sixtus IV undercut its impact almost immediately by sending a fawning communication to the Spanish monarchs. Only days after the Brief of January 29, Sixtus wrote deferentially to Isabella, applauding her pious work with the Inquisition. "We rejoice in our heart, beloved daughter, at the determination and diligence you put into things so desired by us," he wrote. "We should always be diligent in applying the necessary remedies to such pestilential harm. You take upon yourself this cause of God, because in nothing else can you serve him better than this."

Nevertheless, the pope's attention to Spanish affairs was sporadic and deflective. His mind was elsewhere, on problems closer to home, for war had broken out on the Italian peninsula. The Vatican itself was imperiled by soldiers from Turkey, from Naples, and from the Florence of Lorenzo the Magnificent.

"In the Pope's antechambers," wrote an Italian scribe named Sigismondo di Conti, "instead of cassocked priests, armed guards keep watch. Soldiers equipped for battle, and drawn up before the gates of the Papal palace. All court officials are filled with terror and anguish. The fury of the populace is only restrained by the fear of soldiers." The purity of the Church in faraway Spain concerned the pope less than the very survival of the Vatican. In this desperate situation, he would need all the support he could get from the Spanish throne.

On February 11, Sixtus commissioned seven more inquisitors, including Tomás de Torquemada. All were Dominicans, from the order known as the Dogs of God. Significantly, these new inquisitors were to be under the control of the Spanish crown, and not answerable to the Vatican. It was a point that Ferdinand and Isabella had insisted upon.

Sixtus IV made one last effort to impart order and judicious propriety to the Spanish Inquisition. On April 18, 1482, he issued an extraordinary bull concerning the process of the tribunal. Heresy must be tried like any other crime, and the accused must have the right to a fair trial and to simple justice. The names of accusers and witnesses must be revealed to the accused. He or she must be given counsel, must be imprisoned in episcopal jails, must have the right to confess in secret. And finally, most galling of all to Ferdinand, the person convicted of heresy had the sacred right to appeal to the Holy See. He who would block such appeal risked excommunication.

Before this bull could be nailed to the door of a single church in Spain, Ferdinand responded with fury and contempt. The pope had overstepped the bounds of his office. The pontiff was clearly infatuated by the representations of New Christians, Ferdinand wrote. The King of Spain had no intention of allowing the provisions of the bull ever to take effect. He and he alone must exert total control over the Inquisition.

❧

Throughout the summer of 1482, the planning for the war in the south proceeded in concert with the organization of the Inquisition across the

Spanish peninsula. Fleeting contacts with the rulers in the Alhambra were maintained, even as the Christian monarchs schemed about how best to conquer the Moorish state.

In the midst of these epic developments, the royals were in Toledo, and Isabella was pregnant again. If her child was a male, the throne of a conquered Granada would be his. But on June 28, she gave birth to twins, both girls; one was stillborn. Ferdinand left Toledo after the births. Far more than his fatherly duties, his preoccupation was simultaneously the war and the organization of the Inquisition in his ancestral kingdom of Aragon.

Aragon presented the Inquisition with a different challenge than Castile. In this far-flung kingdom, which included not only Aragon, but Catalonia and Valencia, Majorca and the other Balearic Islands, and dependencies in Sicily, Corsica, and Sardinia, the institution had existed since the thirteenth century. Although it had been essentially dormant for many decades, the remnants of its apparatus had to be scrapped if a new, vigorous administration were to be put in its place. Moreover, the spirit of independence ruled there. The nobles of Aragon and Valencia did not easily suffer the interference either of their king or of a foreign inquisition. Resistance to the Inquisition was immediate in the cities of Barcelona, Saragossa, Teruel, and Valencia. At first, Ferdinand proceeded cautiously, respectfully, recommending lenient and nonconfrontational methods to the Aragonese inquisitors.

But in October 1482, a dramatic change took place when Ferdinand got papal approval to appoint Tomás de Torquemada as the inquisitor for Aragon and Valencia. Torquemada's stock was rising. Months later, he was promoted again to Inquisitor-General of both Castile and Aragon, as his jurisdiction over both kingdoms was consolidated.

On January 1, 1483, Torquemada received a letter from the king informing his leading inquisitor of his decision to expel all Jews from Christian Andalusia. The order heralded a new aggressiveness toward the Jews. It was a harbinger of broader measures to come.

With the advancement of Torquemada, the interference of the Vatican ceased. Sixtus IV became irrelevant to the Spanish scene. Before he died six months later, he portrayed the Inquisition as a "great work of purification," and donated its control formally and entirely to the Spanish monarchs. The pontiff compared the effort to the zeal of Jesus Christ who, he proclaimed in stretching a point, had consolidated his holy kingdom on earth by the destruction of idolatry.

With patent efficiency, Torquemada proceeded to break the country down into regional tribunals, dominated by his Dominican brothers. Late in 1483, this sallow Dominican was given a new and unprecedented title to go along with his extraordinary power: Grand Inquisitor-General or simply the Grand Inquisitor.

Among Torquemada's first acts as Grand Inquisitor was the demand that conversos present themselves for confession. He ordered the rabbis of Toledo to swear an oath that they would report any converso who observed Jewish rites and ceremonies, and that these rabbis would expel from their temples any Jew who refused to become a witness against their own people.

In Torquemada, the zeal of a fanatic was joined with superior administrative skills. Every holocaust needs a cold-hearted organization man. To Torquemada, the Inquisition was not about human beings but about organizational charts and clerical appointments and regional commissions, and later about standardizing instructions to his lesser tribunals across the country. In the minds of both the king and the pope, as well as the Cardinal of Spain, González de Mendoza, here was the man to mold this holy enterprise into an engine of purification—purification by fire.

❖

After the capture of Boabdil and the crushing defeat of the Moors at Lucena in April 1483, a few bloodied survivors limped back to Muslim territory. Their bleak news spread rapidly through the land of the Moors. In the seesaw battle for the public's allegiance, Muley Aben Hassan was once again in the ascendant, as the word of Boabdil's humiliating surrender was received contemptuously. From Málaga, Muley returned to Granada and took charge of the Alhambra again. But his high-spirited, determined wife, Ayxa the Chaste, Boabdil's mother, merely moved across the narrow gorge of the Rio Darro to the opposing hill of the Albaicín and took up residence in the fortress there, known as the *alcazaba.*

All support for Boabdil had by no means evaporated, especially among the common people, who well remembered Muley's cruelty. And so on opposite hills in Granada, no more than a few hundred meters apart as the crow and the catapulted artillery fly, the supporters of father and son faced one another. The knights of the realm were for Muley, while the common people supported Boabdil.

Meanwhile, Boabdil languished in splendid captivity in Lucena. There, the count of Cabra lavished royal treatment on him, handling his distinguished prisoner with the honor and respect due a king, while he waited for Ferdinand and Isabella to decide what to do with their prize.

In Córdoba, the court gathered to debate the options. Rodrigo Ponce de León, the marquis of Cádiz, argued for Boabdil's early release, and in this, he was seconded by the Grand Cardinal of Spain, Pedro González de Mendoza. Both these powerful men felt that Boabdil was more useful in Granada than in Castilian exile. The more the internal strife, the more the chance that the Moorish state would implode, rather than have to be conquered. In the chronicle of the Grand Cardinal, the phrase, later made even more famous by others in history was first uttered, "a kingdom divided against itself cannot stand."

From Granada came competing ransom proposals from the competing sides. Muley sent his embassy to Córdoba, proposing a huge ransom if his son could be returned to the Alhambra. It seemed not to matter to the father whether his son came home on horseback or in a box. But the sultana put forward a more attractive alternative, which seemed to appeal especially to Queen Isabella. The queen mother, as well, offered a huge ransom for her son's return, but suggested that he be allowed to retain his crown as a vassal to the Castilian monarchs. The practice of annual tribute would be renewed. A number of Christian prisoners would be returned, and as surety for the deal, Boabdil's only son was offered as a hostage.

To this proposal Ferdinand added a few clever stipulations. Most important, Boabdil must promise to allow safe passage for Christian soldiers marching through territory that El Chico controlled. There must be a two-year truce between the sides. When the provisions were transcribed, Boabdil accepted them gratefully and prepared to return to his homeland. But Ferdinand had one last demand: the king of the Moors must come to him for a ceremony of groveling homage. All must witness his disgrace and subservience. In late August, Boabdil rode magnificently and publicly from his prison to the royal palace in Córdoba. There he fell to his knees before Ferdinand and kissed his hand. Once upon his feet, the Moor delivered a flowery speech of praise for his captor, which went on so long that Ferdinand finally raised his hand for silence.

"Enough!" he reportedly said. "There is no need for these compliments. I trust in your integrity. And I trust that you will do all that becomes a good man and a good king."

With that, a colorful parade gathered for Boabdil's exit. King Ferdinand and his vassal rode side by side through the streets of Córdoba before a cheering throng. A few Moorish knights followed behind, and behind them, a complement of Christian knights, including the marquis of Cádiz. Outside the city walls, the kings parted amid more speeches. Ferdinand turned north toward Guadalupe. Important matters, including the organization of the Inquisition in Aragon, demanded his attention.

At the border, an escort from his mother awaited Boabdil. A dangerous passage lay ahead, and so the king moved warily through his own kingdom under the cover of darkness. At the gate to Albaicín, the king slipped through unnoticed and was soon welcomed in the *alcazaba*. The following morning, the news of Boabdil's arrival spread rapidly. When his father heard about it, his fury was considerable. Through the streets and squares running battles between the supporters of each side raged.

But civil strife carried no glory, and after a few days an uneasy armistice was arranged. Boabdil agreed to leave Granada for the port city of Almería, where his base of support was unequivocal, and where the 500-year-old *alcazaba* rivaled the bastions of Granada.

The House of the Moors stood divided against itself.

❖

Early in 1484, the attention of the Spanish king and queen had shifted to the scrubland of Ferdinand's kingdom of Aragon. In mid-January they convened a Cortes at Tarazona, a town northwest of Saragossa, where the main focus was the final organization of the Aragonese Inquisition. In the previous two years, as the monarchs gained total control over the Castilian Inquisition, they had moved cautiously in Aragon, where the power of local lords was far stronger and deeply rooted in the ancient tradition known as the *fueros*, or powers, of the local establishment. With the extension of Torquemada's jurisdiction over Aragon as well as Castile, the Grand Inquisitor had gradually appointed local inquisitors to his liking. At first, Sixtus IV had attempted to place roadblocks in the way of Ferdinand and Torquemada, lest the Vatican lose complete control over the Aragon Inquisition, as had happened in Castile. But these impediments had been removed one by one, with the quiet help of Cardinal Rodrigo Borgia, the powerful Spanish cardinal, who like Ferdinand salivated at the prospect of seizing the property of wealthy Aragonese conversos.

As his provincial inquisitors, Torquemada had appointed two Dominicans, Gaspar Juglar, and the young canon of Saragossa's cathedral, Pedro Arbués, who had distinguished himself both for his theology and for his zeal. The Grand Inquisitor, in turn, had organized lesser tribunals throughout Aragon. High on the agenda of the Tarazona Cortes was the imperative to accord these tribunals the royal stamp of approval. Catalonia had refused to send delegates to the Cortes, for its leaders opposed the appointment of Torquemada's men. But Torquemada nominated two new inquisitors for Barcelona anyway.

The reaction was immediate. Worthies in Barcelona wrote to Ferdinand that Torquemada's appointments were "against the liberties, constitutions and agreements solemnly sworn by Your Majesty!" and that, moreover, there were very few heretics in Catalonia. "We do not believe," the city councilors of Barcelona were to declare later, "that to be a converso makes one a heretic." The king waved these protests aside. On May 7, Ferdinand issued a directive for his whole kingdom that the inquisitors and their designees were to be honored and assisted everywhere. Any interference would be severely punished.

"There is no intention of infringing the *fueros* but rather of enforcing their observance," the king wrote to the disgruntled Catalans. "If the old inquisitors had acted conscientiously in accordance with the canons there would have been no cause for bringing in the new ones. But they were without conscience and corrupted with bribes. If there are as few heretics as you state, there should not be such a dread of the Inquisition. It is not to be impeded . . . for be assured: no cause or interest, however great, shall be tolerated to interfere with its proceeding."

The way was now clear for action.

On May 10, the first *auto-da-fe* in Aragon was held in the Cathedral of Saragossa, with Gaspar Juglar, one of the two inquisitors for Aragon, delivering the lesson. At this inaugural event, four men were penanced, or "reconciled" to the Church, after their property was confiscated. Then, on June 2, in the courtyard of the episcopal palace in Saragossa, the second *auto-da-fe* was held. This time, the second inquisitor, Pedro Arbués, preached. Two heretics were burned, and a woman was burned in effigy. Within a few days, Gaspar Juglar was poisoned after eating some sweet doughnuts called *rosquillas*. The matter would have to be left to the ecclesiastical police, for Ferdinand and Isabella had left Aragon for Córdoba, where they turned their attention again to the War Against the Moors.

There would not be another *auto-da-fe* in Aragon for eighteen months. A wave of repugnance swept through the populace. Even without additional *autos-da-fé*, the anger against the surviving inquisitor in Aragon, Pedro Arbués, remained high. In lieu of more burnings, influential conversos were forced to take an oath that they would do all in their power to ferret out lapsed Christians. Moreover, attractive offers of vast sums were offered to the crown by wealthy nobles, if the Inquisition would suspend all confiscations.

During the summer of 1484, plague broke out in Rome. In the midst of the public panic over the epidemic, Sixtus IV died. In the election that followed, Cardinal Rodrigo Borgia was narrowly defeated by an Italian cardinal, who took the name of Innocent VIII. But as head of the College of Cardinals and vice chancellor of the Vatican, Borgia's power remained considerable. His day would come.

On November 29, 1484, the Grand Inquisitor gathered the Suprema and his appointed inquisitors together in Seville for the purpose of issuing broad guidelines for their future conduct. King Ferdinand and Queen Isabella were present at this plenary session, and Torquemada made clear that the guidelines were crafted with the involvement and sanction and ultimately for the benefit of the Spanish crown.

Taken together, the "Instructions" laid out an elaborate system for entrapping suspected heretics. They encouraged voluntary self-incrimination by making punishments progressively more severe for those who did not incriminate themselves speedily in the initial thirty days of the local Inquisition's existence. To allow the thirty-day grace period to elapse without a voluntary confession was to risk being accused later by others. The right to confront one's accuser was denied, and the accused was not permitted to see the evidence that was gathered against him. The articles vested the inquisitors with the discretion to decide whether confessions were sincere and complete. If the inquisitors found a confession to be less than the whole truth, the accused could be declared a "false penitent." For that, the punishment was rigorous and extreme. The fifteenth article authorized torture to be administered to an accused person who confessed partially, or persisted in denial, and the eighteenth commanded the inquisitors to be present at the torture.

The Instructions contained elaborate provisions to confiscate land

and property from the accused, since this was to become a vast land grab from wealthy and prominent landholders. A system of treasurers was set up to seize and to record such property. The testimony of slaves and vassals against their lords was protected and kept secret.

"If persons have sold or gotten rid of all their other lands in fear of the Inquisition and are on the run from the Inquisition," the seventh article read, "those people are liable for the amount that they received from the sale of the lands and possessions. This applies to people unless they are treasurers. This is for the reason that the treasurers are the ones responsible for the collection, liquidation, and transfer of the property to the Inquisition."

Confiscation did not apply only to the living. "If it is proven that any person died a heretic, by writings or conduct, he shall be condemned, his body disinterred and burnt, and his property confiscated." Nor were the children and grandchildren of the condemned excluded. They could not hold public office, or join the holy orders or be accorded any honors. "If a man, burnt as a heretic, left children under age," went the twenty-second article, "a portion of their father's property should be grant to them as alms, and the inquisitors shall be obliged to consign their education to appropriate persons."

The process placed great emphasis on efficiency. Any matter not specifically covered by an Instruction was left to the discretion and "prudence" of the inquisitors to determine guilt. Innocence became a near impossibility for anyone accused. The best one could hope for was to be "reconciled" to the Church and merely lose land and property, or to be jailed indefinitely in an ecclesiastical prison.

In January 1485, Torquemada issued a few refinements to the initial Instructions. For "reconciled" persons, the following provision was crafted. "If any person comes to be reconciled and does not tell the truth of their errors as well as of those who took part in said errors with them, and later evidence shows they were lying, proceedings against them will take place with all possible severity and rigor."

Of the sections of Spain where the bureaucracies of the Inquisition had been introduced by 1484, Aragon remained the stiffest in its resistance. After the first *auto-da-fe* in Saragossa in May 1484, one of the two inquisitors for the kingdom had been poisoned, leaving the other, Pedro Arbués, to carry on the detested work alone. Because the resistance was so great, Arbués began the practice of paying for incriminating testimony, and resentment against him exploded. In the south of Aragon, where horseshoe-shaped hills with flat tops, deep ravines, and limestone outcroppings distinguished the grim landscape, the resistance was fiercest. In the fortified town of Teruel, all the town fathers were in open mutiny. When the inquisitor's representatives showed up at the town gates, they were turned away. This defiance led to a series of actions both by the Inquisition and by King Ferdinand himself. The king fired Teruel's magistrates and blocked the flow of royal money to the town, while the inquisitor used his power of excommunication to bring the town to heel. Ferdinand installed an overlord who wielded dictatorial powers. Eventually, over many months, these powerful forces wore down the rebellion; but something more dramatic was needed if the opposition in this fiercely independent section was to be stifled altogether.

In Saragossa, the resistance took on a more desperate shape. A secret conspiracy of the wealthy and influential conversos got under way with a plan to sabotage the Inquisition, violently. If Arbués could only be assassinated, the conspirators argued, no one would dare replace him, and Aragon would be safe. Through the winter of 1484–85, the planning went forward. Secret meetings were held in the homes of the conspirators and in the churches of Saragossa. Assassins were hired, paid a modest fee, and sent out to look for a propitious moment. Several chances presented themselves, but the operations were aborted when Arbués was found accompanied by guards.

On September 15, 1485, the word came that the inquisitor was praying alone at matins in the cathedral. The assassins raced to the church and entered by the chapter door. There, they found the inquisitor kneeling near the altar. He wore a coat of mail and a steel cap, and his lance was propped against a pillar. The assassins fell upon him viciously, plunging their knives into his neck, and leaving him dying in a pool of blood.

The alarm was immediate and shrill. The Holy Brotherhood spread out to apprehend the villains. Some of the assassins were caught immediately, and retribution was swift. Several others fled north to Navarre, where they hoped to find refuge. Fiercely, Ferdinand threatened war against Navarre if the murderers were not turned over.

Both Ferdinand and Torquemada appreciated immediately what a gift they had been given. Contrary to the hopes of the conspirators, public sentiment swung dramatically against the conversos and in favor of the Inquisition. Within a few months the first *auto-da-fe* in eighteen months was celebrated in Saragossa, where a man and a woman were burned for practicing Jewish rites and supping the Jewish broth called hamin. Torquemada quickly appointed replacements for his deceased inquisitors and expanded the sweep of the Inquisition in the kingdom.

Over time, Arbués's assassins were caught one by one. The leaders were literally butchered. One was dragged to the altar where the murder was committed. There, his hands were cut off. He was then taken to the market square to be beheaded, quartered, and burned. The hands of his accomplice were also cut off and nailed to the door of the House of Deputies, after which he too was butchered.

Rumors of great miracles spread immediately through the kingdom, as the canonization of Pedro Arbués was begun. Upon the stones of the cathedral where the inquisitor was murdered, it was said that his blood dried, but then after two days, inexplicably became liquid once again. For the sick who dipped their garments in it, remarkable cures happened. Two days after the assassination, it was reported, the bells of the cathedral rang without their ropes being pulled. Yet another story circulated that the assassins who fled to Navarre became dazed and disoriented at the border, allowing their pursuers to catch up. Lastly and perhaps best, a rumor spread that as the villains were being interrogated by the Inquisition, their mouths turned black and they were unable to speak.

The repercussions from the murder of Arbués were to last for five years in Aragon, time enough to terrify the populace and bludgeon it into submission. Ferdinand manipulated the public's terror skillfully. The traditional independence of the Aragonese nobility faded with each trial and grotesque execution. With its demise, the king's central authority grew stronger.

If the resonance of the assassination had immediate effect in Aragon, it was to last several centuries in the lore of the Roman Catholic Church. A year after the murder of Pedro Arbués, a magnificent tomb was built for his remains. On its side, a bas-relief depicted the scene of the murder. The yellow garments of the heretic, which the assassins were forced to wear temporarily before they were dispatched, were put on public display in the cathedral. The purpose, of course, was to perpetuate the memory of a heinous crime by a group the Church historians called "sham Christians."

Over the next 180 years, a series of attempts ensued at the Holy See in Rome to make Pedro Arbués a full-fledged saint and an official martyr. The notion was controversial. Finally, in 1668, with his beatification, Pedro Arbués was inducted into the pantheon of heroes. His martyrdom and miracles were officially "approved." His relics, though presumably not the instruments of torture, could be put on public display for veneration, although, in a gesture of restraint, the Church barred them from being carried in procession.

Two hundred years after that, in 1866, the infamous Pius IX canonized Arbués as a saint. The inquisitor's canonization fit well into the spirit of the weak, corrupt, and reactionary reign of that pope, who presided over the demise of the Papal States in Italy; who sanctioned, without trial or verdict, the jailing of any dissident against papal authority; and who propounded the doctrines of the Immaculate Conception of the Virgin Mary and the Infallibility of the Pope.

San Pedro's canonization document read: "The divine wisdom has arranged that in those sad days, when Jews helped the enemies of the church with their books and money, this decree of sanctity has been brought to fulfillment." September 17 was declared to be San Pedro's feast day. In the Cathedral of Saragossa, an ornate chapel is dedicated to his memory.

"His name has been associated with acts of wanton cruelty and inhumanity in the fulfillment of his office as Inquisitor," reads his biography in Catholic annals today, "but these have never been substantiated."

Spices and Black Gold

❖

L I S B O N

 In the year 1483, Portugal was the most progressive, visionary, affluent country in all of Europe, and Lisbon was the continent's most vibrant port. In its lovely circumstance, built upon low hills above the broad estuary of the Tagus River, sparkling with white villas and perfumed with jasmine and orange blossom, the city was a breathtaking mixture of Hispanic, African, Moorish, Mediterranean, and Northern European culture. Along the narrow alleys of its Moorish section, called the Alfama, and in its great Alcazar, the remnants of 500-year-long Moorish rule, which had ended four hundred years earlier, were still conspicuous.

On September 7, 1479, Portugal and Spain had formally ended the War of Succession with the Treaty of Alcáçovas. It ended the Portuguese claim to the Castilian throne, but more importantly, it defined the spheres of influence in foreign exploration between the two countries. Portugal would rule the African coastline, and any Spanish vessel had to receive Portuguese permission to trade as far as Cape Bojador. Castile gave up any claim to the Cape Verde Islands, Madeira, and the Azores. But it retained the Canaries, those volcanic islands off the African coast that were named by the Romans for their big dogs.

For two centuries, Lisbon had had a special relationship with Italian merchants. With the emergence of the Ottoman Empire, traders from Florence and Genoa had lost their trading posts in the eastern Mediterranean and had flocked to the western Mediterranean, establishing significant colonies in Seville, Cádiz, Puerto de Santa María, Jerez, and Lisbon, as well as in the newly discovered archipelagos of Madeira, the Azores, and the Canaries. Wealthy Genovese became the financiers of the Portuguese crown. In their less flattering avocation, they were also the principal slave traders in the Mediterranean during the fifteenth century, a trade that included a sizable number of white slaves from Russia and the Balkans. (African slaves were preferred, "black Moors" as they were called, for they worked harder, were easier to convert to Christianity, and were less likely to accomplish a successful escape.) In the shops of the Street of the Genovese in Lisbon, Italian expatriates plied their craft as the best mapmakers in the world.

From its warren of quays along the banks of the Tagus estuary, caravels sailed north to the British Isles and Iceland for fish and to Flanders for cloth, south to Madeira for sugar and timber, to the far reaches of Africa for gold, slaves, and myrrh, west to the Azores for wool and wine, and east to the Mediterranean for almost everything. In dockside foundries, black slaves from Saharan Africa toiled, making heavy iron anchors for the galleys that crowded Lisbon harbor. Within the walls of the royal palace, the Castelo de São Jorge, lions prowled the royal gardens, while garish African macaws and parrots perched on windowsills.

Several generations after the slave trade had begun in the 1440s, blacks comprised about one tenth of Lisbon's population. The business of acquiring and selling slaves was conducted in the *Casa dos Escravos de Lisboa*—the Slave House of Lisbon. "Slaves swarm everywhere," a Belgian traveler of the time would write. "Rich households have slaves of both sexes, and there are individuals who derive substantial profits from their sale of the offspring of their house slaves. In my view they raise them much in the same way as one would raise pigeons for sale in the market place."

The great Prince Henry the Navigator had died in 1460, but his crusading spirit lived on, vibrantly, inspiring Portuguese mariners to press farther and farther south for the magical passage around Africa to the spice kingdoms of India and Goa. That spirit trumpeted the motto: "Crusade, Knowledge, Power." Of these, "Crusade" was the first and most important commandment. The cult of Prince Henry the Navigator was the seagoing offspring of the Templars, the military monks who had fought the Crusades three hundred years earlier to recover the Holy Land from the infidels. The square red cross on the sails of Henry's caravels was the emblem of the Order of Christ and the equivalent of the red cross on the Templar's cloak.

Evangelizing infidels was the highest of Christian callings, and could cover up a multitude of sins. The search for the gold of Black Africa and the muscle of black slaves was always subsumed in the higher and more noble-sounding goal of Christianizing the infidel and attacking heretical Islam. The theology of crusade expressly encompassed slavery. Its pre-Christian roots lay in Aristotle's concept of natural law about the master and the slave. St. Augustine sanctioned the concept when he argued that slavery was a form of divine punishment for man's original sin. St. Thomas Aquinas had expanded this theology still further with the argument that slavery provided a valuable service for both master and slave, for the weak supposedly benefited from being dominated by the strong. A series of papal bulls had given the Church's blessing. In 1452, Pope Nicholas V had issued his bull which specifically authorized the King of Portugal to make war on the infidels, to conquer their lands, and to enslave their natives. Conventional medieval thinking saw blacks as the descendants of the accursed biblical figure of Ham and therefore subject to eternal slavery, and this was melded with the lore of Cain. Medieval observers could recoil at the suffering of blacks at the same time as they rejoiced at the prospect that black souls were being saved from eternal damnation.

Not everyone was fooled by this hypocrisy. The medieval historian Bartolomé de Las Casas wrote of Portuguese slave trading: "To be marveled at is the manner in which the Portuguese historians glorify as illustrious such heinous deeds, representing these exploits as great sacrifices made in the service of God."

The Portuguese caravel was the wonder of the fifteenth-century ocean. Constructed with a frame of dense and hard cork and holm oak wood, covered with a skin of wild pine, manned by a crew of twenty including the captain, the pilot, and the scrivener (who counted the money and served as the prince's watchdog), its draught was shallow so that it could slip across the deltas of African rivers. Except for the captain and the scrivener, who had private closets, the crew slept on deck, lashed down with ropes in bad weather. Through most of the fifteenth century the caravel's sails were triangular, a design well suited for tacking north against the ever strong trade winds. In the best of conditions, caravels sped along at a clip of six knots. One of Henry's most famous captains, a Venetian named Luigi da Mosto (known in Portugal as Cadamosto), wrote in the 1450s that he made the journey of 1,750 miles between the Cape Verde Islands and Lisbon in twelve days. The way down was quicker. Driven before the northeast trade winds, he had covered the distance of 600 miles between Lagos and Porto Santo in three days.

"The caravels of Portugal being the best ships that travel the seas under sail," Cadamosto wrote, "Prince Henry reckoned that, provided they were furnished with everything necessary, they could sail anywhere."

Until a maritime passage to India was discovered, spices from the Orient came by caravan over the vast stretches of Mesopotamia to the Persian Gulf. They were then shipped through the Red Sea, packed on camels over the Sinai, and eventually taken to the ports of Italy. By the time they reached Portugal, if they reached at all, these spices were outlandishly expensive. The lure of spices was more for their use as a food preserver than for their lively taste. To find a way to obtain spices for a reasonable price became a national goal.

Indeed, it was this concentration that set Portugal apart from every other European nation of the time. Not just the kings of Portugal but the entire nation was caught up in a strategic plan to find the passage around Africa to the Orient. It had become a national obsession.

The prowess of Portuguese navigation was renowned in Europe, and the fame of its favorite patron, Henry, spread far and wide. Centuries later, this led to the concoction of one of Portugal's most enduring myths: that Henry founded a school of navigation on the promontory of Sagres, a fist of limestone protruding into the Atlantic on Portugal's southwestern corner. The myth of the Sagres school was a product of eighteenth-century Portuguese romanticism.*

A salon rather than a school might be a better word for Prince Henry's gatherings, for the infante maintained his favorite residence at a place called Raposeira on the high bluffs halfway between Sagres and Lagos on the southern coast. There in the 1450s sea captains, geographers, astrologers, mathematicians, and shipbuilders beat a well-trodden path to his door to consult with and importune their prince.

Nevertheless, wherever they worked, in Lagos, Lisbon, or Oporto, Portuguese masters had labored for decades to improve the charts and instruments of the kingdom's brave explorers. By 1485, most seagoing captains used the square charts called portolan charts, which located the lands of Africa by calculating their positions in relation to the sun and the polar star in conjunction with the landmarks of the coastline. The uses of the compass and astrolabe were studied to liberate the explorers from the coastline so they could navigate by the stars and penetrate deeper into the daunting "green sea of gloom."

New designs had been crafted for narrower, three-masted, rudder-guided oceangoing vessels. After the Portuguese slave raids began in earnest in 1444, with a raid by six Lagos caravels on the islands off the Arguin Bank (in present-day Mauritania), the design of some caravels was modified to carry horses south for barter and replace them with slaves for the return journey (the standard rate: seven slaves for one horse). When transoceanic voyages began, a second generation of caravels called rounded caravels was designed, with square sails for the long runs downwind.

The royal archives in Lisbon boasted the best map collection in the

---

*The story was further promoted by the mythmakers of the twentieth-century dictatorship of Antonio Salazar, who put Henry the Navigator forward as part of the national slogan of "God, Fatherland, and Family." But after the Carnation revolution of 1974 which threw Salazar out, the cult of Henry the Navigator suffered in popularity. He was now called Portugal's "first fascist."

whole world. Included in the collection were the ancient geographical speculations of Ptolemy, which Mozarabs had translated from the Arabic into Latin, and the travels of Herodotus across Asia Minor and Africa four hundred years before the birth of Christ. The work of Herodotus had only been translated from ancient Greek into Latin in 1450. There was also a 1433 map that purported to identify the fabulous kingdom of Prester John, an Oriental Christian monarch who reigned somewhere in northeast Africa or in India. "In this region," read its caption, "there reigns the great emperor, Prester John, Lord of the Indies, who is black by nature."

The myth of Prester John captivated the time and exerted a powerful influence even upon so sophisticated a leader as Henry the Navigator. Prester John was believed to be the most powerful leader in the world and richer than any other leader in gold, silver, and precious stones. He was said to command an army of over 1 million men, some of whom went into battle armored with crocodile skins while the rest were naked. It was reported that these black Christians burned the Cross of Christ into their foreheads as part of their baptismal ceremony. If only these "black Indians" could be found, it was believed, a Christian alliance might be forged, including a marriage, and from this would spring the most powerful empire in the world. Prince Henry had dispatched a mission to Egypt to gather information on Prester John's whereabouts, since his dominion was supposed to lie somewhere to the south in Abyssynia, across a great inland African sea known as Sinus Aethiopicus.

Alfonso the African, the Portuguese king who had challenged the legitimacy of Ferdinand and Isabella in the 1470s during the War of Succession, had died in 1481 of the plague. He was succeeded by his energetic, roughhewn twenty-one-year-old son, João II. The nation rejoiced at this vigorous new monarch and proclaimed him to be the "perfect prince." He was, the court chronicler proclaimed, "a good Catholic, anxious for the propagation of the faith, and a man of an inquiring spirit, desirous of investigating the secrets of nature."

Dom João set out to reinvigorate the push south along the African coastline. In the Treaty of Alcáçovas in 1479 which ended the War of Succession, Spain had recognized Portugal's exclusive rights to the discoveries along the African coast. In 1480, this treaty was strengthened further when the Spanish monarchs agreed to an amendment giving Portugal the right to throw any alien mariner into the sea, if he trespassed into Portugal's exclusive African domain without permission. In 1481, Pope Sixtus IV had sanctioned and blessed Portugal's southern explorations with his papal bull *Aeterni regis*. It granted sovereignty to Portugal "over whatever lands and islands shall be found and acquired south of the Canary Islands and of the vicinity of Guinea." Guinea then designated the entire landmass of Africa.

Among João II's first acts upon gaining the throne was to order the construction of a mighty fortress on Africa's gold coast called St. George of the Mine, not far from a native gold mine. This bastion was to become an emporium not only for real gold but also for "black gold," slaves from West Africa, who were destined for the slave markets of Lisbon and Lagos in southern Portugal. By the time of João II, the rationale for slavery used by Prince Henry—that the practice was a noble effort to save the souls of pagans and savages—had been dropped. Slavery had become pure commerce.

The young king cultivated an atmosphere that encouraged visionary men to propose bold, exploratory missions. In 1484, the king appointed a Junta of mathematicians to advise him on exploration and navigation. Important in this advisory council was a Jewish physician and mathematician, Master José Vizinho. In 1485, the king's Jewish master was ordered to travel on a voyage down the coast of Africa to determine the latitude of landmarks of Africa. Master José hung an astrolabe from a tree limb in the Los Idolos Islands, the Islands of the Idols, just offshore from Conakry, Guinea. He calculated its position as five degrees above the equator and only several degrees off its precise location. Master José presented these findings to great acclaim.

In the audience was a young Genovese sailor named Cristoforo Colombo.

❖

The Portugal of the late fifteenth century beckoned to the dreamers of Europe. Among them was a ruddy-faced, red-headed, blue-eyed, broad-shouldered, tall, and loquacious Genovese charmer named Cristoforo Colombo. The eldest of four children, Colombo hailed modestly from a family of woolcombers. Though in his teens he had been briefly at the University of Pavia, where he dabbled in geometry, geography, astronomy, and navigation, his education was limited. But his mind was lively. His curiosities were deep. And his religious faith was genuine. Like so many of his compatriots, the sea beckoned him. In later life, in a letter to the Spanish monarchs, he would assert that his bent for the sailor's life was divinely guided, as preparation for great and pious endeavors.

At the age of fourteen he shipped out on his first voyage as a common seaman. By the time he reached his twenties, he had seen a considerable part of the known world. "I have seen all the east and west," he would later boast, prematurely. Twice he had sailed on African expeditions. At least once, in February 1477, he had voyaged to Iceland. That voyage to Iceland has been identified as a joint expedition of both King Alfonso the African of Portugal and King Christian I of Denmark. Its purpose was to explore the North Atlantic, and perhaps to find a mythical island called Brasil that was rumored to exist far to the west of the north Atlantic. Patriotic Portuguese historians would later claim that this voyage may have reached as far west as Newfoundland.

Importantly, it was on that voyage that Colombo learned of two strange corpses which had washed up in Galway in the west of Ireland. Their skin was light brown, and their flat faces bore unusual aboriginal features very different from any race then known. Colombo would later think of these exotic creatures as "men of Cathay," for in a note in his own hand, written many years later in the margin of his copy of Pierre d'Ailly's *Imago Mundi*, he would write: "Men of Cathay have come from the west. Of this we have seen many signs. And especially in Galway in Ireland, a man and a woman, of extraordinary appearance, have come to land on two tree trunks."

If this story is true, they were probably Inuit Indians, whose kayak was swamped in the Davis Strait and whose bodies were swept rapidly east to Ireland by the frigid North Atlantic current. Their Oriental looks would become one more piece of important evidence to contribute to the evolution of Colombo's grand vision of what lay across the western horizon.

Colombo's most fateful voyage took place in the summer of 1476, when he was twenty-five years old. In Genoa, he had signed on to a commercial venture consisting of five caravels that were hired to transport a cargo of gum mastic (the essence of wood varnish) from the Greek island of Chios, off the coast of Turkey, bound for Flanders and England. Chios was Homer's island; more menacing, it was also a transfer depot for the Genovese traffic in white slaves from the Black Sea.

After a routine passage across the Mediterranean and through the Straits of Gibraltar, the convoy of small ships was attacked off the southern coast of Portugal by a combined French-Portuguese force made up of massive Venetian warships. Most of the Italian vessels sank, including Colombo's ship, called the *Bechalla*. Though he was wounded, Colombo grabbed onto an oar and swam some six miles to the shoreline near the Portuguese town of Lagos.

His unceremonious arrival in Lagos put him at another spot that was associated with slavery. Lagos was the major port of the southern Portuguese province called the Algarve and the first port of call for the caravels coming north from Africa with their black booty. Here, thirty years earlier, Prince Henry the Navigator himself had been present, watching proudly from his horse as the first cargo of one hundred slaves was offloaded and then divided into lots of five, regardless of family ties. After the process was completed, Henry collected his royal fifth of the value of the treasure as well as one twentieth that would go to the Order of Christ. Uppermost on his mind, we are asked by his chronicler to believe, were the souls that had been saved that day from eternal damnation. "When you saw the captives displayed before you, so great was the pleasure the sight of them gave you that you reckoned as nothing the expenses you had laid out on the enterprise. But a greater happiness still was the one that was reserved for them, for, though their bodies might be in a state of servitude, that was a small matter when compared with the fact that their souls would now enjoy true freedom for all eternity."

After he recovered from his wounds, Colombo made his way from La- gos to Lisbon to find his younger brother, Bartholomew, who was by now well established along the Street of the Genovese as a chartmaker. He stayed for several years in Lisbon, where he was known as Cristóbal Colón. Alternately he worked in his brother's mapmaking shop and shipped out on the occasional commercial voyage, becoming an experienced merchant and widely traveled seaman. By the standards of the time, his reach was global, from the far North Atlantic to the African coastlands to the Azores. And he was expert in the use of the portolan charts.

If his reach was global, his experience vast, his bravery proven, and his curiosities intense, he remained a foreigner and a commoner. But in 1478 he made a decent marriage. Filipa Perestrello e Moniz may have been no beauty, but she belonged to a prominent family in the second rank of Portuguese society. On her mother's side, the Moniz family had been close to the royal families of Portugal for over three hundred years. Filipa's maternal grandfather had fought alongside Prince Henry in the great Portuguese victory at Ceuta, the African Gibraltar, in 1415. Her father, Bartholomew Perestrello, had been an important explorer and colonist who was third in command in the settlement of the Madeira archipelago after its islands were discovered in 1419.

As a reward, in 1446, Prince Henry made a donation of land to Per- estrello, not on the glorious, timbered paradise of Madeira itself (which he divided between his first two colonists) but on its northern sister is- land of Porto Santo. The gift was somewhat ironic, more of a punish- ment than a gift, for Porto Santo, apart from its glorious six-mile beach, possessed very little drinkable water, had none of Madeira's soaring mountains or thick forests, and no lush fertile soil. Perestrello made the place worse by introducing rabbits, which proliferated exponentially and devoured nearly every plant that was cultivated. Nevertheless, on his windswept, rabbit-infested wasteland, the colonist was knighted as Dom Perestrello.

About the Perestrello family there hovered the whiff of delicious scandal. Filipa's father had two sisters, Isabel and Branca, and together, jointly, they had been the mistresses of the archbishop of Lisbon, Dom Pedro Noronhã. The lusty archbishop, a close relative of King João II, had sired a son by Isabel and three children by Branca, and later had them all legitimized. A son of the archbishop by Branca would become the mayor of Obidos and then the Portuguese ambassador to the Roman Curia. Thus, through his wife's naughty aunts, Colón would find entry into high ecclesiastical as well as royal circles.

In the family of Colón's bride, Italian blood ran thick. Her father's family had roots in Piacenza, just north of Genoa, and was said to have been minor royalty. The Italian connection must have smoothed conversation when Colón and Filipa first met at a mass at the Convent of Dos Santos. (The nuns of this convent belonged to the Order of Santiago, whose purpose was to provide for the families of knights away at holy war against African Muslims.) No doubt, in their brief courtship, Filipa fired Colón's imagination by showing him her father's dog-eared charts and the journals of his pioneering voyages fifty years earlier.

Not long after their marriage, the couple moved to the Perestrello estate in Porto Santo. Filipa's brother was the governor, and the island supported itself by its export of sugar and "dragon's blood," the red resin from the rare dragon tree that was used in dyeing. In this outpost the newlyweds lived quietly for several years, during which time their first son, Diego, was born.

Porto Santo and Madeira were way stations for the Portuguese explorers moving down the African coast and for Portuguese slavers who used the Madeiras as their base and supply point. The watering holes of the island teemed with adventuresome seamen and buccaneers including a sizable contingent of Italians. Colón was caught up in the excitement of the new discoveries. As he was able, he basked in the reflective glory of his father-in-law's expeditions.

As the Portuguese navigators pressed farther and farther south along the African coast, they left in their wake prominent stone markers called *padrãos*. On headlands and prominent rivermouths and peninsulas, these markers, along with names and dates cut into dragon trees, were meant to establish Portuguese sovereignty. By 1485, the Portuguese explorer Diogo Cão had discovered the great Congo River and had sailed as far down the African coastline as modern-day Angola. The marker that Cão placed just north of the Tropic of Capricorn read:

"It was 6,685 years after the creation of the world and 1,485 years after Christ that the excellent and illustrious King João the Second of Portugal ordered this land to be discovered and this stone marker to be placed by Diogo Cão, esquire of his house." For his accomplishments, Diogo Cão was knighted and given his own coat of arms, as well as an annuity of 10,000 Portuguese reals. It could not have escaped Colón's attention that discoveries conferred wealth and title on the explorers.

The air of Porto Santo was also full of delicious rumor. One told of a piece of driftwood that had washed up on shore and that bore exotic primitive designs. Mariners gossiped about trunks of huge pine trees, strange sea beans, and immense reeds that were found on the beach in the Azores to the north, and whose species did not exist in Europe or Africa or the Madeira archipelago. Colón immediately assumed these reeds to be the bamboo from India that Ptolemy had described. Sea captains from the Canaries claimed to have seen a large island to the west which some believed to be the island of Antilia, mentioned by Aristotle, and which appeared in the portolan charts as early as 1424. This magical island, where reportedly silver mixed with beach sand, was located far west beyond the grasp of the known world, on the latitude of the Iberian peninsula. In Portuguese lore it was celebrated as the Island of Seven Cities, where seven Christian bishops from the Moorish invasion of Portugal in A.D. 734 had fled and established seven fabulous cities.

To this buzz, Colón could add a personal note. Not long after he settled in Porto Santo, he met a sea pilot in very sorry physical condition who told of being blown far off course by strong winds and powerful currents on a voyage along the African coast. He claimed to have seen strange lands, full of riches and treasure, far to the west. Eventually, his caravel had run aground, and most of the crew had perished. But somehow the pilot and three of his men had made it back to the Madeira archipelago. He gasped to Colón the approximate location of these western lands. Soon after he had unburdened himself, the pilot died. By all accounts, Colón kept this fascinating intelligence safely under his hat, and it would later be referred to as "Columbus's secret."

By the early 1480s, the elements of Colón's grand plan were falling into place one by one. There were the rumors: the Oriental corpses of Galway, the Norse saga about Leif Eriksson's discovery of a land of honey and grapevine far to the west called Vinland, the driftwood of the Azores, the tales of the far western islands of Antilia and Brasil, and now the pilot's tale. To these were added Colón's impressive professional credentials: his experience of the known world, his skill in mapmaking, his knowledge of oceanic currents and trade winds. Then there was the culture of Portugal, with its legacy of Henry the Navigator and its brassy young king, and his emphasis on pressing out the limits of the known world, for the glory both of Portugal and of Jesus Christ.

To all of this Colón could now add a measure of social standing. Yet, even though he had joined a family of explorers, his stature was not quite sufficient to gain him access to the parlors of lords and the chambers of bishops, much less of kings. He might don the role of a gentleman, the lord of a colonial estate, and seasoned merchant, but his social rank was a level below where he aspired to be.

His commanding physical appearance and his congenial, talkative ways served his social pretensions well. At age thirty his hair had turned white, which made his steel-blue eyes and ruddy, freckled complexion all the more striking in contrast. When he strode through the streets of Lisbon and the lanes of Porto Santo, pausing to chat with artisans, fishermen, and gentlemen, he cut an imposing figure with his broad shoulders and aquiline nose, his tanned, round face, and his air of sobriety and piety.

If he knew much, he had a healthy sense of what he did not know and what he could not accomplish. He had, as yet, no standing as an explorer. Portugal's gaze was to the south along the African coast. For those productive expeditions, the Portuguese king had his coterie of indigenous favorites, especially Bartholomew Dias. In 1481, Dias had commanded a royal ship on an expedition to Africa's Gold Coast, but it was merely a preliminary. Upon his return, discussions were under way for a far bolder mission: to take three ships and to press beyond the Tropic of Capricorn as far as the western coastline would take him. Was it really true, as Ptolemy suggested, that Africa stretched all the way to the end of the earth and there was no maritime passage around it?

As a foreigner, Colón could not hope to break into this elite club of African adventurers. But as he looked at the maps of the world and studied the speculations of Ptolemy, which remained the standard authority, he surmised that one third of the known world remained unexplored. The most unknown was the region due west across the great expanse of water where the mapmakers filled empty space with drawings of Neptunean monsters and imaginary islands. For these researches he learned Latin, the lingua franca of intelligent discourse and commercial contracts.

Somewhere along the way, he concluded that he would garner more respect and dignity among the grandees if he Latinized his Italian name to Christopher Columbus. He aimed to be a man of the world rather than merely a citizen of Italy or Portugal.

II

The Pilot of the Argonauts

❖

By the mid-1480s curiosity and experience joined opportunity, as the newly minted Christopher Columbus began to delve into the work of Marco Polo, into the legends of Prester John, and the fabulous tales of the Orient. The most outrageous (and most entertaining) of these storytellers was one Sir John Mandeville, purportedly an English knight of the previous century, who wrote his remarkable book, *The Travels of Sir John Mandeville*, around 1356. It described his imaginative travels to such astonishing places beyond the horizon as the islands of India; Cathay; Amazonia; and Tibet. On his travels he had encountered fantastic creatures: certain men with the skin of snakes who hissed like serpents, beasts with the body of a human and the head of a dog, and still other monsters whose human heads grew beneath their shoulders. He had seen dwarfs with a round hole for a mouth, and men with lips so large and flappable that they could be wrapped around the body like a cloak. He told of pygmies who married and produced children in six months and parrots who played chess with apes and spoke ancient Greek.

To this mind-traveler, the planet was round. Its circumference was exactly 20,435 miles. Africa was half the size of Europe. The earth's center was Jerusalem, which was set in the midst of an earthly paradise. This comported with most medieval maps, in accordance with the biblical verse in the book of Ezekiel (5:5), "Thus saith the Lord God: This is Jerusalem: I have set it in the midst of the nations and countries that are round about her."

In the second part of Mandeville's book, the kingdom of Prester John is described. The lore of an all-powerful Christian emperor in the

Orient dates back to the twelfth century, when this fabulously wealthy kingdom was first mentioned in the chronicle of Otto of Freising. But Mandeville embroidered the legend with fantastic detail. The kingdom was dangerous to approach, for it was surrounded by the Gravelly Sea, which had no water, but whose sand and rock including precious stones rolled and moved like ocean waves. The approach to the Gravelly Sea was dotted with magnetic stones that sucked the nails out of unwelcome ships. Beyond the waterless sea the beaches were guarded by horned wild men, who grunted like pigs.

This lost Christian kingdom comprised fifty-two provinces, which stretched across three Indias and included the Tower of Babel. "In the land of Prester John are great plenty of precious stones of diverse kinds, some of them so great and so large that they make of them vessels, as dishes, goblets, and cups. . . ." The gates of the emperor's palace were fashioned from precious stone, bordered with ivory. Its windows were crystal. The tables where the court ate were made of emeralds and gold, while the palace steps were onyx and burnished coral. Its pillars were gold and precious stone, while the emperor's bed sparkled with sapphire. Atop the main tower of the kingdom's chief city were two balls of gold, which shone brightly in the night.

The fantasy of a fabulously wealthy Christian kingdom somewhere in the African hinterland held a special sway over the imagination of the Portuguese explorers and Portuguese kings. Portugal was a small and isolated nation, forever threatened by its much stronger neighbor to the east, at the hands of which Portugal had just suffered a humiliating defeat. To survive, Portugal needed powerful friends, and the thought of allying itself with a fabulous African king with an army of 1 million set the Portuguese to dreaming. Finding this paradise and its Christian emperor became the chief motivation for the Portuguese expeditions, more important than the spices of the Orient. If their explorers could round the southern tip of Africa, they would turn north along the eastern coast of the continent, north as far as Ethiopia where Prester John's kingdom was thought to reside.

King João II gave enough credence to this story that he commissioned an explorer to travel to Egypt and thence south to Ethiopia to look for this lost Christian empire. If the traveler missed Prester John's kingdom, he might just stumble upon the dominion of the Queen of Sheba or the gold-soaked island of Ophir, which was mentioned in the Bible's book of Kings, or even King Solomon's mines, supposed to be twenty miles long.*

The lore of Prester John was forever linked with the Great Khan of Tartary. For this potentate, Columbus had a much more reliable source. The travels of Marco Polo to the Orient in the mid-thirteenth century, his three years in the court of Kubla Khan, and his descriptions of Cathay and the island of Cipangu (Japan) held a powerful sway over the medieval mind. A copy of Polo's book, with its descriptions of the Great Khan's luminous court and the golden roofs and marble bridges of Cipangu, and lords wearing golden armor and eating upon golden table-cloths, graced the archives of the Portuguese court. Columbus was to ac-quire his own copy, into whose margins he appended copious notes.

But Marco Polo's descriptions remained controversial two hundred years after they were written. Medieval geographers could find no place for so vast a continent and such a grand island as Cipangu in Ptolemy's geography. Columbus did not doubt their existence, however, nor, more importantly, their wealth. And in his acceptance of Marco Polo's dis-coveries, he had an additional reference.

Into his possession had come a letter written by one of the fifteenth century's most distinguished scientists. Paolo Toscanelli was a Floren-tine mathematician, astronomer, and cosmographer, a brilliant figure in the luminous society of Florence that included Brunelleschi, the archi-

---

*It has subsequently been argued that Columbus's fixation with King Solomon's mines proved that he was Jewish, for it was the wealth of the mines, in biblical lore, that would finance the rebuild-ing of the Temple in Jerusalem. In addition, the insinuation of Columbus's Jewishness rested upon seven points: his mother's name was the common Jewish name Suzanna; his father's family might have been related to the Colóns of Pontevedra in northeast Spain, a well-known Jewish clan; there were Jews in Genoa known as Colombo; Columbus himself had once boasted of a connec-tion to King David; his staunchest supporters later were Jewish; he seemed to prefer the company of conversos; and he occasionally dated his correspondence by the Jewish rather than the Chris-tian calendar. Does that prove that Columbus was Jewish? No. Did he have to be careful of scur-rilous rumor and ambitious inquisitors? Most definitely.

tect of the famous Duomo. For decades Toscanelli had studied the heavens and plied his craft of theoretical mathematics.

Among his prodigious scientific preoccupations was a great interest in Marco Polo's book. Toscanelli had talked extensively to Italian merchants and seamen who traded European wool for the exotic goods from China and India in the teeming markets of the Middle East (although the number of these Italian traders was greatly reduced by the demise of the Mongol Empire in Central Asia and the expansion of the Ottoman Empire in the Mediterranean and the Black Sea). From these investigations, he concluded that the landmass of Europe and Asia comprised 230 degrees of latitude, and from this he inferred that the trip across the Atlantic Ocean comprised only 130 degrees, or about 2,000 miles. The Florentine scientist was convinced that the kingdom of the Great Khan of Cathay could be reached quickly by sailing due west.

Toscanelli's certainty about a western route to the Orient was widely discussed in Florentine circles, and in 1474 these speculations had reached the ear of the Portuguese king Alfonso the African, who asked Toscanelli to communicate his theory in writing. In a letter written in Latin and dated June 25, 1474, with which he included a map, the Florentine master laid out his theory.

"It is good," he wrote, "that many others have talked of the short road that there is from here to the Indies, where the spices are borne, by way of the sea, shorter than that way which you have for Guinea [Africa]." The distance between Lisbon and the "great and noble city of Quinsay" in China was 6,500 miles, but in between were the islands of Antilia and Cipangu. In the latter, the temples and royal houses were covered with pure gold. And in Cathay, "one can find not only large profits and many things but even gold, silver, precious rocks and all manner of spices . . . and it's true that sages, doctors, philosophers, astrologers and other great wise men in the arts govern the magnificent province."

Toscanelli's letter was a compelling final piece of evidence informing Columbus's obsession, for it lent the imprimatur of respectable science to his inspiration. The map attached to the letter was more important than the letter itself, since it showed that the continents of Europe and Asia faced one another in close proximity, with the noble island of Cipangu in between.

At the beginning of the new decade, Columbus, restless and anxious that his secret would be discovered by others, moved back to Lisbon. There, courtesy of the lofty if sketchy connections of his wife's family to important prelates and explorers, he was welcomed into Lisbon's high society. Still, his domestic responsibilities weighed upon him, like an anchor, for his wife's health was deteriorating. In 1482, he broke free nonetheless and undertook another voyage to Africa, this time taking his brother, Bartholomew, along as a shipmate. Each voyage seemed to raise his bona fides, moving him into the higher ranks of commercial pilots in a country where sea captains were supreme.

In the coming few years as he waited for his chance, a wide variety of sources stoked the fire of Columbus's obsession still further. With his newfound mastery of Latin, he absorbed literary and scientific rationales for sailing west to reach the spice-rich east. Besides the lore of Prester John and the Grand Khan and the kingdom of Ophir, beyond Marco Polo's descriptions and Toscanelli's encouragement, he consulted the work by Pierre d'Ailly called *Imago Mundi*. It was a richly imagined geography of the world, written in 1410, and mariners seventy years later still accorded it great respect. In the margins of his copy Columbus would, over time, pen copious notes, which he wrote carefully in tiny packed script in his newly acquired Latin.

"The end of Spain and the beginning of India are not far distant but close," d'Ailly had written, "and it is evident that this sea is navigable in a few days with a fair wind." Spain and India were close, the philosopher contended, because each possessed elephants.

Columbus paid special attention to d'Ailly's measurement for the circumference of the earth, where a degree of longitude was measured at 56 ⅔ miles. The world, he believed with ever greater certainty, was smaller than most people supposed. He embraced these deductions with the single-mindedness and determination of a visionary.

Moreover, in a world where bishops and inquisitors were all-powerful, he appended a biblical reference to his list of arguments. For in the book of II Esdras (5:42) in the Apocrypha, it is written that on the third day, God commanded that the waters of the earth occupy one seventh of the world, while land comprised six sevenths of the surface. "Six parts hast thou dried up. . . ," read the text. To the medieval mind it was inconceivable that their God would make a world where only one seventh of its surface was habitable.

And then there was the encouragement of poets. In Seneca's *Medea,* Columbus latched onto a choral strophe and made it his refrain:

> *There will come an age in the far-off years*
> *When the Ocean will lose its chains*
> *And the whole broad earth shall be revealed.*
> *When a pilot of the argonauts shall discover new worlds*
> *And Greenland will no longer be the farthest point on earth.*

Christopher Columbus meant to be that pilot of the argonauts.

❧

In late 1484, only months after the death of his wife, Filipa, Christopher Columbus obtained an audience with the energetic young King of Portugal. By now, the lines of Columbus's vision were sharp and mature. He was a man possessed. To the eager fascination of Dom João, Columbus proposed to sail due west in search of the fabulous island of Cipangu. For his mission, he asked for three caravels, a year's supply of food, and the latest navigational instruments and charts, as well as chestful of trinkets and notions that might be bartered with natives.

He was not modest about the rewards and honors he expected for himself in return, if his mission was successful. Like the discoverer of the Congo River, Diogo Cão, and like his father-in-law, he wished to be knighted, so that for life he would be referred to with the honorific "Dom." This honor was not merely for himself. He demanded that the title be hereditary, distinguishing his family and their heirs. Moreover, he required the official title of "Chief Admiral of the Ocean Sea," thus surpassing the stature of Diogo Cão and Bartholomew Dias, and joining the company of the legendary admirals of Castile. For all the islands and lands he might discover, he required the standing of a viceroy, which would enable him to rake in a tenth of all the gold and profits that came of the venture. But this was not enough. He also demanded an eighth of all profits that might accrue from subsequent trading missions to his discovered lands.

This was a brassy set of demands, especially from a foreigner and the son of a wool carder. But Dom João did not seem overly surprised or put off, for the king was excited by the boldness of his expansive Italian visitor. Given the precedent of Diogo Cão, the titles were the easy part. The gold and profits were matters of pure speculation, and dividing spoils between the king and the sea captain was accepted practice.

If the king was not shocked, Columbus's demands set off a furor when they were put before the king's Junta of Mathematicians. This distinguished group of experts had among them some sixty-five years of superior Portuguese seamanship, and they were not easily swept away. Joining these experts in navigation was the bishop of Ceuta. Already the bishop had qualms about the expense and the diversion of Portugal's African program, for those ventures, he believed, divided a nation already stretched thin by foreign entanglements and domestic plague. Columbus's proposal was "wild" and "chimerical," the bishop cautioned, just as Columbus himself came off as a vainglorious, facile braggart.

"The greatness of monarchs does not arise so much from the extent of their dominions, as from the wisdom and ability with which they govern," the bishop said. "If the king wishes employment for the active valor of the nation, the war in which he is engaged against the Moors of Barbary is sufficient."

The bishop's opposition drew a passionate response from the count of Villa Real, Dom Pedro de Meneses. The count was mystified, he asserted, that the bishop of Ceuta should oppose this undertaking, "the ultimate object of which is to spread the Catholic faith from pole to pole."

"Crowns enrich themselves by commerce, fortify themselves by commerce, and acquire empires by conquest," he said. "While Portugal is at peace with all the princes of Europe, it has nothing to fear from engaging in an extensive enterprise. It would be the greatest glory for Portuguese valor to penetrate into the secrets and horrors of the Ocean Sea, which are so formidable to the other nations of the world. Thus occupied, our country can escape the idleness engendered in a long interval of peace. Idleness is the source of vice, that silent file, which little by little wears away the strength and valor of a nation."

Given these eloquent sentiments and the king's infatuation with Columbus, the bishop of Ceuta put forward an underhanded and ignoble proposition. Why not string Columbus along for some months, require him to produce extensive documentation for the Junta of Mathematicians, and then put his documents into the hands of a Portuguese native to test? What did Portugal have to lose?

To his discredit, João II acquiesced in this unworthy betrayal. A cover story was concocted of a routine mission to the Cape Verde Islands. An experienced captain from the Azores was commissioned to sail due west from Terceira in the Azores. The captain, ironically, was not Portuguese at all, but a Flemish settler named Fernao de Ulmo. Using Columbus's charts (according to an account later given by Columbus's son Fernando), Ulmo was instructed to stay that course for forty days, the time the experts imagined that it would take to reach the supposed Island of the Seven Cities.

A few days out, Ulmo's caravel encountered ferocious storms and the stiff headwinds of the westerlies. Columbus's vision was absurd, he proclaimed. Ingloriously, he turned back.

Portugal had nothing to lose by betraying Columbus, the bishop of Ceuta had argued to the court. In fact, Portugal lost everything. When Columbus caught wind of Ulmo's mission and the king's duplicity, he was understandably furious. The entire circumstantial case he had built over the past six years to support his expedition was exposed to the universe of mariners. In a pique, he began to shift his gaze elsewhere, to other more upstanding patrons and sponsors. He dispatched his brother,

Bartholomew, to England to sound out Henry VII, while Columbus himself made his preparations to leave Portugal.

In the centuries that followed, Christopher Columbus was often viewed as he viewed himself: as an instrument of God. Even his rejection by the Portuguese court was seen as divinely preordained. The estimable historian of Columbus's journeys, Bartolomé de Las Casas, wrote,

"It is best to believe that divine Providence had reserved for the Portuguese the mission of saving the Elect from among the people of the territory we call India, and for the Castilians the mission of showing the way to the Truth to the peoples of the New World."

Betrayed by the Portuguese, Columbus looked east. He would take his proposition to the vigorous young monarchs of Spain.

12

The Court Rabbis

❖

 In his betrayal of Christopher Columbus, King João II of Portugal had proven himself to be less than his original billing as the "perfect prince." Visionary in his support of Portugal's dramatic southern expansion in Africa, stalwart in his goals, courageous personally, he was nevertheless cold, manipulative, and duplicitous in his personal relations. In one respect his domestic agenda paralleled that of Ferdinand and Isabella: he was determined to reassert the absolute power of the monarchy over the Portuguese nobility. During the forty-three-year reign of Alfonso the African, the aristocracy of Portugal had been coddled and appeased and enriched, especially the most powerful house of all, the House of Braganza. The duke of Braganza was the king's brother-in-law and had become the chief executive of the crown. At the time of Alfonso's death in 1481, this mighty lord, wielding his influence from his castle at Vila Vicosa near the Spanish border, held sway over a third of Portugal, including huge acreage devoted to the cultivation of the valuable cork tree. He ruled fifty towns and castles, and was able to muster ten thousand foot soldiers and three thousand cavalry in their defense. Elsewhere lesser nobles governed their domains without royal interference, causing João II to remark in frustration,

"All my father left me are the highways of Portugal."

During the sovereignty of Alfonso the African, especially its second half, when the African was confident in his rule, Portuguese Jews had enjoyed a golden age of prosperity. But now João II sought to tighten the grip on the Jews of Portugal, who he felt were in league with the nobles. Here too Portuguese history mirrored that of Spain. In 1391, as anti-Semitic violence flared up across the border, Portugal experienced a lesser version of the same. Jews were ordered to wear badges of their faith. They were herded into walled ghettos with guarded gates and barred from being out after sunset. In 1404, Jews were declared to be ineligible for royal service. In 1449, as the anti-Jewish rebellion turned violent in Toledo and then spread to other Spanish towns, so too in Portugal were Lisbon's three ghettos attacked. Unlike Spain, however, Jews in Portugal defended their enclaves successfully. Thereafter, Alfonso adopted a more conciliatory policy, bringing Jews into his inner circle and relaxing the restrictions on them.

Among the chief beneficiaries of this benign attitude was the House of Abravanel. Dating back to the fourteenth-century rule of Alfonso X the Learned, and claiming roots in the royal House of David itself, this distinguished Jewish family had provided prominent confidants and financiers to both Castilian and Portuguese kings, as they had in turn been leaders and rabbis of their respective Jewish communities. When the anti-Jewish measures in Spain became intolerable around the turn of the previous century, a branch of Abravanels had fled to the safe haven of Portugal, leaving behind a considerable part of their wealth.

During the reign of Alfonso the African, the scion of this family, Don Isaac Abravanel, was an influential member of the royal inner circle. Born into wealth and privilege in 1437, the son of Don Judah Abravanel, who was the chief financier to the crown, Don Isaac distinguished himself first as a scholar and a philosopher. In his early literary life he wrote a commentary on the book of Deuteronomy, addressed the thought of the great Jewish scholar of the twelfth century, Maimonides, and delved into fundamental questions of political philosophy.

Given the course that Abravanel's own life would later take, his philosophical position on monarchy as a form of government is noteworthy. In the perfect society, a judge rather than a king represented the best leadership for people, he argued, for a judge best reflected the will of God. In the realistic world, however, a king was an acceptable substitute. A king, he wrote, also enjoyed divine sanction and guidance, and he was entitled to absolute obedience, even if that king was a gentile and even if he was a tyrant. In time, this political stance would involve great peril.

As his father grew old, Don Isaac Abravanel was increasingly drawn into the realm of business and politics. Eventually, in the 1460s, he succeeded his father as the king's chief financial officer and head tax collector. By his own account, he lived a charmed life. "Tranquilly I lived in my inherited house in fair Lisbon," he wrote. "God had given me blessings, riches and honor. I had built myself stately buildings and chambers. My house was the meeting place of the learned and the wise. I was a favorite in the palace of Alfonso, a mighty and upright king, under whom the Jews enjoyed freedom and prosperity. I was close to him, was his support, and took delight in being in the king's shade. While he lived, I frequented his court."

In King Alfonso's court, Don Isaac was a popular figure, for he was urbane and voluble. He cut a striking figure: round moonface, piercing eyes, sharply defined nose, high forehead crowned with a yarmulke, and a full white beard that covered his expansive chest. As the scholar gave way to the businessman, he amassed an immense fortune not only through his service to the crown as a tax collector but in the family enterprise of banking and textile trade with Flanders. By the end of the 1470s the Abravanel fortune was so immense that the king applied to him for loans.

Abravanel's devotion to his people had been proven many times over. When Alfonso conquered the ports of Arzila and Tangier in 1471, the victorious Portuguese brought home thousands of captives who were enslaved. Among them were 250 Jews. The thought of Jewish slaves appalled Abravanel, and he set out to buy back their freedom. Gathering a commission of Jewish elders, Abravanel raised the necessary funds and then personally rode through the country to find and free them, and incorporate them in the Jewish fold.

With his independent voice, Don Isaac had opposed the War of

Succession as a war of aggression. Wars of aggression, he had written, were ill-advised and counterproductive, leading often to the bankruptcy of the aggressor state. That described the condition of Portugal after its defeat in 1478. Still, with his credo of strict obedience to the ruler, Abravanel loaned King Alfonso over 1 million reals to finance the nation's recovery afterward.

All this changed in 1481 with the accession of João II to the throne. In his determination to smash the power and independence of the nobles, the young king spread a wide net. At first, João adopted measures that undermined the judicial and economic powers of the nobility. Then he challenged their very nobility by forcing the lords to produce for review the documents that underpinned the claims to their fiefdoms. Naturally, the nobles rebelled at these stiff measures.

Since Jewish financiers had deep ties with the wealthiest lords—ties that ironically had greatly enriched the Portuguese crown—the sentiment in João's court turned sharply anti-Jewish. Always lurking just below the surface in prior reigns, anti-Semitism suddenly became overt, rampant, and fashionable. The court poet, Garcia de Resende, gave voice to it. Jews, he wrote, were two-faced and deceitful. They pretended to serve the king, but really had their own agenda and did not respect or abide by the law. "With their charming ways, they pretend to ingratiate themselves, but behind your back, they will try to cheat you. Beware of their supposed friendship."

For several generations the House of Abravanel had had particularly strong ties to the House of Braganza; quickly Don Isaac fell out of favor and came under suspicion. During the months that the relations between the crown and the nobility disintegrated into open strife and secret conspiracies, Abravanel had been living with his family in the countryside, partly to escape the plague which was still raging through the streets of Portuguese cities. But in the fall of 1482, he returned to Lisbon to find a transformed place. In what he saw, Abravanel gave way to despair.

"From the day our City was laid in ruins, our Temple destroyed and our people exiled, we have known neither peace nor respite," he wrote

QUEEN ISABELLA I
(Museo del Prado, Spain)

KING FERDINAND II
*(Courtesy of the
Library of Congress)*

ENRIQUE IV OF CASTILE
(Biblioteca Nacional, Spain)

TORQUEMADA
(*Biblioteca Nacional, Spain*)

BOABDIL, THE LAST MOORISH KING
OF GRANADA
(*Courtesy of the Library of Congress*)

CHRISTOPHER COLUMBUS
(*Biblioteca de las Indias, Seville*)

João II,
KING OF PORTUGAL
(Museo lisboeta de la Marina)

ISAAC ABRAVANEL
(Courtesy of the Library of
Congress)

POPE ALEXANDER VI
(RODRIGO BORGIA)
(Courtesy of the Library of Congress)

SEVILLE *(Courtesy of the Library of Congress)*

MÁLAGA *(Courtesy of the Library of Congress)*

GUADALUPE *(Courtesy of the Library of Congress)*

St. Dominic
(Museo del Prado, Spain)

Pedro Arbués,
Inquisitor of Aragon
(Courtesy of the Library of Congress)

TALAVERA,
ISABELLA'S CONFESSOR
(Curia Eclesiástica de Grenada)

AUTO-DA-FE *(Museo del Prado, Spain)*

St. Dominic presiding over
the burning of Qur'ans
(Museo del Prado, Spain)

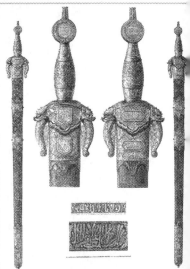

Boabdil's sword
(Courtesy of the Library of Congress)

to a friend. "The nations amongst whom we live do not stop taking council and devising means for assailing and harming us. And if we do enjoy peace for a brief moment, we are soon terrified by frightful news of savage persecution against the remnants of Israel coming from all the corners of the earth. What man who is subjected throughout life to the fear of enemies would grieve when his last hour arrives? Weep not for the dying among Israel and do not bemoan them! Weep for those who are cast from one misfortune to another, and for whom God has blocked all avenues of relief. For honor has departed from Israel, and I wish we were all dead and no more given to scorn and derision, to contempt and humiliation."

In May 1483, when the king's agents discovered secret communications between the duke of Braganza and Ferdinand of Aragon, João had the pretext for the crackdown he coveted. Even though the contacts with Spain were innocent, the duke was immediately arrested and charged with treason. A purge of all the duke's co-conspirators got quickly under way. Within hours of the duke's arrest, Don Isaac Abravanel was summoned to appear before the authorities.

And so the classic dilemma of his forefathers faced yet another brilliant Jew and yet another Abravanel. That the king was capable of the most extreme measures, Don Isaac had no doubt, for he had come to see João II as a greedy and brutal tyrant. That the charges were a fabrication was obvious. "There was no violence in my hands and no deceit on my lips," he would say later. Subsequent events proved him right about the imminent danger, for the duke of Braganza was summarily executed as a traitor in June 1483 and all his lands confiscated. A death warrant for Don Isaac himself was issued. To flee would leave his family in jeopardy, and almost certainly mean the loss of his entire fortune. The king was bent on robbery, Don Isaac believed, for it was absurd to think that he could be a secret agent against the crown he had served so well and faithfully. His writings alone might prove his innocence, for as a matter of belief, he opposed rebellion of any sort against established authority. Later, he would confess to having had discussions about rebellion.

"I discussed with some of the great nobles this question of rebellion against a king. They maintained that a revolt against a tyrannical king is justified. I am convinced it is not." A forthright defense of his honor was out of the question. He had no choice but to flee.

"I forsook the woman whom the Lord designated for me and the children whom God graciously bestowed on me," he said.

On May 31, 1483, under cover of darkness, and with the king's posse close on his heels, Isaac Abravanel crossed over the Castilian frontier. He arrived at the tiny Spanish town of Segura de la Orden, not far from Plasencia.

He was now the subject of a far more powerful Catholic king.

❖

For nearly a year Don Isaac Abravanel settled down in his small border town, where he would find himself comfortably among many friends and co-religionists, for the Plasencia region was filled with Jewish refugees who came there after the expulsion of Jews from Andalusia in early 1483. But Don Isaac was not idle. His presence in the region became quickly known, and he was soon surrounded by admirers from the extensive Jewish communities in the area and importuned to lecture on the early prophets. He threw himself into scholarship, and his literary output was astonishing. In one five-month period alone, he wrote commentaries on the books of Joshua, Judges, Kings, and Samuel, four volumes comprising over 300,000 words.

"When I lived in royal courts, I had time only to dally with books," he would write later. "It was only when I became a wanderer on the face of the earth, going destitute from kingdom to kingdom, that I became a student of the Book of God." During this period in the borderlands, he may not have been entirely destitute. By remaining close to Portugal yet beyond the reach of João's agents, it is likely that he found ways to smuggle out some of his wealth, and to stay in contact with his family.

It was not destined that so talented and valuable a man as this would languish for long in his ivory tower. In March 1484, probably upon the suggestion of the princes of Braganza, Ferdinand and Isabella summoned Don Isaac to the Spanish court. The court was then convened at the Cortes of Tarazona in Aragon, where the recommendations of the Grand Inquisitor, Tomás de Torquemada, about the organization of the Aragonese Inquisition were under consideration, along with other stiffer measures against the Jews and conversos of Spain. Aragon was on the cusp of its first *auto-da-fe*.

Don Isaac seemed blind to the treacheries of the court he was entering. Gratified and flattered to be called to the brilliant court of the Spanish monarchs, and seeing this as an opportunity to build again a fortune such as the one he had lost in Portugal, he seemed to give little thought to who this king was or what the king's long-term agenda might be. The worrisome harbingers of the Jewish future were evident. The Cortes of Tarazona was building on the actions of the Cortes of Toledo two years before, when the establishment of ghettos for Spanish Jews became a strict and enforced policy. The Jews of Seville had already been expelled from the city that was the ancestral home of the Abravanel family. Any resettlement of new Jews there was prohibited. At Tarazona, the Jewish "heresy" and the Jewish "superstition" were phrases on every tongue. The Talmud, wrote the chief chronicler of the Spanish monarchs, "contains very dark, abominable lies against the law of God and against the law of nature and the law of the scripture."

Ferdinand had developed into a mature, energetic, deceptive, and dangerous leader. His messianic vision of himself was taking shape, not only as the liberator of all Spain but as an instrument of God in the coming apocalypse to purify the world. He was beginning to think of himself as the Bat, who would complete the mission of freeing first Spain and then Jerusalem from the pollution of the infidel, whether that non-Christian was converso, Moor, or Jew. And yet the king masked his intentions and his greed in smooth flattery and in high-minded expressions about the common good and Christian charity. Three years after Don Isaac arrived in the Spanish court, the Jews of Castile were still describing Ferdinand as "a just and righteous" leader, even as Ferdinand was exploiting the hatred of Jews and conversos to advance his political aims.

For these qualities of cunning and political clarity, Niccolò Machiavelli would later make Ferdinand a model for his "new Prince." "Nothing makes a prince so esteemed as when he personally accomplishes things rare and exemplary," Machiavelli wrote in his masterwork. To Machiavelli, Ferdinand was the "first king among Christians." "At the beginning of his reign he attacked Granada, and that undertaking was the foundation of his state. First he did it when his country was at peace and without a hint of opposition: he kept the minds of the barons of Castile occupied with this undertaking, and they, thinking of that war, did not consider making any political changes. By this means he acquired prestige and power over them without their becoming aware of it. . . ."

"Besides this, in order to be able to undertake greater enterprises, always making use of religion, he devoted himself to the pious cruelty of driving the [conversos] out of his kingdom and despoiling them—this example could not be more rare. These actions sprang one out of another in such a way that between the two he never gave his enemies space to work in tranquility against him." Ferdinand, Machiavelli concluded, "never preaches anything but peace and loyalty and is the greatest enemy of both."

In Isabella, the metaphor was different but no less grandiose or ironic. As she acquiesced in the Inquisition, she was lionized and deified by the very conversos she was complicit in sending to the funeral pyre. Old and new Christians alike saw her as their strong and generous saviour. Converso poets saw her as the Virgin Mary incarnate, whom God had placed on earth and on the throne to protect them from the howling dogs around them. "You Queen are the figure/who rids us of our evil," wrote a converso friar. "Your gentle beauty is painted/in colors more divine than mortal./If, enlightened queen/God made you/so unique and so great/you must be in everything/as to be the chosen one." And another poet, Antón de Montoro, went further: "Great sovereign queen/from you the son of God/received human form/ How beautiful, saintly, and discreet/that perfect Virgin/accepted by divinity/and that is why through you/we win glory."

To this magical court, puffed up with its own righteousness and sense of messianic mission, Abravanel was being summoned for a decidedly secular task. His skill in extracting vast taxes from the reluctant hands of the powerful and the wealthy was legendary. From his success at raising the support for the Portuguese crown in the War of Succession, his reputation for building a war chest preceded him. The Spanish monarchs were now feeling the pinch of military expenditures. After the defeat in the Axarquia west of Málaga a year before, Ferdinand knew full well that his War Against the Moors would be harsh and protracted. It required the mobilization of all the resources of northern Spain. Don Isaac's talents, therefore, were useful.

It is not surprising that Abravanel overlooked the quiet and sinister process that was well under way against Spanish Jews. To the extent that he took account of it, he ascribed the Jewish suffering to the Jews themselves for their own heresy. The anti-Jewish policy was not instituted all at once, but rather piecemeal over a period of years. In the royal court itself, Jews were still prominent as physicians, treasurers, tax collectors, and lawyers. Had not the Queen Isabella said only a few years before: "All Jews in my realm are mine and under my care and my protection, and it belongs to me to defend and aid them and keep justice"?

The chief rabbi of the court remained the venerable Don Abraham Senior. His special relationship with Ferdinand and Isabella was secure and of long standing, for he had been a matchmaker in their nuptials and an early supporter of Isabella in her conflict with her half brother, Enrique IV. Through Abraham Senior's auspices the fortress of Segovia, his hometown, had been turned over to Isabella's supporters, after the rabbi had persuaded its commander that Enrique was unfit to rule. He became the chief tax collector of Castile, and through that strategic post, the wealthiest man in Spain. As the country's largest landlord, he owned houses, estates, lands, orchards and vineyards throughout the realm, from which he gained income in leases and grants and sharecrops. In Segovia alone, besides his own commodious mansion in the heart of the Jewish quarter, he owned fifteen other houses, including one fine one that he bought after its converso owner was burned at the stake. In Ávila he had four houses on the main square, and elsewhere in the kingdom the crown ceded properties to him to manage.

Beyond his religious post, Abraham Senior was also the supreme judge of Castilian Jews under the Talmudic law, which was recognized by the state. In this capacity he presided over many legal disputes among his people. Though he was more skeptic than true believer, he conducted a house of prayer in his Segovia mansion, at whose services conversos and even some Old Christians were quietly in attendance. Through the 1480s he was a staunch and effective advocate for his people. He did not shrink from confronting the intimidating Torquemada. In 1486, he complained bitterly to the king's supreme court about the preaching of a friar in Torquemada's Monastery of Santa Cruz. The friar, named Antonio de la Peña, had threatened "to set up his pulpit in the Jewish quarter and cause such a commotion that the whole city would not be able to remedy the matter." In another sermon, Peña said, "If the Christians of this city do not light a fire on the hill, the wolves would not be frightened off." After Abraham Senior complained about this scurrilous and incendiary ranting, the ferment quieted down some. A year later, the rabbi did his best, without success, to prevent the expulsion of Jews from Andalusia.

His loyalty to the queen was total, and she, in turn, granted her chief rabbi a lifetime pension of 100,000 maravedis. In 1480, the Cortes of Toledo (as it was handing down stringent measures against the Jews generally) added to this annuity by rewarding him another 50,000 maravedis for his stellar service. He was exempt from the restrictions placed on other Jews for dress and travel. When the aging rabbi traveled, he was accompanied on the road with a retinue of thirty servants and guards on mules, and he wore an immense gold pendant around his neck. Yet, if Senior enjoyed the great favor of the court, he was distrusted by many in his own Jewish community, who protested that the rabbi had not been elected as their leader, but appointed by anti-Semitic rulers. Some Jews questioned the sincerity of his Jewish beliefs, to the point that he was called the "Hater of Light."

At the Cortes of Tarazona, Don Isaac Abravanel was persuaded to enter the royal service as a tax collector, under the supervision of Don Abraham Senior, who was then seventy-two years old; Abravanel was twenty-five years younger. From 1483 onward, they were to become intimate friends and colleagues. Ironically, these two pillars of the Jewish community would be responsible for collecting a heavy tax on their own people known as the *Alfarda*, or Stranger's Tax, to support the war against Granada.

Don Isaac Abravanel and Don Abraham Senior relied on the illusion that they were indispensable to the crown and therefore protected. And in turn, the Jews of Spain labored under the illusion that by virtue of their leaders' privileged position with the monarchs, they too would be protected. As long as they enjoyed the favor of monarchs, Abravanel and Senior would be as a "shield and a wall for their race," wrote Abravanel's son later, "and would deliver the sufferers from their oppressors, heal differences and keep fierce lions at bay."

Not exactly. When the apocalypse finally came for Spanish Jews in 1492, these two leading rabbis, statesmen, and ministers of finance chose radically different paths.

13

The Valiant, the Powerful, and the Unlucky

RONDA

In the two years that followed the major defeat of the Christians west of Málaga in March 1483, and the major defeat of the Moors a month later at Lucena where the sultan Boabdil was captured, the holy war between the two sides had devolved into a struggle over organization for the long haul. On the Christian side, Ferdinand gradually mobilized the complete chivalry of his empire, summoning it with the clarion call of crusade. In April 1484, 11,000 light cavalry and 25,000 foot soldiers gathered in Córdoba for the summer campaign. As they did so, Ferdinand said of the war to his queen, "It is so just and holy an enterprise that among all the Christian princes nothing is more honored, nor can it be. Truly, this war has the help of God and the love of the people."

Perhaps. But two years of conflict had cost his kingdom dearly in men, material, and money. Much ravaging of the countryside had been enjoyed by both sides, but no major bastion had changed hands. Little had been gained.

An unexpected shift in leadership had shored up the weakness of the Moors. The pathetic figure of Boabdil had been marginalized. He languished in splendid isolation in Almería, sunk in self-pity, his treason well understood by the people and his inadequacies deplored even by his tart-tongued mother. "It is a feeble mind that waits for the turn of fortune's wheel," Ayxa de Hora hissed at her son. "The brave mind seizes upon the moment and turns it to advantage. Take the field, son, and you may drive danger before you. Remain cowering at home, and fortune besieges you in your own house. By bold enterprise you may regain your splendid throne in Granada. By passive forbearance, you will forfeit even this pathetic throne in Almería."

Of course, this was the same acerbic advice she had given in prodding her son into action the year before, the action that resulted in catastrophe and capture. How was he to accomplish such a thing, anyhow? He had few followers and no soldiers. "Evil indeed was the day of my birth," he moaned, "and truly am I named El Zogoybi, the unlucky."

At the Alhambra in Granada, his father, Muley Aben Hassan, was old and infirm and incompetent. Nearly blind, surrounded by satraps and sycophants, railing at his fate, he was often bedridden with various ailments, and incapable of action. His fiery, impetuous nature had become a flicker.

And yet between the feeble, treasonous Boabdil in Almería and sick old Muley in Granada, an alternative had arisen in Málaga. He was El Zagal the Valiant, the brother of Muley and the hero of the Moors' great victory west of Málaga. On the streets of the capital, as seemed to happen often in times of grave crisis, the old hermit, Alfaqui, emerged from his cave in Sacromonte to berate the crowd.

"You have been choosing and changing between one man worn out by age and infirmities, unable to sally forth against the foe, and another who is an apostate, a traitor, a deserter from his throne, a fugitive among the enemies of his nation, a man fated to misfortune," he cried. "In a time of war like this, only he who can wield a sword is fit to hold the scepter of power. You need not look far. Allah has sent such a man. You know who I mean. He is your general, the invincible El Zagal whose name stands for the courage of the faithful and who can strike terror in the hearts of the unbelievers."

This was Jihad, the fifth pillar of the faith, the moral duty of all Moors to rise in defense of their homeland and their faith. The flag of Jihad had to be raised against the banner of Crusade. God is Great—*Alihu Akbar*. Of unbelievers who attack you, especially in the Inviolable Place of Worship, the Koran says: "Fight in the way of Allah, against those who fight against you, but do not transgress limits. Lo! Allah does not love aggressors." And in this fight against aggressors, "slay them wherever ye find them and drive them out of the places whence they drove you out, for persecution is worse than slaughter."

Great God He might be, but Allah had not prevented the forces of the unbeliever from penetrating deep into Moorish land the summer before. The invaders had ravaged the meadows around Antequera, burning fields, vineyards, and olive orchards, and stealing whatever livestock they could find. Before the small but significant *alcazaba* (fortress) of Alora, a mere fifteen kilometers northwest of Málaga, the Christians had deployed their terrible new engines of warfare. Brought to Spain by French, German, and Italian mercenaries, the new artillery included a devastating cannon called a bombard, capable of hurling 200-pound boulders and iron-cased, gunpowder-filled shells, which quickly reduced the tall, thin-walled towers of the outpost to ruin and threw the population into confusion.

With this new artillery, the age of the armored knight and the turreted castle was moving into its twilight. The arrow and spear of the chivalrous age had given way to cannon and catapult, fired at a safe remove from the fray. The battle was given over to the engineers. As this devastating weapon of mass destruction became commonplace in the War Against the Moors, a Moorish cavalier would lament:

"What good is all the prowess of knighthood against these cowardly engines that murder from afar!"

After nine days of bombardment, Alora's walls and towers were rubble, and the fortress was in Christian hands. The nearby town of Sentinel and some forty other villages had surrendered without a fight, for their terrified populations had heard about the fearsome new artillery and preferred to preserve their towns intact. Before the Christian forces withdrew, they penetrated into the vega of Granada, coming almost to the gates of the Alhambra itself. The demonstration was effective, for old Muley Aben Hassan promptly reversed himself and offered an armistice and a resumption of payments of vassalage. It was too late. This time, Ferdinand rejected the offer out of hand. Total victory was now his goal.

Meanwhile, El Zagal was consolidating his grip on the Moors' empire. Appearing before the walls of the Alcazar in Almería, he demanded that Boabdil be turned over.

"Where is the traitor, Boabdil?" he shouted.

"There is no traitor more treacherous than you," shouted the feisty Ayxa in reply. "I trust that he is safe and preparing to take revenge on you for your usurpation."

Safe Boabdil was, safe in Christian hands. He had slipped out of his own dominion and was again being toasted by Christian knights in Córdoba. They would soon turn him back with instructions to foment civil war more vigorously.

Thus stood the situation in the spring of 1485 as Christian soldiers flooded the streets once again for the seasonal campaign.

❧

In the council of war that spring, Ferdinand, Isabella, and their generals settled on Málaga as their main objective for the initial weeks of the year's campaign. If they could not actually take the well-defended port, they could at least isolate it and pick up some important satellite towns along the way. At first, this plan seemed sound, as the Christian force of 9,000 cavalry and 20,000 foot soldiers thundered its way through the Val de Catama, taking the towns of Coín and Catama after week-long sieges.

Even before the Christian army moved out of Córdoba on April 5, however, El Zagal the Valiant One knew from spies of his enemy's plan. He had worked diligently to fortify Málaga, knowing that sooner or later his port would be attacked. While the city's defenses were formidable, El Zagal viewed them as inadequate, especially with these reports of Ferdinand's new super weapons of bombardment and Castile's effective boycott of the southern coast.

When the report came that the Christian army was approaching his city, El Zagal gathered a thousand of his best fighters and sallied forth to engage it. The ensuing skirmish was violent and brief; many were killed on both sides. But it caused the Christian side to reconsider its war plan. In the aftermath the marquis of Cádiz, Ferdinand's most distinguished field commander, advised a change of strategy. The Christian force was insufficient for a major siege, he argued. They should ponder their alternatives.

The key to the western defenses of the Moorish state was Ronda, a fortified town some thirty miles north of the coast and sixty miles due west of Málaga. This bastion enjoyed an utterly remarkable natural circumstance which in medieval terms—but for the factor of human folly—practically defined the concept of impregnability. Within a region of wild mountains, the town was set upon a high butte, the sides of which were great chimneys of limestone 200 feet in height. The north side was a yawning ravine, El Tajo, through which the Guadalevín River ran. Across this narrow gorge was a single bridge to a well-fortified gate that was later called "the Moor's armchair." The approach to the lower, more vulnerable southern side of the butte was protected by the massive, turreted *alcazaba,* or fortress. A fierce corps of veteran mountain fighters defended it, and its mayor was an important and experienced Moorish general named Hamet El Zegri.

Ferdinand was still smarting from the breach of intelligence that had undercut his plan for Málaga. If spies had penetrated even his inner circle, he was determined now to trick both the moles and his enemy. He too had his spies. A report had come from Ronda that the morale of the garrison there was low, and that if its defenders could be drawn away by a diversionary action, the place might be easily taken.

The governor of Ronda had been present at the disappointingly short battle for Coín weeks before, and he had returned home to his mountain redoubt itching for revenge. When he learned that the Christian army was heading due north for far-off Loja, he deemed it safe for a quick foray into the fertile pickings of Medina-Sidonia. Venturing out of his town and leaving its defense at about one third full strength, he marched west, where he amused himself for some days by ravaging the fat fields and barns of the Christian grandee.

Meanwhile, the Christian forces marched north from Málaga, moving northeast as if they were heading for the northern stronghold of Loja. At the last moment, in a stealthy maneuver, two thousand cavalrymen under the marquis of Cádiz split off and made a dash west for Ronda. When the foolish ruler of Ronda returned to the outer hills of his town, buoyantly weighed down with booty, he was horrified to find it surrounded by the enemy.

In the distance the banner of the Catholic monarchs waved in the breeze above the smoky encampment of the Christian army. Ferdinand had arrayed his forces in five groups around the town. The largest contingent faced the *alcazaba*, while the left flank was commanded by the marquis of Cádiz and the right by the count of Medina-Sidonia. The artillery was set up to the east of the town. Isabella was already there with her husband, tending to her well-stocked hospital of six tents and to the provisioning of her army. She had planned for enough bread, wine, and meat for a long siege. Characteristic of her attention to detail, she ordered that two piles of flour mixed with pork fat be left in front of each tent. If her supply line to Córdoba was interdicted, her soldiers could stay fit—or at least alive—by ingesting this disgusting medieval version of hardtack.

But Ronda had an Achilles' heel. Its sole access to water was through a secret passageway of 130 zigzagging steps that began in the rear of a noble house and had been cut through the limestone, leading down through dripping anterooms to the river. Known to a few as the water mine, this lifeline, however, was no secret to the marquis of Cádiz. His commandos immediately sealed it off when he arrived in Ronda's vicinity ahead of the main Christian force.

On the outer perimeter, Hamet El Zegri saw that there was no chance to break through the Christian lines, and so he ordered fires to be lit on the hilltops. When darkness fell, the Moors raced down the slopes, screaming their invocations to their God and their curses upon the enemy. The clatter was unnerving, but the Christian lines held.

Ferdinand had ordered his soldiers not to stray from their posts for any reason, since the terrain around Ronda was unfavorable fighting ground.

For four solid days, the bombards and catapults of the Christian army hammered the town without letup. As the gunpowder shells exploded, the screams of women and children added to the confusion. By the fourth day, all the towers were brought down, and the walls were breached. Hand-to-hand combat ensued. The most unusual of these fights took place on the roof of the town's main mosque where, as a kind of metaphor for the entire war, the defenders of the faith fought their hardest against the crusaders atop their inviolable place of worship.

On the tenth day of the siege, the Moors capitulated, and on May 23, 1484, Ferdinand entered the city. There the elders of the conquered town presented him with a letter that contained a rare piece of ecumenism. "O great and powerful King," it read in part. "May God preserve the State and may He always be present in your deeds. Take from our days and add to your own. It is convenient for us to serve you, since God has made you the greatest of kings. Once we place ourselves in the hands of Your Majesty, we trust that we shall be treated with kindness, just as we were treated by other kings, especially since Your Majesty is more powerful, greater, and better than all the others."

If Ferdinand's heart was softened by this flattery, it would harden once again when three hundred Christian prisoners crawled out of Ronda's dank dungeons. One by one these warriors from past battles emerged from their darkness, naked, hungry, with beards to their waists. Despite this, Ferdinand was temporarily magnanimous in his terms. The conquered were allowed to leave with anything they could carry, to emigrate to North Africa, or to Castile where they could go with a royal letter of protection. Ironically, several prominent, non-military families resettled in Seville on property confiscated by the Inquisition from conversos. Otherwise, those conquered could remain in the region, so long as they did not interfere with the occupation of their town and swore an oath of allegiance to the Catholic monarchs. Those who chose to stay were officially designated as *mudéjares*, or Moors who would be permitted to continue their Islamic beliefs, so long as they remained loyal to Ferdinand and Isabella. For them, the royal chronicler proclaimed, Ferdinand promised "on his royal word to preserve and protect the law of Muhammad."

Meanwhile, the encomiums to Isabella poured in. One knight wrote to Ferdinand of Isabella that "she fought no less with her many alms and prayers and by giving order to the things of war than you, my lord, with your lance in your hand." From her quarters in the Palacio de Mondragon, Isabella supervised the transformation of Ronda's mosques into Christian churches. Sacred books and lace and crosses were shipped in wholesale from Córdoba and Seville, along with new settlers to replace the Muslims who had left. The main mosque of the town was inviolable no more. It was consecrated as the Church of Santa María de la Encarnación, while other mosques were purified and renamed for the Holy Spirit, San Sebastian, and St. John the Evangelist.

On June 2, 1485, the feast of Corpus Christi was celebrated in the new Ronda as if to mark its purification and its conversion. "Thus, this pestilent nest of warfare and infidelity, the city of Ronda, was converted to the true faith by the thunder of our artillery," a chronicler later wrote. "The port of Marbella and some seventy-two other places soon followed suit in being rescued from the vile sect of Muhammad and placed under the benign domination of the Cross."

On the following day, Ferdinand dispatched a letter to the pope about the triumph in Ronda, "so that Your Holiness should see and know how Spain spends its time and money." The king was beginning to regard himself as divinely guided. Forces of history were at work, and he was his Lord's instrument. Those around him perceived this vanity and played to it shamelessly. The vision they promoted did not end with the reconquest of Spain for Christianity.

"It is clear that our Lord intends to carry out what has been prophesied for centuries," one important courtier said to him. "Namely that

you shall not merely put these Spains under your royal scepter, but that
you will also subjugate regions beyond the sea."

❧

The celebration over the Castilian victory at Ronda was matched in
the Alhambra by despair and loud wailing. With Muley Aben Hassan
near death and Boabdil consorting with the enemy in Córdoba, the
state of the Moors foundered without a proper king. With the blessing
of the dying king, a delegation was dispatched to Málaga to persuade his
brother, El Zagal the Valiant, to take the throne. El Zagal was reluctant
to do so, for he knew that his legitimacy would be questioned, and he
was more a fighter than a governor. Given the dire circumstance, however, he relented and was escorted grandly to Granada. The procession
needed to be careful, for the road between Málaga and Granada passed
by the Christian redoubt of Alhama, thought to be still under the command of the disciplined, chivalrous count of Tendilla. Unbeknownst to
the Moors, the count of Tendilla had completed his tour there some
months before, and a less chivalrous, less aggressive, and less exacting
knight had taken his place.

When El Zagal's procession of three hundred knights came into the
vicinity of Alhama, instead of well-organized sallies or disciplined harassment, the Moors came upon a hundred Christian soldiers spread out
and sunbathing themselves in an open field, far from their horses.
These easy pickings were too tempting to pass up. El Zagal saw an opportunity to make his entrance into Granada all the more magnificent.
Several days later, his procession passed through the gate of Elvira
below the Alhambra, led by eleven Christian captives, followed by
ninety Christian horses, and by Moorish cavaliers from whose saddles
dangled the heads of slain Christians.

To make El Zagal's installation more splendid and less awkward,
Muley Aben Hassan withdrew to the Costa del Sol before his brother
arrived in Granada. The old king first took up residence in the port
town of Almuñécar, surrounded by his fading star of a wife, Zoraya, and
her children, and what treasure they had been able to haul south with

them. Later, the deposed king moved east to more luxurious apartments in Salobreña, where he died a few weeks later. Before Hassan's death, El Zagal made sure that the treasures Muley had taken with him to the coast were returned to Granada. The old king's death caused little stir. It was reported subsequently that his bones were deposited in a charnel-house and later transferred to a common, unmarked grave.

Rumors of Muley's ill-treatment at the end were coupled with a shocking revelation. Before Hassan's death, no doubt because of his shoddy treatment by his brother, Muley Hassan had changed his will and donated his crown to his son, Boabdil. Overnight, El Zagal's rule became illegitimate. For a considerable portion of the population, re-sentment against the new potentate was rife, as El Zagal was trans-formed from saviour to usurper. And thus, his honeymoon was brief. Old sentiments were rekindled, especially in the Albaicín across the Darro River from the Alhambra, where a contingent of die-hard, for-giving loyalists still dreamed of Boabdil's return. The Unlucky One still languished pathetically in the enemy's camp in Córdoba. Ferdinand had lost interest in him, given the fact that his potential for fomenting civil war seemed to have vanished. But when a delegation from Granada arrived seeking to persuade Boabdil to return home, Ferdi-nand perked up, and after deliberations, he provided Boabdil with enough money to create the illusion of royalty.

Boabdil set up his shadow court in Vélez El Blanco on the far east-ern frontier of the Granadian province and waited for things to de-velop. Though he was just a few miles within the Moorish state, his presence on Moorish soil gave heart to his supporters in the Albaicín, and once again, the Albaicín and the Alhambra faced off against one another across the Darro River. With the renewal of civil strife, no one was particularly happy. But it took the bizarre figure of the old Alfaqui to point the way. Emerging once more from his cave in Sacromonte, looking more ethereal and threadbare than ever, the dervish railed at the gathering crowd:

"O Muslims, beware of men who are eager to govern, yet who are unable to protect you. Why slaughter each other for El Chico or El

Zagal? Let your kings renounce their contests and unite for the salvation of Moorish civilization . . . or let them be deposed!"

But the principals had other ideas. Around El Zagal, the air was thick with treachery. If Boabdil could be assassinated, all problems would be solved. And so with the promise of great reward, four plotters were recruited. Dispatched to Vélez El Blanco as messengers from El Zagal, they carried with them jewels as gifts and a letter which dripped with fake and obsequious sentiments of concession.

"Beloved nephew," it read.

Desirous as I am to forget the origins of our contentions for the kingdom, and conscious that you alone are the lawful king, by virtue of my brother's last will and testament, in which he appoints you his heir, I wish to surrender the government into your hands as rightful king and master, requesting only for myself to be able to spend my days in this abode, to live content and to owe you due allegiance. This I require for Allah's and Mohammet's sake, that the kingdom not be destroyed by its internecine quarrels. Return then as sole king to this city as its lord and master. I sincerely lament the disturbances that have passed and desire to atone by my future conduct for the part I have taken in them.

From Granada, Muley Abdullah El Zagal

When the assassins arrived at Vélez El Blanco, they demanded an audience with Boabdil to deliver their message and gifts from "the king." But Boabdil had been tipped off. Surrounding himself with thirteen of his finest, well-armed guards, he admitted the culprits into his presence, read the letter, and then had the bearers seized. After they were tortured and confessed, they were hung, their bodies displayed from the battlements. And then Boabdil sat down and wrote his reply to his uncle.

The all-powerful God, creator of heaven and earth suffers not the wickedness of man to remain concealed, but causes it to be brought to light, as he has done your horrible conspiracy. Your letter teemed with more treachery than the famous Greek horse at Troy. You offer me friendship and yet you persecute my friends and those who acknowledge me as their rightful king. There actions witness the insincerity of your professions of friendship. But the time will come, I trust, when you shall atone for your crimes. The kingdom was my father's, and it descends to me, and yet you wish me harm, because I have formed an alliance with the Christians. You must admit that by virtue of the treaty I have made with them, the Moors aligned with me are allowed to cultivate their lands and live in security, while the Moors who are aligned with you can do neither, and are constantly attacked and pillaged by the Christians. . . .

The ruffians you sent to me with hearts as dark as your own, who came with the intent to slay me, have died the death of traitors. You will suffer also. Your jewels I have cast into the fire, suspecting treason even in them, treason that is so evil a nature that I confess, it greatly surprises me when I reflect that we are sprung from the same royal lineage.

From Vélez El Blanco, The lawful king of Granada

With the two pretenders to the throne at one another's throats, the wise men gathered and divided the realm in two. The Valiant One was to receive the important cities of the province: Granada, Málaga, Vélez-Málaga, Almería, Almuñécar, while the Unlucky One gained control of the northern provinces, most importantly, the fortress of Loja. With Boabdil in Loja, in close proximity to the Córdoba of his handlers, it was supposed in this end game that vassalage rather than hostility might save the northern part of the kingdom from ruin and create a buffer for the heart of the kingdom, the city of Granada itself. Warily, with strong guards protecting them, the principals gathered in Granada to seal this unholy alliance. Boabdil and El Zagal circled one another like lions. El Zagal regarded his nephew with utter contempt, a weakling, traitor to his land and his faith, and cursed by the fates; while Boabdil saw his uncle as a thief and usurper and assassin. After the stiff formalities, Boabdil mounted his horse and prepared to ride north. But before he moved out, the notorious hermit, Alfaqui, emerged once again from the shadows and detained Boabdil with a parting shot.

"Be true to your country and your faith," he warned. "Hold no further communication with these Christian dogs. Do not trust the hollow gestures of friendship of this Castilian king. He is mining the earth beneath your feet. Choose one of two things: be a sovereign or be a slave. You cannot be both."

Gossamer, Velvet,
and Blue Silk

❖

CÓRDOBA

 In mid-1485, as the Spanish sovereigns savored their victory at Ronda and pondered their next move, Christopher Columbus in Lisbon had concluded that the King of Portugal could not be moved to support his project, at least not any time soon. And so he prepared to leave Lisbon in search of more welcoming patrons. His departure, however, was fraught with anxiety and awkwardness. The most tangible of these difficulties was that in his tireless and seemingly interminable self-promotion he had saddled himself with considerable debt. His savings from his commercial ventures depleted, he had no way to pay his insistent creditors. In all he owed various creditors a total of 220 ducats. To leave precipitously might make him subject to arrest as a fugitive scofflaw.

On the surface, his relations with João II remained friendly. The ruling of the Junta of Mathematicians had not extinguished the king's interest entirely, and this gave Columbus the hope that his project was not so much rejected as tabled. Indeed, three years later, in 1488, calling the Italian his "special friend," João II invited Columbus to return to Portugal from Spain for more discussion. The king promised that on this return trip the would-be explorer would have no trouble with the police over his debts.

But this was on the surface. What was the Portuguese king really thinking? Was this another double deal? If he was not ready to back Columbus's bold adventure, the king was not quite ready for it to be handed gratuitously to someone else, especially not the king and queen of his arch rival, Spain. João's treachery had already been demonstrated. It was entirely possible that the Portuguese king would block Columbus's exit or even arrest him to keep him in Portugal, if only to squeeze more information out of him, that might again be handed to native explorers.

Thus, quietly and secretly, Columbus left Portugal by ship one night. Years later, the mariner imputed divine intervention to his rejection. God had blinded the Portguese king to his arguments, for He had another plan.

The itinerant visionary made his way to the maritime provinces in southern Spain. He came with no introductions and no standing and no prospects. He was a foreign widower, penniless, and dragging behind him his five-year-old son, Diego. To no observer would he look like a worthy sea captain or a royal courtier. But his instincts were true, and his luck infallible. As his ship moved up the Rio Tinto to Palos, Columbus noticed the Monastery of La Rábida on the bluff above the river, and he went there first.

The father and son must have been quite a sight. Dusty, hungry, disheveled, and exhausted from the voyage and the long walk from Palos, Columbus pounded on the door of the monastery. When it was answered, he asked first for bread and water, as if he was an ordinary beggar and his son a pathetic urchin. Consistent with their reputation, the Franciscans welcomed the pair warmly. And then Columbus blurted out his fantastic and improbable story: that he had just come from the royal court of the King of Portugal, that he offered to lead an expedition of discovery across the western ocean, and that he had been ridiculed by courtiers. He had come to Spain in hope of making the same proposition to the Spanish crown, and to Palos specifically, because Filipa's sister and her husband lived in nearby Huelva. As his luck would have it, the monastery had a visiting brother, Antonio de Marchena, who was practiced in astrology. He was intrigued.

Importantly, the monastery's father superior, Brother Juan Pérez, was well connected. He had served Queen Isabella as a youth, and he was friendly with the count of Medina-Sidonia. An audience with the powerful duke was promptly arranged. Columbus's Spanish enterprise was under way. The count of Medina-Sidonia possessed the resources to support the venture, and Columbus made a good impression upon him. But the duke was still trying to mend his fences with the Spanish sovereigns. If he funded the expedition, and if new lands really were discovered, his tenuous relations with Ferdinand and Isabella would be complicated further. Moreover, he had no authority to confer titles on anyone; that could only be done by royals. While the discussions were under way, the duke was abruptly called to the royal court in Madrid on important business.

Under the guidance of his Franciscan patron, Columbus then turned to the count of Medina Celi. At his port of Puerto de Santa María, ten kilometers across the Bay of Cádiz from Cádiz itself, the estimable count owned a prospering merchant fleet. He too was captivated by his visitor. "I should like to have taken a whack at it," he wrote later of Columbus's proposals, "for I had three or four caravels, and he asked me for no more." But the count too realized the complications of supporting Columbus's voyage, especially during a time of war, without royal permission. The proper thing, he suggested, was for him to arrange an audience with the sovereigns. Columbus was not averse. Until the request could make its way through the proper channels, the count of Medina Celi took Columbus and Diego into his house and kept them as his guests for many months.

❧

On January 20, 1486, Columbus arrived in Córdoba for his much-anticipated audience with the monarchs, only to find that weeks before, the royals had moved north to Madrid. He found himself in a city that had become a military camp. Córdoba, the site of the most beautiful mosque ever built by the Moors, the Mezquita, famous for its forest of geometric striated arches, was now the base of operations for the War Against the Moors. Everywhere, drums beat, trumpets sounded, and horses jostled in the armies of the colorful and powerful nobles.

Through the good offices of the count of Medina Celi, Columbus was put in the care of the royal treasurer, Alonso de Quintanilla, who took the wayfarer in as his guest.

In the four months Columbus waited, he was not entirely idle, for he took up with a peasant girl named Beatriz Enriquez de Arana. She was soon pregnant with Columbus's second son, Fernando, later to become his father's biographer. When he was not carousing, he established contacts with a network of royal underlings who might help him press his case.

As Columbus languished in Córdoba, the forces of Spanish history ground forward. Just before the previous Christmas, on December 15, 1485, the royal court was in Alcalá de Henares, fifteen miles east of Madrid. This town had become the home of Don Isaac Abravanel, where the court rabbi busied himself as chief tax collector for the Cardinal of Spain, Pedro González de Mendoza. During these days in Alcalá, Queen Isabella gave birth to a daughter named Catherine, known better in later life as Catherine of Aragon, the unhappy first wife of Henry VIII of England. "The birth of a son would have caused the King and Queen greater happiness," the royal chronicler wrote at the time, "for a succession depending on an only son inspires no small fear, and the fecundity of their daughters presaged difficulties for future relationships."*

While Isabella attended to her newborn, Ferdinand concentrated on the Inquisition in Aragon. In a pious proclamation, he tried to shift the blame for confiscations to Pope Innocent VIII. The king was merely executing the pope's order "by virtue of his obedience to the Holy Mother Church." Such expressions of piety surrounding royal theft would certainly have pleased Machiavelli. Actually, the pope had only provided a vague authority for the confiscations; it was Ferdinand who decided the specifics of what land and property should be seized. Early in 1486,

---

*This was a reference to the problem of a disputed succession. Ironically, Catherine of Aragon proved her fecundity by having six children by Henry VIII before he threw her over for Anne Boleyn. Five, including two princes, were stillborn. The sole survivor was Mary, later known as "Bloody Mary."

the king learned that the assassins of the inquisitor in Aragon, Pedro Arbués, were hiding in Tudela, a border town just inside Navarre. Ferdinand threatened war unless the culprits were handed over, which they promptly were.

Resistance still thrived in southern Aragon, in the lands around Teruel. Blaming the defiance on Jews, Ferdinand resorted to a measure that should have resounded through the land. He expelled all Jews from this area. Thinking he was onto a good thing, he followed by expelling Jews from Saragossa and a half dozen other cities. The royal order of banishment bore the fingerprints of Torquemada. "It appears from experience that the damaging inroads of heresy among Christians have resulted from communication between Jews and New Christians," it read. "The only effective remedy is to remove these Jews from among the New Christians, as we have already done in Seville, Córdoba, and Jaén. A formal order for said expulsion will accordingly be prepared by the devout Father [Torquemada], prior of the monastery of Santa Cruz."

The reach of Torquemada now stretched across the peninsula. In February 1484, Pope Innocent VIII, under pressure from Ferdinand, fired the local inquisitors in Barcelona, and replaced them with Torquemada. The Grand Inquisitor, meanwhile, was staging ever greater spectacles. On February 12, 1486, in Toledo, 750 lapsed Christians were paraded through the streets from the Church of San Pedro Mártir to the cathedral, where they were to be reconciled to the Christian faith. In the freezing cold, the men walked barefoot and hatless, but the women had it worse. They were absolutely naked, adding leering lasciviousness to the other roiling emotions that an *auto-da-fe* induced. All carried candles, as the feverish crowd taunted them along the way.

The royal entourage moved on to the holy town of Guadalupe, where Isabella satisfied her piety by building an oratorio for her prayers, commissioning the building of a royal hostelry to be funded by the inquisition, and speaking with Church officials about the three friars who had recently been burned in the town square. In late April, the sovereigns arrived back in Córdoba.

Under the guidance of his benefactor, the royal treasurer, Columbus shed his shabby clothes for the velvet and brocade that suited a royal supplicant, and early in May 1486, he was brought into the royal presence. The audience had been offered as a courtesy to the count of Medina Celi, for the minds of the king and queen were focused elsewhere, the king's on the upcoming spring offensive against several Moorish strongholds, the queen's torn between her duties as a mother and as the quartermaster for the army. Moreover, they were disturbed by stirrings of rebellion far to the north in Galicia; this would soon have to be addressed. A fantastic plan for discovery across the foreboding dark sea was scarcely on the fringes. Queen Isabella had signaled as much to the count of Medina Celi.

"She did not hold this business likely to come off," the count wrote later.

Still, this brash, handsome, eloquent Italian commanded attention. In the royal court, his was a fascinating presence. Most of all, he was earnest in his representations and in his certainties, and he had thought out carefully how he might be most persuasive. His presentation blended science and evangelism, wealth, geopolitics, and mystery. The science might bore them, he imagined, but it would lend weight and gravitas to his pitch. A noble quest to bring Christianity to the horde of benighted infidels in Marco Polo's Orient would appeal to Queen Isabella, just as would his more soaring flights of fantasy, while dreams of conquest in the golden-roofed reaches of Cipangu would appeal especially to Ferdinand. The king too would surely see how such a brilliant stroke of discovery could catapult Spain beyond its arch rival Portugal in its global reach. If Spain could find a shortcut to the Orient, the discovery would trump all the plodding Portuguese expansions down the coast of dark Africa.

The monarchs listened to this fascinating personage attentively. Columbus and Isabella were the same age, and an instant bond seemed to spring up between them, a bond that may even have possessed the blush of sexual attraction. At this infatuation, Ferdinand was characteristically and understandably standoffish and inscrutable, shielding his first favorable impression behind a stony countenance. When the time came for them to respond, the monarchs did what all decision makers do when a tangential matter takes up their valuable time. They dispatched the proposition into lesser hands. The man was interesting. His theories had merit. The matter should be pursued. A commission of experts should be gathered. Perhaps Columbus should meet the Grand Cardinal, Pedro González de Mendoza, the "third king of Spain." Since a decision would rest on the technical and scientific merits of the case, he should also meet Archbishop Hernando de Talavera, the reigning intellectual of the court.

Columbus went away from this first meeting with real hope. The sovereigns had not said no. They were opening more doors. A commission was to be established, and hopefully, it would have on it no bishop who would mock him.

Within days the monarchs stood before the battlements of Loja, Boabdil's lair, on the northern frontier. The meeting with Columbus had been quickly forgotten. It was not even mentioned by the court chronicler. The defeat of the Moors was their first and all-consuming preoccupation.

✦

With the warning of the old hermit to be a sovereign rather than a slave still ringing in his ear, Boabdil took charge of his northern garrison of Loja and promptly attempted to be both sovereign and slave. He sent an obsequious message to Ferdinand, informing the Castilian king of his arrangement with El Zagal, and reconfirming his status as a vassal. As such, Ferdinand was not to attack Loja. In return, beyond the annual duty and the return of captives, Boabdil promised safe passage through his lands for the Castilian armies as they moved against the strongholds of his uncle in the south.

So absurd was this shameful offer that Boabdil himself could scarcely have expected it to be taken seriously. It was hard to say who had more contempt for Boabdil now, Ferdinand or El Zagal. The only questions were how brief would be this partition of the Moorish kingdom, and who would take over the north first.

Ferdinand's reply dripped with scorn. By his union with his uncle, Boabdil was no longer a vassal but an enemy combatant, the king scrawled furiously. By this alliance Boabdil had forfeited his rights of protection and forbearance. Granada would be Spanish. Boabdil should prepare to be attacked. Within days, Ferdinand's armies were moving on Loja. As usual, the marquis of Cádiz, the formidable Rodrigo Ponce de León, was the field general, now with five thousand cavalry, twelve thousand foot soldiers, and most important, a battery of bombards. Ferdinand's determination was great. The memory of his humiliation at this place three years earlier fueled his passion further.

Three years had made a big difference. Within Loja's walls was no fierce old defender like Ali Atar, but a wimpering, muddleheaded weakling. Still, Boabdil had reinforced his garrison in anticipation of the coming fight by deepening the trenches and raising the berms higher around the outside walls. Loja would be no easy prize. In short order, the marquis of Cádiz took over the hill of the Albohacen overlooking the fortress and brought his catapults and bombards forward. To his credit, Boabdil did not cower, but sallied out flamboyantly on a magnificent steed across the bridge over the Genil River. He fought capably until he was twice wounded by the thrust of a spear and had to be carried from the battlefield. The terrible bombardment then began, and the Battle of Loja was over in two days. It ended yet another humiliation for El Chico. The wounded Boabdil was brought out of the battered town on a stretcher. Before Ferdinand, he stooped to grovel, finally falling on his knees to kiss Ferdinand's feet, before he was sent off south to cause more trouble.

These sieges began to take on a certain sameness. Loja was handed over to Ferdinand; again bedraggled Christian prisoners of war crawled out of their dungeons. The defenders were permitted to leave for Castile or Granada or exile abroad, and new settlers were brought in to populate the town. And then Isabella's religious police moved in to transform the mosques into Christian churches.

After the fall of Loja, the bastion of Illora to the north—known as the right eye of Granada—fell. The Christians then stood before the more important fortress of Moclín, only thirty miles north of Granada. A year before, the count of Cabra had been ordered to take this bastion with a hundred knights and three thousand soldiers, but El Zagal had been ready with an even greater force of cavalry and foot soldiers, and the Christians had been turned back. But in July 1486 Ferdinand, with a greater force, was determined to push the conflict forward to its final resolution.

Outside of the Alhambra itself, Moclín was perhaps the most awe-inspiring of all the Moorish fortresses. It perched on a spire of rock atop a mountain 5,000 feet high. The expanse of Granada's plain stretched out dramatically to the magnificent, snow-covered peaks of the Sierra Nevada, which scored their sharp lines along the southern horizon. Moclín commanded the road to Córdoba and overlooked one of the few deep passages through the mountains. Its walls circled the mountaintop in coils, and its square towers were among the most imposing in the Islamic kingdom.

As if they were anticipating a last stand, the Moors had emptied the fortress of its women, children, and elderly, for it was now appreciated that the terror of these groups at the falling bombs had contributed to the confusion and chaos in Ronda. Once again, the new age artillery carried the battle. Here, the gunners timed their shots so that eight or ten balls would land at once. One memorable projectile from a bombard went spiraling through the air, giving off sparks, and landed on a tower that housed a magazine of Moorish gunpowder. The resulting explosion was so spectacular and awe-inspiring that, when the smoke cleared, only a pile of rocks remained. It was later asserted that the Christian God had guided the projectile toward its direct hit. When the Battle of Moclín was over in a day, the strains of the *Te Deum* filled the air, followed by Christian soldiers falling to their knees and mouthing the words *Benedictum qui venit in nomine Domini*—Blessed are those who come in the name of the Lord.

After the sad evacuation of the town, and when it was safe for ceremony, the queen arrived in glory. Isabella rode on a mule, seated upon a saddle of silver. In her hands were reins of silk, embroidered in gold.

She wore a luminous velour dress and a black hat. A gossamer veil hid her face. Behind her rode her daughter Isabel, similarly dressed, also upon a mule whose tack was silver and whose reins were embroidered in gold. Behind the princess came ten ladies-in-waiting. Victorious soldiers lined the sides of the road. As their gracious queen passed, they lowered their colorful battle flags in reverence and affection.

From the opposite direction came the king, dressed in a suit of yellow silk and also wearing a hat. Behind him rode various knights, including a number of foreign nobles who had been drawn to this noble cause of Crusade. Notable among them were masters of artillery from Lombardy, France, and Switzerland, and an Englishman, Count Scales of Lancaster, who was dressed entirely in white, a French hat festooned with gaudy feathers cocked rakishly on his head, while his chestnut horse was draped in blue silk to the ground. When the monarchs met before the assemblage, Ferdinand dismounted and Isabella removed her gossamer veil. He kissed her lightly on the cheek, and then turned to his daughter Isabel, kissing her hard on the mouth.

When they were finally in the royal tents, they spread the map of Al Andalus before them and rejoiced at their successes. The forces of Christ the King now held all the towns and castles west of Málaga.

15

The Learned Men
of Salamanca

SALAMANCA

 In the fall of 1486, the Spanish monarchs were well satisfied with their military accomplishments. Releasing their army for a winter of rest, they packed up and moved north to Salamanca, where they put their minds to other pressing business. An obstreperous renegade-knight was acting up in Galicia in the northwest corner of the peninsula and needed to be silenced. There was a succession rivalry in the vassal state of Navarre that needed to be straightened out. A knight had unjustly sentenced one of his subjects to death, and when the queen sent her adjudicator, his interference was resisted. Not to be trifled with, the queen ordered the houses of the rebel destroyed. And tensions with France remained high along the northeastern frontier with Catalonia.

One aspect of their rule did not seem to worry Ferdinand and Isabella during this winter of contentment. The Inquisition was in capable hands, and grinding forward with its papal and royal approval. In his dealings with his Grand Inquisitor, Ferdinand sounded almost deferential. With language crafted in Torquemada's own dark chambers, the royal order had gone out in 1486 to expel Jews from six major towns, including Ferdinand's own capital of Saragossa.

The wholesale expulsions of 1486 were the first major steps toward the apocalypse of 1492. Even this draconian edict was clothed in strange charity. Teruel in southern Aragon remained a hotbed of resistance, and when Jews there complained that they did not have enough time to sell their property, Ferdinand generously granted them a six-month delay in their departure date, that is, with the proviso that Torquemada agree. To his inquisitor, Ferdinand asked,

"Look into this, and if it is agreeable to you, let it be done."

The monarchs arrived in Salamanca on November 7, 1486, and settled in for a comfortable stay of three months. This ancient and venerable university town, captured by Hannibal two hundred years before Christ and by the Moors in the ninth century, had been the beacon of Spanish learning and culture since its famous university was founded in 1230. This made Salamanca the oldest of Europe's great universities, predating the first college at Oxford by twenty years. Always significant for its cross-fertilization of Arabic and Christian knowledge, the university at Salamanca had led the movement to translate Arabic science, philosophy, and mathematics into Latin, and to spread this Eastern knowledge north into backward Central Europe.

Ferdinand and Isabella were arriving in Salamanca at an especially propitious time in its intellectual life. Their very own political reforms, not to mention the growing importance of the Spanish Empire on the European stage, had stimulated artists and thinkers and drawn them here. Isabella was particularly interested in advancing Spanish learning, art, music, and literature. When printing was invented during her early life, she had appreciated immediately its impact. By 1487, printing presses in Salamanca, Toledo, Seville, Barcelona, and Valencia were churning out classics and religious works. By her order, German and Italian printers paid no taxes, and foreign books could be imported without duty. Her own library reflected her interest; her titles ranged from religious treatises to Latin and Greek classics by Plutarch, Livy, Virgil, and Aristotle, to more modern writers like Boccaccio. This literacy in turn resulted in chronicles of her reign that were more fluid and accessible, far more polished and textured than the wooden annals that had chronicled reigns of the past.

More important perhaps was the luminescence of the Italian Renaissance. From Florence, it radiated outward with the starpower of

Donatello, Brunelleschi, and Ghiberti. In his thirteen-year papacy from 1471 to 1484, Sixtus IV may have approved the Spanish Inquisition and ratified the choice of Torquemada to lead it, but in Rome he had also been a great patron of the arts. At his direction the Sistine Chapel was built, and for its decoration he summoned the greatest painters of Italy. Most significant was Sandro Botticelli, the Florentine painter who was lent to the Vatican by Lorenzo the Magnificent and who painted the fresco representing the history of Moses. Other great painters of the time also contributed to its decoration, including Pinturicchio, Rosselli, Perugino, and Ghirlandaio. The decoration of the ceiling by Michelangelo would come twenty-four years later.

The real ambassador of the Italian Renaissance to Spain was an Italian humanist named Pietro Martire d'Anghiera, or Peter Martyr, as he was better known. This luminary was brought from Rome to Saragossa in August 1487 by the hero of Alhama and now the Spanish ambassador to Rome, the count of Tendilla (Iñigo López de Mendoza). In his correspondence to Rome later, Martyr stated his reasons for leaving Italy for Spain. Italy, he felt, was self-absorbed and divided into warring factions, whereas Spain was united, vibrant, and outward-looking. He was attracted to the great deeds that the Spanish monarchs had undertaken against the enemies of Christianity, especially the war against Granada, which he compared to the Trojan War and Caesar's campaigns in Gaul. He admired the ambition and self-reliance of the Spanish sovereigns.

Instantly, Spanish humanists gravitated to this Italian thinker. The university at Salamanca invited him to give a series of lectures on the revolution in thought and culture and philosophy that was sweeping through his native land. Their impact was seismic. During this winter when the royals were in Salamanca, this great mind was brought into their company and, not surprisingly, the education of young nobles in the court was soon entrusted to him. It is also not so surprising that the Italian was later captivated by his countryman, Christopher Columbus.

Martyr was to write the first major work on the discoveries of the New World.

Without doubt, sessions with Peter Martyr in Salamanca inspired the queen to build great churches throughout the land as "sermons in stone" and, not incidentally, as monuments to her great and pious reign. If their decoration was sometimes excessive, it was meant to show the depth and elaborateness of her faith, as well as the awesome power of the Almighty. Magnificent churches sprang up throughout Spain; to decorate them, painters were encouraged to imagine and paint the scenes of Christ's life. Schools of painting were established in Toledo and Andalusia. Isabella's own taste drew her to the Flemish masters, such as Rogier van der Weyden and Hans Memling.

A musical repertoire of distinctly Spanish character also evolved dramatically under Ferdinand and Isabella. Past Spanish monarchs had imported foreign musicians for their entertainment, but Isabella insisted upon solely Spanish performers. The result was an explosion of new songs and dances, both religious and secular, which were eventually compiled in *El Cancionero de Palacio*, the *Song Book of the Palace*. Secular songs were especially popular at court, particularly when they pined upon the themes of courtly and platonic love as well as idealizing the simple shepherd or the pretty maiden lost in the mountains, or—most significantly—the perfection of the lady in contrast to the cruelty and boorishness of a hapless lover. The original compositions employed unique Spanish forms, divided between the romance and the *villancicos*. The romance usually told a long narrative tale, expounding upon current events. The war against the infidel was a popular standard.

> *What has become of you, unhappy one,*
> *What has become of your land and your Moors.*
> *Reject now Mohammed*
> *And his evil doctrine*
> *For to live in such folly*

Is a ridiculous joke.
Return good king and restore
Our venerable laws
Because even if you have lost your kingdom
You can at least save your soul.

The *villancico*, by contrast, had the feel of a jaunty village song, with a refrain at the top that was repeated with each strophe.

Alas, sad, you see me
Overcome with love
Although a simple shepherd
I would have been better off
Had I not gone to the market
Whence I returned
So smitten by love
Now here I am, miserable
Overcome with love
Although a simple shepherd

Salamanca was the center of this musical revolution. Most enduring of its maestros was a genius named Juan del Enzina. Born in Salamanca, and educated in law at its famous university, he was to account for hundreds of these songs. For many years before he moved into the royal court, he had served the duke of Alba de Tormes, whose castle was several leagues to the south of Salamanca. Throughout this long service he aspired to the post of choirmaster to the royal choir in the Cathedral of Salamanca, a high honor. But the position was denied to him. Perhaps being passed over led to his bittersweet *villancico*:

Whoever rules and whoever is ruled
Without wisdom
Can only be badly ruled

Badly ruled is he who is not prudent
Because everything goes wrong;
And to rule perfectly is
To know how to command wisely;
Whoever rules and whoever is ruled
Without wisdom
Can only be badly ruled.

It has been said in retrospect that the land of Ferdinand and Isabella was in the throes of transition between the Middle Ages and the Renaissance, that the religious crisis over the Inquisition moved the nation into the modern age, and that the ferment in Salamanca dramatized that transition. If the Inquisition inspired terror, it was accompanied in intellectual circles by a great sense of personal liberty. Instead of the peon's dismal, short existence as part of a community of sufferers, the individual could determine or at least influence his own fate.

The evidence of the first glimmerings of this wider personal freedom came in literature, especially in the form of Spain's first prose masterpiece, *La Celestina.* Not quite a play and not quite a novel, it is a dialogue, divided into sixteen acts, with no narrative or description or stage directions, which deals in essence with the conflict between highflown moral ideals and the reality of everyday living, the conflict between courtly love and sensual erotic love. The work was written in Salamanca at about this time by a law student named Fernando de Rojas. Rojas found his inspiration in the mood of the times and in his own early life. He had personally experienced the hard hand of the Inquisition. He was a converso, and his father had been imprisoned, tried, and burned as a heretic by the Holy Office. Told in an earthy, comic style, *La Celestina* portrays the impossible love affair between an Old Christian of pure blood and a conversa whose blood is polluted by her Jewish ancestry. It ends in the tragic death of the two lovers. As such, the story prefigures *Romeo and Juliet.*

"In the end," the male lead, Calisto, says wistfully, "we are all children of Adam and Eve."

Full of anxious expectation, Christopher Columbus followed the court from Castile to Salamanca that fall. During this winter of tranquility, his visionary proposal was on the royal agenda. Friar Hernando de Talavera, the court theologian and confessor of Queen Isabella, had been placed in charge of the Commission of Inquiry into Columbus's proposition. That so important a prelate and one so close to the queen had been chosen to lead the investigation inspired false optimism in Columbus.

The commission consisted of three types of "experts": sea captains experienced in oceanic navigation; professors of astronomy, cosmology, and astrology at the university (though there cannot have been many of these specialists to choose from in Castile); and distinguished men of letters and science like Rodrigo Maldonado. He was a physician, a member of the royal council, and the scion of one of Castile's most illustrious families. Over the years, he had been entrusted with a number of sensitive missions. In the early 1480s, he had ruthlessly overseen the relocation of Jews in Ávila and Segovia into their cramped and putrid ghettos. (In Ávila, the ghetto was situated next to the leather tanneries.) More recently, he had been the royal emissary to Navarre and France concerning the marriage of a royal daughter.

In Salamanca, Columbus took up residence in the Dominican monastery of San Esteban. While he prepared his papers for presentation, his companions at table and in prayer pursued the heretics and secret Jews of the region. Within a few years, the Inquisition in Salamanca would police the student body at the university, to be sure that any marriages consummated there were pure and "legitimate." Living in such close proximity to the dogs of God must have caused Columbus no small measure of anxiety, for one wrong word might have turned the investigators onto him. He could, after all, serve as an instructive target for the Inquisition.

Columbus's very proposal might be interpreted as having elements of Jewish lore and passion. To the monarchs and to the Commission of Inquiry, he was suggesting that he search for King Solomon's mines or the biblical Ophir in the Indies or in the fabulous Orient. (In 1499, he did indeed assert to the sovereigns that he had discovered Ophir.) It had taken King Solomon's ships three years for the voyage to Ophir. The length of Columbus's voyage might be just as long. Solomon's ships had returned with cargo of gold, silver, ivory, apes, and peacocks. Columbus was promising to do the same. The wealth of Ophir was used to build the First Temple, and the quest to find the long-lost treasure of King Solomon's mines was in part motivated by the desire to rebuild the Second Temple after it was destroyed by the Romans.

A suspicious Dominican might have wondered why Columbus clung to this scripture so dear to Jews. Was it not true that Columbus had developed a number of close relationships with conversos? Could it be that the supplicant was secretly Jewish? The mariner needed to be careful.

In the meetings at St. Stephen's College at the university, Columbus put forward his proposition with a prophet's sense of absolute certitude. He asked again for three ships and proposed to sail them first to the Canary Islands before turning due west along the 28th parallel. That course would be safely above the dividing line between the Portuguese and Spanish spheres of influence that had been set in the Treaty of Alcáçovas in 1479. Marco Polo's island of Cipangu lay 750 leagues or about 2,000 miles due west, he stated confidently, and the golden kingdom of the Grand Khan was 1,125 leagues. If he was successful, he demanded lofty titles and a fortune that must have seemed to some commissioners like all the gold in China.

From the outset, Columbus confronted a skeptical lot. In a sense the queen had stacked the deck against him, for she had let it be known that, as much as she was charmed by this silver-tongued, handsome, and sensitive foreigner, she did not think his proposal had legs. Despite their lofty titles and pompous airs, the "wise" geographers and university astronomers on the commission spoke from ignorance rather than enlightenment. The prelates on the commission were stuck in the conventional interpretations of the Bible. How could the world be a globe? they wondered. If that were true, men on the opposite side of the globe would walk with their feet opposite to ours and would be hanging downward. Had not St. Augustine in his *City of God* denied the existence of the Antipodes? Had the saint not said that it was impossible to pass from one hemisphere to another? And the poorly paid men of letters were appalled at the price tag that this sea merchant and would-be admiral placed upon his mission. If his jury was full of doubt, Columbus himself was guarded in his presentation. The treachery and mockery that had marked his reception in Portugal still had its sting.

Later, his second son, Fernando Colón, described the dynamics of the Salamanca deliberations. "In all the thousands of years since God created the world," Fernando wrote in characterizing the resistance of the commissioners, "those lands remained unknown to innumerable learned men and experts in navigation. It was most unlikely that the Admiral should know more than all other men, past and present. Others, who based their opinion on geography, claimed the world to be so large that to reach the end of Asia, where the Admiral wished to sail, would take more than three years."

The ocean might not be infinite, but it was too large to be navigated; and even if it could be crossed, who could say that habitable and wealthy lands existed on the other side? When Columbus showed them his revised map of the world, modified from the Toscanelli map to support his vision, and redrawn in his brother's mapmaking atelier in Lisbon, the stony-faced commissioners were unmoved. An expert in navigation remarked that, since the earth was round, Columbus would not be able to return to Spain once he dipped over the western horizon. For he would be sailing downhill, as if off a mountaintop. Even the strongest wind could not propel Columbus's ship back uphill to the motherland. At this argument, Columbus could only roll his eyes. He had heard this nonsense in Portugal.

The Commission of Inquiry met periodically through the Christmas season and into the new year. By the time the royal court left Salamanca on January 30, 1487, it was clear enough that Columbus's proposal was not going anywhere. Still, he followed the monarchs to Córdoba, holding on to the slender reed that his plan had not been rejected outright. In Córdoba, the commission held a few more perfunctory meetings before the members tendered their opinion to the monarchs. Holding to Ptolemy's estimates for the earth's dimensions, they noted that Asia was 2,495 leagues or about 7,500 miles away (rather than the actual distance of 14,000 miles). This distance across an empty expanse was simply too great to be navigated safely. Columbus countered with his assertion that resting places might well be discovered along the way. Many medieval maps displayed legendary islands of Brasil, Antilia, and St. Brendan on their western fringes in the unknown Ocean Sea. How grand it would be to discover these islands on the way to the Orient!

The commission did not buy it. In the end, Fernando Colón wrote sourly, "they condemned the enterprise as vain and impossible and advised the Sovereigns that the proposal did not comport with the dignity of such great princes to support a project that rested on such weak foundations."

It was time to brush Columbus off gently and gracefully. On May 5, he was given a payment of 3,000 maravedis for his trouble and his expenses. The stipend was meant to soften the blow of rejection, and yet still keep him in their employ. Apart from his proposal about the west, he might prove useful in a few delicate matters of intelligence. Perhaps, the monarchs told Columbus, they could revisit his proposition when they were less distracted.

The battle plan for the summer was now their focus. A voyage across the Dark Ocean to some imaginary land of treasure was far from their minds.

16

Do What Is Most Convenient

❖

MÁLAGA

 Málaga was the second city of the Moorish empire, its principal port, its entry point for troops and money from Muslim North Africa, the lair of El Zagal the Valiant. Its wealth was great, especially that which was vested in the hands of its powerful sea merchants, who despite the evident hostilities between Christian and Muslim Spain carried on a lucrative trade with the Aragonese ports of Barcelona and Valencia. Málaga was, first and foremost, a city of commerce, and it valued money above mere international imbroglios.

The metropolis of eleven thousand inhabitants had been Islamic for nearly eight hundred years. Its defense depended upon its daunting double fortress, which occupied a lower and upper hill in the center of the city and which was connected by a double wall. The citadel on the lower hill had been built 250 years before, and then the immense castle on a pinnacle of rock above it called Gibralfaro had been added. Taken together, these connected fortresses were every bit as awe-inspiring as the Alhambra itself. Málaga's harbor was wide but unenclosed and unprotected from high seas and high winds. Now that the Christians owned the sea, the Islamic defenders of Málaga considered the liability of its open harbor to be to their advantage.

As he studied his war maps for his campaign of 1487, Ferdinand had to choose his summer strategy, whether to move directly on this well-defended city or to concern himself first with its outposts. Vélez-Málaga, a fortified town thirty miles east of Málaga, was the logical first target, since it was slightly inland and astride the road to Granada. To allow Vélez-Málaga to remain in Islamic hands was to ignore a staging area and rallying point for the Moors. In consultation with the marquis of Cádiz and his other generals, Ferdinand decided that Vélez-Málaga would be the first objective of the campaign, for its capture would deny the Moors a base and resupply depot in the principal assault on the port of Málaga itself.

The requisition for troops and money was the largest yet. Soldiers signed up by the thousands for an eighty-day tour, while the great overlords from Medina-Sidonia, Cádiz, Benavente, and central Castile ponied up millions of maravedis. El Zagal the Valiant, however, commanded numbers equal to the Castilian king, and he would be fighting on his home turf. The outcome was by no means foreordained.

On the political front, the news was good for the attackers. The divisive, internecine competition between El Zagal and his nephew and Ferdinand's vassal, Boabdil El Chico, continued hot and heavy. Boabdil had been holed up far to the east in Murcia, in his border castle called Vélez El Blanco. There, his uncle had sent ambassadors to go through the motions of negotiation, but their real mission was to put before Boabdil certain official-looking diplomatic papers that were poisoned with deadly herbs. When this assassination attempt was discovered before it did any damage, Boabdil was angry, but his anger was nothing compared to the fury of his passionate mother, Ayxa the Chaste.

"For shame to linger timorously about the borders of your kingdom while the usurper is seated in your capital!" the sultana is supposed to have said. "Why look abroad for treacherous aid from the Christian when you have loyal hearts beating true to you in Granada. The Albaicín is ready to throw open its gates to receive you. Strike home vigorously. A sudden blow may mend all. A throne or a grave: for a king there is no honorable in between."

Secretly and dutifully, El Chico stole out of Murcia with several hundred minions and made his way west to Granada. He was indeed admitted to the citadel of Albaicín, if not with hearts throbbing, at least with sufferance, and soon enough the old skirmishes in the narrow alleys of Granada between the partisans of the nephew and his uncle began anew. In narrating these events later, the chronicler of the Christian court saw the hand of God at work.

"As guards opened the gate of the City to him, so God opened the hearts of the Moors to receive him as their king."

Meanwhile, on Palm Sunday, 1487, Ferdinand's army moved out of Córdoba. Initially, the auguries were worrisome, for on that day a terrible earthquake rocked Córdoba. Torrential rains and floods followed in the days ahead. At these bad omens, so upsetting to the superstitious, Ferdinand was not cowed, for there was much work to be done. The rains presented practical problems, especially in transporting his heavy guns over the rutted and washed-out roads. Nevertheless, by mid-April, he stood with his army before Vélez-Málaga.

In Granada, El Zagal now had a dilemma, and he risked losing his kingdom whichever way he chose. If he allowed the Christian invaders to take Málaga, the 800-year-old Moorish empire was lost. If he left Granada, he risked a takeover by Boabdil. His only hope was to leave and to win a spectacular victory. He chose this latter course, confident of victory, as he left the Alhambra with a force equal to Ferdinand's: one thousand mounted cavalry and twenty thousand foot soldiers. To coordinate his assault on the invaders, he sent a messenger ahead to the defenders of Vélez-Málaga about his place and expected date of arrival. But the messenger was captured. Under interrogation, he revealed the contents of his dispatches. When El Zagal arrived at the narrow pass that leads into the bowl of Vélez-Málaga, the marquis of Cádiz was waiting in ambush for him. Within hours, the Muslim forces scattered in disarray, abandoning their weapons and fleeing back to Granada.

When the first stragglers reached Granada, the news of El Zagal's defeat spread rapidly. Once again, confused between resistance and accommodation, the fickle populace flip-flopped, switching loyalties, escorting Boabdil across the gorge and into the Alhambra, and barring El Zagal when that warrior returned, breathless and bedraggled. Within a few days, El Zagal took up residence thirty miles east of Granada in Guadix, and did his best from there to marshal his forces.

Boabdil in turn sent a triumphant message to his lord and master Ferdinand about his possession of the Alhambra. In it he renewed his vassal's pledge of obedience. El Chico now proposed a new double cross: he would surrender Granada to the Catholic monarchs in exchange for dominion over the Moorish towns of Guadix, Cenete, Ugíjar, and Mojácar in the Alpujarras Mountains southeast of Granada. The great prize thus seemed to be within Ferdinand's grasp. He was not quite prepared to accept it just yet, however, largely because El Zagal was still dangerous and in charge of large portions of the province of Almería.

Meanwhile, the defenders of Vélez-Málaga were in difficult straits. The torrential rains had ruined much of the provisions that had been stored away. The inhabitants lived a few anxious days under the delusion that Ferdinand would be unable to bring his fearsome artillery pieces through the mud to their town. But when the heavy guns showed up, it was the equivalent of the Inquisition showing the instruments of torture. The mere sight of the heavy bombards was enough to quell resistance. On May 3, Vélez-Málaga surrendered.

As Vélez-Málaga was merely the forerunner to the main battle, and since the town's resistance had been brief and light, Ferdinand offered its residents a graceful exit. No doubt he wished to send a message to Málaga. So long as all Christian captives were returned safe and unharmed, the Moors of the town were free to leave and to relocate. When the town was secure, Ferdinand entered it with the usual fanfare. Characteristically, he went immediately to the main mosque, which he reconsecrated as a Christian church and within which he placed the cross of Holy Crusade.

To the king was brought a most interesting captive. He was a former servant of the marquis of Cádiz, Mohamet Mequer, who had left the marquis's service to become successful in business in Vélez-Málaga. Now a man of considerable property (which he fervently hoped to retain), he offered to help in the surrender of Málaga itself. When the marquis proposed this gambit to the king, Ferdinand replied to his field marshal sweetly,

"I leave this matter in your hands. I will entrust the treasures of

Málaga to you, to distribute them as you will, if you can bring that city under my name."

And so the marquis dispatched Mequer to Málaga with the offer of 4,000 gold doubloons to the commander of Málaga's castle, if he would surrender the town. With the surrender he would guarantee the liberty of its inhabitants and the right to retain their property and possessions. But the commander was now the great warrior El Zegri, the bitter former governor of Ronda, and he replied, politely but firmly, to get lost.

"Tell Ferdinand that if I were to comply with these demands, I would be the worst and most cowardly of Moors," he said. "The city has not been entrusted to me to surrender it to King Ferdinand, but to defend it."

Ferdinand would have to win Málaga the hard way.

❦

On May 6, 1487, Ferdinand encircled the city, and the siege of Málaga got under way. The king's forces numbered 2,500 mounted cavalrymen and 14,000 foot soldiers, as well as scores of warships that lay just off-shore. Several hundred small bombards were deployed on the perimeter, along with seven of the king's largest cannons. At first, Ferdinand was restrained in the use of his doomsday weapons. Wealthy as it was, Málaga was more useful intact than in ruins.

Substantial though the encircling forces were, Ferdinand's opponent, Hamet el Zegri, was confident in his defense. Behind the walls, the lower citadel, and the castle of Gibralfaro above, he commanded six thousand soldiers, a considerable portion of whom were awe-inspiring black Gomeres from North Africa, along with highly motivated Jewish refugees from Seville and Moorish refugees from the battle of Ronda.

Days stretched into weeks with no surrender, and anxieties rose in the Christian camp, for not only was the wait expensive but Ferdinand's forces were unaccustomed to long sieges. Moreover, El Zegri's frequent raids kept the Christian forces off guard. When the siege dragged into July, many of the Christian soldiers had fulfilled their eighty-day commitment to the crown and wanted to go home. Rumors of discontent and rampant desertion in the Christian ranks spread rapidly, fueled by

the presence of a "holy Moor," a dervish who had slipped into the be-
sieged town and claimed to have been blessed by Allah with a revelation
of a Moorish victory. This would-be prophet roamed through the streets
hectoring the assemblage and rousing the defenders to greater efforts.

"Allah has commanded that tomorrow morning you shall sally forth
to the fight," the dervish is supposed to have said. "I will bear before you
the sacred hammer and deliver your enemies into your hands. Remember that you are but instruments in the hands of Allah to take
vengeance on the enemies of the faith. Go into battle with pure hearts.
Forgive each other all past offenses, for those who are charitable toward
each other will be victorious over the foe."

When Ferdinand caught wind of these destructive rumors, he sent
for Queen Isabella, thinking that her presence would inspire his troops
and dispirit the opposition. With the queen in the ranks, there could be
no doubt of the determination of the Christian invaders.

But this gambit had no effect, and even the Christian chroniclers
admired the sturdy defense. "Who does not marvel at the bold heart of
these infidels in battle, their prompt obedience to their chiefs, their
dexterity in the wiles of war, their patience under privation, and un-
daunted perseverance in their purpose?" wrote one.

Things turned ugly. One summer night, 150 Moors stole through the
enemy lines with gunpowder and provisions, only to be apprehended
before they reached the city walls. One of these Moors insisted on an
audience with Ferdinand, professing to have important intelligence
about the sorry state of the defenders. As the king and queen were not
nearby, the Moor was ushered into the tent of a Portuguese nobleman,
Dom Alvaro, the brother of the duke of Braganza. Impressed by the
knight's noble appearance and thinking him to be Ferdinand, the Moor
pulled out his dagger and proceeded to stab the Christian knight until
other Christian nobles rushed in and literally sliced the assassin to
pieces. When the king returned, he ordered the dead assassin to be
sewn back together and catapulted over the city wall. In proportionate
reprisal the Moors killed a Galician captive, strapped the body to the
back of a donkey, and sent the animal loping through the gate.

By August, the defenders were indeed in a sorry state. It was rumored that the inhabitants were eating the flesh of dogs, cats, and horses, and baking bread made from the fronds of the palm tree, a confection that was killing them. Amid the disintegrating situation, the emir, El Zegri, seemed to be going mad before his citizens' eyes. Word spread that he was considering killing all the women, children, and old people within his walls and then launching a final, desperate suicide attack on the Christians. Worried about these signs of madness, prominent men of commerce stepped forward to take charge. Their leader was a merchant named Ali Dordux, a man well known to the traders of the Mediterranean, especially Genovese traders, for his levelheadedness.

Ferdinand saw an opportunity to circumvent El Zegri, but he needed to know more about these Muslim merchants. Who had information on them? Abruptly, the name of Christopher Columbus flashed back into the king's mind. The starry-eyed petitioner was languishing in Córdoba, and he was already on the king's payroll. Had he not been on countless trading voyages whose caravels had called in Málaga? Was there not a significant contingent of Genovese commercial traders in the port? Perhaps he could be useful. And so Columbus was summoned from Córdoba to the muddy Christian encampment outside Málaga. He had been paid an installment of 3,000 maravedis in July. When he arrived in Málaga, he received an additional 4,000.

Whatever representations Columbus may have made about Dordux, a backchannel correspondence did begin between the merchant and the king, a correspondence whose first missive was freighted with deference and with references to past merciful generosities by Christian kings.

"To Your Majesties, the King and Queen, greater than all Kings and all princes," Dordux's letter began. "Trusting in the greatness of your state, and kissing the ground beneath your feet, your servants and slaves of Málaga, old and young (may God redeem them!), beg your royal highnesses to visit us with your pity and compassion, as did your ancestors who were great and powerful monarchs. You are aware of how Córdoba was sieged for a long time until half of it was taken, and the Moors were confined to the other half until they ate all the bread and begged King Fernando who showed mercy and allowed them to keep their belongings. Likewise, in Antequera, your grandfather sieged it for six months and a half until the water ran out and then listened to the people's supplications and secured their escape with their goods. And Your Majesties, more honorable than all monarchs, your fame and honor and mercy is well known and have manifested themselves in your treatment of people before us. This reputation has spread among Christians and Moors.

"We, your servants and slaves, place ourselves in your hands and entrust our persons to your favor. Do with your serfs what is most convenient to you. And may God make you act well toward us. May God extol Your Majesties."

But the long, bloody, and costly siege had hardened Ferdinand. He was no longer in an accommodating mood. With Boabdil's offer of the Alhambra itself, a total victory for Jesus Christ, his divine mission, was at hand.

"I the King have read your letter in which you propose to surrender this city with all its belongings on the condition that you be free to leave whenever you want," Ferdinand replied. "If you had sent me this plea when I first contacted you from Vélez-Málaga or as I was arraying my forces around you, I would have been able to satisfy your wishes. But as it stands now, your only option is to surrender yourself."

Dropping all the flatteries of their first letter, the Moors answered cryptically. They wanted only a guarantee of liberty in return for the surrender of the city. If the king did not agree, the defenders would hang the five hundred Christian men and women whom they held captive. Then they would burn the city and launch one final, desperate attack on Ferdinand. Ferdinand was unimpressed. If you harm a single Christian captive, he replied, no Moor would survive the inevitable surrender. He would slaughter them all.

The protracted correspondence between Ali Dordux and Ferdinand advanced to the fine points until Dordux was negotiating only for himself. So long as none of the defenders was executed, the merchant was prepared to surrender the city. For his efforts, Dordux and his family were to be rewarded with his liberty to remain in Málaga as a *mudéjar*, or Muslim under Christian rule, to retain his property and his business. That settled, the town was handed over, except for the castle of Gibralfaro, which remained in the clutches of the desperate El Zegri. From the parapets the old warrior would watch the sad spectacle of surrender below him for two days, before he too capitulated and was led away in chains. Why had he held out so long? he was asked.

"Because I was commissioned to defend the place to the last extremity," he replied. "If I had been properly supported, I would have died sooner than surrender now!"

After three months and eleven days of siege the stench of Málaga was unbearable, and Ferdinand refused to enter the putrid place until it had been cleaned and sanctified. With the job half done, Hernando de Talavera, now the bishop of Ávila and the queen's confessor, entered the town to provide the Christian blessings. As before, the main mosque of the city was reconstituted as a Christian church and renamed as yet another Santa María de la Encarnación. It was consecrated as a cathedral whose dominion would cover the captured towns of Ronda, Vélez-Málaga, and Coín. When all this was accomplished, the King and Queen of Castile along with the Cardinal of Spain led a solemn procession to the cathedral for a mass of thanksgiving.

Meanwhile, the residents of Málaga were herded onto the plain and divided into groups like cattle. In all, over four thousand were sold into slavery. One group was sequestered to be exchanged for Christian captives who had been taken to Africa. The second group was distributed among Ferdinand's courtiers and any commander who had distinguished himself in battle. The Cardinal of Spain himself got seventy slaves, while fifty Moorish maidens were sent to Ferdinand's sister, the Queen of Naples, and thirty lesser maidens went to the Queen of Portugal. The third group was sold to slave merchants of Andalusia to cover the costs of the battle. And finally, one hundred prize Gomeres were sent to Pope Innocent VIII. Some of these black slaves no doubt served in the lavish wedding ceremony for the pope's son in November of that year, when for the first time the son of a pope was publicly introduced and extravagantly celebrated in the Vatican.

Within a few days, the solemnity and enslavement in Málaga turned to bloodthirsty revenge. In a public spectacle, twelve Christian turncoats who had been found among the defenders were fastened by reeds to poles in a public square, and Christian knights galloped past, discharging cane spears into the victims until they were dead. The deadly game was said to be of Moorish origin. After that, for good measure, a few lapsed conversos were burned at the stake.

"These were the feasts and illuminations most grateful to the Catholic piety of our sovereigns," wrote an eyewitness from Aragon.

A few matters remained to be dealt with. What, for example, was to be done with the 450 Jews captured in Málaga? Here, the chief rabbi of the court and its chief tax collector, Abraham Senior, along with his lieutenant, Don Isaac Abravanel, stepped forward, for they could not bear to see Jews enslaved. Raising a considerable sum from the Jews of Castile and supplementing the ransom fund by selling the jewelry of Málaga's Jewish women, the court rabbis succeeded in purchasing the freedom of their brethren for a royal price.

And what was to be done with the empty houses of the enslaved? With the help and encouragement of the crown, thousands of loyal Christians from Old Castile flooded in to repopulate the city, along with a phalanx of priests to deal with the Moors who remained. And so down through the ages came the saying from the Church,

"Mother, here is your son. You gave him to me a Moor, and I hand him back to you a Christian."

17

Upstaged

❖

LISBON

 If Christopher Columbus hoped that supplying the Spanish court with commercial intelligence on the businessmen of Málaga might help his proposal for a western voyage, he was quickly disabused. Though he received a fourth payment of 3,000 maravedis in October 1487, the monarchs were preoccupied with weightier matters. That fall they had left for Saragossa, where through the winter lull in the war they were to concern themselves with various problems in Aragon. By 1487, the Inquisition had spread its reach to Catalonia under Torquemada's rule.

Barcelona greeted the new year with its first *auto-da-fe* on January 25, 1488. In the plaza in front of the Royal Palace, attached to the Palacio del Lugarteniente (the Palace of the Lieutenants) where the Inquisition had its offices, twelve effigies of refugees were consumed by flames and four people were burned at the stake. Four months later, on May 23, three more persons were burned along with forty-two effigies of accused who had fled. Meanwhile, down south, the head of the Commission of Inquiry into Columbus's project, Hernando de Talavera, was busy organizing the episcopal see at Málaga.

Now thirty-seven years old, his hair turned a snowy white, Columbus languished in Córdoba, watching vainly for the royal messenger. Restless and frustrated, he cast his gaze toward other monarchs in Europe, especially those in France and England, who might welcome his proposal. The English king, Henry VII, was the wealthiest potentate in

Europe. He had forged an alliance with Ferdinand and Isabella, and Columbus's friendliness with the Spanish court might open doors. Consequently, Columbus dispatched his brother, Bartholomew, to the north, armed with maps and persuasive arguments. The French court would be a harder sell. The King of France was Charles VIII, then merely seventeen years old. The power behind the teenager was his sister, Anne of Beaujeu. Yet the traditional antagonism between France and Spain might work to Columbus's advantage. If his intuition proved correct, the state that backed him could instantly become the preeminent empire of Europe.

But before receiving word from any of these monarchs, he got a surprise invitation from the King of Portugal to return there for further discussions. João II referred to Columbus as his "special friend" and promised that if he would come, he would be safe from the creditors to whom he still owed money. Eagerly, Columbus scurried back to Lisbon.

But Columbus's relations with Portugal seemed destined always to be star-crossed. No sooner had he arrived in Lisbon and attempted to shift João II's attention away from Africa and toward an audacious, if desperate, thrust across the unknown sea toward the western sun than he was eclipsed by a spectacular event. Through the mouth of the Tagus came triumphantly two caravels of the naval commander Bartholomew Dias, returning from a sixteen-month voyage of discovery down the African coast. The news spread rapidly. Dias had navigated his way to the end of Africa, around a glorious cape, and some distance up the northern coast of eastern Africa. So, Africa did not extend all the way to the South Pole. Ptolemy had been wrong! A ship could pass between the hemispheres! The way to India was open around the tip of the African continent!

This impressive commander was soon brought before his king. Christopher Columbus was once again forced to the wings as a silent witness to history.

The tale Dias had to tell was riveting. In August of the previous year, 1487, he had set out with three caravels with orders from his king to navigate beyond the Tropic of Capricorn, beyond the last stone marker of Diogo Cão, and to follow the African landmass as far as it went. Along the way, he was commanded to find the magical land of Prester John.

The commander had taken with him six black slaves, four of whom were female. In the female slaves the Portuguese rested special hope, for it was surmised that a woman could pass harmlessly through hostile tribal lands of darkest Africa, while a strange man would more readily be attacked. They were to be dropped off one by one as the fleet moved down the African coast, and they were to hike inland as far as they could go in search of the magical kingdom while they spread the word of the glorious white king named João. As they encountered African natives, they were to distribute trinkets of gold and silver, and samples of spices from the civilized north.

Dias's caravels called at St. George of the Mine on the Guinea coast, inched through the doldrums of the equitorial low-pressure belt, and past the great Congo delta. Along the way the black scouts were dropped off as ordered. When the explorers were near the Tropic of Capricorn, they left their smaller supply ship (which was under the command of Dias's brother, Pero Dias) at a place known as the Bay of Tigers (in southern Angola).

After this, the voyage turned ominous. The two caravels pressed southward another 5 degrees toward the horse latitudes, until bad weather drove them into a large bay they named Bahia das Voltas (Bay of the Tacks) because of the many tacks it had taken to reach calm water. There they had tarried for five days waiting for the weather to break. When it did not, Dias ventured out anyway, only to find himself blown south and west far out to sea by squalls, known to subsequent mariners as the "roaring forties." This tempest lasted for thirteen full days.

With Columbus on the fringe of the royal audience, the king and his entourage listened raptly to this presentation. Dias told his story matter-of-factly, with marine charts spread out on the royal table. By Columbus's later estimate, Dias's position at its most southerly was 45 degrees (or halfway between the tip of Africa and Antarctica). Once back in control of his vessel, Dias had charted a course due east, tacking across the prevailing westerlies in hopes of reaching the safety of the African coast once again.

When he did not, he turned north and finally came upon land at about 34 degrees south. On the headlands the Portuguese spied a number of cattle grazing and tended by shepherds. The shepherds were "negroes with wooly hair like those of Guinea," a Portuguese historian would write several decades later. The explorers landed, only to find themselves pelted with stones by the native Hottentots. The sailors reacted by killing one of the shepherds with a bolt from a crossbow, prompting the natives to run away before the sailors could interrogate them. Even so, the encounter held an important revelation. To its very end, the African continent was populated by blacks.

Dias named this place the Bay of the Cowherds (now Mossel Bay in South Africa). From there, the caravels followed the coast eastward past Algoa Bay (the present location of Port Elizabeth) and onward as the coastline turned north to a major river. This Dias named Rio Infante, after the commander of his second ship, *João Infante* (later renamed the *Great Fish River*). By the warmth of the current, Dias knew that he had entered the Indian Ocean.

Having weathered the terrible, thirteen-day cyclone, the captain now encountered a storm of a different sort. His men, including his officers, had become increasingly querulous. The scent of mutiny was in the air. With one voice, the crew advocated that the ships turn back. Supplies were running low; the men were tired and cold; and the seas were dangerous. Dias argued with them, for they had not found Prester John, and therefore, had not accomplished their primary mission. When he could not tamp down the dissension, he ordered everyone ashore where, according to procedures, the sailors were administered an oath and then asked to vote on what they should do "for the service of their king." The vote was unanimous for turning back. Dias made them sign their name to a document, which he now showed to João II, as if to deflect any royal questions about the authority of his command.

It was well that Columbus listen carefully to this tale of near mutiny on uncharted seas. He would face the same in a few years.

Now the caravels had retraced their path along the coast of South Africa. Well past the Bay of the Cowherds, they came upon a glorious cape with lovely prominent headlands. Dias gave it the banal name of the Cape of Storms to mark the perils of his journey. At this, João II scowled. Why not name it Cabo de Boã Esperancoã, the king said, the Cape of Good Hope? As a result of this remarkable voyage, there was good hope, if not absolute certainty, that India could now be reached by sailing around Africa.

The excitement over Dias's revolutionary voyage consumed the Portuguese court. How should they proceed? Who should command the next voyage? Were the caravels of current design large enough to navigate across the Indian Ocean, about which nothing was known? What would be their destination in India, if Portuguese caravels were lucky enough to reach that fabulous, spice-rich land?

João II was far ahead of them, for he had been thinking about these questions for some time. Several months before Dias's departure from Lisbon in August 1487, the king had authorized a very different mission. Its objective was to reach India by an overland route, from Egypt and then across the Middle East. As with the Dias voyage, the maps for this epic undertaking were prepared by the king's Jewish cosmologist, Master José Vizinho. For this mission, the king tapped one of the most accomplished members of his inner circle, a man named Pero da Covilhã. This bold confidant had handled a number of sensitive missions for the king before, and he spoke several languages, including Arabic. Once he reached India, he was to discover where the great ports were, how Arabic ships conducted trade along the Indian and East African coasts, where the valuable spices were principally grown. Everywhere he was to listen for tales of a great Christian king called Prester John.

And thus, the king was in no hurry to launch the next mission around the Cape of Good Hope, until his emissary could return from the Orient. Only then could he know what the purpose of the next sea voyage of discovery should be, and what its true destination was. The king was a careful planner. He wanted his ships to navigate on real intelligence, not on blind and dumb luck. This was not the time for celebrations and ceremonies. The next mission had to be done right, and when it was, it would become the crowning achievement of João II's reign.

As Columbus watched from the sidelines while the court became consumed with Africa and India, his importance began to shrink. He had been flattered by his royal invitation, but what was its real purpose? It occurred to him that he had been used. Perhaps he had not been summoned to Portugal at all to present again his proposal for a voyage of discovery due west across the unknown sea but to provide intelligence about the royal court of Spain, Portugal's traditional enemy, and about the current situation in the war against Granada. The contempt and even mockery of the king's advisers lay just below the surface: Columbus was seen as a navigator of no particular skill or prominence, an average cartographer, a hustler from humble roots, a foreigner who was secretive about his origins, a braggart and exaggerator . . . and worst of all, the promoter of a very weak proposal.

Against the accomplishments and the deportment of Bartholomew Dias, the contrast was all too clear. With the discovery of the route to India by this impressive commander, Portugal was close to realizing the dreams of Henry the Navigator and four Portuguese kings. A national goal of fifty years' standing was at hand. Why take a flyer on a far-fetched proposal that was based on hypotheticals and fantastic tales? By the technical advice of his worthy advisers and by the evidence of his own intuition, João II knew full well that the Orient could not be reached by sailing due west. Let this Italian romantic flee back to Spain. Let him infatuate the monarchs there with visions of Cathay and Cipangu. João II wanted no interference with his route to India. In Portugal, there was much work to be done on the real and the tangible. By establishing trade with India and by allying itself with Prester John, Portugal stood to be the most powerful empire of Europe.

The Dias triumph was a pivotal point for Columbus. Dispirited, he turned back to Spain. Ferdinand and Isabella were now his last and best hope.

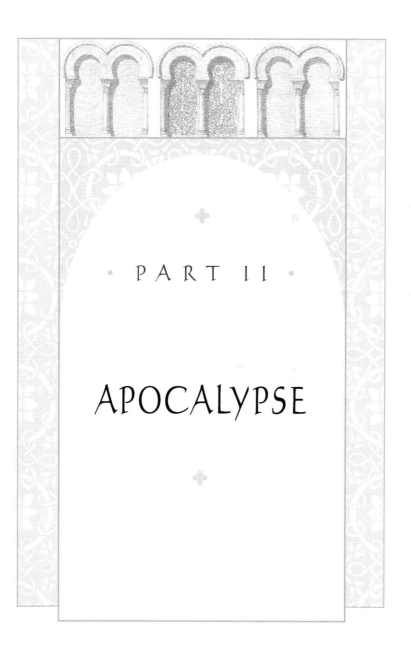

· PART II ·

APOCALYPSE

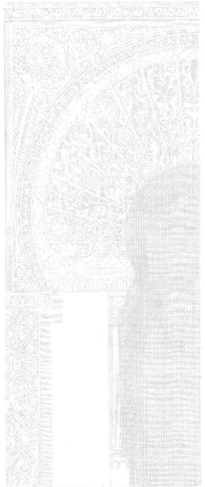

18

The Holy Innocent

 In May 1490, a supplicant named Benito Garcia traveled to the great pilgrimage site of Santiago de Compostela in the northwest corner of Spain with the ostensible desire to worship at the font of St. James the Moorslayer and thereby to defray half of his allotted time in purgatory. He was an itinerant woolcomber and, as it happened, a converso who was reasonably well off by the standard of the time. He had been baptized a Christian thirty-five years earlier, but it had not been a happy occasion, for his father had cursed him for abandoning the faith of his Jewish ancestors, and thereafter, Benito had consigned all his problems in life to this paternal curse.

On his return journey to his home in the village of La Guardia in the province of Toledo, he stopped overnight in the Roman town of Astorga. At an inn there he fell in with a rowdy crowd of locals, drank too much, and when he passed out, he was robbed. The thieves fell greedily upon his knapsack. As they were rummaging through it, a communion wafer fell out on the floor.

Recoiling in fear, the thieves sensed something sinister, even by their grubby standards. And yet this seemed like a piece of special good luck, a chance to get in the good graces of the authorities to cover up their petty crimes. The scoundrels shook their prey back to consciousness and hustled him along to the ornate cathedral and into the presence of the most powerful prelate in town. He was the bishop's vicar, an ambitious upstart named Pedro de Villanda, who had fond hopes of becoming an inquisitor one day. The vicar saw the possibilities immediately, most especially for his own career. More than sinister, a communion wafer in the possession of a false Christian who was returning from a sham pilgrimage to the most holy site in all of Europe: this smacked of heresy, sacrilege, and conspiracy . . . and the chance of advancing the vicar's career in the Church.

The woolcomber protested his innocence vigorously, even after he was dragged to the dungeon and administered two hundred lashes. And so the vicar resorted to more stringent measures. Under Article 15 of Torquemada's Instructions, torture was acceptable if a heresy was only "half proven." Under no circumstances was the priest to shed blood, for this would contravene the laws of the Church. If the suspect should happen to die under torture, the priest would be held responsible and would have to seek absolution from his bishop. This could be embarrassing and might harm a career.

And thus, "the Question," as torture was called, was put to Benito Garcia cruelly but bloodlessly. Given the gravity and the potential of the suspicion, it is likely that the vicar was impatient and put his suspect through an accelerated version of the five normal steps. First torture was merely to be threatened. If that did not compel a confession, the culprit was to be taken to the torture chamber and shown the instruments. If the stout fellow was still untalkative, he was then to be stripped in readiness; and if that was not enough, the naked person was to be strapped onto the rack. Only then, in step number five, which was rarely needed, was the winch on the rack actually to be turned.

But Benito Garcia was stubborn and unyielding—a five-step man all the way. Even as his body was "prolonged" several inches in the "Question of the First Degree," or put more precisely, as his muscles began to rip and his bones began to crack, he remained silent.

When the rack did not produce the desired result, the churchmen turned to the water torture. In this hideous remedy, the prisoner was tied to a ladder that was sloped downward, so that the head was lower than the feet. The head was held fast in position by a metal band, twigs were placed in the nostrils, and ropes winched tightly around his appendages.

The mouth was forced open with a metal piece and a cloth placed over the mouth. Then a pitcher of water was brought, and water poured over the cloth. With each swallow, the cloth was drawn deeper into the throat, until in gagging and choking the victim nearly asphyxiated. The terror of suffocation was extreme, and the process was repeated endlessly, bloating the body grotesquely until the victim was ready to confess. If the suspect was still uncooperative, his body was turned over, causing unimaginable pain in the heart and the lungs. From the inquisitor's standpoint—for he was there to record every detail—the treatment was easy to administer and left no telltale signs.

Garcia had been able to hold his tongue for a few days, but on the fifth day of torture, his resistance crumbled. Yes, he had been baptized thirty-five years before, he confessed, but five years ago he had lapsed back into Judaism. For the vicar this confession was not enough, for this was more than a run-of-the-mill case of false faith. The prelate sensed there was more to the story. With whom did he practice Jewish rites? For what purpose did he have a communion wafer in his possession?

Under the threat of more torture, Garcia blurted out an astonishing tale: At some time in the past two years, he, along with several Jews and conversos in his town, had engaged in a secret and magical rite with a human heart and a consecrated communion wafer. This powerful mixture was meant to create a toxin of mass destruction with marvelous results: the Inquisition would be blocked; all Christians would die raving mad; Jews would seize their property and take over the world. Whether in fact Benito blurted this out, or whether the tale came from the fertile imagination and ambition of the vicar, is unclear.

As usual, Garcia's interrogator demanded the names of his co-conspirators as a signal of the prisoner's sincerity, and the prisoner complied. Among the cohorts he named was a twenty-year-old Jew called Yuce Franco. When this young man was brought to Segovia and jailed there, he abruptly fell ill and appeared to be dying. Brazenly, he asked for a rabbi to be with him at death . . . and not just any rabbi, but the chief rabbi of the royal court, Abraham Senior. (This very request would later be held against Senior as the Inquisition attempted to undermine the power and influence of the court rabbi with the Spanish sovereigns.)

To the Inquisition, Franco's request seemed like a stroke of good luck. The inquisitors regretted that they could not produce Abraham Senior, but instead a Dominican priest who was fluent in Hebrew was brought forward, dressed as a rabbi and sent to the dying man. The wolf in sheep's clothing oozed with comfortable words. Before the dying man met his maker, he should unburden his conscience. Why had he been arrested? "For crucifying a child," was Franco's answer, but the sick man would say no more, except that he wanted to see Rabbi Abraham Senior. That appeal to the most influential Jew in Spain ended the farce.

Still, the outlines of a fantastic story were taking shape. Five years previously, Yuce Franco and Benito Garcia along with seven other men had supposedly participated in a secret diabolical rite known famously as "ritual murder." The blood had come from a Christian boy whom they had murdered in a mock crucifixion to insult Christ, the story went.

And thus, the vicar's torture chamber and the Jew's deathbed had conjured up the most powerful and popular anti-Jewish myths of the past three hundred years into a single case. The background is important. In 1215, at the Fourth Lateran Council (widely regarded as the most brilliant synod of the medieval Church to consider Church doctrine), the concept of transubstantiation (the transforming of the communion wafer into the actual body of Christ) had become official Church dogma. From that point forward, the communion wafer had taken on far-reaching magical importance. Within a few years of the Council, rumors of Jewish rites to mock and desecrate the consecrated host with nails and knives had become popular fare throughout the medieval Christian world. Because of the transformative properties of the consecrated Host, it was suggested that Jews who falsely professed to be Christians would often hold the wafer in their mouths, and then secretly remove it, place it in their pockets, and later, use it for diabolical incantations. Jews whose conversion to Christianity had been forced were especially afraid that by ingesting the wafer, their conversion might become sincere. For Benito Garcia, overwhelmed with guilt for having forsaken the faith of his fathers and finally having sought to recover his ancestral Judaism, a consecrated wafer in his mouth was a desecration in reverse.

"Ritual murder" had popularly come to mean the actual murder of a Christian boy at Easter time or at Passover in a cynical mockery of Christ's Crucifixion. Occasionally, the libel was linked with the Jewish celebration of Purim, when events in the book of Esther in which Queen Esther rescued the Jews from a threat of massacre by the king's lieutenant, Haman, are commemorated; the feast features a reenactment of the execution of an enemy of the Jews. The myth of ritual murder, or "the libel," as it is sometimes called, was a thousand years old, and rumors of murder and mock crucifixion throughout Europe had wide popular currency.

In the first rudimentary laws of Christian Spain, known as *Las Siete Partidas*, there was specific language forbidding the practice. "We have heard it said that in certain places on Good Friday the Jews do steal children and set them on the cross in a mocking manner." A hundred years later, Geoffrey Chaucer gave ritual murder a place in literature in the story entitled "The Prioress's Tale" in his *Canterbury Tales*. The desecration of the Host and the ritual murder were linked with yet another myth known as the "blood accusation," in which allegedly Jews mixed Christian blood into their recipes for unleavened bread at Passover time. Therefore, supposedly, Jews needed Christian blood every year.

And so in the Garcia case, all three myths were combined in a powerful blend of magic, heresy, superstition, murder, poison, blood, and sacrilege, whose purpose was the very destruction of Christianity itself. The great sorcerer himself, the Devil, or his agent, the Antichrist, were supposed to be behind these evil practices. In the mind of the Jew hater, the reappearance of the Antichrist on earth was said to be the equivalent for Jews of the return of Jesus Christ for the Christians. And when the Antichrist returned, he and his Jewish agents would take over the world.

To support this relationship between the Devil and the Jews, and to rationalize their extreme hatred of Jews, medieval clerics, including the ambitious vicar of Astorga, found support for their rabid hatred in several biblical references. They pointed to chapter 8, verse 44 in the

Gospel of St. John about the Jews: "Ye are of your father the devil, and the lusts of your father ye will do. He was a murderer from the beginning, and abode not in the truth, because there is no truth in him. When he speaketh a lie, he speaketh of his own: for he is a liar, and the father of it." Or even more pointedly, they invoked two verses in the book of Revelation: "I know thy works, and tribulation, and poverty, (but thou are rich) and I know the blasphemy of them which say they are Jews, and are not, but are the synagogue of Satan" (2:9) and again at 3:9: "Behold, I will make them of the synagogue of Satan, which say they are Jews, and are not, but do lie. . . . "

And thus, in some remote cave outside the village of La Guardia, the synagogue of the Devil had produced this profane sacrilege. As the strands of the story came together in Astorga, the investigation would take complicated twists and turns. Yuce Franco recovered his health and refused to say more. The other ritualists, however, told widely different stories. Between them, probably through repeated tortures, enough wildly salacious and highly imaginative quotes were elicited. One witness reported that at the point of the boy's crucifixion, the young Jew, Yuce Franco, had exclaimed,

"Die, little traitor, enemy of ours who goes about deceiving the world with your lies, and who calls himself the savior of our world and the King of the Jews."

To which another cries out, "Crucify this charlatan who calls himself our King and who says that he has within him the power to destroy our temple, and who through spells and magic claims to be able to kill us and carry out revenge upon us. Crucify him, the dog, crucify him!"

And when it was over, the heart was placed in a box and mixed with the consecrated Host, and the sorcerer of the group waved his arms and said his magic words over the confection to conjure up the destruction of Christianity.

The case had become too big and important to be handled locally. And so, with pride in his vigilance in the face of heresy, the vicar of Astorga sent his report directly to the Grand Inquisitor, Tomás de Torquemada.

❖

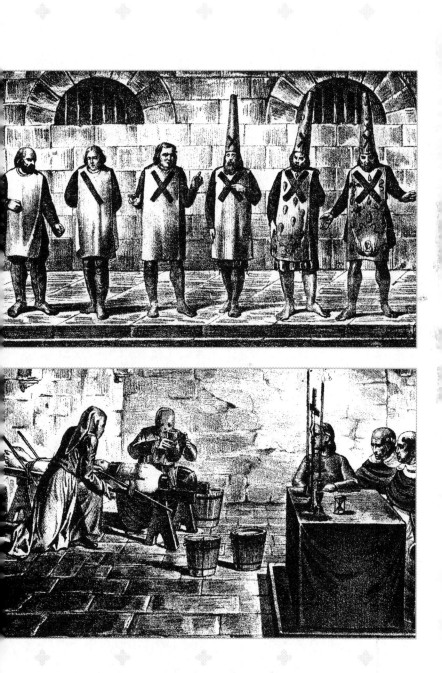

SCENE FROM
THE INQUISITION
(Courtesy of
the Library of Congress)

EXPULSION ORDER,
MARCH 31, 1492
(Ávila Municipal Archives,
from Beth Hatefutsoth Photo
Archive, Tel Aviv)

TORQUEMADA CONFRONTS THE CATHOLIC KINGS OVER
EXPULSION COMPROMISE
(Ya'akov Brill, from Beth Hatefutsoth Photo Archive, Tel Aviv)

JEWS EXPELLED FROM SPAIN
(Beth Hatefutsoth Photo Archive, Tel Aviv)

MOORISH EMIRS
APPEAL TO THE
CATHOLIC
MONARCHS
(*Real Academia de Bellas
Artes de San Fernando*)

COLUMBUS AT
LA RÁBIDA

COLUMBUS'S ROYAL LETTER OF INTRODUCTION TO ORIENTAL
POTENTATES SUCH AS THE GRAND KHAN OF CATHAY
(*Archivo de la Corona de Aragón*)

CARAVELS SAILING
(*Museo Naval de Madrid*)

ALEXANDER VI's BULL DIVIDING THE WORLD *(Biblioteca de las Indias)*

THE DEATH OF ISABELLA, 1504 *(Museo del Prado, Spain)*

In the latter half of 1490, the Grand Inquisitor was well pleased with the situation. He had become the third most powerful man in Spain and virtually independent from his titular leader in Rome. His institution was well established in all of Christian Spain, and he essentially had a free hand while the sovereigns were preoccupied with the war in the south. In the nine years of the Spanish Inquisition, some three thousand heretics had been burned at the stake, and thirty thousand lesser strays had been "penanced" with lighter sentences. His home base remained the Dominican monastery of San Tomás in the suburbs of Ávila. As he let his mind rest on his national reach, he must have been flattered not only at the millions who feared him but also those legions who hated him.

He was, of course, in constant danger of assassination. As a result, in what seems like a touch of uncharacteristic whimsy, his desk was adorned with a sculpture of a unicorn's horn that was believed to ward off the effects of poison. When he traveled, which was often, an escort of fifty cavalrymen and two hundred foot soldiers accompanied him. He slept in palaces throughout the land, but usually on the floor in his hair shirt.

In one respect, Ferdinand and Isabella had frustrated his ambitions. As part of the purification of Spain and the final victory of Catholicism there, Torquemada passionately wanted to drive all Jews from the peninsula. Across Europe there was precedent for this extreme measure. England had expelled its Jews in 1290; France had tried the same measure several times (though its sway was temporary); and a number of provinces in Germany had expelled their Jews, accompanying the expedient with bloody pogroms.

Isabella especially was resistant to the idea of expulsion, no doubt in part due to the influence of the powerful court rabbis, Abraham Senior and Isaac Abravanel. But Torquemada knew how to manage the monarchs. With Ferdinand, he could appeal to money. With Isabella, he could appeal to her piety, her desire for public happiness, her stature as the Virgin Mary incarnate or the Spanish version of the Apocalyptic Woman, portrayed in the book of Revelation, chapter 12, verse 1: "And there appeared a great wonder in heaven; a woman clothed with the sun, and the moon under her feet, and upon her head a crown of twelve stars. . . ." He remembered well that Isabella had also been adverse to the establishment of the Inquisition itself, but she had been won over by outside pressure. What Torquemada needed now was a lurid event that might inflame public hysteria against the Jews.

In the nine conspirators of La Guardia who were in his possession, the Grand Inquisitor saw a gift. Torquemada took personal charge of the investigation. For the hands-on interrogation of the case, he appointed three inquisitors, awarding the vicar of Astorga, Pedro de Villanda, one of the posts. Six months of interrogation ensued, sometimes individually, sometimes collectively in groups of three. Along the way, torture was frequent, pitiless, unrelenting. In the process, three of the Jewish suspects died. The problem with so much torture was that the victim was predisposed to say anything, having constantly to guess what magic words he might utter to stop the winches.

Inevitably, nine different stories emerged. The nine could not agree on the year of the supposed crime, nor the age of the victim who was professed to be somewhere between three and eight years old. There was no good answer to the question of motive: why would Jews who were not subject to the Inquisition risk involvement in so dangerous a ceremony? Some confessed that only the human heart had been brought to the cave, others that there were two hearts and two communion wafers. Still others testified that the boy had been brought alive and crucified in the cave, while another desperate babbler added the neat detail that the boy had been lashed 5,500 times on his way to the cave, five more than Jesus Christ was believed to have received on his way to Calvary.

From somewhere else a bit of interesting dialogue was salted into the ever-embroidered story. With the martyr's chest wide open, Benito García searched around in the gore, while the boy said calmly,

"What are you looking for, Jew? . . . if for my heart, you will find it on the other side."

Besides the inconsistencies, absurdities, and contradictions of the testimony, there was the problem of the martyr's identity. The Inquisition initiated a widespread manhunt. By one account the boy hailed from Quintanar, a town southeast of Toledo. But no report of a missing child had been filed there. Indeed, no child had been reported missing anywhere in the province of Toledo. No grieving mother turned up. One prisoner confessed to having buried the child after the ritual and provided the coordinates of the grave. But no grave and no body were found, only a little disturbed dirt at the designated spot. Finally, the Inquisition settled on the canard that Benito García had picked up an urchin in front of the Cathedral of Toledo. Predictably, they gave the martyr the name of Cristóbal. To account for the lack of a distraught mother, it was announced that the holy child was the offspring of a blind woman!

After sixteen months of investigation and torture, the Inquisition gave up on blending the testimony into a consistent, plausible story. Plausibility was no hurdle, and there was no court of appeal. Two juries examined the case. The first comprised seven noted scholars from Salamanca University who proclaimed the guilt of the accused. The second comprised five "learned men" from Ávila who seconded the decision of the first.

Their decision was unanimous.

A day after the sentence was announced, the Inquisition warned the local populace not to talk about the discrepancies and insufficiencies of the testimony. In so doing, a proverbial phrase was used. One should not gossip, *"porque el asno está enalbardado—*

. . . because the ass is saddled."

❖

The veneration of the child martyr began immediately after the execution of the conspirators. The Holy Innocent of La Guardia was compared to St. Hugh the Little, the nine-year-old boy from Lincoln, England, who had supposedly been the victim of a similar ritual killing in 1255 and had continued to sing sweetly, due to the intervention of the Virgin Mary, even after his throat had been slit. Nineteen Jews had been executed for that act, and the case was later invoked by Geoffrey

Chaucer in the *Canterbury Tales*, when he referred to the Jewish quarters as the "waspish nest" of Satan and proclaimed, "O cursed folk of Herod come again/Of what avail your villainous intent?" The Prioress concludes her tale this way:

> O yong Hugh of Lincoln, slayn also
> With cursed Jews, as it is notable,
> For it is but a litel whyle ago;
> Pray eek for us, we sinnful folk unstable
> That of his mercy, God so merciable
> On us his grete mercy multiplye,
> For reverence of his moder Marye. Amen.

According to the Church, miracles followed quickly on the heels of the sentence. The holy child-martyr became the patron saint of the village of La Guardia. It was reported that the boy's mother had come forward and was found to have recovered her sight! The devout prayed for the recovery of the child's bones, but when they did not turn up, it was proclaimed that from the spot of disturbed earth, the Almighty had taken the remains to heaven on the third day after the boy's crucifixion. It was added that his mother had regained her eyesight exactly three days after her son's death, or at the very moment when her son's body was being lifted to heaven by God. The consecrated Host, which had been found initially in Benito Garcia's knapsack, had been secretly kept within the leaves of a Book of Hours. The purported book was put on display in Torquemada's Convent of San Tomás and was later credited with protecting Ávila from an outbreak of the plague. Several hundred years later, the book was still on display, its pages still sparkling and limber and uncorrupted as if they had been printed the day before.

In time, the Holy Innocent of La Guardia moved from religious fable into Spanish literature. The story was to have lasting power, especially in later centuries when the flames of anti-Semitism were fanned. Passion plays were written about the episode, as well as poetry. A hundred years after the episode, in 1592, a Spanish poet named Jerónimo

Ramírez wrote an epic poem in Latin, divided into six books about the "passion of the Innocent Martyr of La Guardia." Written in the first person as verse directed to the Almighty, four lines convey its spirit.

La Guardia turns its devoted face to You
and watches the body of the boy carried over the rocks
devoured alone after he has survived many blows
He saturates a vast nation with his blood.

❧

The case of the Holy Child of La Guardia was exceptional in many respects, not least of which was the speed with which it moved from interrogation to trial and disposition. The propagandistic and psychological value of the case accounts for this dispatch. But the majority of cases took far longer to be adjudicated. If nothing else, the Inquisition was patient. To mold all the hearsay and confessionals into a coherent and plausible form took time. There was no rush. And sometimes when coherence and plausibility could not be achieved, condemnation came anyway.

For the thousands upon thousands of suspects, the bulk of incriminating evidence rested upon reports of the converted Christian being caught secretly observing Jewish rites and customs. Sins of both commission and omission could get a converso into big trouble. The list of forbidden acts was long. First, there were the revealing dietary practices.

If a person abstained from eating fat or lard, it was probably due to the Jewish requirement to avoid pork in any form. Since it is difficult to distinguish bovine fat from pork lard, both were forbidden.

If a person made a habit of cooking a stew containing vegetables, meat (if available), and spices for twenty-four hours and served it at midday, this was probably hamin or the traditional Shabbat warm meal of the Jewish Sabbath.

If a converso was caught eating matzo at Passover, he was surely a secret Jew commemorating the swift exodus from Egypt and slavery when the Jews barely escaped the wrath of the Pharoah.

If a woman removed the sinew before cooking a piece of meat, she was surely thinking of the episode, beloved in Jewish lore, when Jacob wrestled with the angel of the Lord, and the angel touched the hollow of Jacob's thigh, and it went out of joint, and the angel proclaimed that Jacob's name would no longer be Jacob but Israel. In the Book of Genesis it is written: "Therefore the children of Israel eat not of the sinew which shrank which is upon the hollow of the thigh unto this day because he [the angel] touched the hollow of Jacob's thigh in the sinew that shrank."

If someone was seen eating raw eggs upon the death of a loved one, he was probably observing the Jewish belief in eggs as the source of life. This was a custom peculiar to Spanish Jews of the time.

If someone else was noticed tossing bits of dough into the fire while he was kneading bread, he was probably thinking of the days of the Temple in Jerusalem when sacrifice was the means of worship.

And if a converso ate meat during Lent or was seen fasting on Jewish holy days of Yom Kippur and Purim or going barefoot on these days, he or she was in trouble. For according to the Talmud, four things are forbidden on Yom Kippur, the major fast day in the Jewish calendar: eating, drinking, sexual intercourse, and wearing footwear. On Purim, a minor fast day called the fast of Esther, Spanish Jews also went barefoot.

Then there were the suspect signs involving cloth. It was dangerous to be seen putting out a fresh tablecloth for Friday night dinner and wearing clean clothing on Saturdays, for this was surely a sign of welcoming the Jewish Sabbath and celebrating it in a festive atmosphere. Other dangerous practices were the presence of a Hebrew Bible in the house or a grandfather blessing a child by passing the hand over the forehead. The latter suggested the Jewish emphasis on the veneration of the elders and came from the incident in the Bible of Isaac blessing his son Jacob. A grandfather blessing a grandchild, usually on the eve of Sabbath, was (and is) a Jewish tradition of transmitting the blessings of the elder, accrued during a long life, from generation to generation.

It was perilous to speak well of Jews or give them alms; to rest on Saturday and work on Sunday. It was deadly to ignore the Lord's Prayer at a Christian service or not know the words to the Nicene Creed, to neglect to make the sign of the cross or fail to kneel when the Eucharist was raised heavenward by the priest. For the eyes of the inquisitional police were everywhere.

The case of one Brianda de Bardaxi is representative of the process. She was a thirty-year-old housewife and conversa who lived a quiet, ostensibly pious, reasonably comfortable existence in northern Aragon. But Brianda's relationship with her mother was troubled, for the matriarch seethed with resentment over her belief that her daughter had taken too large a portion of the family estate. The seventy-year-old mother lived in Barbastro with her widowed daughter-in-law, who also passionately disliked Brianda.

After the Inquisition was established in Aragon in 1484 under the leadership of Torquemada, Brianda de Bardaxi was called to the Holy Office. Given the threat implicit in the Edict of Grace, she presented herself promptly for questioning. Being assured of the secrecy of her testimony, encouraged to demonstrate her sincerity by providing evidence against others, and governed by the transcendent instinct to protect herself and her property, she provided a few seemingly harmless and trivial anecdotes from her childhood. When she was five years old, she said, she had once witnessed her mother fasting until nightfall. At age ten she remembered hearing a woman named Violate Fayol utter a few words in Hebrew and had seen her barefoot. When the girl asked the woman why she was barefoot, the woman replied that this was a day for Jews to fast. And then at age fifteen she had again seen her mother fast, together with her boarder, Brianda's sister-in-law. Promptly, the mother and sister-in-law were called in for questioning. There could scarcely be any doubt about where the testimony against them had originated.

Several years passed, years in which the first inquisitor of Aragon had been poisoned, and the second, Pedro Arbués, had been murdered at the altar in the Cathedral of Saragossa. In the reign of terror that followed, Brianda's mother and sister-in-law were brought to trial and sentenced to do penance for their lapses. In their interrogations, they named Brianda and charged that she had been an enthusiastic participant in the fasts about which she had originally told the inquisitors. And so Brianda was brought in for depositions both in 1485 and 1486. Two years later, on February 9, 1488, charges were filed against her, and the case moved to a more serious stage.

Now an acquaintance named Gilabert Despluges stepped forward with his two daughters. Also a converso, he was under suspicion for apostasy, and his wife had already been burned at the stake. The Despluges family testified to having heard Brianda proclaim herself to be a secret Jew. Yet another acquaintance swore that she once heard Brianda say about the assassinated and martyred inquisitor, Pedro Arbués, that "his only fault was that he purchased testimony." This of course would constitute a libel against the famous martyr of the local church.

Three more years passed. But then on February 17, 1491, she was examined for the sixth time. In this interrogation, Brianda added a few details to her prior testimony. It was true that when she was five or six years old, she had actually ingested one or two mouthfuls of matzo, but she had not found the stuff tasty. Further, she remembered that at age twelve she had been offered the Jewish stew, hamin, on the Jewish Sabbath in the household of her accusers, Gilabert and María Despluges, but had refused it. This refusal had nearly caused a fistfight with Gilabert's daughter, María Despluges. (María Despluges had been penanced in 1488 when at her *auto-da-fe* she was pardoned and avoided the confiscation of her property as a reward for her pious service of providing testimony against Brianda. For his part, her father, Gilabert, accomplished little by his accusations against Brianda. Ten years later, he followed his wife to the scaffold and was burned at his own *auto-da-fe*.)

As the case was referred to inquisitional headquarters in Saragossa, the Bardaxi matter was getting serious enough that a counsel was appointed to defend her. By regulation, the Inquisition provided him. But the lawyer put up a surprisingly spirited defense. He drew up a list of forty witnesses who swore under oath that Brianda de Bardaxi was a sincere and devout Christian, who observed the obligations of Catholicism faithfully, prayed every day, frequently ate fat and lard, contributed her money generously to the benefit and succor of the Church, and had applied to the pope to provide her with a confessor. Further testimony swore that upon the murder of Pedro Arbués, she had sent a servant to dip a cloth into the miraculously liquefied blood of the martyr, had kissed the cloth and forced her household staff to do the same.

With this body of exculpatory testimony, the preponderance of the evidence was now weighted in Brianda's favor. By the Inquisition's math, however, the charges against her were only half proven. In order to condemn her, a fresh confession was needed. One last time she was commanded to confess and confess more or she would be tortured. Stoutly, Brianda maintained her innocence and professed her readiness to be tortured. However, she said with incredible courage, anything she might say in the torture chamber would be invalid, for it would be the fruit of fear and agony. When it was over, she would deny everything she had said.

This was taken for impertinence and disrespect, and she was hustled off to the torture chamber. Over the next three days the water torture was administered repeatedly, with predictable results. On the trestle, she was commanded to enumerate the Jewish rites she had observed. She replied that she would need some help. What were the those Jewish rituals anyway? The inquisitor enumerated them. By the third day she was saying that she had observed them all. Which ones? The ones you mentioned.

On the third day she was again brought before the chief inquisitor and yet again commanded to confess the Jewish rites she had performed. You can torture me a hundred times, she said, and a hundred times I will confess and afterward I will recant my confession.

Such contempt for the inquisitional court could not be tolerated, and so she was returned to the torture chamber, where they stripped her naked. Instead of the water treatment, she was prepared for the bone-crushing remedy called the *strappado* (in which the wrists are tied, the body hoisted, and then dropped the length of the rope). But the fear and pain of the past three days had taken their toll. At these preparations, she fainted unconscious to the floor, her body temperature turned cold, and she had to be returned to her prison. The charges against her remained unproven.

On March 28, 1492, the year of the apocalypse in Spain, Brianda mounted the scaffold at the Church of Our Lady of Grace. At last, the Inquisition had moved its suspect to the place it wanted. At this *auto-da-fe* she mumbled the words that the Inquisition required: that she had in fact eaten lard, that she learned the Jewish rites at the home of her accuser, Gilabert Despluges, that she had rejoiced at the death of the inquisitor, Pedro Arbués, and had said that his only fault was that he purchased testimony, and that as a child she had eaten Passover bread.

At this litany of sins, the inquisitor condemned her in the name of Christ: "We find that we must declare and pronounce her suspect of the crimes and heresy and apostasy which she has abjured. As these suspicions must not remain unpunished, we assign to her as penance that she never again commit these crimes and errors. We condemn her to imprisonment at our discretion, reserving such other penance as we may see fit to impose. We condemn her in the costs of the case, the taxation of which we reserve to ourselves."

She was sent to the tower of Saldaña, where she was to confess and receive the holy sacrament three times a year. One third of her property was confiscated.

And so in the grand scheme of things, Brianda de Bardaxi had done her part to support the war against Granada. The proceeds of her property, along with the stolen wealth of tens of thousands of others, was tossed into the war chest that the Inquisition was providing to the Catholic monarchs to complete the Christian Reconquest of Spain. In the last few years of that historic war, the Inquisition was the Christian army's paymaster.

19

The Will of Allah

❖

 After the fall of Málaga in 1487, half of the last Moorish kingdom was in Christian hands, while the greatest prize of all—Granada and its Alhambra—was in the hands of Ferdinand's lapdog, Boabdil the Unfortunate. East of the Alhambra, however, Boabdil's uncle, El Zagal the Valiant, still ruled the last three Moorish strongholds of Guadix, Baza, and Almería, as well as large portions of the Alpujarras hills south of the towering ridgeline of the magnificent Sierra Nevada. The valleys of these hills, fed by the snowmelt from the Sierra Nevada, were among the most fertile and prosperous in Iberia. Besides the orchards and fertile fields of the Alpujarras, the finest silk in Spain was spun here.

Even in this shrunken domain, El Zagal remained powerful and dangerous, and he was soon to demonstrate it. From the cities and villages, he could still mobilize an impressive army of fifty thousand tough, battle-hardened mountain soldiers, who moved fast and who were expert in the tactics of surprise and ambush. After Málaga, the old warhorse called a complement of these fighters to arms for an expedition to the northwest, as much to bolster the spirits of his despondent followers as to recover lost ground. Slipping out of Guadix, he marched north of Granada into the province of Jaén, where he burned villages and rampaged in the countryside around Alcalá la Real, slipping away to Guadix again, heavy-laden with booty, before the Christian side could mount a counterattack.

To Ferdinand, it was pointless to accept the gift of Granada from Boabdil until El Zagal was subdued, and his three strongholds captured. And so, secretly, Ferdinand and Boabdil negotiated a devil's agreement: the keys of the Alhambra would be handed over only after Baza, Guadix, and Almería came into Christian hands. When the exchange was consummated, an extensive fief east of Granada would be conferred on Boabdil, and he would be able to live luxuriously in peace and security as Ferdinand's vassal. Only Boabdil's mother, the sultana, Ayxa the Chaste, knew of this cowardly deal, and she was none too pleased. Already Boabdil was so loathed by his subjects that they would certainly rip him limb from limb had they known what treachery was afoot.

In the spring of 1488, Ferdinand mobilized his army east of the Moorish dominion in the city of Murcia. His force was smaller than usual, fourteen thousand foot soldiers and four thousand cavalry; worse, the Christian soldiers were bursting with overconfidence. They entered Moorish lands along the coast, easily took the seaside village of Vera, and made for Almería. This ancient, proud port had been founded by the Phoenicians before the time of Christ, and since the Moors captured the city in the eighth century, they had built a formidable *alcazaba*, or fortress, on a bluff above the port during the reign of the great Abd ar-Rahmān III in the tenth century when Almería was the eastern jewel of the Umayyad dynasty in Córdoba. In the first centuries of Moorish rule, Almería eclipsed Granada in glory, epitomized by the rhyming couplet *"Cuando Almería era Almería, Granada era su alquería*—When Almería was Almería, Granada was her farm." The governor of the city was El Zagal's cousin and brother-in-law, Prince Cidi Yahye, a proud and seasoned warrior.

As the Christian force drew close to Almería, it encountered increasingly formidable resistance. When King Ferdinand came within sight of the city itself, he appreciated its strength immediately. His current force was wholly insufficient to mount a substantial assault on the bastion. After gathering the intelligence he might need for a future campaign, he withdrew and directed his army north to Baza.

There he was in for a bigger surprise. In this equally formidable bastion, El Zagal personally awaited him. As the marquis of Cádiz and his advance guard came whistling into the valley, El Zagal pounced upon it ferociously, driving the Christian soldiers into the warren of gardens outside the town and proceeding to slice the invaders up. As with the first Battle of Loja, Ferdinand was administered an instructive horse-whipping. He had made the mistake of entering hostile territory, short on men and artillery, full of empty pride. Before he lost more of his finest chivalry for no reason, he gave the order for a speedy withdrawal.

The entire fighting season of 1488 had been squandered in over-weaning pride. The king would not again underestimate the enemy. He took his army back east to Murcia and disbanded it. To gather his thoughts and concentrate on the embarrassment of this wasted season, he withdrew to the holy sanctuary of Caravaca to reflect and pray.

For such a trauma the pilgrimage site of Caravaca de la Cruz was an appropriate retreat for the chastened king. Its fame derived from an episode that was believed to have taken place 250 years before. Then, so the legend goes, a Moorish lord was intrigued by the Christian faith and asked the local priest to celebrate a Christian mass, so that the Moor could witness the liturgy and make up his mind about whether to convert. Reluctantly, the priest agreed. But when he assembled his holy implements, he found that he did not have a proper cross. Without this essential, the priest was about to call the whole thing off, when two angels flew through the window bearing a silver cross.

The relic was there still to remind both the holy and the powerful to make their preparations full and complete before they appealed for salvation or triumph.

❖

In the spring of 1489, the Christian army mobilized in Jaén with renewed determination and greater wisdom. The rains were frequent and heavy well into May, a condition that made all roads to Jaén slick, rutted, and often washed out. It was not until the end of that month that the army was ready. This time, the force had ballooned to forty thousand foot soldiers and thirteen thousand cavalry. With the Cardinal of

Spain standing beside them, Ferdinand and Isabella looked on with satisfaction. For what they hoped would be the final assault on Granada and the consummation of a 500-year-old quest to reconquer Spain for Christianity, the monarchs were confident that the mistake of unpreparedness would not be repeated. For Ferdinand, the king, the code of the warrior reigned: he wished to avenge the humiliation of the year before.

Baza now lay in their sights as the first objective. If Baza fell, the monarchs expected Guadix and Almería to topple quickly after.

Some fifty miles to the east of Jaén, the town of Baza presented an awesome fortress. Protected by high palisades, it was built on the slope of a hill, enclosed by massive walls with immense towers and a small stream at its foot. Beyond the stream, outlying residences stretched for half a mile; and beyond them lay the complex of walled gardens and groves that had so confused and bedeviled the Christian forces the year before. Of special pride to Baza's citizens were the groves of stately oak, mulberry, and wild pine trees that graced the gardens and provided many pleasant walks for the citizens.

The town itself was constructed around an ancient central plaza; narrow alleys and streets radiated outward haphazardly. On one of these narrow byways was the famous atelier where magnificent silk prayer rugs of great renown were woven. The approach to the town was across a wide basin of undulating ground, striated by small streams. The high ground on the western road to Guadix was guarded by a number of conical, brush-covered hillocks that greeted the traveler and the invader alike as sentinals.

When El Zagal got word in Guadix of the Christian mobilization in Jaén, he guessed that Baza was the Christian objective. Though Guadix was only thirty-five miles south of Baza, the old warrior was loath to leave his bastion for fear that the unpredictable, flighty Boabdil might venture out of Granada and take advantage. El Zagal called on his most trusted comrade, Prince Cidi Yahye, the governor of Almería, to assume the command of Baza. Cidi Yahye was El Zagal's cousin and brother-in-law, and he rose to the call enthusiastically. El Zagal was grateful.

"You are my second self," El Zagal wrote his cousin affectionately. "Happy is the monarch who has his kinsman to command his armies."

Cidi Yahye did more than avail himself of this important last-ditch command. In his port of Almería, he gathered a force of ten thousand Moorish fighters and marched them double-time to Baza. Meanwhile, El Zagal sent out the call to Jihad. All true believers in Islam were called to the defense of their homes, their liberty, and their religion.

O you who believe! Answer Allah by obeying him and His Messenger when he calls you. To fight in Allah's cause is your third best deed! And by this deed, you make Allah's Word superior! He who avoids this duty dies a hypocrite, and say not of those who are killed in the Way of Allah, "They are dead." Nay, they are living, but you perceive it not!

There was a sense on both sides that Islam was approaching its final apocalyptic battle with Christianity. From the far corners of the last Moorish state the soldiers poured into Baza, including a number who had slipped out of the Granada of El Zagal's nephew, Boabdil. Between Prince Cidi Yahye's troops from the south and El Zagal's jihadists, the garrison of Baza doubled.

As the rains delayed the arrival of the Christian army, Baza became an immense stockyard, grainery, storehouse, and armory. When the gardens and the groves were picked clean, the spring wheat in the surrounding countryside was cut prematurely to salvage whatever nutritional value it might have and to deprive the invading army of sustenance. Meanwhile, the stockpiles of weapons and munitions filled the stone caverns of the walls. Toward the end of May, Cidi Yahye calculated that he had enough food and firepower to survive a siege of fifteen months. To his gathered soldiers, he proclaimed,

"We fight for life and liberty, for our families, our country, our religion. Nothing is left for us to depend upon but the strength of our hands, the courage of our hearts, and the almighty protection of Allah."

Meanwhile, only a few miles to the north, the clatter of hoofbeats, the grave, basso thump of kettledrums, the din of a holy army massing filled the air of Jaén. And in this furtive atmosphere, the Catholic monarchs issued a most curious order. On May 12, they put out the following summons: "The King and Queen to members of the court, justices, knights, squires, officials and all honest men in all cities and villages of our kingdom: Christopher Columbus must come to this court to concentrate himself on certain matters in our service. We command that when he should pass through cities and towns he must be given good lodgings for himself without charge, if not at inns, and provided maintenance at fair prices. You must not quarrel with him, or hinder him in any way, under pain of our justice and a fine of 10,000 maravedis."

Why Christopher Columbus? Why now? In the preparations for Armageddon, what possible impulse could have motivated the monarchs? When terrible realities faced them in the coming days, they could scarcely have been interested in fantasizing yet again about the magical island of Cipangu, the golden pagodas of Cathay, or the jewels of the Great Khan. After the conclusions of the Talavera commission, most of the court viewed Columbus as a suave gadfly and insufferable boaster; not the "Christ-bearer," as he would later like to think of himself, but the bearer of bad science. Was he summoned as entertainment, as diversion, from the terrible anxieties of the moment?

A partial answer may lie in Columbus's possible value as an agent of intelligence about the enemy. Just as he had been summoned to the war camp at Málaga two years before, presumably to impart his knowledge of that port and its defenders, so now the Spanish army had the port of Almería as a war objective. In his many commercial ventures, trading goods and slaves in the Andalusian ports for various Genovese concerns, had Columbus also called at Almería? What did he know of Cidi Yahye? Had Columbus had any direct dealings with the prince?

Still, Columbus had his important boosters, few though they may have been. The faithful count of Medina Celi, for example, kept his offer in place to provide 4,000 gold ducats for the construction of three caravels and the wherewithal to supply them with sailors and supplies for a year. Columbus's commanding presence in court fascinated and amused Queen Isabella, and she liked to have him around. If he was to be supported at all, she insisted on doing it. His stately bearing re-minded some of a Roman senator, even if his suave ways reminded oth-ers of an oily huckster.

Once in the royal presence he knew how to adapt his grandiose dreams to the timbre of the court. If Spanish Christianity was on the verge of the final apocalyptic battle with Spanish Islam, his proposal could add to the glory of a Christian victory. As Spain was reconquered for Christianity, so a New World might be unveiled in the dawning of a new golden age. In a cosmic drama, Discovery must join Reconquest and Purification. Together, the three fitted into the new heaven and the new earth that was promised in the book of Revelation. Ferdinand, Torque-mada, and Columbus were to be the queen's—and God's—instruments in this passion play.

Columbus was not the only exotic visitor to contribute to this mag-nificent vision. At about the same time, two friars from the Convent of the Holy Sepulchre in Jerusalem arrived with a terrifying ultimatum from the Mameluke sultan in Cairo. Unless the Catholic monarchs ceased their assault on Islam and the Moorish empire of Granada, the sultan threatened to execute all the Christians in his empire, destroy all the convents and churches, and level the Holy Sepulchre itself.

At this menacing threat, Columbus put forward a new argument to Queen Isabella. If she would fund his adventure, and if it were to prove successful, he would contribute its profits to fund a glorious new crusade to the Holy Land to wrest the holy Christian sites from the infidel.

Columbus's offer summoned yet again the fondest dream of King Ferdinand. His destiny, the king believed, was to drive the infidel from Spain, to purify its religion of heresy and superstition, and then, as a modern-day King David, to return the Ark of the Covenant to the City of David, heralding the Second Coming of Christ and the kingdom of heaven on earth. It would be he, clothed in fine linen, hailed with cor-nets and shouting, who would sanctify himself and his brothers and then bring the Christian Jubilee to the Holy Land. He, Ferdinand V of Spain, would fulfill the prophecy of the twelfth-century Italian mystic and apocalyptic theologian, Joachim of Fiore,

"He who will restore the ark of Zion will come from Spain."

In early June, Ferdinand entered the basin of Baza with his grand and colorful army and pitched his tents just beyond the expansive warren of gardens and orchards that buffered the city. Brazenly, he sent a message to Prince Cidi Yahye to surrender or die. This haughty communication infuriated the Moor, and he was for sending back a petulant, snappish reply. But one of his generals calmed him down.

"Let us threaten what we know we can perform," he said. "And let us endeavor to perform more than we threaten."

Within a day, Ferdinand launched his attack. With some trepidation, Christian knights entered the fearsome labyrinth of gardens and orchards. Between its many walled enclosures, its small canals, its tall and densely packed orchards, cavalry was useless. The Christian knights were immediately attacked by Moorish foot soldiers, and they were forced to dismount and fight on foot hand-to-hand. A hundred separate battles broke out in the various enclosures, a situation that favored the clever and well-commanded Moors, who knew the terrain and knew how to communicate from one garden to the next, one grove to another. The fighting was fierce, and the battles lasted twelve hours, until darkness fell and contact was broken off.

The next day, Ferdinand surveyed a scene of desolation. His confused and battered forces had withdrawn beyond the gardens once again, too far from the walls of the city for his artillery to have any effect, just as his cavalry was powerless within the gardens themselves. His council of war gathered to analyze the situation. Uncharacteristically, the marquis of Cádiz, hero of so many Christian battles in the war against the Moors, argued for realism. Baza was simply too well defended, its situation too advantageous to the defenders, its commanders too experienced and clever for the Christian side to prevail. To subdue the town would take weeks, if not months, and the problems of sustaining and supplying an army of fifty thousand in a protracted siege were both overwhelming and novel. Where was the money to come from to fund such an effort? They should withdraw, argued the marquis, and concentrate on the minor outposts not only around Baza but around Guadix and Almería, so that the three bastions could be completely isolated and starved out in the following year.

Other generals disputed their field general. To withdraw would reinvigorate the enemy, not weaken him, and make him more formidable rather than less in the following year. The battle had been joined, Christian against Muslim, Spain against Africa. This was no ordinary war but a crusade, and they, in the name of the Christian God, must persist.

There was a conflict within the high command. Given his aggressive nature, Ferdinand tilted toward the voices of perseverance, but he was wary of deciding one way or another without Queen Isabella's input. A messenger was dispatched to Jaén, where Isabella had remained with her children, the Cardinal of Spain (and Christopher Columbus). Her reply was gracious and deferential. Ferdinand and his generals should resolve their differences. She would not do it for them. But if their decision was to continue the siege, she would step forward to take charge of the titanic undertaking of supplying the great army.

This missive was sufficient to end the dispute. From the parapets of the town, the Moors cheered as the Christians struck their tents and began to withdraw. Once the soldiers mustered in the open basin, however, the army split into two, with the two flanks commanded by the king and by the marquis, and then returned to reposition itself on either side of Baza's extensive gardens. In the coming days, despite constant harassment from squads of Moorish commandos, the engineers went to work building an extensive system of defensive canals, berms, and towers. Later, an effort was made to divert the stream at the base of the town. Knights decorated their tents colorfully, fashioning makeshift roofs and walls to protect them from the weather, until the encampment looked less like a tent city than a colorful slum of shacks.

Weeks stretched into months. Within the town, Cidi Yahye did his best to buck up the spirits of the defenders. "The Infidel king builds his hopes on our growing fainthearted," he told them. "We must show unusual cheerfulness and vigor. What would be rashness elsewhere becomes prudence for us now."

In Jaén, meanwhile, Isabella worked feverishly to meet her side of the bargain. The rear area began a huge supply depot through which reinforcements tramped daily, and wagon trains passed with loads of flour, meat, and wine, followed by an army of tinkers and artisans ready to sell their wares or provide their services to soldiers with nowhere to go but a few maravedis to spend. Young bloods spent lavishly to outdo one another in outfitting themselves in colorful helmets or brocaded caparisons for their steeds.

Shiploads of wheat and barley from Catalonia and León came through the captured port of Vera. The number of beasts of burden the queen hired was estimated to be fourteen thousand. She muscled merchants and wealthy churches in Castile and Aragon for every last ducat. Where outright requisition was not possible, she resorted to loans. To demonstrate her personal investment in the holy siege, she even hocked some of her most precious jewels. The vital task of overseeing the fair distribution of these supplies was put in the hands of the eminent physician and courtier Rodrigo Maldonado. He had been on the commission to investigate Christopher Columbus's proposal, but more important, immediate business pressed on him now.

Summer bled into fall, and the defenders were heartened. "The rainy season is at hand," Cidi Yahye told his soldiers. "The floods will soon pour down from the mountains. The rivers will overflow their banks and inundate the valleys. The Christian king already begins to waver. He dare not linger and encounter such a season in a plain, cut up by canals and swollen rivers. A single wintry storm from our mountains will wash away his canvas city and sweep off those colorful pavilions like wisps of snow before the blizzard."

After five months of confinement this was a brave front, but the strains were beginning to show. Secretly, Cidi Yahye wrote to El Zagal in Guadix that if the grip of the siege was not loosened soon, he would be forced to open negotiations with the infidel. He wrote in the spirit of the Koran: *Make ready against them all you can of power, including steeds of war, to threaten the enemy of Allah and your enemy, and whatever you shall spend in the cause of Allah shall be repaid unto you, and you shall not be treated unjustly.* El Zagal had his own problems, however. He had no steeds of war to give. *But if they incline to peace, you also incline to it, and put your trust in Allah. Verily, He is the All hearer, the All knower.*

Ferdinand had his own strains. Between the daily harassment, the boredom, the deprivations of camp life, the army was growing restless. Desertion was becoming a problem. In fact, in October, as the Moor had predicted, a ferocious storm did sweep over the area, washing away the makeshift shacks and colorful pavilions of the Christians, leaving pennants and battle flags to be carried away in rivers of mud. Surveying the damage, the king, not the Moor, took the initiative toward an accommodation. He sent a message through to Cidi Yahye offering liberty and the security of property, as well as huge rewards for him and his top generals, in return for surrender.

"Leader of the Arabs: you are well aware of how many deaths and damages have been inflicted upon your city over the past six months. For your people as well as the soldiers of my own royal army, in addition to those who will soon be arriving, we must find an honest compromise. . . ."

The Moor high command rejoiced. The message was an expression of desperation.

"A little more patience," a Muslim commander said, "and we shall see this cloud of Christian locusts driven away before the winter storms. Once they turn their backs, it will be our turn to strike, and with the help of Allah, the blow will be decisive."

The apparent stalemate could only be broken by some dramatic surprise, and that was to take place in November with a roll of kettledrums, a flash of color, and a rustle of taffeta in the far distance. Up the valley came a procession of Christian knights in their finest costumes of velvet, silk, and brocade, with colorful plumes flowing from their steel helmets and banners streaming from their lances. And in the midst of this column, dressed in an extravagant gown, accompanied by the Cardinal of Spain and her eldest daughter, Isabel, rode Queen Isabella herself. For all the pomp, the shrill blaring of clarions, clatter of steel and hoofbeat, the queen rode demurely on a mule.

The Moors watched this amazing pageant in awe from the walls. Hotheads implored their superiors to venture out and attack, or at least unleash a volley of artillery to disturb this flaunting of Christian power and elegance. But Cidi Yahye forbade it. It was an enduring irony that among the Moors, for all their desperation, the figure of Queen Isabella was honored almost with reverence. The Moorish soldiers were reduced to the role of gawking spectators, as if this were a field of sport, and they were the fawning audience. They watched meekly as the king greeted his lady.

It was as if the whole army longed for her presence, as if it were her collective lover. The poetry in her honor showed this yearning for this woman and symbol, and the sentiment seemed especially apt during the stalemate at Baza.

> My *soul is starving. I appeal*
> *For your help. I'm near to dying.*
> *All the world knows*
> *That you alone can heal my predicament.*

This psychological masterstroke had an immediate effect. With the arrival of the queen, the passion for conflict waned. There could be no further doubt of the Christian resolve to see the siege through, regardless of weather or season or duration. Within a few days, Cidi Yahye requested a parley. With courtesy and respect two representatives, the master commander of León and the mayor of Baza, met between the lines, in full view of both camps. The king's legate renewed the offer of liberty and the security for property if the town was honorably surrendered. In his presentation, he was a bit long-winded.

"If you, honorable caudillo, think that, with the remaining forces you have, you can defend the city of Baza against the might of the King and the Queen, then allow me to tell you that even though you are known to be a noble and brave knight, you would be making an ill-advised mistake. Since, as you know, it is a common law among all humans that we obey the Mightiest One, if you should choose to disobey, it will be more fitting to say of you that you are a man of greed and death, not a lover of true liberty . . . ," and so on.

The populace within the walls must evacuate the city, but its citizens would be permitted to remain in peace in the outlying environs. If the defenders did not accept these generous terms, he pointed to the fate of Málaga. There, truculence and resistance to the bitter end had resulted in slavery, confiscation, imprisonment, death, and exile for its inhabitants.

The spokesman from the Arab side was no less flowery and long-winded. "Noble gentleman, not the lack of our provisions or the weakness of our walls or the lack of Arabs guarding them will compel us to render to the King Don Fernando and the Queen Doña Isabel the city of Baza. But we are moved by the great virtue and nobility of your appeals, which allows us to choose the manner in which we should act in response to this supposed relinquishment . . . ," and so on.

Upon hearing the terms, Cidi Yahye wavered. In good conscience he could not surrender the city without the approval of El Zagal. He requested permission to send a message through the Christian lines to the old warrior, explaining the situation. Crumpled in despair within his fortress walls at Guadix, El Zagal was powerless to act. He could offer no relief. Granada was hopeless, and his trusted alter ego had spoken. Cidi Yahye should surrender the city on the best terms he could get.

It was done promptly. On December 4, 1489, Cidi Yahye rode magnificently out of his fortress and was received grandly by Ferdinand and Isabella. The monarchs loaded him down with gifts and lavished him with praise and honors. The queen seemed genuinely to be taken with his exotic ways and elegant manners, and the Moor in turn was smitten with her. How pleased the queen would be, if the Moor would honor her by becoming a permanent figure of her court. Before long, he was vowing never again to draw a sword against the Christian side.

He went further. Soon he was offering to go to Guadix and try to persuade El Zagal to give up. At this welcome offer, Ferdinand conferred upon the Moor the fertile lands around the town of Marchena southeast of Seville, where he could live in comfort as a vassal of the king. And before long, the queen prodded and induced the Moor to take the final plunge of converting to Christianity. The conversion must be kept secret, Cidi Yahye insisted, so that his Muslim followers did not feel abandoned, and El Zagal did not feel betrayed. And then the Moor departed for Guadix.

There he found El Zagal sullen and incommunicative. Undeterred, Cidi Yahye laid out the case. Further conflict and slaughter was pointless. The old warrior should trust in the justice and generosity of these all-powerful monarchs. He should remember the horoscope of Boabdil at birth that it was written in the stars that his weak nephew would be the last Muslim ruler of Granada. This was their destiny, their fate, and it was the will of Allah.

El Zagal listened, emotionless, and when Cidi Yahye had finished, he finally spoke up.

"From the decision of Allah there is no appeal," he muttered. "I now see that this is indeed the will of Allah, and what Allah wills must come to pass and be accomplished. If it had not been written in the decree at Boabdil's birth that the kingdom of Granada should fall, He would have supported this hand and this sword."

At El Zagal's acquiescence, events moved rapidly. Ferdinand had moved to the vicinity of Almería, just in case. Cidi Yahye brought El Zagal to him there, and they concluded a treaty. As with Baza, the people of Almería and Guadix must evacuate their bastions, but could remain in peace, with their property, outside the city walls.

The appearance of the ferocious warrior in the Christian camp greatly impressed and touched the scribes of the Christian king. Though they regarded El Zagal as a barbarian, he had evinced great heroism in defense of his country and faith, and he was respected for that. The Moor wore a simple loose *abornoz,* or cloak, and a fulsome white turban. His posture was erect and proud, his visage pale and grave, his expression one of deep melancholy.

Ferdinand treated his royal foe with abundant courtesy. When El Zagal dismounted before him, Ferdinand scowled at this humiliation and insisted that the Moor remount. When El Zagal offered to kiss Ferdinand's hand as an act of homage, Ferdinand pulled his hand away. El Zagal responded by kissing his own hand in the manner of Moorish sovereigns. If these acts showed great sensitivity, they were undermined by forcing El Zagal to stand and witness as the standard of Islam was lowered from the tower of Almería's fortress, and the Christian standard was slowly raised.

Meekly, El Zagal gave up the last great bastion of his kingdom in exchange for a slender valley northeast of Almería in the Alpujarras hills called the Taa of Andarax. (*Taa* means "obedience" in Arabic, the equivalent of vassalage.) Grand his new fief was not, but dry, remote, and poor.

Now, of the great Moorish civilization in Spain, only the bastion of Granada itself remained.

20

The 4th Day of the Moon, Rebie Primera

 During the moons of Muharram and Safer in the Muslim year 895, these calamities befell the Muslims of Andalusia. Only the King of Granada himself seemed at first to view the events in Baza, Guadix, and Almería positively. When Boabdil heard of El Zagal's capitulation, he rejoiced and gave thought to putting on his finest robes, caparisoning his favorite steed in silk and brocade, and strutting triumphantly before his people. His father was dead; his uncle had surrendered; his cousin, the Prince of Almería, had gone over to the Christian side. Now, at long last, Abu Abdullah Muhammad El Zaquir, otherwise known as Boabdil, reigned as the sole king of Granada.

"The stars have ceased their persecution," he said in a reference to his natal horoscope. "Henceforth let no man call me The Unfortunate."

His joy was momentary. Outside the amber walls of the Alhambra, the mood was ugly and violent. The news of El Zagal's surrender sent shudders of fear and rage through the populace. El Zagal, at least, had resisted stoutly until the very end. His warriors of Baza had comported themselves brilliantly, harassing the enemy tirelessly, in the finest tradition of Islamic holy war, and they had wilted in exhaustion only when Allah finally showed them that further strife was pointless. If the traitor in the Alhambra had come to his uncle's aid, the kingdom and the true faith would surely have been safe.

A wave of revulsion for Boabdil swept through the streets of

Granada. Throngs poured out of the Albaicín, their numbers swollen by the hardened refugees from the battles in the east. They came down the narrow gorge of the Rio Darro from the Sacromonte and through the Arch of Elvira, until they stood in front of the Puerta de la Justicia and demanded the head of Boabdil as their justice.

Boabdil cowered in the ornate Hall of Kings, peering through the slats of his jalousied arched windows at the gathering mob, retreating to his throne room in the Hall of the Ambassadors, where he was rebuked by his domineering mother and hectored by the wailing women of his harem. As he scurried to the Tower of the Comares to look far down on the mob, he passed the exquisite, intricate facade which bespoke the greatness and the wisdom, the learning and the piety of the Nasarid kings who had come before him.

"My position is that of a crown and my door is a parting of the ways," read the inscription from one of his radiant predecessors. "The West believes that in me is the East. Allah has entrusted me to open the way to the victory that has been foretold, and I await his coming just as the horizon ushers in the dawn. May God adorn his works with the same beauty that resides in his countenance and his nature."

While Boabdil quailed before the ferment, the situation in the city was close to getting out of hand. In the vacuum, various high officials, viziers and mayors and generals, took it upon themselves to interpose themselves between the angry mob and their paralyzed, terrified king. From the crenellated walls, these officials argued with the hotheads below. This catastrophe was not the sole doing of their king, they shouted, but was in part the fault of all. Did not they, the people, remember their own cowardice and fickleness? Had they not fought continuously amongst themselves in past years? Had they not switched their loyalties from one leader to another, while the infidel made his inroads against a fractured nation? Thus, they had only themselves to blame. Their disunion as much as the enemy's strength or their king's weakness had led to this desperate turning point. Their only hope now was to set aside their anger and unite against the common foe.

For the moment, the multitude was mollified, but Boabdil knew he was not safe for long. With great urgency, he dispatched a secret envoy to Ferdinand, describing his desperate situation and requesting the Christian king to send troops immediately to rescue his loyal vassal. Ferdinand responded promptly by pouring troops into the vega in front of the city. This had an instant miraculous effect, but not the one that either Ferdinand or Boabdil foresaw. Instead of intimidating the populace, it emboldened it. The spectacle of Christian battalions arrayed across the fertile plain united the Moors more effectively than anything the windy viziers could say from the walls of the Puerta de la Justicia.

Once his soldiers were in place, Ferdinand sent his formal reply to Boabdil. Remember your agreement after your capture in Loja. Remember the renewal of your promise in the past year. Once Guadix, Baza, and Almería had fallen, once El Zagal was subdued, Granada and the Alhambra would be handed over. The time for that final act has come.

Boabdil was a weed in the wind. Turn over the Alhambra to the infidel king? He scarcely had control of the keys that led to the Courtyard of the Lions. His viziers held the power now, and they were in no mood for surrender. And so, Boabdil sent his reply to Ferdinand's ultimatum. He must be excused from his promise, he wrote, for it was not in his power to hand over the city and its great bastion. His own generals and close advisers would not submit to deference and fealty. And so, if it please the king, he should be satisfied with the many gains that he had made and leave Granada alone.

Meanwhile, the spirit of insurrection was spreading. In the suburbs of Guadix, the natives were dissatisfied with being displaced from their city, and they rose up against its occupation. The same thing happened in the tiny consolation prize for El Zagal, his Taa of Andarax, over the ridge of the Sierra Nevada, in the south. His own citizens turned against the old warhorse and would have killed him if he had not gone into hiding. Like Boabdil, El Zagal the Valiant begged Ferdinand to subdue these insurgents. Ferdinand offered help, but El Zagal changed his mind. Rather than be hassled in his old age, he now proposed to sell his tiny fief back to the Christian king. This was done: the valley and its twenty-three villages for the firesale price of 5 million maravedis.

At that, El Zagal packed his remaining belongings and sailed for Africa, where he lived out the rest of his life in the emirate of Tlemcen (in present-day Algeria). He surely found peace there. The emirate of the Abd-el-Wahid was the capital of the Berber dynasty and a model of amity between the people of the Book. Jews, Muslims, and Christians lived comfortably side by side in this crossroads between the Mediterranean and the Sahara. The jewel of the trading city of 125,000 was the mosque of the Sweetmeat Maker (El Halawi), whose eight minarets of Algerian onyx sparkled in the blistering sun.

Back on the vega of Granada, Ferdinand scoffed at Boabdil's letter contemptuously. The Moor's proposal was unacceptable and impertinent. Ferdinand had run out of patience. He declared war and called for more soldiers to flood into Granada's plain.

With nowhere to turn, Boabdil suddenly found religion. At long last, he appreciated the consequences of his weakness and subservience over the years. He must stand up and lead. He must join with his advisers and resist this Christian invasion. He called a council of war.

And so, late in the year 1490, the call to Jihad went out once again through the hilltowns and pastures that remained in Islamic control. The sultan was reinvigorated now with the passion of vengeance. The true believers were approaching the Day of Judgment. The signs were everywhere that the Hour of the Great Battle was upon them. Boabdil would lead the Mahdi army that would return in glory to restore justice after the oppression of the infidel. The end was near. The words of the Koran were luminous:

And when the sacred months have passed, kill those who join other gods with God wherever ye shall find them. And seize them, besiege them, and lay wait for them with every king of ambush. Slay the infidels. The fire of hell shall not touch the legs of him who shall be covered with the dust of battle in the road of God.

The effect was incendiary. In many places, Moors rose in rebellion against their occupiers. Control over Baza, Guadix, and Almería suddenly was cast into doubt. Especially important was the last port in Moorish hands, the tiny town of Adna, which fell quickly back into the Islamic column. Meanwhile Boabdil, suddenly emboldened, rode out of the Alhambra, invested and took the town of Alheudin, and proceeded south, ravaging through the Taa of Marchena, until he reached the more important port west of Adna called Salobreña.

Salobreña had mythic as well as strategic importance. Its tenth-century castle was perched on a rugged rocky outcropping above the town and was considered impregnable. Over the centuries it had been used as a treasury, but also a notorious Moorish prison, and not always for the enemy. Legend suggested that the Moorish king Mohammed IX, who ruled briefly in the middle of the fifteenth century, had three sultry daughters who sizzled with the names Zaida, Zoraida, and Zorahaidan. Their disconcerting astrology suggested that the three princesses were susceptible to worldly temptation, and so their protective father locked them up in the castle of Salobreña for safekeeping. But then the sentimental old fool made the mistake of missing them and summoning them to the Alhambra. Along the way, the royal party happened upon three Christian soldiers and pounced upon them. But the Christians turned out to be better lovers than fighters.

Now Boabdil was in no sentimental mood. He came angrily, full of newfound religious indignation. The townspeople, who had submitted to Christian control as sheep, were inspired at the sight of the Muslim horde and drove their occupiers off the streets and into the rocky fortress. But this bastion rose to its reputation, and the Christian defenders were able to hold out until word got to Ferdinand. Knowing that he had no time for a protracted siege, Boabdil was unprepared to face the full wrath of Ferdinand. In disappointment, he withdrew, ravaging the fields around other Christian outposts as he returned to the Alhambra.

Another disappointment came quickly. The apostate, Cidi Yahye, the erstwhile defender of Baza who now carried the perfumed scarf of

Isabella the Queen into battle on the Christian side, approached Adna. Combining the power of Ferdinand's army and the wiles of a Moor, he outfitted a fleet of dhows and dressed its sailors in turbans to look like a rescuing squadron from Morocco. Tricked, the defenders admitted the Trojan seahorses into the harbor, and the town quickly fell back into Christian hands.

Having reversed Boabdil's temporary successes, Ferdinand now turned his full wrath on the rebellion in the countryside. Iñigo López de Mendoza, the count of Tendilla, was put in charge of pacification. If any town or village offered resistance to the Christian king, its fields and storehouses were ravaged without pity. To deal with the insurgency at Guadix, Baza, and Almería, the count adopted a brilliant tactic: anyone in the towns who had conspired in the rebellion must face the Christian judiciary; at the same time, any resident was free to pack all his worldly possessions and leave with no questions asked. Since most residents were conspirators and rebels, the three towns emptied. As Arab refugees fled to Africa and to Granada, Christians from the north soon replaced them. This tactic of voluntary rather than forced ethnic cleansing accomplished several purposes at once. The three Moorish bastions became securely Christian, and Granada was flooded with unruly and discouraged refugees.

After the terrible season of siege in 1489, the Christian forces had been exhausted, and it had taken a year for the king's resources to be replenished and his soldiers to regain their fighting trim. But in the spring of 1491, some sixty thousand strong, they mobilized in the Val de Velillas northwest of Granada and returned to the battlefield with ferocity. Faced with such overwhelming power and resolve, Boabdil's Jihad evaporated as quickly as it had begun. Into the summer of 1491, Ferdinand would brook no further delay. He stood on the verge of fulfilling his providential destiny.

On the vega outside Granada, the king now prepared for the assault on the Alhambra. Some six miles from the walls of the Alhambra, and in full view of its defenders, he began to construct a mock city. Its four streets were laid out in the shape of a cross, with a gate at each point, and a plaza in the center where weapons were stacked. Each quarter of the town was named for the knight who had overseen its construction. The army wished to name the town itself for Queen Isabella. In her modesty, she declined the honor. At her command the town was named Santa Fe, or Holy Faith.

From afar, the Moors marveled at this mirage, for it seemed that the Christians could construct a city overnight. Its walls appeared to be of brick, but they were made of wood and covered with a wax cloth that looked like masonry. Towers of significant height also appeared quickly, draped with the same cloth, and garrisoned with expert crossbowmen. Of this a poet wrote a generation later:

> Santa Fe is round encirc'd,
> The walls of waxen cloth are made,
> Tents within it shine resplendent,
> Tents of silk and rich brocade
>
> Dukes are here, and Counts, and nobles,
> Knights and Squires of valor great;
> These King Ferdinand assembles
> To decree Granada's fate.

Over the summer, despite regular sallies from the Alhambra, Santa Fe took on a more permanent look. The spark for this permanence came from a lady in Queen Isabella's court who inadvertently kicked over a lamp and set the draperies of her tent on fire. The blaze spread quickly, threatening the elaborate pavilion of the queen herself. After the conflagration was contained and the ruined gowns and jewels inventoried, the queen expressed the hope that pavilions should be improved to prevent any such accidents in the future. Wooden houses replaced tents, and then brick houses replaced the wooden ones, and within eighty days deep moats paralleled its reinforced walls. The wood for the houses and walls was taken from fruit trees in the surrounding orchards.

In horror, the Moors watched as their great breadbasket began to disappear before their eyes. For centuries the magic of Granada lay in the nexus between the Alhambra, the Sierra Nevada, and the vega. "Fresh and comfortable vega," read a Moorish poem, "sweet recreation of ladies and men of immense glory." And now that beloved and glorious expanse swarmed with locusts that devoured their crops, felled their orchards, and threatened the survival of their city and their faith.

Supplying Granada became the desperate concern. With the refugees from the east, the population of Granada had swollen to 200,000. The wagon trains from the Sierra Nevada and the granaries and fertile valleys of the Alpujarras were increasingly interdicted by Christian raiding parties. With the disruption of these supply lines, the city began to feel the pinch.

Still, during the summer, there was time for chivalry. Young bloods from the Alhambra regularly staged raids on the Christian forward positions, defying the sharpshooters in the battle towers, just as Christian rangers scoured the mountain roads for Moorish supply trains. It was not infrequent for the greatest of the fighters to venture out into the median ground, dressed to kill, plumes and banners waving in the wind, and to engage in single combat, with enthusiastic spectators on both sides. The chronicles report that King Boabdil himself witnessed the heroic fight of a Christian knight whose small band was overwhelmed by a superior Muslim force. The next day, Boabdil sent to the defeated Christian knight his very own scimitar, magnificently mounted and packaged, as a sign of his admiration.

The presence of Queen Isabella added to the luster. Much involved as always in logistics, she regularly ventured out among her troops, mounted on a great steed and clothed in full armor, to encourage them. Of her beauty, her piety, and her courage, the poets and minstrels crooned eloquently:

Where we part
Departs my heart.
Glory hides:
Sorrow abides.

Victory vanishes:
Memory languishes
And my grief is great.

Once, her curiosity got the better of her, when she insisted on getting a closer look at the Alhambra. Joined by the king and protected by a significant detachment under the command of the marquis of Cádiz, the reconnaissance took the expedition to the hamlet of Zubia, which provided a fine view of the great bastion from the east. The queen had laid down stiff orders to the marquis not to engage the enemy, for she wanted no Christian life lost on account of her sightseeing, not to mention that her eyes were to be shielded from witnessing actual bloodshed. But, seeing this force hovering so close, Moorish fighters poured out of the city, and a brief but quite bloody encounter took place, with the royals scurrying to safety. Later, the marquis apologized to the grateful queen for breaking her orders (and for saving her life) and the episode became known as "the Queen's Skirmish."

There were other diversions, for who should turn up yet again at a war encampment but Christopher Columbus. To many in the court, even perhaps King Ferdinand himself, the Italian seemed like the proverbial bad penny. In Málaga, in Jaén, and now in Santa Fe, here again was this eccentric, prattling on about gold pavilions and Great Khans in Cipangu when there was serious work to be done on the terra firma beneath their feet. At least in Málaga and Jaén a few snippets of useful intelligence might be extracted from him, but the price was his endless blather. The man would not take no for an answer!

Still, he cheered and warmed Queen Isabella, and that was enough to reduce these grumbles to a whisper. And he came now in the company of the queen's confessor, Friar Juan, from the Franciscan monastery at La Rábida near Palos. The detractors were well advised to suffer their annoyance in silence or just to ignore the visitor in his borrowed clothes. Ferdinand also kept his counsel, but he was less than enthusiastic about his wife's deepening commitment to this threadbare dreamer.

Into the fall of 1491, the situation grew more grave for the defenders of Granada. Boabdil held emergency council of war with his top advisers. Alone among them, his impressive field general, Musa Ben Abil, was petulantly opposed to any talk of giving up. There was still hope, he argued forcefully. The refugees might be a burden, but with them had come another twenty thousand soldiers from the east. The resources were still adequate. The subject of surrender was premature.

But he was overruled. "What remedy remains to us but surrender or certain death?" proclaimed one vizier.

With great sadness the council dispatched a venerable governor to King Ferdinand to open talks. Ferdinand received the Moorish envoy graciously. Over the succeeding days, discussions between envoys were held in secret, sometimes in the Alhambra itself and sometimes in the tiny village of Charriana, three miles from the city.

By mid-November, an agreement was reached. It contained ten key provisions. If Boabdil received no relief in two months, the city and its fortress would be handed over on the following conditions. Boabdil and his generals were to swear perpetual fealty to the Catholic monarchs. All Christian captives were to be released. No tribute would be exacted from Granada for three years. Three hundred sons of the noblest Granadine families, including the son of Boabdil himself, were to be presented immediately as a guarantee of good faith. Boabdil could choose between certain valleys of the Alpujarras hills as his final domain.

And then came the more important social provisions, the ones that were to haunt Spanish history for generations. Residents were permitted to remain in their houses and retain their property. Soldiers could retain their arms and horses. And the most important of all: free exercise of religion was guaranteed, including the sanctity of mosques. There was to be no prohibition of Muslim dress or custom, and no interference with the use of the Arabic language. Islamic law would continue to govern the province.

This agreement was signed on the 22nd day of the Moon of Muharram in the Muslim year of 897, or, as bitter Arab historians of the future would write, "by computation of the Infidel," on November 25, 1491.

When the documents were returned to the Alhambra, Boabdil gathered his full council in the Hall of the Ambassadors, the throne room that was the epicenter of Nasarid magnificence. The councilors entered, some for the last time, through the hallway that bore the inscription: "Be brief and live in peace," the epigraph that had awed so many councilors of the past as they moved into the presence of the sultan. Awed now only by the majesty of their palace and the glory of its passing into history, they sat on the floor before Boabdil the Unfortunate and gazed upward at the magnificent arabesque ceiling of concentric designs. "He who created seven heavens, one above the other," read one inscription. "You will find no discord in the creation of the Merciful One." And another:

"The only conqueror is God."

Their great general, Musa Ben Abil, looked around at the downcast, embarrassed, tearful visages of his cohorts and was nauseous.

"Leave this useless weeping, men of Granada, to the eyes of children and delicate maidens," he hissed. "Let us be men and expend our emotions, not in the shedding of unmanly tears, but in pouring forth our blood even to the last drop. Let us go forth with the strength of desperation in our muscles and offer the breast of brave men to the enemy's lance. I am ready to lead you with a heart that will show no hesitation. Let us display valor and dignity that will make our names resound for eternity. Let posterity view us as glorious defenders of our homeland rather than hypocrites who chose only to surrender and save our own skins. Why should we refuse the honorable death of the battlefield?"

The faces of his audience remained fixed in silence on the polished stone beneath them. "Death is the least of the evils that threaten you. More fearful are the humiliations that are being prepared: plunder of our houses, desecration of our mosques, violation of our wives and daughters, cruel intolerance," and, in a reference to the Inquisition, " . . . the burning pile of the bigot."

He paused, waiting for a response. But there was none. "Do you believe for a minute that the Christians will be faithful to the promises they have made to you?" he continued with contempt. "Will the king who led them to conquest be as generous a victor as he is a fortunate enemy? Be certain he will not. Do not deceive yourself. These Christians are thirsty for blood. . . ."

"Let the will of God be fulfilled," Boabdil mumbled. "The heavens have decreed the ruin of our homeland in the unfortunate horoscope of my birth."

"I see well that the spirit of the multitude has become feeble," the general responded deflectively. "Their hearts have sunk. But there is ever one refuge for the true noble. He can seek shelter in death. I for one prefer to die in freedom, rather than to live for the sorrows and humiliations that are coming. For myself, by Allah! I will not see them."

With that he strode out of the hall, mounted his horse, and rode away through the gate of Elvira.

❖

There would be no succor for Boabdil. No legions of an African emir or an Egyptian sultan appeared to rescue the Unfortunate One. The grip on the last bastion of Spanish Islam was tight and complete. There would be no miracles. Secret though the negotiations were meant to be, word of the capitulation slipped out, and once again Boabdil's life was in imminent danger. He sent word to Ferdinand that the date for the handover should be moved up. January 2, 1492, or the 4th day of the Moon Rebie Primera in the year 897, was set.

At dawn that day, all the treasures of the Alhambra that could be packed up were loaded onto wagons. Boabdil, his mother, and family were ready for their journey into obscurity, exile, and death. At the appointed moment, by prearrangement, three volleys of cannon roared from the fortress as a signal. Out of the low, gray eastern light the advance party of the Catholic monarchs came into view. Leading the procession was the Cardinal of Spain, Don Pedro González de Mendoza. Behind came the king's group. On the banks of the Genil, it stopped. The cardinal proceeded warily up the incline, known as the Hill of

Martyrs, and toward the great bastion. From the Alhambra, accompanied by fifty knights, Boabdil came down to meet the prelate. When they were face to face, Boabdil said,

"Go, sir, and occupy these walls and fortresses in the name of your powerful kings. God, who is all powerful, has chosen to give this city to them for their deserving merits, and for all the sins of Arabs."

As his final request, Boabdil asked that the gate by which he had left the Alhambra for the last time in the Tower of the Seven Floors be closed up and never used again.

They rode on to King Ferdinand. When he was close, Boabdil made to dismount as a sign of homage, but Ferdinand raised his hand to stop him. This time, there was to be no groveling. When they were side by side, Boabdil kissed the king's right arm—and then handed him the keys of the city.

"Since Allah decrees it, take these, my lord, the keys to this paradise. Myself and all those who are inside are yours. Use your success with clemency and moderation."

"Do not despair in your adversity," Ferdinand responded graciously. "What bad fortune has taken from you will be restored through our friendship." And then he added, significantly, "And do not doubt the sincerity of our promises." At this point, Boabdil's hostage son was brought forward and reunited with his father. Boabdil then asked to be introduced to the knight who would govern Granada. The count of Tendilla rode forward. Boabdil slowly removed from his finger a magnificent gold ring in which a precious stone was mounted and on which was etched the stamp of authority.

"With this stamp Granada has been governed," Boabdil said. "Take it so that you too may govern. May God give you more fortune than I."

The cardinal took the keys, and his party passed calmly back up the hill, along the gorge of the Rio Darro, toward the gypsy caves in the Sacromonte, and entered the fortress by the Gate of Justice. Above the delegation, the houses and narrow streets of the Albaicín were deathly silent, for the populace had shut themselves up in darkness. After an anxious hour, as the royal party watched from below, the standard of the Nasrid dynasty was lowered on the Tower of the Comares and the banner of Castile was hoisted up in its place. Upon that banner the motto of the messianic kingdom fluttered in the wind: *Unum ovile et unus pastor*—One flock and one shepherd. And after that, the great silver crucifix which the late pope, Sixtus IV, had given to Ferdinand, and which the king had carried in his train from the beginning of the crusade, was raised on the crenellated wall.

At this sign, the situation was safe. The queen, dressed now in a long, elaborately embroidered Moorish caftan, rode forward to join her husband. Once they were together, knights knelt to express their homage to the new King and Queen of Granada. A witness was to write later, "They appeared more than mortal, as if sent by Heaven for the salvation of Spain."

In the next four days, under the supervision of the count of Tendilla, the army secured the city. Swiftly, the count proceeded to break the cardinal promise of the monarchs to respect Islam and its sacred sites, as the main mosque of the city was reconstituted as a Christian cathedral. General Musa's prophecy was coming true much more quickly than even he might have expected. On January 6, the day of Epiphany, the Catholic monarchs entered Granada. The heroic and bombastic strains of *Te Deum laudamus* (We praise Thee, O God) wafted through the empty stone streets, belted out by the royal chapel choir.

Meanwhile, Boabdil's sad procession took a back road to avoid passing through the city and wound its way south. At the rise of the hill called *La Cuesta de las Lágrimas* (the Hill of Tears) that would take the Moors to the valley of Purchena that Boabdil had chosen as his domain, the party stopped. Boabdil cast his eyes back over the valley for his last look at his city and wept. A councilor rushed to comfort him.

"Consider, my lord, that a great and memorable misfortune, when it is endured with fortitude, does sometimes render men famous."

Boabdil was not comforted. "Where then shall be found a misfortune greater than mine!" he wailed.

At the sight of her wretched son, his mother spat out her contempt.

"Because you knew not how to defend your country like a man, you weep for it like a woman."

❖

In concluding his story of the end of the 800-year-old rule of Islam in Spain, the most important of the Arab chroniclers attached a final epitaph: "Praised be God! who exalteth kings and who casteth them low, who giveth power and greatness at his pleasure, who inflicteth poverty and humiliation according to his holy will. The fulfillment of that will is Eternal Justice which regulates all human events."

Christian chroniclers, meanwhile, exulted. The fall of Granada was compared to the fall of Troy. "It is the end of Spain's calamities," Peter Martyr declared. Isabella had "redeemed Spain, indeed all of Europe," wrote another scribe. January 2, 1492, was "the most distinguished and blessed day there has ever been in Spain."

News of the Christian triumph raced across Europe. When it reached Rome, there was jubilation and even whimsy. The Spanish cardinal, Rodrigo Borgia, only a few months away from becoming the next pope, treated the Roman people to the novel spectacle of a bullfight. The ailing pope, Innocent VIII, led a solemn procession from the Vatican to the Piazza Navona and the Church of San Giacomo degli Spagnoli, the Church of Spain, which had been built forty-two years before. There, he proclaimed Ferdinand and Isabella to be officially "the Catholic monarchs."

They were, the pontiff said, "the athletes of Christ."

21

Promiser of Kingdoms

❖

THE ALHAMBRA

 In the days after the surrender of Granada, the royals wandered in amazement through the decorative halls and spacious courtyards of the fabulous Alhambra. In the Hall of the Mexuar, hailed by the fourteenth-century poet Ibn Zamrak as "the haven of counsel, mercy, and favor," Isabella must have wondered whether this too for her would be the place to entertain supplications and to dispense mercy. "Enter and ask," read the calligraphy in marble. "Do not be afraid to seek justice for here you will find it." Could she emulate the wisdom and the elegance and the humility of the best Muslim rulers who had come before her? To remind the mighty of their place, the motto of the Nasrids—"The only conqueror is God"—was repeated above the windows over and over in Magrib script.

The soft, feminine imagery of the legends in the tracery in a niche that led to the Courtyard of the Myrtles must have appealed to the queen. "I am a wife in my bridal gown, sublime in my perfection. Look at this jar of water and you will understand how true my words are. Look too at my crown. It will seem to you like the new moon. . . ." Equally, she must have been appalled by the ghosts of the concubines and slave girls who had inhabited the Courtyard of the Harem.

Within the roseate walls, the air of celebration lasted for many days. For a time the romance of the place captivated the new occupants as if, as a great storyteller once put it, they "expected to see the white arm of some mysterious princess beckoning from the gallery, or some dark eye sparkling through the lattice." The prelates did their best to exorcise the spirit of the infidel from the place. In the Hall of Justice an altar was erected, and the Cardinal of Spain celebrated his somber high mass there for the giddy conquerors. Atop the watchtower known as the Torre de la Vela, bells tolled for the great victory of Christianity over Islam. To the Christian newcomer, this was the sweetest of sounds.

> I want to live in Granada
> If only to hear
> The bell of the Vela
> When I go to sleep.

Outside the walls, a harsher reality was at work. The count of Tendilla had been appointed military governor, and he went about his business of transforming the city with his customary diligence and arrogance. Cidi Yahye, once hero to the Muslims at Baza, now became their oppressor. After his infatuation with Isabella and his conversion to Christianity, he had changed his name to Don Pedro de Granada. Now he was a cavalier of Santiago and had been made master of the Muslims. Meanwhile, the queen's confessor, Hernando de Talavera—formerly prior of Prado, bishop of Ávila, propagandist for the concept of *limpieza*, or pure Spanish blood, and head of the Commission of Inquiry into Columbus's proposal—had been appointed archbishop of Granada.

It is likely that Columbus was a witness to these exuberant events, if at the back of the room and in dark corners. He had returned to Granada for the final decision on his proposal. All the impediments had been removed. There could be no further excuse for postponement. He had waited six long and frustrating years for this infernal war to be over, and now, with something of a chip on his shoulder, he demanded a clear and definitive answer. He would give the Spanish monarchs one last chance.

In his last sessions with Talavera's commission, he had been fighting a defensive battle against pseudo-scientists, religious ciphers, obfuscating "philosophers," and contradictory reservations. Their specious arguments infuriated him, and he exercised an almost superhuman patience. Five objections had been raised against his proposal. The voyage to Asia across the vast eastern sea would take three years, a duration far in excess of anything that had ever been attempted and which would be impossible to supply. If he managed to reach the opposite side of the earth, the Antipode, it would be impossible for him to return, for the Antipodes were contradictory and opposite and defied interconnection. Conversely, the Antipodes did not exist since, as Talavera himself had often said, according to St. Augustine, the globe consisted primarily of water. Moreover, the Bible identified five zones in the world and made three of them uninhabitable. Finally, at this advanced stage of the world, some four thousand years after Creation, it was unlikely that mysterious undiscovered lands still existed.

Now Columbus had surrendered to his annoyance and anger and resentment. Compared to the practical Portuguese, this collection of Spanish quacks was hard to suffer. They were, as Don Quixote would say later, a little short of salt in the brainpan. If they were dense and cynical, they were also vain and arrogant, and he had run out of patience with them. He had presented his hard clues and tantalizing rumor. He had invoked the theories of world-class thinkers like Toscanelli and Pierre d'Ailly. He had conjured up mountains of gold, mounds of spices, coasts of pearls, and continents of Christian converts. He had spoken of St. Nicholas of Myra, the patron saint of mariners from the fourth century, who watched over divinely sanctioned voyages and had once caused a tempest to abate on a trip to the Holy Land. Columbus had appealed to national interest, to providential destiny, to the glory of Spain and the Church. He had prodded Ferdinand's greed and Isabella's piety. He had nursed relationships with bishops, dukes, and counts. At this last, maddening stage, he was thrown back on the poetry of Seneca, predicting that the age had come when the ocean would lose its chains, and a new world would be revealed.

That the war was over had removed the final objection of the monarchs. Since the count of Medina Celi was still offering to pick up the tab, the venture would cost the crown nothing. That Portugal controlled the coast of Africa and had discovered a passage to India could tip the balance of power in Iberia. Even the Cardinal of Spain himself was wavering. Nicholas of Myra might have been an important saint and Saint Augustine a giant of the Church, he was overheard to say, but neither was a good geographer.

For six months as the end game of the war played out, Columbus had been on the verge of abandoning Spain entirely and taking his proposal elsewhere. Since the summer he had been living at the Franciscan monastery of Santa María de La Rábida outside the town of Palos on the Tinto River. There, he poured out his frustrations about the disrespect and mockery he had suffered at the Spanish court. In time, he made two great friends: Brother Antonio de Marchena and Brother Juan Pérez. Brother Antonio was an amateur astrologer and Brother Juan had been the queen's bookkeeper as a youth before he became her confessor. By day, Columbus had enthralled these men with the grandeur of his vision; and by night, he had fascinated them with a display of how he planned to navigate across the ocean by the stars.

The Franciscans admired and believed in this dreamer. In those months they did their best to calm his frustrations and to dissuade him from taking his proposal to France where his brother, Bartholomew, was even then pleading their case at Fontainebleau. They beseeched him to give the Spanish monarchs one last chance. Just a little while longer; just a few more conversations, they had argued. To keep him active and eager, they had introduced him to shipbuilders and sea captains in Palos, now an important harbor on the southwestern Spanish coast.

"During the six years I traveled in Castile I found protection from no one, other than eternal God and Friars Antonio and Juan Pérez," Columbus would say later. "Only these two Brothers have been loyal to me."

With Friar Pérez at his side, Columbus waited for his answer. The queen reconvened her ponderous philosophers, and they repeated their well-worn objections, barbing them with the usual mockery. Cardinal Mendoza and Archbishop Talavera, focused now on other excitements, had lost interest. Talavera in particular, as head of the inquiry, was actively working to undermine Columbus's proposal. As much as anything, Talavera had come to view Columbus as a gold digger and social climber. The new archbishop was still aggravated by what he regarded as Columbus's appalling demands for titles and monetary rewards.

"Such demands smack of the highest degree of arrogance," Talavera told the monarchs, "and would be unbecoming for Your Highnesses to grant to this needy foreign adventurer."

Within days of the fall of Granada, the supplicant was summoned into the presence of the queen and informed that his proposal was formally, conclusively, and terminally rejected. Angrily, Columbus threw his belongings on his horse and rode north on the road to Córdoba—and France.

Sprinkled in the second rank of courtiers, Columbus had his admirers. One was Luis de Santángel, a wealthy Aragonese financier whose family had served the crown of Aragon for generations as merchants and lawyers and who was then serving as treasurer of the *Santa Hermandad*. Upon hearing of Columbus's departure, he rushed into the queen's presence to launch a passionate protest. He was surprised and disappointed that so great and high-minded a queen had dismissed this man of quality when his project involved so little risk to the crown, and yet, if successful, would bring such glory to Spain and to the Church. Columbus's proposal would allow the Spanish Empire "to grow beyond all imagination."

If another European country, such as France, sponsored Columbus, and he discovered even half of what he imagined, Spain would be the great loser, Santángel said. There would be "much damage to your Kingdom . . . and our enemies would not lack reason to insult Your Highness and affirm that Your Majesty had gotten what she deserved." The Spanish monarchs would be ridiculed for their timidity and lack of foresight. "Your successors will be deprived of what could have been theirs." Even if the enterprise turned out to be a failure, the monarchs would be praised for their efforts to penetrate the "secrets of the universe." Think of Alexander the Great and other great kings in history, he urged. "When they did not succeed in everything they tried, this did not diminish the grandness of what they tried." If the royal expenditure was huge, that would be one thing. But Columbus was asking for only 5 million maravedis. Let it not be said that a great queen rejected a grand and noble enterprise over such a pittance.

Santángel's passion must have been extraordinary, for his speech shook and moved Isabella. For once, the appeal to her vanity won the day, not only as a queen but as the Woman of the Apocalypse. She thanked Santángel for his service to Spain. "If you still feel that this man will not be able to wait any longer," she said, "then I will provide some jewels from my chest to lend the necessary money. . . ."

"That will not be necessary, my Lady," Santángel replied. "If I may render you the smallest service, I will offer my home as collateral. But please, Your Majesty, send for Columbus, because I fear that he has already left." Immediately, she dispatched a bailiff to ride after Columbus and bring him back to court.

Sixteen miles up the road at the Bridge of the Virgin over the Cubillas River in the town of Pinos Puente, the bailiff caught up to him. Suspicious and still resentful, Columbus turned back reluctantly. At Santa Fe, Santángel greeted him effusively. The queen had changed her mind. She had instructed her scribe to draw up the necessary documents, giving Christopher Columbus everything he had asked for.

There is an ironic footnote to Santángel's pivotal contribution to the Columbus saga. Queen Isabella did indeed reward his service to

Spain, for the financier was a converso. His family, both the Jews and the converted Jews, were to be spared the horrors of the Inquisition, she ordered. Five years later, in 1497, Ferdinand as King of Aragon formalized the arrangement with a personal grant. It exempted Santángel and his sons from the ministrations of the Holy Office and guaranteed his heirs the safety of their personal property.

❖

Queen Isabella's capitulation was a testament to Columbus's unshakable persistence, to his single-mindedness, to his certainty in the correctness of his vision. Having waited so long, having suffered so many disappointments and so many indignities, having endured great poverty and dislocation in those endless years of dubiety, he suddenly stood taller than any sea captain in Spain. He had spent many years in pursuit of this dream: it had been thirteen years since he first conceived it. Now forty-two years old, the son of a wool carder had been raised legitimately to nobility.

And thus, even before his departure, his story was the stuff of legend and of poetry. A hundred years later, an Italian poet named Gabriello Chiabrera would capture the spirit of this moment:

> Surely from the heart such a great destiny he did not choose;
> Beautiful souls to beautiful works are chosen
> For they know how to rejoice in exceptional efforts.
> Neither can popular reproach enchain them
> Nor quest for accolade slow down their course.
> For such a long time in vile ways,
> Did Europe despise his illustrious hope
> People and kings scoffed at him together
> This bare, exposed leader, promiser of Kingdoms.

The queen, in turn, deserves her due. Over the years she had left the door open to Columbus. Despite her lack of technical knowledge, she alone had seen his quality. She alone had risen above the sniping and the derision of her wise men. Later, after his third voyage, Columbus was still bursting with gratitude for his queen, and once again credited divine guidance.

"In the midst of general incredulity," Columbus wrote, "the Almighty infused into the Queen, my Lady, the spirit of intelligence and energy. Whilst everyone else in his ignorance was expounding only on the inconvenience and cost, her Highness approved it on the contrary and gave it all the support in her power."

In the weeks that followed the queen's reversal, the necessary documents were drawn up. Friar Juan Pérez acted as Columbus's attorney in the negotiations over the language and the fine points. The town of Palos was charged with providing and equipping three caravels, two of which would be offered at taxpayers' expense, while the funds for the third would be provided, through donations, by Columbus himself. In the royal decree, the town was commanded to provide the ships to Columbus within ten days of receiving the order. Not surprisingly, four months rather than ten days would end up as the actual time it would take to find and outfit the vessels.

In the "Capitulations"—as the articles of agreement were formally and appropriately called—Columbus was granted the title not only of Admiral but of Viceroy and Governor-General of any lands, specified as islands or mainlands, he might discover. He would be entitled to one tenth of all "pearls, precious stones, gold, silver, and spices" he might find or seize, while the crown would take the remaining 90 percent. Of any commerce that might subsequently be conducted in lands he discovered, Columbus would be entitled to a cut. Henceforth, he should be addressed with the honorific "Don Christopher Columbus," and his heirs would be entitled to enjoy the privileges of his admiralty.

After these essential provisions came the fine points. Under no circumstances was he to call at the Portuguese possession of St. George of the Mine in Africa or conduct any trade with Portuguese agents. "For it is Our pleasure to abide by and enforce the terms which we agreed upon and convenanted with the Most Serene King of Portugal, Our brother, on this matter." Amnesty was granted to any criminals who might ship out with the voyage, since it was not entirely clear whether it would be easy to recruit a crew. No taxes were to be assized on the supplies for the voyage, and any supplies and repairs to the ships must be provided at reasonable prices. Any attempt to exploit or overcharge would be punished with a fine of 10,000 maravedis.

On April 30, the Admiral was summoned to the Hall of the Ambassadors in the Alhambra. There, in the golden glow of the arabesque and beneath the intricate ceiling of mysterious, starry design, he collected his broadsheet parchment documents, embossed with the seal of the Spanish monarchy, and received his official sendoff. In this official sendoff, Columbus was, as usual, deft in stressing the themes that he knew were close to the royal heart. In a startling aside, he said,

"I plead with Your Majesties to spend all the treasure from this enterprise on the conquest of Jerusalem." He meant to be a part of the full, absolute revelation, not merely a partial one. That Revelation, prophesied in the last book of the Bible, would involve the New World, the New Heaven, the New Jerusalem. This suggestion was well received, especially by Isabella, but it played to the apocalyptic longings of both monarchs.

One final document was requested: an official introduction to imaginary Oriental potentates like the Great Khan or other Kings and Lords of India or the Emperor of the island of Cipangu or even the elusive Prester John. Three such introductions were provided, with the name left blank, for no one knew by what titles these exotic Brahmins might like to be addressed.

"To the Most Serene Prince [blank], Our Dear friend, Ferdinand and Isabella, King and Queen of Castile, Aragon, León, Sicily, etc. greetings and increase of good fortune," the document read. "From the statements of certain of Our subjects who have come to Us from Your Kingdoms and Domains, We have learned with joy of Your esteem and high regard for Us and Our nation and of Your great eagerness to be informed about things with Us. Wherefore, we have resolved to send you Our Noble Captain, Christopher Columbus, from whom you may learn of Our good health and Our prosperity."

The Catholic monarchs made one final gesture. They appointed Columbus's son Diego as page to Prince Juan, the heir apparent to the Spanish throne. This was a seminal honor that was accorded only to the sons of the most distinguished families in the realm, and it was evidence of how completely they had now swung over to Columbus.

If in that last session in the Alhambra, Columbus pandered to the apocalyptic dreams of the monarchs—first Spain, then the New World, finally Jerusalem—he also flattered them on their victory over the infidel. He proposed to be the right arm of their crusade. "I saw the Moorish King come forth to the gates of this city," he would say, "and kiss the Royal hands of Your Highnesses. As Catholic Princes devoted to the Holy Christian faith and propagators thereof and enemies of the sect of Mohamet and of all idolatries and heresies, you resolve to send me to regions of India to see princes and peoples and lands and to determine the manner in which their conversion to our Holy Faith may be accomplished."

Isabella and Ferdinand had made him join them as a dog of God. Theirs was a great crusade to purify the world of heresy and idolatry, as it advanced the glory of Spain. Columbus would rejoice in the fact that his glorious undertaking coincided with the monarchs' decision to deal decisively with the superstition of Judaism.

On March 30, 1492, a month before Columbus's final sendoff at Granada, the Catholic monarchs issued a royal decree to expel all Jews from Spain.

22

The Pit and the Snare

❖

On November 16, 1491, six weeks before the fall of Granada and two months before Columbus was given his authority, an *auto-da-fe* was held outside Ávila in a meadow called the Brasero de la Dehesa (Brazier of the Pasture). At last, the case of the Holy Child of La Guardia came to its gruesome consummation. A formal condemnation was read, and then the prisoners were handed over or "relaxed" to their executioners. Some relaxation. The effigies of the three deceased Jews were burned first. Then the conversos, including Benito Garcia, who had repented of his sins and had asked to be taken back into the Church, were accorded the mercy of being strangled to death before being burned. Then came the climax of the spectacle: the bodies of the Jew, Yuce Franco, and his eighty-year-old father, were torn with hot pincers before their mutilated bodies were burned at the stake.

Whether Torquemada was present for this gory Act of Faith is not known, but his ghostly figure hovered like the Fourth Horseman of the Apocalypse over the entire case from start to finish. The Grand Inquisitor had a larger agenda. The case of the Holy Child of La Guardia was central to his strategy for the final solution of the Jewish problem. The case was his catalyst. The condemnation of Benito García and his Jewish co-conspirators, Torquemada insisted, must be read from the pulpits of churches throughout Spain, accompanied by a warning to conversos not to associate with Jews, lest their minds be contaminated again by Jewish superstitions.

Popular loathing for Jews was inflamed throughout the country, as Torquemada hoped. Women and mothers were especially incensed.

Inevitably, Jewish quarters were attacked. A Jew was stoned to death in Ávila, and the situation threatened to get out of hand.

At first, no doubt from the prodding of her court rabbi, Abraham Senior, and his brilliant cohort, Don Isaac Abravanel, Queen Isabella's instinct was to protect her Jewish subjects from this hate campaign. Indeed, she issued a decree to that effect. But the popular outcry over the La Guardia case raged beyond her control.

Torquemada, meanwhile, went about laying his groundwork quietly and methodically. In early December 1491, he sent a portentous memorandum to the monarchs in which he complained that the restrictions on dress for Jews, including the wearing of the Jewish badge, were not being enforced. For one who himself wore the hair shirt, the clothes of both the Jew and the penitent seemed inordinately important to the Grand Inquisitor. He had become a specialist in garments of shame and discomfort. The year before, he had approved a new fashion for the penitent to replace the drab yellow of the traditional penitential cloak known as the *sanbenito*. The new style featured black or gray sackcloth, eighteen inches long and nine inches wide, on which a large red cross was to be displayed prominently front and back. Another point in the memo sought to restrict how Jews could exercise authority over Christians in the business of tax collection. If the crown were, by some chance, to lose its master tax agents, like Abravanel and Senior, who could replace them? Torquemada needed to plan ahead.

By implication, these provisions targeted the special privileges of the two court rabbis, for their power had to be undercut if Torquemada was to realize his ambitions. The Grand Inquisitor was all too aware of the influence Senior and Abravanel wielded with the monarchs. Senior's association extended back farther than Torquemada's, to the days of royal courtship. His faithful service, his tax collection and war loans, his loyal embassy to his people for the crown, made him a formidable adversary and a significant impediment to Torquemada's plans. Abravanel, in turn, had become the queen's personal financial adviser and the crown's main tax collector in central Castile, as well as the tax collector for the Cardinal of Spain, Pedro Gonzales de Mendoza. Importantly, with the royal treasury virtually empty as the royal army stood before the walls of the Alhambra, Abravanel had personally loaned 1.5 million maravedis to the queen to support the siege. The queen was deeply in his debt.

At the time of the Torquemada memorandum, the negotiations with Boabdil for the surrender of Granada were well under way. One hundred and ten Jewish families lived in that city. The Inquisition insisted that they must be expelled as part of the final surrender agreement. One month would be given for them to settle their affairs and leave. The monarchs bowed meekly to this demand, and Torquemada and his new archbishop in Granada, Hernando de Talavera, watched closely as the families disposed of their property and packed up.

Granada was to be a test of Torquemada's wider master plan. But the actual launch of that master plan was a closely held secret between the monarchs and their principal prelates, the Grand Inquisitor, the new archbishop of Granada, and the Cardinal of Spain.

If the immediate and indeed longer-range signs of impending catastrophe for Spanish Jewry were obvious and unmistakable, neither Senior nor Abravanel seemed to notice. Comfortable in their personal luxury, living grandly in the last vestiges of their golden age, secure in the knowledge that they had valiantly served the War Against the Moors with their loans to the crown, they were blind to the portentous rumblings. When the catastrophe hit them in March 1492, the blow seemed to come as a complete surprise. In the waves of anti-Semitism, the talk of pure Spanish blood, the ghettos, the fury of the Inquisition, the restrictions, the identifying cloaks, the expulsions in Andalusia and Aragon and Granada, the *autos-da-fé*, the greed of Ferdinand, the sanctimony of Isabella, the passion of Torquemada, the preparation for the Second Coming—all this, the burden of the past twenty years of Spanish history, was coming to fruition. Yet the two rabbis went blithely about their business.

In his writings later, Rabbi Abravanel would insist that when the dire portent finally dawned on him, he had met three times with the sovereigns and vociferously protested to the king and a host of his ministers.

"Three times with my own mouth, I implored him, 'Save us, O King! Why do you do this to your servants?' " At the rabbi's protests, King Ferdinand remained stonily silent, his ears deaf as a viper. Queen Isabella stood "on the King's right to lead him astray." Piously, she whispered that God had put this obsession in the king's heart. There was nothing she could do about it. She invoked Proverbs 21:1,

"The king's heart is in the hand of the Lord, as the rivers of water: he turneth it whithersoever he will."

"Do you think that we were the ones who said this to you?" she continued. "It is the Lord who placed that word in the king's heart."

By contrast to Abravanel, Abraham Senior did more than employ empty words. Perhaps cold cash could speak louder. And so the most powerful and wealthy Jew in the land, perhaps in concert with Abravanel, offered 30,000 gold ducats to the Catholic king and queen if they would stay their hand. This was an enormous pile of money, nearly 4 million maravedis, truly worthy of a royal bribe, especially to a crown that was virtually broke. Ferdinand wavered, and it seemed for some days that the monarchs were reconsidering. Soon enough, Torquemada sniffed out this rumor and flew into the royal presence, brandishing a cross, his normally sallow face red with rage. He slapped the cross on the table before the startled monarchs and shouted,

"I know what you are up to, King. Behold the crucifix of our Savior whom the wretched Judas sold for 30 pieces of silver to his enemies and betrayed our Lord to his persecutors. If you approve that deed, at least sell him for a greater sum. I resign from all my power. Nothing shall be imputed to me, but for this wicked deed, you will answer to God!" With that, he turned and stalked out.

His theatrical raving had its intended effect. The monarchs looked at one another thunderstruck. There would be no more talk of Judas gold. Torquemada had won. Ferdinand contemplated the windfall. The heart of Isabella hardened. It was God's will that Spain should be thus cleansed and purified, as a beacon to the world. This was preparation for the Second Coming, after which, guided by Spain, the New Heaven would be revealed on the New Earth.

On March 31, 1492, they issued their formal Edict of Expulsion. The Jews of Spain were continuing their evil ways, "seducing faithful Christians to their own damnable beliefs and opinions, instructing them in the ceremonies and observances of Jewish law, holding meetings where they read to them and teach them what to believe, advising them of the Jewish fast days to observe, teaching them the histories of their law, instructing them about the Passover and other Jewish ceremonies, supplying them with unleavened bread and ceremonially prepared meats and persuading them to observe the Law of Moses, giving them to understand that there is no true law except the Law of Moses."

Nothing would dissuade the Jews from their hideous conspiracy against the true faith except their complete removal from the province of the faithful.

"To this end we issue our Edict, by virtue of which we command all Jews, of both sexes and all ages, who live, dwell, and are in any way present in our kingdoms and lands, both natives and foreigners who in whatever manner or for whatever reason have come or are now here, that by the end of July of this present year of 1492, they be gone from all our kingdoms and lands, together with their sons, daughters, Jewish servants and familiars, without regard to rank or station, and of whatever age they may be, and that they not presume to return or even to pass through these realms nor any part of them under pain of death and confiscation of all their property."

A month after the Edict's publication, heralds fanned out across the country to announce the edict in the cathedrals and town squares, accompanied by trumpeters and drummers. The action would have to reach many people. It affected all of "Jerusalem in Spain," the traditional Hebrew designation for Sephardim. Spanish Jews were the descendants of Judean royalty who had lived in Spain for nearly one thousand five hundred years and graced Iberia with a long line of poets, scientists, diplomats, and philosophers. The shock was enormous. Because it took some days for the edict to be broadcast to the far corners of Spain, Torquemada, in the fullness of his generosity, extended the deadline for departure by a few days, to August 2. For his victims, the choice of that day was horribly appropriate. In the Jewish calendar it was the 9th day of Av, the day of mourning, which commemorated the destruction of the Temple and which became a portentous day for many subsequent catastrophes of the Jewish people.

The people of Abraham, Jacob, and Isaac had one option only to avoid exile: to convert immediately to the Christian faith. How many Jews took this plunge no one can say, but the offer caused its own havoc, as the churches were swamped with simple peasants who were terrified and had suddenly seen the light. On one morning in Teruel alone, while the local rabbi was detained in his house under house arrest, one hundred persons were baptized. Elsewhere, prominent and influential rabbis were given one day to leave their communities, and three days to leave the country. The number of the converted was higher in Aragon than elsewhere, since Torquemada, with the sufferance of Ferdinand, insisted on the disposal of Jewish property there being handled directly by the Inquisition. Each Jewish household was required to appraise the value of its property and report the figure to the Inquisition. Across Ferdinand's ancestral realm, Christians were forbidden to trade or to have contact with departing Jews.

With the country in chaos, Ferdinand, with no hint of irony, wrote to Torquemada: "I have been informed that the banishment of the Jews is now public, and that many of them want to become Christians, but are suspicious of doing so out of fear of the Inquisition. They worry that the most minor error that they commit will result in the execution of grave penalties against them." Royal orders were quickly drawn up to facilitate conversion and give the new converts time to adapt to the ways of their new faith. Guarantees were given that no harm would befall the converts. And Torquemada himself, in the sweetest of tones, encouraged Jews to return to the Mother Church, "whose arms are always open to embrace those who return to her with repentance and contrition."

As individual Jews considered their horrible fate—to leave or convert, to flee to Italy, Portugal, North Africa, or Turkey, to sell their land

and houses to scoundrels and parasites for a pittance—the spiritual police, the *Santa Hermandad*, pondered the immense logistical problems of
the exodus. Ironically, Abraham Senior, as treasurer of the *Hermandad*,
was drawn into the planning for the deportation of his own people. As
the titular leader of all Spanish Jews and the chief magistrate of
Jerusalem in Spain, it fell to him to oversee the disposal of Jewish property. While the regulations announced that Jewish property was to be
sold at "fair and equitable prices," a vast rip-off got under way. Its essence
was distilled in a sentence by the court chronicler, "they exchanged a
house for a donkey or a vineyard for a piece of woolen or cotton cloth."
Royal storehouses filled with silverware, china, jewelry, goblets, and
valuable textiles. (Some of these were later sold to finance the second
voyage of Christopher Columbus.) Debts to Jews were supposed to be
paid promptly, but most delayed their payment until after the deadline
for departure and thus avoided the obligation altogether. Synagogues
and their cemeteries were turned over to the royal treasury or converted
to Christian churches. Gold-embroidered and silk-covered Torah scrolls
were confiscated. No gold, silver, or precious stones could be taken out
of the country.

At this colossal disaster, the emotions of the deportees ran the
gamut: anger, fear, uncertainty, confusion, despair, self-loathing.

To most of the victims, King Ferdinand was the arch villain, the incarnation of this evil, the messenger not of God but of the Devil. He
was the new Nebuchadnezzar, the King of Babylon in the sixth century
before Christ who destroyed Jerusalem and "who dimmed the beauty of
our light and threw down from heaven the pride of our glory." He was
like unto Nabal in I Samuel (25:25), a man of great power but of churl-
ish and evil ways and disobedient to King David. "Nabal is his name
and folly is in him. . . . His heart died in him and he became as a stone
and ten days later, the Lord smote him and he died." Ferdinand was
Sennacherib, the Assyrian king of the eighth century B.C., "who min-
gled the nations and scattered Jews across the earth." The refugee who
made that remark might only hope in his anger that Ferdinand would
suffer the same fate as Sennacherib, that his host would be destroyed

when field mice again might devour all his quivers and bowstrings and the thongs that bound his soldiers' shields.

Isabella came in for her share of criticism in the Hebrew chronicles as well. In her complicity in the expulsion, she was likened to Jezebel, the wicked and evil genius of biblical Phoenicia, symbol of feminine depravity and betrayal. Some regarded the queen as the pure anti-Semite who was provoked by Torquemada and became the real instigator behind the expulsion, and whose problem was to overcome the softness in her husband's heart, because of his Jewish blood.

Why would the king and queen have done such a terrible thing? The question tormented the wise men among the Jews, and a number of explanations were put forward. One of the most interesting came from a rabbi and scholar named Solomon Ibn Verga. To him, Ferdinand was ashamed after the conquest of Granada and wondered how he could find favor in the eyes of his God, who had given him victory on the battlefield. "In what way can I promote my Creator who has given me the city of Granada into my hands," the rabbi imagined the king saying to himself, "except by bringing under my wing the nation that walks in darkness, the lost lamb Israel, to return the silly, wayward daughter to my faith? I will say to the Jews, 'If you will denounce God, be baptized and bow in worship to my God, then the fat of the land you will eat like me. But if you refuse and rebel, I will exile you far away to some other land. After three months, there will not be even a crumb left of anything that is called Jacob.' "

If many vented their anger at Ferdinand, others were mired in terror and self-pity and self-loathing. They were living once again the prophecy of Moses. For their disobedience and transgressions, the Lord was scattering them and making them serve other gods, even ones of wood and stone which neither they nor their fathers had known. They would have no rest, but rather a trembling heart, the failing of eyes, the languishing of soul. King Ferdinand was an instrument of a vengeful God wielded against a sinful people. "In God's hatred of us," wrote one deportee, "He made Ferdinand King over all of Spain. In his evil decrees, the king did what his fathers and his fathers' fathers had not done. . . . And the Lord's word was in the conflagration. The land of Spain burned with the fire of God." From such divine vengeance there was no escape. Another writer found certification in the words of the prophet Jeremiah (48:43–44), "Fear, and the pit, and the snare shall be upon thee, O inhabitant of Moab, saith the Lord. He that fleeth from the fear shall fall into the pit; and he that getteth up out of the pit shall be taken in the snare: for I will bring upon it, even upon Moab, the year of their visitation, saith the Lord."

The year 1492 was the year of their visitation.

Christian commentators naturally saw things differently. They too regarded Ferdinand as an agent of providence. The king had ordered the expulsion "in the love of God, when he could no longer bear the actions of those who had crucified Jesus." Andrés Bernáldez, the scribe of the monarchs, the friend of Columbus and chronicler of his voyages, felt Ferdinand had done the Jews a great favor. In his chronicle he described how the rabbis of Spain explained Ferdinand's action to their people. "They bade them know," wrote Bernáldez, "that this thing came from God, who wished to lead them from servitude and bring them to the Promised Land. In this departure they would see how God would do many miracles for them and bring them from Spain with wealth and great honor, as they hoped; and that if they encountered any misfortune or setback along the way, they would witness how God would lead them as He had done for their fathers in Egypt."

Another Christian commentator felt that the expulsion touched upon the glory of religion. The edict might be cruel, he admitted, that is, "if we regard Jews not as animals but as human beings and creatures of God." The Renaissance man, Pico della Mirandola, was ambivalent. "The sufferings of the Jews, in which the glory of Divine Justice delights," he said, "were so extreme as to fill us Christians with commiseration." And years later, Machiavelli in *The Prince* saw the expulsion not as a religious but as a rare act of political daring. Perhaps the edict was "pious cruelty," but it was an example of how a successful prince can make good, if cynical, use of religion, thus enabling him to undertake greater and more heroic enterprises.

As France closed its borders to the refugees, the path of least resistance led to Portugal. For a handsome price, João II had agreed to accept the deportees temporarily. After the refugee paid his exit fee to Spain, he faced an entry fee at the Portuguese frontier of 8 gold cruzados per person. More than half the Jews took this route.

And so the sad procession began. Even the most rabid Jew hater could not but be moved by the spectacle. Three days before their departure, the Jews of Segovia gathered at the graves of their forefathers and shattered tombstones to carry away the shards into exile with them. The sight of the bedraggled, wretched refugees along the dusty roads evoked great admiration. "Over the fields they pass, in much travail and misfortune, some falling, others standing up, some dying, others being born, others falling sick, that there was not a Christian but felt sorrow for them," a witness wrote. "And always where they went the Christians invited them to be baptized. Some in their misery would convert and remain, but very few. The rabbis continually gave them strength and made the women and girls sing, and play tambourines and timbrels, to raise the people's spirits."

The remainder left by sea, embarking upon whatever rattletrap tub they could find to take them. From Cádiz and Almería, they headed for North Africa, from Barcelona and Valencia to Italy or Turkey. As their property had been stolen from them in their own villages, and on the road to their embarkation points, so too many were attacked and robbed by their sea captains or by pirates once they were in open waters.

"Half dead mothers held dying children in their arms," wrote one commentator. "I can hardly say how cruelly and greedily they were treated by those who transported them. Many were drowned by the avarice of the sailors, and those who were unable to pay their passage sold their children."

If they made it safely to their destinations, thieves and slavers awaited them onshore. All suffered; many died; until, as one said, only a few remained of the many.

And so on the 9th day of Av, they sat on the ground, wherever they were, tore the cloth from their Torah scrolls, dimmed their lamps, and read from the book of Lamentations. As Jerusalem was destroyed in the days of Nebuchadnezzar and Titus, so Jerusalem in Spain was destroyed. They were paying for their disobedience to the Law of Moses once again. Their affliction was of their own doing. Yet another generation was paying for the sins of their fathers, enduring the curse of Moab, finding themselves scattered even to the geographical limits of the known world.

*

And what of the court rabbis, Don Abraham Senior and Don Isaac Abravanel? What would be their choice? To leave and take up the wanderer's staff or to stay and betray one's faith? The choice was Hobbesian in its horror and its impossibility, a Jewish version of the choice between the pit and the snare.

For Don Isaac Abravanel the horror seemed the worse of the two, for he agonized about it more publicly. Because his faith was deeper, his disillusionment was more intense, and at first, he would seem ripe for apostasy. Later he wrote profusely about his initial confusion and bitterness. His anger was raw and vivid. Yet it was directed not at his royal tormentors but inward, at himself, at his own people, at the failure of his ancient texts, even at his vengeful God. His first reaction was to despair that all hope had been lost.

The catastrophe was so much worse than anyone could ever have imagined. At first he seized upon the passage in the psalms of praise in the Haggadah (116:11): "I said in my haste all men are liars." It seemed to Abravanel that in this disaster all the prophets, Moses with his promises, Isaiah in his words of comfort, Jeremiah and Ezekiel in their prophecies—all were liars. "Our hope is lost," he despaired, "the anointed God of Jacob is dead or broken or imprisoned. His sun will not shine."

The pressure on him to convert was enormous, since he was famous in the land and vital to the financial well-being of the realm. When ordinary measures failed to work, harsher tactics were tried. His grandson was kidnapped and secretly taken to Portugal, where he was held ransom to conversion. Later, the boy's father, Isaac's son Judah, wrote a poem about the kidnapping.

> At the same time that exiles fled from Spain
> The King set up an ambush and bespake
> That I be barred from safely passing through,
> So that he might my youngest suckling take
> And make of him a convert to his faith.

But the ploy failed.

For one so devout as Don Isaac Abravanel, only one path was possible. It was consistent with the fate of his people and his fathers and himself. His forebears had fled Castile after the persecutions in 1391. They had gone to Portugal, settled and prospered, until he personally had been forced to flee the King of Portugal in 1483 in the purge of dissidents. Since Don Isaac now stood convicted of the capital crime of conspiracy there, Portugal was closed to him as a destination. He would take his family to Italy.

In the weeks after the edict, he worked feverishly to liquidate his assets. His holdings were vast and complicated: leases, mines, lands, herds of cattle, properties, commercial ventures, tax fees. From the towns under his supervision in central Castile alone, he was owed more than 1 million maravedis. To collect these debts and to settle the books in good faith for the cardinal and the Queen of Spain was a gargantuan task, especially in an environment where debtors were stalling for time. Ironically, Abravanel sought help from the officers of the law to pressure his debtors to pay up.

In late July, only days before the deadline, the clan of Abravanel gathered in Valencia for its departure to Naples. After all his trouble to salvage a vestige of his wealth, he would be permitted to leave the country only if he renounced his claim to funds owed to him by the crown itself. As a special dispensation to him, the crown relaxed its more stringent provisions and allowed him to leave with 1,000 gold ducats. (Later, Christian writers would tell of the anatomical marvel of Jews smuggling ducats out of the country in their stomachs. Women were said to be especially amazing. Some of them, it was claimed, could swallow 30 ducats at once!)

The departure of the Abravanel family was delayed several days, since Don Isaac's brother, Yose Abravanel, was called to testify at a trial of the Inquisition. Inquisitional trials in Valencia had the reputation of being spirited affairs. For Yose Abravanel, this last brush with the Spanish Inquisition was a detail, and he gave his testimony freely, to the prosecution. His affairs were in order. He had sold his house to the other court rabbi, Don Abraham Senior.

The mind of Don Isaac Abravanel rested upon the larger tragedy. Of Spanish Jewry, he would write eloquently:

"There never was such a chosen people in beauty and pleasantness. There will never be another such people. God is with them, the children of Judea and Jerusalem, many and strong . . . a quiet and trusting people, a people filled with the blessing of God with no end to its treasures."

❊

In mid-May 1492, Ferdinand and Isabella left Granada and traveled north to the holy retreat of Guadalupe. Remote in rugged country of sharp defiles and mesas, the village was famous as a pilgrimage site. Its Monastery of Santa María de Guadalupe on the town's plaza was dedicated to the Virgin of Guadalupe, whose statue there was believed to have been carved by St. Luke and which had miraculously survived the Moorish occupation until it had been discovered by a shepherd in 1330. Somehow it seemed appropriate that at this pivotal moment of religious history in Spain, Isabella and her crusading husband should surround themselves with pious friars and incense and sacred music and legends of saints and virgins, as they pondered the purification of their realm. The place exuded its evangelizing piety and had inspired the saying,

He who is a count and wishes to be a Duke
Becomes a priest in Guadalupe

The royal retinue was joined by the court rabbi, eighty-year-old Don Abraham Senior. The pressure on him to convert was no less than it had been on Abravanel, and there were indications after the edict that he too was leaning toward exile. Queen Isabella was confident that she could persuade him otherwise. At his advanced age, twenty-five years older than his protégé, Senior was less able to endure the hardships of exile. He had even more wealth to lose, and his reach was national rather than regional. Should he defect as well, the finances for the nation would be thrown into total chaos. But he was also less inclined to choose his faith over his position in the court. If his love for his people was above question, the pleasure in his vast financial empire was great. More importantly, the sincerity of his religious beliefs had always been in doubt. A fellow rabbi had said of Senior that he "lacked knowledge and a fear of God."

The monarchs needed to be sure, and Queen Isabella stepped into the breach. If Senior did not convert, she threatened coldly, she would obliterate the Jewish community totally and pulverize their properties. And so, the apologists wrote later, Senior "did what he did to save the lives of many people, and not of his own desire."

On June 15, 1492, six weeks before the deadline, in the apse of the Church of Santa María de Guadalupe, Don Abraham Senior was baptized in the Christian faith with the grace of the Holy Spirit. They made of it an extravagant affair. The royal council was in attendance, including Rodrigo Maldonado and the converso and Columbus saviour Luis de Santángel. The Cardinal of Spain officiated, as the papal nuncio stood at his side. The king and queen assumed the role of godparents as Senior took the aristocratic name of Fernando Núñez Coronel. The very name was an amalgam of all the right touchstones: Fernando, after King Ferdinand; Núñez, a common forename in the House of Mendoza; Coronel, suggesting a colonel or a person of rank. Within a few weeks, in addition to his normal duties in the exchequer, he was appointed the alderman of Segovia, a political post that only a Christian could hold.

The conversion was a great victory for the crown. The cash flow to the royal treasury was safe. The message spread rapidly that the most prominent Jew in Spain had become a Christian. In the Jewish communities the reaction was amazement and sadness, but most of all, embarrassment. Senior, nay Coronel, stood alone, an anti-leader and heretic to Judaism. Among the thousands who converted, compared to the tens of thousands who went into exile, only he had stature and influence. He would be cursed as the "enemy of light," and a number of his own immediate family rejected his path.

For many, the word of his conversion fired their determination further.

"Let us be strong, for our religion, for the Law of our fathers before our enemies and blasphemers," one of their wise men proclaimed. "If they will let us live, we shall live; if they kill us, then shall we die. We will not desecrate the covenant of our God. Our heart shall not fail us. We will go forth in the name of the Lord."

23

The Curse of Palos

PALOS

 On May 12, 1492, Christopher Columbus left Granada for Palos. He traveled the coach road 170 miles due west to Seville, descending from the plateau of Granada into the luxuriant breadbasket of the glorious and now fallen Caliphate of Al Andalus. Through the foothills and fertile fields of the Genil Valley, past ancient olive orchards and wheat fields and groves of scarlet oak and palmetto, the towns he passed had been of stategic importance in the War Against the Moors: Santa Fe, Loja, Antequera, and Marchena, where the hero of the war, the paragon of medieval chivalry, Rodrigo Ponce de León, the marquis of Cádiz, had retired to his ducal palace and would soon be dead of weariness. In Moorish Marchena, thoughts of both the past and the future raced through the Admiral's head. Here Boabdil had made his last gasp, one that had made Columbus's journey across the Ocean Sea possible. The town was also the birthplace of his ever faithful Franciscan friend Antonio of Marchena, the amateur astronomer of the monastery at La Rábida in Palos.

His journey was slow, for Jews choked the roads. If Columbus was touched by the sight of these wretched refugees, there is no suggestion of it in his writings or those of his son. What he did write to his patrons in this prologue to his voyage was his self-serving celebration of their actions against the Moors and the Jews, praising the king and queen as "enemies of the sect of Mahomet and of all idolatries and heresies." He gloried in the fact that the monarchs had approved his voyage in the same season as they had exiled all Jews from the realm.

Columbus then came into the great valley of the Guadalquivir. After tarrying briefly in Seville with his mistress, Beatriz Enríquez de Arana, he continued west 40 miles into the valley of the Rio Tinto, arriving at Palos on May 22. The journey of 300 miles had taken him ten days.

At the Monastery of La Rábida the brothers Antonio and Juan Perez greeted him excitedly, for his arrival at last as an official agent of the crown and an Admiral of the Ocean Sea was a personal triumph for the friars. Having been Columbus's constant advocates throughout, the brothers had always hoped that Palos and their monastery would share in the great glory they imagined lay ahead. No doubt, the candles burned late and low that night, as the map of the known world was spread out on the heavy walnut table in the refectory, and the difficulties of finding the ships and recruiting a veteran crew were discussed into the wee hours of the morning.

The following day, on a promontory overlooking the Tinto just outside the village, a formal assemblage of local dignitaries, the mayor, alderman, and constables of Palos, gathered on the steps of the Church of St. George. The church had once been a mosque, its Moorish arch still visible within a later Christian makeover, and it stood in the shadow of a Moorish castle on higher ground. With Columbus and the friars at his side, the notary public stepped forward to proclaim the royal decree in important, stentorian tones. The officials of the town stiffened as the preamble of the decree was read. "You will know that, because of certain acts performed and committed by you to Our detriment, you were condemned by Our council and obliged to provide Us for twelve months with two caravels equipped at your own expense, whenever and wherever by Us, under fixed penalties, as is provided in detail in the aforementioned decree which was pronounced against you."

And so this foreigner with his royal documents, his important airs, and sanctimonious friends was coming as the agent of a royal rebuke to Palos. The punishment for the town's transgressions (which were left unspecified in the decree, though all in the audience knew what they were) was to provide two caravels (the third somehow to be commissioned by the Admiral himself), a year's provisions, and a crew of ninety. The royal language was harsh: "We warn you that if you do not render performance as specified, we shall order the execution of the penalties against you and your property. None of you shall contravene these provisions in any way under pain of forfeiting Our favor and 10,000 maravedis to our exchequer for each infraction."

The mission of the voyage had been left deliberately vague in the royal decree: "a voyage with three ships to certain parts of the Ocean in order to fulfill duties at Our Service." But in the coming days the true nature of the commission became known, and when it did, the mockery began. Palos and the larger village of Moguer upriver was full of oceanic sailors and sea captains. These veterans scoffed at this royal endeavor as vain and pointless. One claimed to have been on a Portuguese mission of the same sort—was it Dulmo's misadventure?—that attempted to sail due west from the Azores and had found nothing.

At the outset, the scolding tone of the royal decree alienated the townspeople of Palos, but the royal scold had a sound basis. The mariners of Palos had always been an unruly lot, and they were persistent in the practice of illicit slave trade. Their ships had encroached upon the Portuguese province of Guinea in Africa, had sacked the village of an important African king, taking slaves to be put to work in the copper and silver mines of Andalusia, thus jeopardizing relations with Portugal. In their endeavors, the outlaws avoided royal taxes and sanction. This was the basis for their punishment of providing two caravels for royal use, and the fact that the royal decree punished the whole town suggested that more than just a few men were involved. So the shores of the Río Tinto teemed not only with veteran sailors but unsavory pirates and cutthroat slavers as well, and Columbus was well advised to be cautious both in his recruiting and in his business dealings. Still, skepticism and guilt were also tinged with fear at this dangerous adventure. *El mar tenebroso*—the Gloomy Sea—held more than a few terrors. No one stepped forward, certainly not the owners of caravels in the area.

In desperation, Columbus sent word of this non-cooperation to the monarchs in Guadalupe. They responded by dispatching an officer of the royal council named Juan de la Peñalosa to twist some arms. But at first he too had no success with the sour and resistant locals.

Not everyone in Palos thought that Columbus's venture was futile, however. As it happened, an old salt named Pedro Vasquez de la Frontera lived in the village. Forty years earlier, in 1452, he had been the pilot of a voyage west of the Azores whose mission was to search for the mythical islands of St. Brendan, the "Promised Land of the Saints," that were supposed to exist somewhere in the vast, watery expanse. Ancient as he was, the old mariner still possessed a vivid imagination and a visceral excitement at all voyages of discovery. He told Columbus about sailing into a weedy expanse of ocean west of the Azores, and reassured the Admiral that, notwithstanding the sea monsters that usually populated the unexplored area on medieval maps, he should not fear it. This later became known as the Sargasso Sea, a huge oval of the central Atlantic clogged with floating seaweed or gulfweed that was carried by the circular currents of the ocean, beginning with the Gulf Stream. His ships would be able to sail safely through, Vasquez told Columbus.

The break for Columbus came with his introduction to the Pinzón family. The three Pinzón brothers were the gentry of Palos. They had considerable oceanic experience and owned several ships. Indeed, they were probably implicated in the illicit slave trading for which the whole town was being punished. The eldest and most esteemed of the three was Martín Alonso Pinzón. In 1492, in his mid-forties, he cut a fine, athletic figure. He was thin and wiry, with dark, doe's eyes and a somewhat faraway look to his visage. Along the banks of the Río Tinto, he was regarded as the most capable sea captain in the region, and he was a veteran of sea battles of the War of Succession with Portugal fifteen years earlier.

He was also ambitious and curious. Indeed, as Columbus arrived in Palos, Martín Pinzón was returning from a voyage to Rome. The ostensible purpose for his journey to Italy was to trade sardines; but while there, through a friend who served as a cosmographer in the archives of the Roman Curia, he had perused certain maps of the world, and it is not out of the question that he may have come across the Toscanelli map that had been so important in firing Columbus's imagination initially. But another map transfixed Pinzón: it came from a mythical voyage across the Gloomy Sea to Japan by a mariner of the biblical kingdom of Sheba. From these researches, Pinzón developed his own ambitions to be an explorer. As he came into contact with Columbus, he saw himself not so much as an equal but as a superior. His credentials as a sea captain were far better. Soon enough he would prove himself to be a treacherous rival.

Still, Columbus had the money and the royal licence. And so, for whatever personal reasons, greed and ambition primarily, Martín Pinzón signed on to the voyage enthusiastically. As a bonus, he brought with him his two younger brothers, Vicente Yañez Pinzón and Francisco Martinez Pinzón, both fine and experienced commanders. This moral support was pivotal, for the family carried with it considerable cachet along the riverbank. With these local eminences on board, the magistrates could now enforce the royal prerogatives. First, they commandeered the *Pinta*. This sturdy, square-rigged caravel was impressed into duty over the strenuous objections of her owner, Cristóbal Quintero, and this reluctance was soon to emerge as a real problem. Next they found a sleek little beauty called the *Niña*, which had been built in Ribera de Moguer in the Río Tinto estuary. With triangular rather than square sails, she was configured along the lines of the Portuguese caravels that cruised the coast of Africa and could tack handsomely against prevailing headwinds. Vicente Pinzón became her captain, and Juan Niño, the ship's owner, agreed to be his first mate.

Meanwhile, the Pinzóns fanned out into the taverns and homes of Palos, Moguer, and Huelva to tap the most experienced seamen. "Friends, come away with us," Martín Alonso Pinzón exclaimed in one town plaza. "You are living here in misery. Come with us on this voyage, and to my certain knowledge, we shall find houses roofed with gold and all of you will return prosperous and happy." The twinkly-eyed old salt Pedro Vasquez came along as a booster, encouraging the able-bodied to sign on, for they were certain to find "a very rich land." (Unfortunately, this spry mariner would not live to greet Columbus upon his return. In the rough-and-tumble seacoast life, he was murdered a few months later.)

Beyond the able-bodied, there was a need for specialists: pilots, boatswains, scriveners, stewards, a barber-surgeon, a physician and an apothecary, comptrollers, constables, as well as carpenters, caulkers, coopers, blacksmiths, a silversmith to assay the gold they expected to find, and the translator, Luis de Torres, a Jew who had only recently converted to Christianity. Torres would never get to use his Hebrew and Arabic in conversation with the Great Khan of China or Arabian mariners in the Indian Ocean, but he would gain the distinction of becoming the first European to smoke tobacco.

In Granada, the monarchs, together with Columbus, had anticipated difficulties in the raising of a crew. As a result, just in case, a royal decree had been issued to pardon any criminals who were willing to join the expedition. Their sentences would be suspended, and they would be guaranteed safe conduct throughout the duration of the voyage. Columbus was unenthusiastic about this ploy, reluctant to use his power of pardon, skeptical of inviting ruffians onto his crew. He did not broadcast the opportunity widely. Still, four fugitives came out of hiding to take advantage of this offer of amnesty. Their crime had been to spring a comrade from jail, after the jailbird had murdered the town crier of Palos. Contrary to the legend which later grew up—that the entire crew was comprised entirely of thugs and cutthroats—there were only these four. They were scarcely desperados; they would serve well and honorably; and they would be formally pardoned by the king and queen upon their return.

From the beginning, greed rather than Christian evangelism proved to be the prime motivator for recruitment. The fantasy of gold, pearls, and spices as far as the eye could see was played up, while the more noble impulses were discarded. Indeed, despite Columbus's lip service to saving souls—a principal goal of his expedition was to find the Great Khans of the Orient and to determine "the manner in which their conversion to the Holy Faith might be accomplished"—there was scant talk of religion in Palos. The absence of an evangelizing prelate on the manifest was telling. It was an especially strange and glaring omission since a crew facing the unspeakable terrors and uncertainties of the Gloomy Sea would certainly be consoled by regular supplication to their maker.

❧

With the *Niña* and the *Pinta* in hand, and eighty crewmen including four conversos recruited, the town of Palos had fulfilled the letter of its sentence. But the plan called for three ships, and while the town was charged with the responsibility to ensure that all three ships were suitable for exploration, it was left to Columbus to find and charter the third. By a somewhat mixed fortune, a Galician trading vessel called *Marigalante (Frivolous Mary)* happened to be docked in Palos in May, and, having no better choices, Columbus chartered her reluctantly from her owner, Juan de la Cosa. Square-rigged, with a raised quarter-deck, and a capacity of about 100 tons, she came with a largely Basque crew of forty men. Piously, Columbus renamed her *Santa María*.

Next to the *Niña* and *Pinta*, the *Santa María* was larger, heavier, and slower. She was to gain her prominence as the flagship of the flotilla by virtue of her size alone; but Columbus never liked her. When she came to a bad end, Columbus blamed the town of Palos for not providing a ship that "was suitable for discovery" as the crown had required them to do.

With the addition of the *Santa María*, the financing of the entire voyage came into play. Columbus estimated its cost at 2 million maravedis, and yet the king and queen, using confiscated Jewish gold, had provided only 1.14 million. For a man who had been impecunious just five months earlier, this foray into high finance was daunting. From the moment he received the royal imprimatur on March 31, he went to work on raising the extra funds.

But who had that kind of disposable cash lying around? Naturally enough, the Admiral gravitated to his native countrymen in marine commerce. In 1486 in Córdoba, as he languished on the fringes of the royal court, Columbus had met an Italian slave trader named Juanoto Berardi, with whom he had established a close and productive relationship, and from whom he now secured a loan for the lion's share of the extra money he needed. Berardi was happy to become involved, for his involvement would go a long way to legitimizing his commercial ventures. He, in turn, put Columbus in touch with several other Italian merchants who operated out of Palos on the fringe of the law in the lucrative slave trade. Ironically, the friars at La Rábida facilitated these contacts. By the early summer, Columbus had raised the funds he needed both for the charter of the *Santa María* and the provisioning of his fleet.

For his supplies, especially the food for the voyage, the Admiral was disadvantaged by the calendar. By the time he arrived in Palos, the harvest of spring wheat had taken place and had long since been distributed. The second harvest would not take place until late July. Since sea biscuit or twice-baked bread was the staple for long sea voyages, this was a problem. On this front the presence of the royal constable, Juan de la Peñalosa, was helpful, for he had the power to commandeer needed supplies, despite the resentment this caused. In estimating how much wheat he would need, Columbus had before him the example of Bartholomew Dias and his sixteen-month voyage to the Cape of Good Hope. Columbus thought his requirement would be less. He estimated six months to reach Asia, and guessed that he could not count on resupply in the islands he encountered along the way before he reached fabulous Cipangu. If the roofs were painted in gold there, its Grand Khans were certain to have bread and water.

By late July the preparations were in full swing, and departure was set for early August, the prime season for long-distance sailing. Trouble dogged the process, however, especially in the readying of the *Pinta*. Her owner, Cristóbal Quintero, dragged his feet and groused and beefed, sowing dissension and undermining the captains. Worse, as the departure date approached, it was discovered that the caulking on the

Pinta had been done sloppily. The whiff of deliberate sabotage was in the air. In being ordered to redo their work, a number of workers deserted the project, as did several prospective crewmen.

As the Admiral dealt with this mischief and supervised the loading of supplies, he was also attentive to outward appearances. He commanded that the badge of the Templars, the Cross Pattee (often thought incorrectly to be the Maltese Cross), be painted large and bold and red on the sails, so that in the far distance there could be no doubt that ships of a Christian crusade were approaching. In case gentle persuasion was not sufficient, the caravels were also armed with small cannons, stone cannon balls, crossbows, and primitive muskets.

As the day of departure arrived, a funereal gloom settled over Palos. If August 2 was the 9th day of Av in the Jewish calendar, it was the Feast of the Virgin for the Christians of Palos—a day, appropriately enough, to settle accounts and get one's affairs in order. Dutifully, the practical man, Columbus, paid his crew four months' wages in advance, and then withdrew with his friars to the Monastery of La Rábida to contemplate with awe the monumental odyssey ahead.

They viewed him as a radical visionary, but had not the prophet Daniel coupled the vision with the end? "Understand, O son of man, at the time of the end shall be the vision," and was it not written in the Gospel according to St. Matthew, "And this gospel of the kingdom shall be preached in all the world for a witness unto all nations . . . and then shall the end come." Was he that witness?

Before dawn, on the beach, he knelt before his friends to confess his sins, receive absolution, and take the holy sacrament. At 8 a.m. with the sun well up, the three vessels slid past the bar of Saltes into the Gloomy Sea. The wind filled his topsails, and Columbus set his course for the Canary Islands.

But the Fortunate Islands, as the Canaries were known, would not to be so auspicious after all. On the first leg of the journey, there were more bad omens, and the fear and dread of the crew deepened.

24

Angels of Retribution

❖

ROME

 In the few years before the Great Jubilee of the year 1500, the God-fearing people of Europe had a quickening sense of time's passage. With the invention of the printing press the calendar was among the first items to receive mass distribution. Coupled with the widespread dissemination of the calendar was the invention of the coil spring in clockmaking. This made it possible to mass-produce small, lightweight clocks for the home. Between the calendar and the clock, suddenly the medieval man had a fresh and intimate awareness that time was moving quickly and inevitably toward an appointment with an epochal year.

To the northeast in Nuremberg, Germany, a precocious young painter named Albrecht Dürer would perfectly represent the religious foreboding as the year 1500 approached, when he began to imagine scenes from the book of Revelation. His disturbing visions of the Apocalypse would replace the abstract, mythical, almost comical images of past representations by blending realism with fantasy. Best known is his woodcut etching, *The Four Horsemen of the Apocalypse*. In this shocking portrayal, the agents of retribution—War, Death, Famine, and Disease—are portrayed dynamically as they gallop across the sky, vying with one another for position and trampling their victims underfoot. If his *Four Horsemen* is the most famous of his Apocalypse woodcuts, his portrayal of the opening of the Fifth and Sixth Seals in the book of Revelation dramatized the paranoia of the coming cataclysm. When the Sixth Seal was opened, a shower of burning stars would rain down upon a cowering humanity, as the sun turned black "as a sackcloth of hair," and the moon became blood red.

The signs of the End Times seemed everywhere, either in the glory of Revelation or the disaster of Apocalypse. In Spain, this sense was especially acute. After five hundred years, the infidel in the south had finally been conquered upon the fields of Armageddon. The Jews had been expelled. The Woman of the Apocalypse sat triumphant and resplendent upon the throne, with her magnificent Holy Warrior at her side. Christopher Columbus had been sent forth, and if he was successful, a New World, a New Jerusalem stood to be revealed.

There was a sense that history had arrived at a pivotal turning point. The earth was on the cusp of renewal, renaissance, reformation, purification . . . or disaster. Good was in a death struggle with evil, faith with heresy, glory with corruption. If the right side prevailed, the rewards were manifest. To Christian optimists, prophecies were being fulfilled. The strands of the past were coming together. Could the confluence of these epic forces be a factor of random chance? Surely not. For events so earth-transforming, all to happen at the same time, only divine providence could be responsible.

But could it be that this spasm of good news was merely preparation for the end?

In midsummer 1492, as Columbus made his final preparations, as the Jews boarded their ships, as the Christianization of Al Andalus went forward, the news from "the capital of the world" was bleak. Rome remained the fulcrum of European geopolitics. When events shook the Eternal City, all of Europe shook with it. Now came the report of the deteriorating health of Innocent VIII. As the public perception grew that the pope was dying, lawlessness broke out. Murders and assassinations became commonplace around the Piazza del Popolo and near the Spanish Steps. The Church feared for its treasures. Finally, things grew so desperate that rival factions took the extraordinary step of declaring a truce to quell the disorders.

The more important tournament went forward ferociously behind the scenes. As the pope dwindled, the cardinals jockeyed for position. In the early going, as Innocent VIII moved into his death throes, the Spanish cardinal, Rodrigo Borgia, ran a feeble fourth. His greatest liability was his Spanishness, for in Rome, Spaniards were considered barbarians by the *cognoscenti*. But Borgia had considerable advantages. As vice chancellor, virtually the second pope, he had been a powerful and capable, if controversial, force in Rome for thirty years. His roots were in Valencia, where the Borgias hailed from mixed Moorish stock, and he had been well educated in law at the University of Bologna. His head for business had been evident from an early age. His uncle had been Alfonso de Borgia, the pope Calixtus III, whose achievements were an unsuccessful crusade against the Turks to recapture Constantinople and the cleansing of Church history by declaring St. Joan of Arc officially innocent twenty years after her burning. Calixtus had made his nephew a cardinal at the age of twenty-four and the commander of papal forces.

For a cardinal, Borgia was a wild and rambunctious roué. He was tall, with an athletic build, and his face was full and fleshy, dominated by a curved, aristocratic nose, sparkling eyes, and a full mouth that broke easily into a mischievous smile. While his manner was amiable, he exuded a certain animal energy. He had a honeyed, mellifluous voice, and his words were often laced with well-turned phrases. And he was, in the words of a contemporary, the "most carnal of men."

"He attracts beautiful women to love him and draws them to him like the magnet draws iron," his teacher, Gaspar of Verona, wrote. But Borgia was also a cad. "He leaves them as he found them." In 1460, two years after Calixtus's death, the new pope, Pius II, felt compelled to issue a stern rebuke to the young Spanish cardinal for scandalous behavior.

"My dear Son:

"We have learned that your Worthiness, forgetful of the high office with which you are invested, was present four days ago in the Gardens of Giovanni de Bichis, where there were several women of Siena, women wholly given over

to worldly vanities. Your companion [another cardinal] was one of your colleagues whom his years, if not the dignity of his office, ought to have reminded
of his duty. We have heard that the dance was indulged in with much wanton-
ness. None of the allurements of love were lacking, and you conducted yourself in a wholly worldly manner.

"Shame forbids mention of all that took place, for not only the things
themselves but their very names are unworthy of your rank. You and a few
servants were leaders and inspirers of this orgy. It is said that nothing is now
talked of in Siena but your vanity, which is the subject of universal ridicule!
We leave it to you to decide whether it is becoming to your dignity to court
young women and to send those whom you love fruits and wine, and during
the day give no thought to anything but sensual pleasures."

Though he clearly had no intention to change his rakish behavior,
Borgia apologized, and the pope forgave him. "So long as you do good
and live becomingly, you will find in me a father and a protector whose
blessing will also fall on those who are dear to you," the foolish old pope
replied.

Cardinal Rodrigo Borgia would never lose his passions; but at least
in the year of this rebuke he settled into a permanent, though scarcely
exclusive, relationship with a shrewd and voluptuous beauty named
Vannozza Cattanei. She was said to be a lusty combination of Venus
and Juno, and she parlayed her relationship with the cardinal into a
substantial commodious house on the Via del Pellegrino, the Street of
the Pilgrim. Predictably, it was not far from the cardinal's own magnificent palace, known as the Palazzo Sforza-Cesarini, located aptly
enough on the Via Banchi Vecchi, the Street of the Ancient Banks.
With its tower and three-story loggia overlooking a courtyard, and its
staff of two hundred minions, the Borgia palace was compared to the
golden house of Nero.

In the years ahead, Vannozza bore the cardinal five children, including his favorites, Cesare and Lucrezia Borgia. Between these notorious
villains of history, they were alternately rumored to be masters of the
poison cup, the incest bed, fratricidal dagger, garrote, and, in Cesare's

case, the model, even more than King Ferdinand of Spain, for Machiavelli's ruthless Prince, partly because he terrorized his own father and thus harnessed the power of the pontificate.

If Rodrigo Borgia's lifestyle was lurid, it differed from the other princes of the Church only in minor degree. All the eminent cardinals lived lavishly and extravagantly in the great palaces of Rome, accompanied by musicians and mistresses, guarded by scores of braves. They strutted about in martial garb, dangling elaborately decorated swords from their belts. Treating the red cape of their office merely as the garb of nobility and commerce, they vied with one another in the splendor of their entourage. The children of popes populate pages of Catholic history, but Innocent VIII may have been the first to acknowledge his children openly. His illegitimate son was worthy enough to marry the daughter of Lorenzo de Medici, and the marriage ceremony was held in the Vatican. This was, as one wag put it, "the golden age of bastards."

Meanwhile, over the years in which Ferdinand and Isabella took charge of the Spanish monarchy, Cardinal Borgia made himself the wealthiest man in Rome. As vice chancellor of the Holy See, he assigned to himself the wealthiest abbeys and bishoprics and towns across the southern Mediterranean from Oporto to Majorca to Naples, and raked in their taxes and revenues greedily. In Spain alone he possessed sixteen episcopal sees, including the greatest and richest of them all, Valencia, which he would eventually turn over to Cesare Borgia. Despite the Inquisition and the War Against the Moors, he had cut a number of lucrative business deals with Moors, Jews, and Turks over the years.

His lavish Sforza-Cesarini palace was considered the finest house in all of Italy. Its loggia and great hallways were decorated with scenes from history; its side rooms filled with gorgeous tapestries, sumptuous objects of art, elaborate furnishings and draperies of velvet, brocade, and silk. At his extravagant banquets, the table was set with plates of gold and silver, and if the Spanish cardinal sometimes forgot the words of the ceremonial blessing before the feast, his eminent guests did not seem to mind.

By mid-July 1492, Innocent VIII hovered near death, and knowing the end was near, he summoned his cardinals to his deathbed. In a weak and halting voice, the pontiff apologized to them for his shortcomings and pleaded with them to choose a more worthy successor than he. In the following few days, the most extraordinary measures were applied to revive the dying man. Reportedly, the pope's Jewish physician had consulted a most unusual source for his last desperate measure. It was the writings of the early Christian writer, Tertullian, who in the second century A.D. had prescriptions for everything from arguing with heretics (never use scripture) to rejecting idolatry (it is the principal crime of mankind) to the mistake of the Jews (they had voluntarily rejected God's grace and thus it was offered to gentiles). In the ninth chapter of his *Apology*, he had also addressed the matter of human blood. At gladiator games, Tertullian had pointed out, there were those who drank the blood of brave slain fighters to cure epilepsy.

And so, as the story goes, three boys, ten years old, were purchased for 1 ducat each, killed, and their blood brought for the dying pope to drink. Whether or not Innocent VIII took the ghastly potion, the measure failed, the doctor fled, and the patient died on July 25.

Cardinal Rodrigo Borgia was now sixty years old and ready to throw his considerable clout into achieving his life's ambition. Whoever succeeded Innocent VIII was likely to be the pope to carry the Holy Church through the Jubilee of 1500. For that distinction, the millennial pope was sure to be remembered forever, a goal Borgia certainly achieved. On the more prosaic level, the Jubilee was sure to be a monetary bonanza for the Church, and for whomever led it, in the emporium of selling indulgences.

As the late pope lay in state in St. Peter's and the cardinals rendered their obsequious eulogies, the streets of Rome degenerated into mayhem. It was estimated that some two hundred assassinations took place in the two weeks after the pope's death. The scourge abated only when the cardinals finally gathered in the Sistine Chapel.

The envoys of foreign powers entered the contest with gusto. The Papal States of Milan and Naples squared off with opposing candidates. Charles VIII of France offered 200,000 ducats in support of Giuliano della Rovere as Innocent's successor, while the duke of Genoa sweetened the offer with another 100,000 ducats. But money alone was no guarantee: the support of France was as much a liability as an advantage, and della Rovere was resented for his influence over Innocent VIII. "The intrigues are innumerable and change every hour," wrote the envoy from Florence, whose lord, Lorenzo the Magnificent, had died two months earlier.

On August 6, the Conclave began. Of the twenty-three cardinals, a two-thirds majority was required for election. Della Rovere led with eleven votes, but stalled there a few votes short, and he soon faded. Ascanio Sforza looked strong, as did a Portuguese cardinal, but when Sforza too saw that he would fall short, he began to listen to Borgia's sweet propositions. Mysteriously, four cartloads of silver were delivered to Sforza's palace, with the excuse that perhaps in the unrest the silver would be safer there.

Very quickly the gathering resembled not so much a holy Conclave as a grubby bazaar, and in the trading Rodrigo Borgia had the best goods. To Sforza, he offered the lucrative vice chancellery, his Roman palace, and castles and episcopal sees outside Rome. To the other eminences, he offered estates and abbeys and fortified towns only slightly less valuable, until he found himself one vote short. This last vote was secured by strong-arming a ninety-six-year-old cardinal who had seemed confused by the whole proceeding.

On August 11, the window of the chapel was thrown open and Rodrigo Borgia's election was proclaimed to the world. Two weeks later, he was invested as Alexander VI. Rome had rarely seen a papal ceremony more lavish or outlandish, and it was soon being compared to a Bacchanalian orgy.

"I think," said one chronicler, "that Cleopatra was not received with greater magnificence by Mark Anthony."

Everywhere the Borgia coat of arms, a bull grazing on a gold field, was on display. Flowers and velvet hangings were draped from the buildings, and triumphal arches proclaiming the coming golden age spanned the route from the Vatican to the Lateran Basilica where the investiture took place. Huge crowds lined the procession route, as the resplendent pope-designate rode past on a snowy white stallion. At the Basilica of St. Mark's, one of the ancient titular churches of Rome, an immense sculpture of a bull was erected. From its horns, eyes, ears, and nostrils streamed water, and from its forehead gushed sweet wine. Poets waxed eloquent and profane. "Rome was great under Caesar, greater under Alexander," wrote one. "The first was only mortal, but the latter is a God."

So overwhelming was the pageantry that it went to the head even of the new pope himself. At the Lateran, under the weight of his magnificent and heavy robes, in the sweltering heat, he fainted and had to be revived by splashes of water. Two stalwart cardinals hoisted him up and held him by the armpits for his investiture.

After the official hoopla died down, the backlash over this bought election came immediately. The details of the bribes quickly became public knowledge, evoking widespread disgust and outrage. "Oh, Jesus Christ, it is in punishment for our sins that Thou hast permitted Thy vice-chancellor to be elected in so unworthy a manner!" moaned a Roman notary. It was reported that the King of Naples burst into tears when he heard, even though he had never been known to weep before, even at the death of his own children.

The legitimacy of the election was widely questioned, even by his countrymen Ferdinand and Isabella. The obedience and authority of the Vatican was in jeopardy, and, no doubt, this contributed to Alexander's tolerance and promotion of the tactics of terror so monstrously practiced later by his son, Cesare Borgia. The Catholic monarchs would dispatch one of their most distinguished warriors, Gonzalvo of Córdoba, to Rome to express the indignation of Europe at the election; and still later, a joint delegation from the kings of Spain and Portugal came to protest against papal scandals. Alexander received the envoys in the presence of five cardinals, brandished the threat of excommunication against their kings, and still more menacing, threatened to unleash Cesare Borgia against them.

The disgrace of his simoniacal election would come to define Alexander's twelve-year pontificate. It seemed in character that the new pope soon turned on the very cardinals who had assured his election, banishing a few, imprisoning others, and ensuring the death of others. "Now we are in the power of a wolf, the most rapacious perhaps that this world has ever seen," remarked the scion of the Medicis, Giovanni de Medici. "And if we do not flee, he will inevitably devour us all."

A second theme was also prominent in his rule: the pope's relentless efforts to promote and enrich the House of Borgia. His relatives descended on Rome like starlings to feed on the papal berry tree. So rampant became his nepotism that a noble was heard to say,

"Ten papacies would not have sufficed to provide for all these cousins."

❖

No multitude of complaining Roman notaries or teary-eyed despots or indignant ambassadors could inspire fear or anxiety in the brazen new pope. There was one who could. He was the prior of the Dominican monastery in Florence called San Marco, and the yelping of this dog of God had already shaken kings and potentates. Through the reign of Lorenzo the Magnificent, Florence lay beyond the reach of the Roman Curia. And thus, Girolamo Savonarola could preach his fiery sermons from the high pulpit of the fabulous Duomo without fear of interference from a meddlesome, corrupt pope.

The friar had begun to preach his sermons promoting fundamental reform of the Church and freedom for the people of Florence as far back as Lent in 1485. Indeed, it was the occasions of Lent and Advent that became his stage, and it became his habit to preach on the book of Genesis during Advent. His popularity was immense, his sermons much anticipated. Pico della Mirandola, the brilliant savant of the High Renaissance, spoke of the cold shivers that ran through him and of how the hackles on his neck stood up when he listened to Savonarola preach. Like all demagogues, Savonarola fed on the emotional and psychological impact of his preaching on his listeners. The cavernous Duomo was packed for his riveting performances, which blended charismatic rhetoric with Christian theology, homey pastoral advice, and magical prediction. He had opposed Lorenzo de Medici without fear, excoriating Lorenzo's tyranny and greed, as he advocated for democracy to the masses. Nor did he spare Rome. It was, as his standard reference of Psalm 73 mentioned, a slippery place, where the wicked were prosperous. He cared not for them, for " 'they that are far from Thee shall perish. Thou hast destroyed all them that go a whoring from thee.' "

"We are living in evil days," he proclaimed. "The devil has called his followers together, and they have dealt terrible blows on the very gates of the temple. It is by the gates that the house is entered, and it is the prelates who should lead the faithful into the Church of Christ. Therefore the devil hath aimed his heaviest blows at them, and hath broken down these gates. Thus it is that no more good prelates are to be found in the Church. See how in these days prelates and preachers are chained to the earth by the love of earthly things. The preachers preach for the pleasure of princes to be praised and magnified by them. The new church is no longer built on living rock, but built of sticks, by Christians dry as tinder for the fires of hell."

Besides his passion, Savonarola's courage and honesty and austerity were much admired.

In 1492, a new element came into his arsenal, which scared princes and commoners alike even more. Savonarola prophesied the deaths of Lorenzo the Magnificent and Innocent VIII. In the spring, the first of these "conclusions" came about with the demise of Lorenzo. As the Magnificent One languished on his deathbed in April 1492, he shocked his satraps by calling for Savonarola to administer the last rites.

"I know no honest friar save this one," he murmured, scarcely able to speak.

Though astonished at the summons of one he had so pilloried, Savonarola came dutifully. God is good, God is merciful, he said, but for the Magnificent's soul to rise to heaven, three promises must be given. First, he must truly believe in God's mercy. That was easy. Lorenzo nodded. Second, Lorenzo must return all his ill-gotten wealth to its rightful owners. Still strong enough to feel shock and dismay, Lorenzo reluctantly muttered his agreement. And then, as the legend is told,

Savonarola rose and towered ominously above the deathbed. And lastly, the friar said, Lorenzo the Magnificent must grant liberty to the people of Florence. At this, Lorenzo turned his back to the friar. So be it. Savonarola left the room without receiving the prince's confession and without granting him absolution for his sins. His doctor then gave Lorenzo a potion of dissolved diamonds, and he died, his soul left to languish in brilliant limbo.

When, three months later, Innocent VIII died as well, the prophetic powers of Savonarola were broadcast throughout Italy. Did he truly speak for God? Did he possess the power of life and death? Could he truly be the messenger of God's wrath against the tyrant and the false Vicar?

On Good Friday, 1492, only two weeks after Lorenzo de Medici's death, Savonarola ascended to the pulpit of the romanesque Church of San Lorenzo that was so associated with the Medici dynasty. There, he announced that he had seen a vision. In it a black cross had risen from the city of Rome and reached all the way to heaven, its arms stretching across the earth, and on it was written the inscription *The Cross of God's Wrath.* Thunder and lightning and hail filled the sky. And then he saw Jerusalem, incandescent in the morning light, and from the Holy City, he had seen a golden cross rise, radiating its brilliant rays outward across the world, and upon it were written the words *The Cross of God's Mercy.*

In that Lenten season, he began a series of sermons on Noah's Ark and the Deluge. In Savonarola's allegory, the Ark represented the gathering of the faithful. His Ark was built upon the planks of Christian virtue, and on Easter morning in 1492, he concluded his sermon by saying, "Let all hasten to enter into the Lord's Ark! Noah invites ye all today, the door stands open. But a time will come when the Ark will be closed, and many will repent in vain of not having entered."

Savonarola's words had a terrifying, magnetic effect on his audience. Months later, during Advent, the time supposed by many to be the season when Christ would return for a second time, Savonarola had another vision. Now, in the great Duomo, he spoke of seeing a gigantic hand in the sky, holding a great sword pointed toward the earth, and on the sword were the words "*Gladius Domini super terram cito et velociter*— The Sword of God over the land, quickly, with speed." He heard voices proclaiming mercy for the clean of heart and punishment for the wicked. The angels of retribution were coming, and the wrath of God was at hand. And as the sword hovered above the earth, fire rained down from heaven, and all the world was overtaken by death and pestilence and famine. A great voice commanded Savonarola to proclaim what he had seen, to inspire fear in the people, and to offer hope to those who had lost their way.

"The only hope that now remains to us," he proclaimed, "is that the sword of God may soon smite the earth."

And as he brandished his sword and his Ark and his tempest from the pulpit, so in his tiny austere cell in the Monastery of San Marco, he wrote poetry which sharpened his terrible jeremiad:

> *Soon shalt thou see each tyrant overthrown,*
> *And all Italy shalt thou see vanquished*
> *To her shame, disgrace, and harm.*
> *Thou, Rome, shalt soon be captured:*
> *I see the blade of wrath come upon thee,*
> *The time is short, each day flies past . . .*

> *My Lord will renovate the Church,*
> *And convert every barbarian people.*
> *There will be but one fold and one shepherd.*
> *But first Italy will have to mourn,*
> *And so much of her blood will be shed,*
> *That her people shall everywhere be thinned.*

While Savonarola was preaching in Italy about "one fold and one shepherd" and about converting "every barbarian people," Ferdinand and Isabella in Spain were doing something about it.

25

Harvests Bitter and Sweet

BARCELONA

 In the latter half of 1492, King Ferdinand and Queen Isabella retreated into the Castilian heart of their new and unified Iberian empire. It was as if they realized from the beginning that this year, this *annus mirabilis*, was a historic turning point and that a new epoch, if not a golden age, in Spain, if not in all of Europe, had begun. They did not call it the Renaissance, but all around them, in language, in literature, in music, in art and architecture, as well as politics, were the signs of bursting energy and creativity. As they made their way north, the first modern grammar of Castilian Spanish was presented to the queen, and she understood this linguistic standard immediately to be a powerful tool of imperial consolidation.

The transformation of Granada and Al Andalus was left in the capable hands of the count of Tendilla and the queen's scholarly and pious confessor, Hernando Talavera. In the fall of 1492, the honeymoon for the Muslims of the Old Caliphate was graced and certified with a formal expression of tolerance by the monarchs. On November 29, they officially proclaimed the principle of religious freedom for the Moors. All believers in Islam were guaranteed full liberty to practice their faith, to maintain their laws and customs, to work and trade unmolested by the religious police. Christian women who married a Moor were free to choose which of the two religions they wished to follow. Muslims who had fled to Africa were free to return and reclaim their property. Those Moors who wished to emigrate were to be treated fairly in the disposal of their property.

A honeymoon only it would be. At the recommendation of the Cardinal of Spain and archbishop of Toledo, Pedro González de Mendoza, Hernando Talavera was replaced as the queen's confessor. That he had presided over the discredited Commission of Inquiry into Columbus's proposal, which had recommended against the adventure, was only one aspect of Talavera's diminished standing. More important, his policy toward Islam was gentle and respectful. He believed that Moors should be converted to Christianity through persuasion and example rather than coercion, and he was to devote his energies to missionary work, even encouraging the translation of the Gospels into Arabic. He himself learned the language and required his assistants to do so as well.

But this enlightened stance soon fell out of favor. Cardinal Mendoza and other princes of the Spanish Church argued that the true model for the Moors should be the ultimatum of Jews: baptism or exile. As this idea gradually took hold, Talavera, predictably, would end his career as a victim of the Inquisition, with his own Jewish blood brought to light, and with an accusation, bred of torture, that the archbishop was secretly preaching the return of the prophet Elijah.

Meanwhile, the adoration of the king and queen went forward. The royal choir of twenty young boys and two organists that traveled with the royal entourage sang their praises, accompanied by the triumphal sound of cornet and kettledrum, shawm and sackbut. Juan de Anchieta, Isabella's chaplain and lead singer, composed a romance on the fall of Baza and a mass in celebration of the conquest of Granada. Plays that cast the queen as the heroic lead were written. The queen's prayers and the king's soldiers together had accomplished this historic victory, the heralds exclaimed. She was "the grand lioness," who was feared and loved, the "great and prosperous Queen," who had inspired great courage in the soldiers, "the generous virgin" through whom "the golden centuries" had now begun. The king, in turn, was the illustrious knight who carried a crimson cross and a sparkling sword, whose hosts perturbed the air with dust and glory, devastated the fields of the Moors, and made parish

churches of the mosques of Mohammed. Together, the Catholic monarchs had been guided from above. "As God did His deeds," wrote their
musical propagandist, Juan del Enzina, "defense was unavailing, for
where He put his hand, the impossible was nearly nothing."

Early in 1493, the royal court moved east into Ferdinand's domain
of Catalonia and settled down in Barcelona. Catalonia had long been
troubled by constant military threat from France and even more so by
the fierce independence of its people. Deeply proud of their separate
identity, they held doggedly to their traditions and language, and they
had stoutly resisted the Inquisition for eighteen months. To tame this
beast, Torquemada had personally taken charge as inquisitor in 1486.
From the Palace of the Lieutenants, adjoined to the Royal Palace, the
Suprema had cracked down brutally. In 1487 alone, two hundred
heretics had been—in one of the greatest euphemisms in the history of
language—"relaxed," that is, burned at the stake. Ferdinand viewed the
Inquisition as his best method of social and political control. Only
through the Inquisition's brutal ministrations had the province been
brought to heel.

Now, as the monarchs arrived and took up residence in the Great
Royal Palace, the city presented a woeful face. Once the Venice of Spain
and the rival of Constantinople, with its thriving trade and bustling
commerce, Barcelona suddenly was stagnant. For the Jews of Barcelona
had provided the intellectual energy and the financial backbone of the
city, and they had left en masse. "Today no trade at all is practiced,"
lamented a local dignitary, "not a bolt of cloth is seen. Clothmakers are
unemployed, and other workers the same." The Jewish quarter had
graced the city with its finest schools, its best doctors, its poets and
philosophers, and in the blink of an eye, they were all gone.

In the stagnation of Barcelona lay the bitter harvest of the expulsion.
The city's demoralization was all too evident, even to royalty. From its
windswept streets and dormant quays, the hill behind the city seemed
like a symbol of the wicked edict. For the hill, Tibidabo, took its name
from the Latin words "I will give you," a phrase derived from the biblical
passage on the Temptation of Christ when the Devil takes Jesus up into

the mountain and shows him all the kingdoms of the world. In their greed, the monarchs had given in to the Devil's temptation.

In the deflowering of its populace, Spain had paid a monumental price.

On December 7, 1492, King Ferdinand spent his morning indulging his pleasure in listening to cases in the law court of Barcelona. When the session broke up, he ambled down the steps of the court in languid conversation with his treasurer, Luis de Santángel, surrounded by a crowd of knights and commoners. He tarried for a minute on the last step, and then concluded his conversation, moving toward his mule, which was tied there in the King's Square. Suddenly, an avenging Moor burst from the throng and with all his might struck the king in the head with a three-foot-long scimitar. Ferdinand slumped to the ground with a terrible wound that sliced from the top of his head, across his ear, to his shoulder.

They carried him to the Great Royal Palace, and when she heard the news, the queen could barely look at the wound. She repaired to St. Agatha's Chapel in the palace to pray and then wrote to her confessor,

"I had no heart to see the wound. It was four fingers deep and so long that my hand trembles to say it . . . but all the strings and the neck bone and all that was mortally dangerous was spared."

The gold chain that the king wore around his neck on the day of the attack had arrested the path of the scimitar.

❖

In late February 1493, as the king recovered from his wound, the *Pinta* blew into the tiny Galician port of Baiona in northeast Spain and announced the discovery of the New World. She was a battered, intrepid explorer, with her caulking leaking and her mast loose. In worse shape was her captain. Martín Alonso Pinzón was gravely ill and had to be carried ashore. He was suffering from a strange, unknown disease. Sores covered his body. But the condition of their captain did little to restrain the euphoria of his crew, nor did it suppress their admiration for Pinzón's accomplishments. Had it not been for him, they proclaimed to their amazed audience of fishermen and townspeople, the mission of the foreigner, Columbus, could never have succeeded.

Throughout the many crises of the journey, Pinzón's hand had been steady and reliable, they said. They told of how only four days out of Palos, the rudder of the *Pinta* had jumped its sockets, and how Captain Pinzón had cleverly jerry-rigged the steering with ropes, so that the caravel could limp another 200 miles into Grand Canary. The crew spoke of how bad omens had spooked their mates—early on, they had passed an active volcano in the Canaries and later, a meteorite had fallen within a dozen miles of the little fleet. It had been Martín Pinzón, not the foreigner, who had calmed their fears. They told of how the Admiral had tried to trick his captains and crew about how far they had sailed across the Gloomy Sea, as if the perception of a shorter distance would allay their fears. But Pinzón knew the truth, and Pinzón was not tricked. And it had been Pinzón, some 400 leagues still from land, who had carefully considered the flight of birds that skirted the fleet.

"Those birds breed on land," he said comfortingly, "and to land they go to sleep." From the direction of their flight, Pinzón had suggested a change of course from southwest to southwest by west, and that course had eventually brought them to land.

Still, after four full weeks of sailing across the seemingly endless sea, through sawgrass and doldrums, the crew had grown anxious and combative. They were terrified that the prevailing winds blew in a single, westerly direction, so they would never be able to retrace their path home. Mutiny was in the air. The mariners told their gawking audience of how Columbus was discouraged and on the verge of turning back, as the frightened crew demanded that he do so. At a meeting of captains, he asked the Pinzóns, "What shall we do?"

"Come, sir, we have hardly left Palos, and you are already discouraged." Martín Alonso Pinzón spoke up cheerily. "Onward! onward! that God give us victory, that we discover land, that God does not wish us shamefully to turn back!"

This had inspired Columbus. "Good luck to us then," he said, resigned.

And when the glorious moment came, it was the vigilant Martín Pinzón who had been the first to sight land. It had been he who had fired off his cannon in celebration to alert the Admiral, who tarried far behind. And when Columbus finally came alongside, he had shouted gleefully,

"Martín Alonso, you have sighted land!"

"And my reward, sir?" Pinzón parried.

"I give you five thousand maravedis as a bonus!"

And then they had seen the most astonishing things: islands with beautiful white beaches and palm trees and remarkably clear water, noisy, garishly colored plumed birds, plants that one lit with fire and whose smoke you inhaled with the most sensuous pleasure. They had encountered some natives with coffee-colored skin who walked about entirely naked, without shame, and who had welcomed them effusively, especially the women. Their men had hair as long as women from Castile and festooned with parrot feathers, and they knew how to make safe and palatable bread from the poisonous yucca root. Other natives called Caribs were hostile, shot poisoned arrows, and ate human flesh. In the lagoons, they had seen mermaids with disappointingly ugly faces and unshapely bodies and fish that looked like pigs. They watched the natives fish for very large snails and eat snakes and lizards. They had heard of one island inhabited entirely by beautiful women and of another island where the natives had no hair. In the west of the island Columbus had named Juana (Cuba) after the firstborn son of the monarchs, they had heard that people were born with tails.

They told of how they had explored those smaller islands, how Martín Alonso had been the first to sight the island Columbus called Hispaniola, and then a huge landmass that the Admiral said was Asia and gave the apocalyptic name Alpha and Omega. While the Admiral gabbled incessantly about the island of golden roofs called Cipangu and a king called the Great Khan, and allowed their flagship, the *Santa María*, to run aground in his search, it was Martín Alonso Pinzón who had found the gold of the New World. To prove it, the sailors showed the fishermen the little bag of gold nuggets that each one had, and joked about the simpleminded natives who gave up their treasure for trinkets of colored glass and tiny copper bells.

Lastly, Martín Alonso, the heroic Spaniard, had brought them home safely, ill as he was, through terrible ocean storms. The *Pinta* with Pinzón and the *Niña* with Columbus had stayed together across the expanse, communicating with bells and lamps, until they reached the vicinity of the Azores and were driven apart by a violent storm. Of what happened to the *Niña* and to Columbus, none could say.

Even as their captain was barely conscious, the glasses were raised to him in toast, and to Spain, and, almost as an afterthought, to the Almighty.

The monarchs in Barcelona must be informed.

Dutifully, a letter about the discovery was written, and once it was approved by the sick man, a messenger set off, to ride on horseback the 600 miles across the dusty roads of Galicia and León and Aragon and Catalonia to announce the glory to their majesties and the triumph of the Pinzóns from Palos.

❖

Two weeks after the *Pinta* limped into Baiona in Galicia, the *Niña* appeared in rough seas 200 miles to the south off the Rock of Sintra, at the mouth of the great Tagus River. In a sense, the rude buffeting that Columbus received in the last month of his first journey fit the grandeur of his discovery. Nothing in this adventure had come easily for the discoverer of the New World; yet his difficulties only glorified his accomplishment.

After the *Niña* lost contact with the *Pinta* on the terrible night of February 13, 1493, somewhere in the vicinity of the Azores, the tempest of cross swells and hurricane-force winds increased. The tiny caravel was in desperate peril of being swamped as the waves crashed over it from all sides. To save his craft, Columbus had the yardarms lowered as far as he dared, so the sails would still propel the craft forward but would not be ripped by the savage waves. He allowed the *Niña* to run before the gale, wherever the gale might take her.

The battle with the elements raged outside, but also within Columbus himself, for not only his life but his revelation was at stake. His terror was great. With his mystical nature, he saw his plight as biblical, and he was beset by contradictory emotions, his worries and hopes as crosshatched as the winds and the waves outside. Was his God punishing him for his lack of faith in divine providence? Had he been permitted to see the paradise of the New World, only for his God to kill him? Where was the meaning in that, if his sons were now to be orphaned, and his sovereigns were never to know what had been discovered? Or perhaps as humiliating, that he should perish, and Pinzón should live to take all the credit. Mysterious indeed were the ways of the Lord.

Yet, within his inner prayers, he drew confidence from the honor he had been accorded. He should not fear the squall but only his own inner "weakness and anxiety." His God had granted all his prayers. He had overcome despair and mutiny and Pinzón's betrayal. Many wonders had he seen. After he had been allowed "so great a triumph in discovering what he had discovered," surely his God would allow him to complete what He had begun.

Even as the waves crashed over the *Niña* and the tiny vessel swayed dangerously from side to side, the Admiral sat in his cramped cabin, furiously scribbling down all he remembered about what had been revealed to him in the past three months. When he had finished, he enclosed his parchment in a waxed cloth envelope, put it in a barrel, and threw it overboard.

Then he called the crew together for a collective supplication. For each crew member (but probably not for the Indians they had with them), a garbanzo bean was placed in a cap. One bean was scored with a cross. Whoever drew the cut bean promised to make a pilgrimmage of thanksgiving to the shrine of Santa María at Guadalupe, if they survived this ordeal. The pilgrim was to go "in his shirt" as a sign of humility. Columbus drew first—and drew the crossed bean. Twice more during the night, they gathered to encourage one another, making vows to send a pilgrim to Santa Maria of Loreto in Ancona, Italy, where according to legend, the Holy House of the Virgin Mary had been carried by angels after the twelfth-century Crusades and which as the patron for mariners was supposed to spawn miracles. And later, in a vow they came to regret, they promised to visit the first church of the Holy Virgin that they encountered once they were safely on land.

They did survive the tempest, only to find themselves with a different predicament. At sunrise on February 15 they saw land, and fantasies abounded. Pilots thought it might be Castile or Portugal, but it turned out to be the southernmost island of the Azores, called St. Mary's. This outpost had no good refuge from the raging winds, though it was a regular way station for caravels traveling down the coast of Africa. Its governor immediately jumped to the conclusion that the *Niña* was another of those Spanish pirate ships from Palos that were poaching on Portuguese territories in Africa. Word that Pinzóns of Palos were involved in the expedition only deepened his suspicions. When the ship's grateful pilgrims came ashore to fulfill their vow of giving thanks to their Saviour, the governor promptly threw them all in prison. It would take a week for the Admiral to sort out this annoyance, a time when he sought vainly and without success in the continuous bad weather to take wood and ballast on board for the last leg of the journey.

At last the storm subsided, and when a patch of blue appeared overhead, they sailed for Spain, lightheaded and light-weighted. None was more impatient to reach home than Columbus, for he remained in high anxiety that Martín Alonso Pinzón had arrived before him and was spreading lies about the journey. His resentment against his captain was great. Only ten days after they arrived in the New World, Pinzón had sailed off on his own without Columbus's permission, in the company of an Indian who said he knew where the gold was. It had been a miracle that the *Niña* and the *Pinta* happened upon one another two months later on the southern coast of Hispaniola. Columbus had dressed Pinzón down furiously for his "cupidity" and insubordination and threatened to hang him from the yardarm.

"This is what I deserve for having raised you in the honor in which you now stand," Pinzón replied bitterly. He had found gold, and he supposed that this might excuse his independence and assuage the Admiral's anger. It did not, and now, as Columbus fretted about the possibility that Captain Pinzón was being lionized in the company of the king and queen, he must have berated himself for not hanging Pinzón when he had good cause. Especially grating was the memory of Pinzón's remark that he had raised Columbus to the honor he now enjoyed.

On March 3, another bad omen presented itself as swallows landed on the railings and yardarms of the *Niña*, and a whale raced by them for the outer ocean. That could only mean that heavy weather lay ahead, and they promptly found themselves in a second storm. Now they huddled once more for mutual support and vowed a third time to dispatch a pilgrim, this time to the shrine of La Cinta in Huelva, a shrine much revered by the local seamen of Palos. Again Columbus drew the lucky bean.

But there was no luck that day. The wind and waves were so fierce that it seemed to the mariners as if the caravel was levitating off the surface of the ocean. In one blast, the working sails were shredded. If the caravel came near shore, it would surely be dashed to pieces against the rocks. Dry-masted and unballasted, they were in the gravest peril.

Still, at sunrise on March 4, as if some benevolent pilgrim had gone to the House of Loreto for them, land was sighted, and Columbus recognized the great promontory as the Rock of Sintra, at the mouth of the Tagus River outside Lisbon. If his working sails were in tatters, the square storm sail was still intact; and so, despite his anxiety about how he would be received in the land of Spain's bitter rival, he made for the rivermouth. At the village of Cascaes, the first anchorage in the river, fishermen turned out in amazement to see the battered wreck. From them, the crew learned that the winter's storms had been especially harsh, and that some twenty-five ships had been lost at sea off Flanders. As the wind was still up, the *Niña* moved farther upriver to an anchorage at Belém.

As Columbus anticipated, it was not long before an imposing military launch from a nearby warship approached the *Niña*. Standing in her bow was none other than the great commander and discoverer of the Cape of Good Hope himself, Bartholomew Dias. It is understandable that Dias assumed this bedraggled Spanish craft to be a poaching pirate ship blown off course. Moreover, Dias was not to be trifled with. He had become an aggressive, difficult character, for he languished in a subordinate role in the Portuguese navy and resented the fact that he had never been properly honored for his African discovery. Recognizing Columbus, he commanded the Admiral to board his launch forthwith and be taken ashore. Columbus refused ostentatiously. He was an Admiral of the Sovereigns of Spain, he shouted back importantly, and he would not leave his ship, unless compelled to do so by force of arms. Then send your master, Dias barked. Columbus refused again. To send him or any other member of his crew would be the same as going himself.

"It is the custom of Admirals of the Sovereigns of Castile to die before they yield themselves or their people," Columbus said grandly.

Getting nowhere, Dias backed off and requested with somewhat more respect to see Columbus's credentials from the Spanish sovereigns. On board, these documents seemed to satisfy Dias as he cast a skelly-eye at the flatheaded creatures from the New World—the five Indians, as Columbus was calling them—three of whom were decidedly under the weather. (A sixth had died on the passage over.) After Dias left, it was not long before a higher-ranking sea captain arrived with trumpets and pipes to accord the Admiral a more dignified welcome.

Word spread rapidly, and the scene became a spectacle. Crowds gathered along the shoreline to gaze at the intrepid discovery ship. Skiffs swarmed around the caravel. Dignitaries clamored to come aboard to see the Indians and the parrots and the strange weed called tobacco. While some grumbled that their king had allowed so great an opportunity to slip through his fingers, many gave thanks to their Christian God "for so great and good an increase of Christianity."

Meanwhile, Columbus penned a letter to King João II about his discovery. The king was then staying at a monastery thirty miles north of Lisbon called Val do Paraiso. The news stunned him. On the one hand, he blamed himself for his shortsightedness four years earlier when he rejected Columbus's overture. More important, he suspected that the lands Columbus had found fell within the Portuguese sphere of influence, as it had been determined in 1479 at the treaty with Spain at Alcácovas. The papal bull *Aeterni regis* in 1481 had certified the terms of the treaty at Alcáçovas and had confirmed grant of Portuguese sovereignty over all territories south and west of the Canary Islands.

Thus, it was entirely possible that, if the discoveries lay south of the agreed-upon demarcation line for the Spanish and Portuguese spheres—the 28th parallel, which ran through the Canary Islands—the new discoveries were Portuguese! The king had a point. The island of Hispaniola lay astride the 20th parallel. The king supposed that this was the mythical island called Antilia, the Island of Seven Cities which was peopled by the ancestors of the Christian refugees who had fled Portugal after the Moorish conquest of the eighth century.

In an even grander sense, Columbus's disclosure connected with João II's dreams about a global Portuguese empire that would span the globe and eclipse the power of the newly consolidated Spanish Empire to his east. At about the time that the *Niña* appeared off the Rock of Sintra, Pero da Covilhã, the Portuguese emissary whom João had dispatched overland to India four years earlier, returned to Lisbon. From him, the king had intelligence about the significant ports and places of wealth in the subcontinent to which the next great Portuguese mission around the Cape of Good Hope might go. (It would be Vasco da Gama's voyage.) Covilhã had left his companion, Afonso Paiva, in Cairo, with instructions to travel south into Ethiopia to find the kingdom of Prester John (which Paiva did, to Covilhã's great disappointment). And so dancing in João's mind was the grandest of designs: a Portuguese dominion that stretched from India to Ethiopia and now to the New World.

Between his regret and his anger, his imperial ambition and his affection for Portuguese myth, João II was a dangerous man. The court around the king was even more dangerous to Columbus. The royal advisers were getting reports of Columbus boasting about his triumph to the visitors who now flocked to the *Niña* and scoffing at Portuguese discoveries by comparison. He was, the courtiers heard, telling tall tales about the riches of the "Japan" that he had found. This penchant for

grandiosity and exaggeration and self-congratulation was highly annoying and well remembered from four years ago. No wonder they had rejected this show-off.

These unpleasant traits might be turned to the advantage of Portugal. Why not, someone suggested, provoke the Admiral into a fight and
kill him? Since he was discourteous and conceited, they could fix it so
that "one of his shortcomings could seem to be the true cause of his
death," as the chronicler of the Portuguese court later related it. The assassination could be done discreetly. "With his death the prosecution of
this enterprise by the Sovereigns of Castile would cease with the death
of the discoverer." With Columbus out of the way, a Portuguese expedition to the New World could quickly be mounted to claim the lands
that were rightly theirs.

Of João II's ruthlessness no one could be in doubt. He certainly had
no scruples about political murder. In the revolt of the aristocracy in
1483, he had had the duke of Braganza beheaded, and when a second
conspiracy dared to arise a year later, seeking to replace João with his
wife's brother, the duke of Viseu, João had killed his rival with his own
hand.

Within a day, Columbus received a warm response from the king.
The royal letter oozed praise and congratulation and invited the explorer to come to Val do Paraiso to visit and to tell everything about
the great adventure. The Admiral was skeptical; he sensed the danger.
He accepted, perhaps thinking that in the crowds and with the news
now so widely public, he had achieved a measure of safety. As a further
safeguard of his security, he had dispatched a letter to the count of Medina Celi, then in Madrid, telling him of the discovery and saying he
was in Lisbon. Columbus remained on his guard.

The royal reception in the country, however, was warm and replete
with expressions of admiration. The king commanded that every courtesy and honor be accorded to Columbus. They talked at length,
Columbus insisting that he had returned from "Cipangu and Antilia,"
the islands that formed the approaches to India. In their conversation,
the king did not mask his opinion that by virtue of treaty and papal bull

the discoveries were Portuguese. To this challenge, Columbus professed ignorance about such lofty matters of state diplomacy, saying only that he had scrupulously followed his orders from the Spanish sovereigns to avoid the Portuguese stronghold on the Guinea coast called St. George of the Mine. This satisfied the king, at least on the surface. These matters would be amicably worked out between the nations, João assured his visitor.

On the way back to the *Niña*, Columbus stopped at another monastery for a visit with the Queen of Portugal. And then safely back on board on the evening of March 12, he received an odd letter from João II. If Columbus wished to travel overland to Castile, the king would be glad to provide the escort and the horses. The letter reeked of danger. How easy it would be to arrange for the convoy to be attacked by brigands. And how easy for the King of Portugal to deny responsibility.

Columbus politely demurred and then secretly put his pilot ashore with 20 gold doubloons and orders to make his way, humbly on a mule in disguise, overland into Castile, there to seek out the royal court with the news.

The following morning, as the sun rose, the *Niña* slipped out of Belém unceremoniously and, unimpeded, rode the strong ebb tide out into the open sea.

Two days later, on March 15, 1493, the *Niña* rode the flood tide gently over the bar of Saltes and docked at Palos. With the completion of his first voyage, Christopher Columbus wrote the last words in his journal, pointing to the many "signal miracles" from which he had benefited, swiping again at those who had considered his undertaking to be folly, and trusting that his voyage would redound to "the greater glory of Christianity." For a month he had had the draft of his formal letter to Ferdinand and Isabella ready. He polished it now, adding a postscript about the storms he had survived from the Azores and about his detour in Lisbon.

"Finally," the letter concluded, "Your Highnesses can see that I shall give you as much gold as you want, if you will give me a little help; as much spice and cotton as you command; and gum mastic as much as you order to be shipped which, up to now, could only be found in Greece on the island of Chios; and aloe wood; and slaves, as many as you shall order, who will be idolaters." It would not be correct, this last phrase implied, to enslave natives who had converted to Christianity. When the letter was right, he made several copies, and sent duplicates to the royal comptroller, Luis de Santángel, who had changed the queen's mind, and to the treasurer of Aragon, Gabriel Sánchez, who had provided part of the funds.

The excitement at La Rábida, in Palos and Moguer and Huelva, was predictably extravagant and unbridled, and reached an even higher pitch when, within hours, the *Pinta* followed the *Niña* over the bar and into Palos. Bittersweet was the spectacle of Martín Alonso Pinzón being carried ashore and taken to his house in Moguer. Grotesque, coppery pustules covered his body. He shook with fever. His heart and nervous system were shot. He had five days to live.

As Columbus watched from a distance, his anger toward his captain drained away. They had logged many miles together. Pinzón had been central to the success of the mission. Columbus could admit that now. And through the tempest of the winter seas, he had brought home the sons of Palos safely. In Pinzón's present condition, it was easy to forgive him. Though it is not recorded, it is probable that the two seamen met for the last time, either at La Rábida or, more likely, at Pinzón's bedside. The Admiral of the Ocean Sea had to be wary, for Pinzón's illness was highly contagious. The captain was in the third, last, and awful stage of a new and unknown illness. Only two decades later, around 1512, would an Italian poet named Girolamo Fracastoro write a poem about the scourge and give it its name, syphilis.

> *Say, Goddess, to what Cause we shall at last*
> *Assign this Plague, unknown to Ages past;*
> *If from the Western Climes 'twas wafted o'er,*
> *When daring Spaniards left their native shore;*
> *Resolv'd beyond th' Atlantick to descry,*
> *Conjectur'd Worlds, or in the search to dye.*

And so, in the year of 1492, Columbus's men had crossed yet another barrier besides the sea: the blood barrier. It was as if, from the medical standpoint, the Antipodes did exist, and it was not meant for the peoples of the different hemispheres to interact with one another. Syphilis had long existed in a mild form among the American Indians, and they had a natural remedy for its annoying symptoms: the resin with a faint balsamic odor that came from the guaiacum tree of the bean-caper family. But Pinzón and the others on the first voyage had no resistance to the venereal disease, and no resistance to the young women with beautiful bodies who welcomed them, "as naked as the day they were born," to the shores of Cuba and Haiti. Men were men, and they did not practice, as a historian of the time put it quaintly, the "virtue of chastity."

"Here neither wench nor woman wears a thing," the normally prudish Columbus wrote in his journal, thinking, no doubt, about what Queen Isabella would think when she read the entry of December 20, 1492. "The women have very pretty bodies, and they were the first to come to bring what they had, especially things to eat, bread of yams, and nut-colored quinces, and five different kinds of fruit." Columbus could not believe that in this wider world there existed "such good-hearted people so free to give, and so timid that they were all eager to hand the Christians as much as they had. When the Christians arrived, the natives ran up to bring them all."

Within three weeks, Columbus was taking captives, including women and girls, into the cramped quarters of his tiny caravels. And when he left forty men behind to build a Christian village in the New World called La Navidad out of the wreck of the *Santa María*, each man demanded five concubines. With this first European colony, Columbus left a doctor, Maestre Juan Sánchez, to treat the Europeans with sores.

Of the American origin of syphilis, historians of the time had no doubt. From Pinzón and others of the crew who were now carriers, as well as the five Indians in Columbus's entourage, the disease traveled to Barcelona, where the first general outbreak was recorded in 1493. From that port city, it was to spread to France and Italy. When, a year later,

Charles VIII of France (known as "Fathead" for his oversized head) invaded Italy and occupied Naples, the army brought with it legions of public women, and syphilis reached epidemic proportions.

If Europeans were to suffer from New World syphilis, it was nothing compared to what Native Americans quickly suffered from European diseases. Smallpox, measles, bubonic plague, diphtheria, influenza, yellow fever, and typhoid among others devastated the native peoples and quickly led to the eradication of entire populations, including the sweet-natured Tainos who had been the first to greet Columbus with open arms. When Columbus invaded the New World with seventeen ships in his second voyage, his crews were immediately laid low with disease. Instead of six individuals, the fleet of the second voyage endeavored to bring back 550 slaves; but 200 died along the way, and half of the remaining 350 were sick and dying when the fleet reached Spain. On the island of Hispaniola alone, where Columbus founded his first settlement, the native population of the island of 300,000 in 1492 was cut in half in four years. In 1508, 60,000 remained; and four years later, only 20,000. By the mid-sixteenth century, the Tainos were exterminated.

In this first contact between the Old and the New World, trade in disease marked and marred the "Columbian exchange."

26

Theatre in Barcelona

❖

BARCELONA

Columbus's path to glory began in humility. For surviving the winter tempest around the Azores, it had fallen to him to make the crew's official expression of thanksgiving. For surviving the equally ferocious storm off the Portuguese coast, he too had, improbably, drawn the crossed garbanzo bean. Now in his simple shirt, alone, he went to the tiny convent of Santa Clara in Moguer, passed along its Moorish corridor, and into the chapel of the nuns of St. Clare. There, he spent the entire night in prayer. A day later, he rode a mule to a whitewashed sanctuary on a bluff outside Huelva overlooking the sea called Santa María de la Cinta. In fulfilling his promise there, he knelt before the icon of the Virgin, whose manifestation, it was believed, had saved seamen from drowning in the past, and perhaps in the present.

With these obligations dispatched, the time for pride had come. A letter from Barcelona arrived on March 30, addressed to Don Cristóbal Colón, our Admiral of the Ocean Sea, viceroy and governor of the islands he has discovered in the Indies. "We wish you to come soon," the monarchs wrote effusively to him. "You should hasten your coming as much as possible, so that everything may be arranged. The summer is with us. We must not let the best time to return to the Indies slip away. See if some preparations for your return to the lands you have discovered can commence in Seville. And write soon, so that we can prepare for your arrival, so that all may be ready."

The anxiety of the monarchs was palpable. Columbus must come quickly, must receive his due from his sovereigns and the nation, but once these joyous festivities were over, he must be dispatched quickly and mightily back to the New World to secure the claim of the Spanish kingdom.

They had good reasons for high anxiety, for they had received important intelligence from their powerful vassal, the count of Medina-Sidonia, about Portuguese intentions. The duke had learned that in the wake of Columbus's departure, João II was highly exercised by the Spanish discoveries, rebuking himself for his negligence and myopia. Now he meant to rectify his mistake swiftly. In the spring of 1493, as Columbus was still in Palos, an armada was being mobilized in Lisbon for an expedition of discovery, under the command of a formidable captain, Dom Francisco Dalmeyda.

The Spanish monarchs were well acquainted with Dalmeyda. A nobleman and son of Count Abrantes Dom Lopo, he was Portugal's premier warrior-statesman. He had distinguished himself in the Battle of Toro during the War of Succession with the Spanish in 1476; he had performed delicate diplomatic missions for two Portuguese kings; and he had sought permission from King João II to fight alongside the Spanish in the War Against the Moors. At the siege of Granada, this gallant Portuguese knight had comported himself so brilliantly that the Spanish monarchs wished to heap honors upon him. But he had refused them all. "My king will reward me," he had replied grandly. Now this impressive cavalier was preparing to undermine the claim to the New World by his former allies. (Later, he would sail around the Cape of Good Hope, become the first Portuguese viceroy of India, and be killed by Hottentots on his way home.)

In the face of this stiff challenge, the Spanish royals replied urgently to the count of Medina-Sidonia, ordering him to arm and provision all the caravels in his domain for a major expedition. Speed was now of the essence. In addition, they tapped Juan de Fonseca, archdeacon of Seville, a prelate with an unusual talent as outfitter of armadas, to begin planning for the second voyage.

By the time Columbus arrived in Seville in the first week of April, his fame had spread far and wide. Throngs turned out to watch his colorful procession pass. Strange Caribbean masks, fashioned with fishbone and decorated with precious jewels, were held aloft for the crowds. Small pots, molded into vacant moonfaces and said to represent the spirit gods of the aborigines, were passed around. Iridescent, cackling parrots, yellow and green and red-collared, glistened in the sunshine. Coyly, sailors allowed glimpses of their personal gold. The surviving Indians were displayed like circus creatures, as if they had two heads or sprouted tails.

In fact, to the European eye, the creatures of the New World were something unworldly and inhuman, for besides their coarse, black hair and their dusky skin, their foreheads were bizarrely large and wide and their heads abnormally flat. This apparent deformity was actually the fashion of the time in the Caribbean, for wide foreheads and flat heads were much admired among the Taino Indians. The look was achieved by a mother squeezing the skull of her newborn between two boards, when the tiny skull was still soft and pliable. Add to this flatheadedness the red and white body paint and the plugs in the noses and the ears, and the result was a kind of freak show.

From Seville's balconies, flowers and compliments rained down on the heroes. Bells rang, banners were on display, and churches held solemn masses of Corpus Christi. The Admiral might well have sailed to Barcelona in a few days from either Seville or Palos and heeded the monarchs' plea for haste. But that would have denied him the ballyhoo he required. The monarchs had asked for time to prepare for a conqueror's welcome. So be it. He was now a master of ceremony and propaganda and self-promotion.

In Seville, the colorful procession pitched its tent appropriately near the Arch of the Images and in the shadow of the Giralda, in a barrio of narrow streets called El Postigo. There was much to do. For the coming extravaganzas, a tailor needed to be found to design modest but exotic garb for the Indians: red breeches, loose shirts, and headpieces over their waist-length hair that could be festooned with feathers and shells, to complement their gold earrings and the gold sticks that adorned their nostrils.

The orders of the monarchs had reached Juan de Fonseca, and the discoverer and the military archdeacon met about the plans for the armada. Another communication from the king and queen had requested Columbus to put his mind to his vision for the coming colonization. On April 9, he did so. Most of his letter concerned gold: who could search for it, how it was to be safeguarded from theft and embezzlement, what percentage of its worth should go to the Church to support its missions, even how it should be stored in treasure boxes, locked with two keys and guarded by two men on the journey home. Emphasizing these details left the impression that tons of the stuff lay around everywhere, just to be scooped up; this fantasy, useful though it was for Columbus's immediate purpose, would get the discoverer in trouble with the monarchs later when the pickings of subsequent voyages were slim. Three or four towns should be established, Columbus recommended, consisting of several thousand colonists.

To this April 9 letter, for the first time, he affixed his mystifying signature, with its mixture of Greek and Latin letters, random dots and slashes, and apparent mystical cryptology. It was a pyramid of letters, always with an S over an X, an A over an M, a Greek S over a Y, and an S at the apogee of the pile. Dots separated the letters. That the letters should always be in the same configuration was clearly intentional and important to him, for he signed his letters this way to the end of his life and even instructed his heirs to do the same, "preserving," as he wrote, "the relation of the lines and points." At the base of the pyramid of this elaborate monogram were the markings:

COLUMBUS'S MYSTERIOUS SIGNATURE.

It is generally assumed that the S's and A in the upper arrangement stand for the Latin phrase *"Servus Sum Altimissimi Salvatoris*—I am Servant of the Most Exalted Saviour," and that the last line is the Greek and Latin form of his first name, suggesting himself as the bearer of Christianity to pagan lands. Given the immense significance of the discovery, there is no doubt that Torquemada and his Inquisition were now poring over every dot and tittle that Columbus produced, especially if the rumor of Columbus's possible Jewish origins had reached their ears. If he presented himself now as the proselytizing hound of the Christian faith, he was safe. But there is also no doubt that the Admiral of the Ocean Sea, as he languished those days in Seville before his inauguration into the nobility, was keen on participating in the way his immortality was shaped.

What better way to start than with a conundrum for the ages.

❖

On April 31, 1493, exactly one year to the day after the Edict of Expulsion for the Jews from Spain, the dazzling spectacle of Revelation took place in the Great Royal Palace of Barcelona. The site was the Salon del Tenill, the principal reception hall of the palace, with its curved ribbed ceiling, its frescoes glorifying the Spanish conquest of Majorca, its Gothic and romanesque appointments. All had been made ready. The monarchs sat upon a dais: Isabella magnificently dressed and jeweled; Prince Juan, the heir apparent, by her side; and Ferdinand, still bearing the raw, grotesque scar from the assassination attempt. Below them clustered the chivalry of the New Spain: an eager and excited assemblage of knights and prelates. The Cardinal of Spain was there, along with the Grand Inquisitor. The naysayers who had been unable to recognize a prophet a year before were pushed to the fringes, while Peter Martyr d'Anghiera, the Italian humanist and philosopher, took a prominent place, his pen poised to spin the wondrous discovery into providential legend and Columbus himself into a human God.

The discoverer entered—a magnificent, noble figure now, striding along the carpet to the dais, kneeling before the majesties, and kissing their hands, before he was directed to a stool next to them, an honor so great and rare that it was reserved only for the occasion of great deeds by great men. Up until this time, the "famous men of Spain" achieved eternal life only through bravery and sacrifice against the Moors, a poet of the time, Jorge Manrique, wrote. But now there was a different way. "He looked like a Roman senator," a contemporary chronicler wrote; "tall and stately, gray-haired, with a modest smile on his dignified face betraying his pleasure and glory."

To the report of trumpets and thump of drums, the doors were thrown open and minions came forward, bearing large silver plates piled with gold nuggets, strange gold-decorated masks, and figurines. Sailors followed with the skins of huge lizards and snakes, and exotic dried plants, some with aromatic and medicinal properties, some merely novel, like tobacco leaves and corn ears.

And then the climax. The audience gasped as the flatheaded Indians entered in their foppish, Sevillian getups, their noses pierced with gold needles and their faces painted savagely, carrying cackling parrots. Their skin, a witness wrote, was the color of "cooked quinces"; to some, they looked like a mixture of Moors and Norse. Their appearance was all the more bizarre for their fear and their sickness and their drunkenness, for they had been plied with wine night and day to calm their jitters and shakes. At this overwhelming scene, they sobbed and howled in terror and despair, as Columbus barked orders for them to kneel and keep quiet.

Soon enough, the celestial strains of the *Te Deum* drowned out these wails and sobs, as the royal choir burst into song. In their declamations, the monarchs and their councilors competed with one another in their superlatives. Columbus was Heracles and a modern Dionysus. He had indeed fulfilled the prophecy of Seneca. To this argonaut, in search of the Golden Fleece, the chains of the ocean had been loosed, the boundaries of Christendom extended, the riches of Spain increased. In finding huge freshwater rivers with wonderful natural harbors, he had also fulfilled the prophecy of Isaiah:

"Their land is filled with silver and gold, and there is no end to their treasures, in a place of broad rivers and streams where galleys with oars can go, and stately ships can pass."

The soaring rhetoric of queens and bishops and councilors challenged the eloquence of the argonaut himself. From his stool he gave a stellar performance in encapsulating his glorious deeds. In describing the wonders of Hispaniola and Juana (Cuba), he evoked the loveliest valleys of Castile and Andalusia and sugarcoated his descriptions with a biblical veneer. He had discovered no less a place than Ophir, the biblical land of gold, and he had found Cipangu, the land of Marco Polo. It was true that he had found no great cities and no palaces with gold-covered roofs, nor had he been able to meet the Great Khan of Cathay. Time had been short—the spring season approached, and he had been eager to return home to announce the good news—but he had heard rumors of them to the south and the west. He could not be sure whether the land he called Juana was the mainland, or a very long island of several thousand miles. It could be the island that Marco Polo had called Java.

From his stool Columbus captivated his audience, and Peter Martyr, the legend maker, took his notes. "The ancients, to show their gratitude, used to respect as gods men whose vision and toil revealed lands which had been unknown to their ancestors," Martyr wrote later. "We, who hold that beneath his three persons there is only one God to be worshipped, can nonetheless feel wonder at men such as these, even if we do not worship them. Let us revere the sovereigns under whose leadership and auspices it was granted these men to fulfill their plans. Let us praise to heaven sovereigns and discoverers, and let us use all our powers to make their glory seen as is right and proper."

With Peter Martyr's sheen, the legend took shape. The wreck of the *Santa María* had been a blessing, for it had led to the first settlement of the New World. At the first sight of the Spaniards, the natives had fled "like timid hares fleeing greyhounds." But the fleet-footed Christian dogs had given chase, and caught one woman, "naked and content with nature." They had brought her back to the caravels, had fêted her with food and wine and clothed her magnificently before setting her free.

Her own people had been so amazed at "her wonderful apparel" that they all came running to the shore, proclaiming that the Spaniards had been sent from heaven. And they swam out to the caravels bringing gold, as much gold as the explorers could ask for.

But then there were other hostile and dangerous natives. They ate human flesh. "They castrate the boys they catch, in the way we do cock chickens or pigs, if we want to rear them to be fatter and more tender for the table," Martyr imagined in a form of medieval pornography. "When fully mature men come into their hands, they kill them and divide them into portions; they make a feast of their guts and their extremities while they are fresh; they pickle their limbs in salt, as we do hams, and preserve them for later occasions. Eating women is for them a sin and disgusting. If they do acquire any young women they tend them and confine them, just as we do hens, ewes, heifers, to breed from them." The description of these terrible savages inflamed the imagination of the Spanish warriors in Martyr's audience to think of military conquest, colonization, and slavery. How else was a conquistador to deal with man-eating savages armed with poisoned arrows?

Still, marvels abounded. Martyr spoke of the native food, especially the yuca plant whose juice was as deadly as hemlock but whose pulp was baked into a tasty bread. As a staple, the natives grew a tall plant whose ears are as thick as one's arm, and whose white seeds are arranged in "marvelous order." And in the ground, they cultivated tubers with sweet, orange flesh called potatoes. To fish the natives had boats they called canoes, some so large that they held eighty oarsmen. The parrots, he said, resemble those of India, and prove therefore that as Aristotle and Seneca "and others skilled in cosmography" had testified, "no great stretch of sea separates the shores of India from Spain."

In Martyr's tale of heaven and earth, of good and evil, of light and darkness, of civilization and barbarism, the gentle tribe had a pliant and sensitive king named Guacanagari, who had shown great friendship to the discoverers and had taken great care for their safety. In embracing Columbus upon his departure, the native king had wept with sadness and pity, especially for the Spanish men who would stay behind to build the town of Navidad and not be able to return to the mother country. (And well he might have wept, for within months, at one another's throats over gold and women, the first colonists would all be dead.) In turn, he had granted the wish of ten natives who longed to see the civilized world, to sail to Spain with the discoverers, so that they might teach the Europeans the language of the New World. (For these ten slaves the gentle king might have wept more.)

As the festivities of the discovery carried on for some days, the arrival of Columbus did much to revive the sullen spirits of Barcelona. The discoverer himself could be seen riding through the streets at the side of King Ferdinand, as Prince Juan rode on the other side. Within a few days, the discoverer's elevation to royalty had begun. The cardinal of Spain threw a great banquet for Columbus, according him the singular honor of having his food tasted for poison beforehand. On May 20, his coat of arms was unveiled, displaying a castle and a lion, both symbols of royalty. Three days later, he was given the reward of 1,000 gold doubloons or 335,000 maravedis. On the same day, at his own insistence, a royal order officially authorized for him an additional reward of 10,000 maravedis as the first man to have sighted land in the New World, although he knew perfectly well that a common seaman on Pinzón's vessel had done so. And on May 28, a ceremony was held to confer the title of "Admiral of the Ocean Sea" upon him formally.

With that, the "Capitulations" of Granada had been fulfilled.

27

The Division of the World

❖

ROME

As the summer of 1493 approached, the civilized world of Europe was mired in its customary turmoil, its various leaders in the grip of grand designs and seething resentments. Charles VIII, the only son of Louis XI, had succeeded to the French throne in 1483 at the age of thirteen. When he became a man in 1492, he set out to reclaim the right of the House of Anjou to the Kingdom of Naples and to use this as a springboard to capture Constantinople from the heathen Turks, setting himself up heroically as the conquering Christian emperor. Since the King of Naples was a relative of Ferdinand of Spain in the House of Aragon, Charles's fantasy was bound to cause trouble. Ferdinand and Isabella had other issues with France over the borderlands in the Pyrenees. For years they had been spatting over the province of Roussillon and its principal town of Perpignan. Some years before, the Spanish throne had ceded this province temporarily to France as surety for a debt. But when the debt was repaid, Charles had refused to return the province. Roussillon stayed then and ever as a part of France.

To the east, Maximilian I, the emperor of the far-flung Holy Roman Empire, and son of a Portuguese princess, had spent his early years in various skirmishes with France and the Netherlands, but in 1493 became the sole ruler of Germany and the head of the House of Hapsburg. Glorying in his victory over the infidel Turks at Villach in southern Austria in 1492, he made an extravagant appeal to the Christian monarchs of Europe to help him drive the Islamic scourge from Europe. He meant to shift the clash between Christendom and Islam 500 miles east to the Balkans. But the appeal fell flat. Holy war in the Balkans would be left to the next generation.

To these imperial imaginings, the fantasy of Ferdinand had to be added. In the Spanish version of the apocalypse, the Antichrist would appear in Seville, but he would be defeated by a messianic king, identified as "the Bat" or "the Hidden One." The Bat would go on to conquer Granada, but this was only the first step. After that, the Bat was destined to lead a great crusade to recapture Jerusalem and the Holy Land for Christianity. With the conquest of Granada now accomplished, Ferdinand the Bat began to savor the grander historical destiny that awaited him.

In the dreams of these Christian champions lay a tacit recognition that after the fall of Granada, the center of gravity for Islamic power in the Mediterranean had shifted to the Ottoman East. The clash of civilizations and faiths for the coming decades and centuries would be fought in the Levant over the rugged Slavic terrain of ancient Macedonia, as the Turks pressed to the gates of Vienna.

Dreams were dreams, but more immediate problems concentrated the mind of the Spanish monarchs. Spain and Portugal faced off against one another with formidable armadas over the discoveries in the New World. Who was to be the arbiter of these disputes? Who would act as peacemaker? Or alternatively, as the true leader of an aggressive, messianic Christian faith?

Beneath these internecine tensions, greater forces of history were at work. With the completion of the Spanish Reconquest and the unification of the Spanish nation, Spain epitomized the rise of the modern state. After over fifty years of expansion down the coast of Africa, with the passage to India now open, with the instant expansion of the geographical horizon that Columbus's discoveries provided, the age of colonialism and colonial competition had dawned. As the Inquisition reached its orgasm of violence in Spain, it had begun to spread to other European nations. With the voyages of the Portuguese and Spanish explorers cast as Christian crusades, the role of religion in political and geopolitical affairs moved to center stage. The arrival of Jewish refugees in Italy and Moorish refugees in Turkey and Africa heightened the tensions between nations and faiths. The need for some form of international law was more important than ever.

Who was to act as the world's mediator? Who had the wisdom and the authority to manage this altered world? There was only the papacy. The earthly Vicar of Jesus Christ.

In the wake of Columbus's discovery, that holy father was the Borgia pope, the purchaser of the papacy, the Spanish swindler, the disgraceful Alexander VI. In the initial months of his decadent reign, another force of history advanced rapidly—the decline of the papacy. One Vatican scandal after another weakened the Holy See, undermined its moral authority, encouraged contempt among Christian nations, and ultimately set the stage for the revolt of Martin Luther two decades later. Criticism, in the form of apocalyptic poetry, predicted the end of the papacy in 1493. An Italian poet, Girolamo Malipiero, saw the end clearly:

> *The light arms of the Gauls will administer justice to the Germans.*
> *The disorderly weight of Italy will drown the Gauls.*
> *Gaul will surrender.*
> *The victorious sign of the eagle will adorn the world.*
> *In 1493 that eagle will rise up to greatness.*
> *The earth will move, in what respect it is impossible to prophesy.*
> *Horses will be made of marble.*
> *Statues of Augustus will be erected, and many Roman palaces.*
> *Constantinople will fall.*
> *The pope will die quickly.*
> *Caesar will reign everywhere.*
> *The empty glory of the clergy will cease.*

It was to the illegally elected, degenerate pope, Alexander VI, that Ferdinand and Isabella now appealed in the spring of 1493 to settle the epic question of who owned the discoveries of Christopher Columbus: Spain or Portugal? The Borgia pope would decide the future of the Americas and the western hemisphere. He must divide the world between the two great naval powers of Europe.

A year into his papacy, the disenchantment with Pope Alexander was considerable. "He leads without respect for the seat He holds, that is abhorred by all," wrote an Italian prince. "From the beginning of His pontificate he has done nothing but disturb the peace. He cares for nothing at all, save to aggrandize his children by fair means or foul. As is his nature, the impostor operates fraudulently in all things, and to make money sells even the smallest offices and benefices."

Indeed, in the first year of his papacy, Alexander VI was much preoccupied with his domestic affairs. His mistress was now the great Roman beauty Giulia Farnese, known as Giulia la Bella, who had replaced the passionate, high-spirited, but aging Vannozza Cattanei, and who had golden hair that, when let down, stretched to her feet. Giulia la Bella had been deposited in the Palazzo Santa Maria in Portico, contiguous to the Vatican, and in late 1492, she bore the pope a daughter named Laura. She was said to be the last child of a pope to be born in the papal apartments, and the papal offspring too was destined to be a great beauty.

Half a year later, on June 12, 1493, the marriage of the pope's daughter by Vannozza, the notorious Lucrezia Borgia, was celebrated in the Vatican. The bridegroom was Giovanni Sforza, of the powerful Sforza family to whom the pope was beholden for his election. Young Sforza was twenty-six years of age. He was also illegitimate, had been married before, and was known as the Tyrant of Pesaro, a region in the Italian province of Romagna. Lucrezia was fourteen and said to have all the charms of beauty and even the golden hair of the pope's stunning mistress. As a lady-in-waiting in the netherworld of papal entertainments and diversions, she was a fast learner.

On the same day to the west, far across the Ligurian Sea and the Golfe du Lion, the Spanish monarchs fretted in Barcelona. They had heard nothing from their envoy in Rome about their appeal to the Holy

Father concerning the Spanish claim to the New World. It was more than a month now since the emissary had been dispatched. Nor did they have any fresh news from Portugal about the Portuguese armada under the command of Dalmeyda, a fleet that was surely ready to challenge the Spanish somewhere on the Sea of Darkness. In this war of nerves, the threat of a naval clash in the Indies hung ominously in the air, with each nation claiming that the other was encroaching upon its territory without permission. Columbus was in the south, Córdoba probably, and he must hurry. How were the preparations for the Spanish armada of the second voyage proceeding? The royals did not know.

And so on June 12, the day of Lucrezia Borgia's wedding far away, Ferdinand and Isabella sat down and wrote an anxious, almost paranoid, letter to their "Admiral of the Islands and terra firma of the oceans near the Indies." He was now an Admiral in the full sense, a military commander as much as a discoverer, and they hoped to spur him forward to quicker action. "Now Herrera, the messenger of the King of Portugal, has come to us. He has said that the King of Portugal plans to send ships to the Islands and lands that we have discovered, so that each may have what belongs to them. He has said that Portugal will let us know when its ships will depart for the new world. When we learn more, we will advise you of their intentions. . . .

"You must proceed with your journey very soon. If in the interest of haste, you deem it necessary to leave a few ships and a few sailors behind, by all means, please do so. They could join you later."

Events seemed to be moving rapidly toward disaster and mayhem in the waters around Cipangu.

❧

Fully two months before Lucrezia Borgia's wedding, Ferdinand and Isabella had dispatched their envoy to Rome with the request for a papal blessing on Spain's claim to the New World. To underscore the importance of the mission, the Cardinal of Spain, Pedro González de Mendoza, accompanied the ambassador. In the Eternal City, the delegation was greeted by Spain's resident ambassador to the Roman Curia, Mendoza's nephew, Cardinal Berardino de Carvajal. Already they had seen to it that the news of Columbus's and Spain's triumph was broadcast far and wide. Columbus's letter to the monarchs about his discovery was recast as a public document for public consumption. More than twenty years had passed since the printing process had been invented in Germany, and so the presses hummed with the public version of the discovery letter. Among the first tasks of the Spanish ambassador on his mission to the Vatican was to ensure that an Italian translation of the letter also be printed and widely distributed in Rome and elsewhere in Italy.

To distinguish Columbus's discovery from the Portuguese claim that everything below the 26th parallel belonged to it, Peter Martyr announced that Portugal had claim to the "southern antipodes," whereas Columbus had discovered the "western antipodes." The large, transoceanic islands of the Indies were imagined to be, in the physical sense, a counterbalance or a counterweight on the one side to Portuguese Africa, and on the other side, the Eurasian continent. They were therefore entirely different, separate and distinct. Columbus himself suggested that the Spanish position at the Vatican assert a claim to sovereignty in these "western antipodes" from North Pole to South Pole.

They were confident of success. The pope, after all, was Spanish, and there was a long history of feathering his nest. Ferdinand had permitted the previous cardinal, Rodrigo Borgia, to add the lucrative bishoprics of Cartagena and Majorca to his already golden see of Valencia. Borgia's son had fought valiantly in the War Against the Moors, especially the battle for Ronda. In gratitude, King Ferdinand had given the duchy of Gandía to the cardinal's son, making the papal bastard one of the most prominent members of the Aragon nobility. Ferdinand had legitimized the pope's favorite son, Cesare, in 1481, had sanctioned his accession to the see of Pamplona, and then had promoted the villain to the archbishopric of Valencia upon Alexander's investiture as pope. Alexander, in turn, had made a Spaniard the general of the papal bastion on the Tiber, Castel Sant'Angelo, and had appointed a Spaniard as his confessor.

How could the Spanish pontiff not rule in favor of Spain?

On the other hand, the new pope, in his haste to reward everyone who had helped him secure his office, had allowed himself to become sucked into the machinations of the French king, Charles VIII. By siding with France's allies in Italy, Venice, and Milan, against Naples, the pope seemed to be encouraging Charles's plans to invade Italy and capture Naples. And the pope had turned a blind eye toward the Spanish demand for the return of Roussillon. These papal actions had annoyed and embarrassed the Spanish crown.

Thus, the Spanish emissary was directed to adopt an offensive strategy with the pope. He was to demand rather than beseech, to insist rather than beg or implore. Weeks later, the envoy arrived in Rome. In his audience with the Holy Father, after offering his pro forma "homage and obedience," the Spanish envoy proceeded to scold the pontiff for his various transgressions against his native country. Why, for example, was the pope permitting asylum in Italy to Spanish Jews and conversos who had been driven from Spain, with papal approval, as enemies of the Christian faith? Was it not true that these infidels and devils were camped in perfect freedom amid the ancient Roman tombs along the Appian Way? Why was the pope encouraging Charles VIII in his designs on Naples, and why had he embarrassed Spain by not insisting upon the return of Roussillon to its rightful Spanish owners? As for the pope's scandalous personal behavior, Queen Isabella was especially affronted, and it would not be long before this indignation was bitingly committed to writing:

"You have achieved your limited purpose of gaining the papacy, even if illegally. Now you have taken unfettered license, and you have committed disgraceful acts. You have tarnished sacred matters at a great price to the faithful. Promise us, the most unworthy, that your habits have changed, and that you will lead the Holy See in the future with honor and true piety."

This was scarcely the meek homage and obedience that the pope might have expected, and no doubt, he was taken aback. But the broadside worked splendidly. The defensive pope became almost fawning in his expressions of regret and apology. He assured the ambassador that he was eager to restore friendly relations. What could he do to please the king and queen? He "desired that the bond with his Spanish allies remain entire and inviolable." He made excuses for his tilt toward France.

"Tell them distinctly with what care we lay ourselves out to satisfy them in all things," the pope said. "We are eager to furnish to all the world the proofs of the paternal affection we have for them."

It was time to get down to the business at hand. The ambassador had just the idea of how the pope could furnish proof to all the world of his affection for Spain.

On May 3 and 4, that proof was forthcoming. On May 3, Pope Alexander VI issued the first of two bulls entitled *Inter caetera*, "in the plenitude of his apostolic authority." The first was to supersede and abrogate any papal bulls that might have been issued previously, a reference to the pronouncements of three popes—Nicholas V, Calixtus III, and Sixtus IV—that had granted sovereignty to Portugal over "southern regions" in the Ocean Sea and which were meant to include the mythical island of Antilia. The bull of Sixtus IV had confirmed the Treaty of Alcáçovas in 1479 in which Spain had ceded to Portugal dominion over the southern regions. That was now abrogated.

The new bull granted Spain sovereignty over the lands and islands it had discovered in the west, as well as others yet to be discovered in that direction, providing that these territories did not already belong to any Christian prince (an oblique reference to the elusive Prester John). It forbade any person or nation to enter those lands and their contiguous waters without permission. The Spanish sovereigns were to assume their powers to be equivalent to those that the Portuguese kings exercised along the coast of Africa, that is, exclusive rights to trade and for colonization.

The document was extraordinary. Implicit in it was the authority of the pope as the overlord of the Christian world. He had dominion over the souls of all men, and therefore, only he could decide who and what nation would conduct the evangelizing of the Lord's children. In the preamble, the pope praised Ferdinand and Isabella for their service to the Catholic faith in the reconquest of Granada. He had always hoped that new and unknown islands and lands might be found, so that the Catholic faith might be brought to their inhabitants. Discovery was, by its nature, a holy enterprise. And now with these new discoveries, "All things considered and especially the exaltation and expansion of the Catholic Faith, you are to subject these lands and islands and their inhabitants, and with the help of God's mercy, bring them to the Catholic Faith."

A day later (at least by its official dating), a second amending bull was issued. In it the question of west versus south was addressed. Now, the pope drew an imaginary line across the globe, north to south, beginning 100 leagues or about 300 miles west of the Azores, partitioning the oceanic world between Spanish and Portuguese spheres of influence. Everything west of that line, from the North to the South Pole, was given to Spain. This had been Columbus's specific recommendation to Ferdinand and Isabella, and its language was now reproduced almost exactly in the papal bull as it had been proposed in Barcelona. On his second voyage, Columbus had every intention of exploring farther south than he had on his first, for he had heard rumors from Indians of a large mass of continental lands there.

Three weeks later, on May 28, even before the Spanish royals learned of the papal sanction, they asserted their right to the entire Western world.

✦

The all-important papal bull that drew the line of demarcation was officially dated May 4, 1493. But it was actually crafted many weeks later, on June 28, and then backdated to make it appear to be an afterthought to the first bull of May 3. Mere sanction of sovereignty was not enough, and the Spanish embassy was dissatisfied. Negotiations for the amendment stretched on for weeks. Given his preoccupation with his personal affairs and with the French saber-rattling and the tensions in the Italian Papal States, it was hard to get Alexander to focus. Once the careful language of the second bull emerged from the papal office, it made its way slowly through the arcane bureaucracy of the Roman Curia. Under the watchful eye of the pope's personal secretary, it needed to be drawn up by the papal "abbreviator" and then sent to the Bureau of Scribes to be beautifully and painstakingly written up for the ages. That the pronouncement was of tremendous historical significance, no less perhaps than the discovery of Tarsis or Cathay or Ophir or the Rivers of Paradise, no one had any doubt. Once the papal scribes produced the document as a work of art, with the magnificent calligraphy of careful, packed lettering, sweeping capital letters, and marvelous decorative flourishes, it had to be registered and collated and taxed. The process took many more days. So, news of the papal donation did not reach Spain until early August.

In the interim, Ferdinand and Isabella remained in a state of high anxiety about what was happening. A favorable papal sanction would be immensely helpful in a political sense, but it was not essential to their right of discovery and conquest. They had already taken their own steps to assert the right of Spain to undiscovered lands on May 28, 1493, proclaiming, in the so-called "privileges" to Columbus:

"This sea belongs to us to the west of a line passing through the Azores and Cape Verde Islands and extending from north to south, from pole to pole."

Nor was the decision of a Spanish pope, illegally elected and personally corrupt as Alexander VI was, likely to stay the hand of Portugal. They supposed that a Portuguese armada was already on its way to the New World, prepared to plant the Portuguese flag in the new territories and then claim its own right of dominion, based upon previous treaties and papal bulls, produced by more honorable popes. Meanwhile, their own admiral was still dawdling in Cádiz outfitting his fleet.

On July 27, the sovereigns wrote again to Columbus to spur him along and maybe even to scare him a little. "The truth is we have been told that the Portuguese fleet left from the ports of Portugal a while ago. It is possible that inclement weather has slowed them. As you have speculated, it is also possible that the armada from Portugal is waiting to leave until you have left on your journey for the New World, but we doubt that this is the case. As a result, we suggest that you stay the course of your present agenda and not modify any plans to adapt to anything the Portuguese may do. Please expedite your departure, and keep us advised of any further needs that you may have for your journey. We can supply you with any of these further needs through a second armada. Please leave as soon as possible." If Columbus had little credentials to be a discoverer before his first voyage, he had even less to be a naval commander now in a bloody sea battle between armadas.

At last, on August 4, the bulls arrived from Rome, and the exultant Spanish monarchs informed Columbus. "The authority has come today, and we send you an authentic copy of it to publish, so that all the world may know that no one can enter into these regions without authorization from us. Take it with you that you may be able to show it in every land."

The news of the papal donation to Spain reached Portugal at about the same time, and João II must have appreciated immediately that he had been effectively outmaneuvered. In fact, the Portuguese armada had not left Lisbon. Nor, in light of the papal bulls and in recognition of the priority of first discovery, was it ever to leave. For the priority of first discovery was a principle Portugal was eager to maintain with its African dominion and forthcoming voyages around the Cape of Good Hope to India. Africa and spice-rich India were far more important than this new land of blockheaded savages. Still, the Portuguese king saw that he had a strong position to bargain from. For his restraint and high-mindedness, he was owed. If Spain would enter into negotiations, he would not challenge the Spanish on the high seas, nor would he quarrel with the abrogation of past treaties and papal bulls.

On August 18, only two weeks after the papal bulls reached Iberia, Spain and Portugal entered into formal negotiations over their respective rights in the New World. At first, King João seemed to be in a conciliatory mood, for he was now engaged in an internal battle over succession, and he was eager to arrange a marriage of his son to the daughter of the Spanish sovereigns, the infanta Isabel. To a king, the perpetuation of his dynastic line could be more important than ruling half the world.

Hard bargaining lay ahead for the negotiators, and the talks dragged on for months, into the spring of 1494. The main sticking point was the placement of the pope's line of demarcation. Portugal was unwilling to accept a line only 100 leagues west of its domain in the Azores. It held out for a line considerably farther west. Eventually, the Spanish relented and agreed to move the line another 270 leagues or over 500 miles farther into the ocean. With that concession, the Treaty of Tordesillas was signed and ratified on July 2, 1494.

❖

Christopher Columbus had taken to Cádiz the royal patents and licenses that authorized the fleet of the second voyage. With this authority, the voyage of conquest and colonization and conversion was ready. Besides its provisions for securing and arming, its seventeen ships, with a total manpower of twelve hundred, the royal "Instructions" breathed good intentions and lofty pieties. Since the Indians of the New World espoused no serious religious dogma or doctrine, other than their pagan spirit gods, and since the sovereigns had been informed that they were therefore "very ripe to be converted," the principal concern of the mission was to be the increase of the Holy Catholic Faith.

The Admiral was given wide latitude to strive for this conversion "by all ways and means." Assisting him in this endeavor was a Benedictine friar, Father Bernardo Boil. (Boil's main efforts in the second voyage were to attempt to execute the Taino chieftain, Guacanagari, and to lead a mutiny against Columbus. He converted no Indians.) The Indians "must be carefully taught the principles of Our Holy Faith," read the Instructions, "for they must already know and understand much of our language." In case the tens of thousands of natives did not understand the Spanish language (or in case something had happened to the wretches who had stayed behind in Navidad), the one Indian who had remained healthy after the transatlantic voyage, and who had been baptized with the name Diego Colón, would be sent back as the fleet inter-preter. All who sailed on the second voyage, the sovereigns demanded, were to treat the Indians "very well and lovingly, abstaining from doing them any injury, so that both people could hold much conversation and intimacy, each serving the other to the best of their ability."

On September 25, the fleet of the second voyage was ready. Cheer-ful colors and flowing banners draped the seventeen ships, while pipers and trumpeters and harpers serenaded the brave sailors. After twelve ecclesiastics performed the customary rites on dockside, anchors were weighed, and the fleet was escorted out of Cádiz harbor by Venetian galleys. The Christian crusade for America had begun. The great dis-coverer had joined the inquisitors and the Iberian conquerors as one of God's most important hounds.

It was a moment to savor. Columbus was at the zenith of his power and glory. From here out, his course would be decidedly downhill. These noble sentiments in the royal Instructions would soon enough be discarded, as the subsequent Columbian voyages dissolved into a tale of greed, slavery, disease, genocide, shipwreck, disappointment, and for Columbus himself, narcissism and humiliation. And yet, as consola-tion, the bad news that came in the following years would be largely overlooked in popular imagination.

It is the Revelation of 1492, its triumphant celebration and the con-sequent division of the New World into Spanish and Portuguese spheres, that has been remembered through the ages. World history was lurching into a new epoch.

The Age of Empire had begun.

In the years that followed 1492, the seeds that had been planted in the run-up to that epochal year grew and flourished. Some, like the Inquisition, propagated wildly and uncontrollably like poison ivy throughout Europe, and it would be another two hundred years before the hideous practice of burning human beings for supposed heresy from Catholic doctrine was finally stopped.

On the diplomatic front, the tough stance of Portugal in the negotiations at Tordesillas in mid-1494 seems utterly prescient. Four years later, in 1498, Vasco da Gama made his way around the Cape of Good Hope to India and claimed that spicy paradise for his tiny kingdom. Two years later, in the Jubilee of 1500, in order to secure its claim to India militarily, as Columbus had done for America with his second voyage, Portugal dispatched a formidable armada to the rich land of spice, under the command of Pedro Alvars Cabral. Drawn up by Vasco da Gama, Cabral's route adopted a southerly course far out to the west of Africa to avoid the doldrums in the Gulf of Guinea and the strong headwinds off the southern shores of the African continent that had so bedeviled Bartholomew Dias. In this far westerly course, on April 22, 1500, Cabral's fleet came upon the coast of Brazil by accident and immediately claimed it for Portugal under the terms of the Treaty of Tordesillas.

In the skill of the Portuguese negotiators at Tordesillas emerges another sidelight of history. A second clause of the treaty provided that each party was not to explore in lands reserved to the other and was to yield any territory it might discover by chance in the dominion of the other. In fact, earlier in the year 1500, and by chance, Vicente Yañez Pinzón, the commander of the *Niña* on Columbus's first voyage, came upon the coast of Brazil before Cabral. But in this case Spain made no claim of first priority.

And thus, by 1500, Portugal reached the height of its empire, one that stretched from the spice islands of the Malay peninsula to India to the African coast to Brazil. In that mix, which realized the dream of King João II of a worldwide empire, there would be one major disappointment. In about 1520, the stout explorer whom João II had dispatched overland in 1486 in search of the great and powerful Christian emperor called Prester John finally found his quarry in Ethiopia. Far from the Christian potentate in a magical land of precious stone and gold that was imagined, the Ethiopian prince was a poor and bedraggled character, living in a dusty wasteland. So there would be no broadshouldered ally for tiny Portugal to challenge Spain and rule the world. The Ethiopian was indeed Christian, and his sect has come down to us as the Coptic religion.

What then of the other major players in the drama of 1492?

By 1495, Tomás de Torquemada was growing old and feeble. In May 1498, the Grand Inquisitor issued his last instructions to his Inquisition before he died a few months later. As Torquemada receded from the scene, an equally scary figure took his place. In 1492, Queen Isabella had discharged her scholarly and sensitive confessor, Hernando de Talavera, and with that sacking, the hope for a tolerant, inclusive policy toward the Moors began to die. Talavera was replaced by a stern, inflexible, and austere Franciscan named Francisco Jiménez de Cisneros. Surpassing even Torquemada in his self-denial, Jiménez wore the hair shirt, doubled his fasts, and scourged himself regularly. He was attached to the Monastery of San Juan de los Reyes in Toledo, which had been established by Queen Isabella in fulfillment of a vow she had made during the siege of Granada. Jiménez eschewed the convivial fraternity of monastic life and chose instead to live alone as a hermit in a hut in a grove of chestnut trees where he slept on a plank.

Upon the death of Cardinal Mendoza in 1495, Jiménez became the archbishop of Toledo, the richest and most powerful of the Spanish sees. After the death of Torquemada, Jiménez was made Inquisitor-General of Castile. In this bloodless fanatic were combined the three most powerful positions in the land: Grand Inquisitor, queen's confessor, and archbishop of Toledo. To him was entrusted the final and complete betrayal of the promise of religious freedom made to Islamic Spain in 1492.

Not long after Jiménez's appointment as Inquisitor-General, with the approval of Ferdinand and Isabella, the principle of religious tolerance was replaced with the principle of "the unity of faith." The forced conversion of Muslims to the Christian religion began. In Granada, various threats and inducements and punishments were used to secure conversion of the recalcitrants. The mosque of the Albaicín was converted into the Church of San Salvador, and the famous public baths by the Río Darro were closed, for the Inquisition considered bathing to promote erotic behavior (although for the pleasure of the royal entourage, the baths in the Alhambra were quietly restored).

These measures inevitably created great tensions. When one royal constable entered the Arabic barrio to arrest an apostate, he was killed, and the Muslim community rose up in arms. The governor, Count Tendilla, moved in mercilessly, and Ferdinand, ever the paragon of Machiavellian intrigue, used the insurgency to issue the proclamation that everyone must convert and that "there is no salvation for the soul in any other law, only that of Jesus Christ." On December 18, 1499, with evocations of hellfire hanging in the air, three thousand Muslims were baptized into a faith they knew nothing about. A few months later, in the Rambla square of Granada, the acrid smell came from burning Korans. On one occasion alone some five thousand Korans, many of which possessed exquisite, priceless calligraphy and decoration, were burned in a public spectacle.

On February 12, 1502, Isabella administered the coup de grâce with a royal order that gave all remaining Moors in realms of the new unified Spain the choice she had given the Jews ten years before: baptism or expulsion. And the sad process of history repeating itself went forward.

Boabdil the Unfortunate was not there to witness the final humiliation of his people. Ten years before, after he swiveled around on his horse for his last glimpse of the Alhambra—and uttered his last sigh—

his melancholy retinue had passed down a slope of the Sierra Nevada to the village of Lanjarón and turned into the long, narrow valley of the Alpujarras, known to the Moors as "the Hills of the Sun and the Moon." The party passed through the fertile fields that had been his breadbasket in his final years as sultan and beneath the shadow of Mulhacén, the 13,000-foot peak that was named for his ferocious and foolish father, Muley Aben Hassan.

In the dry eastern portion of the valley, his exile was in the village of Fondón. In his Taa of Purchena, smaller and more remote than the Taa of Andarax that had been the temporary dominion of his uncle, El Zagal the Valiant, Boabdil remained for only a year. With nothing to do, a figure of shame and scorn, depressed and grieving, deserted by all but a few followers, he soon tired of his imprisonment. Through his spies, Ferdinand kept a close watch on his prisoner, doing what he could to make life difficult and to encourage Boabdil, with both carrot and stick, to leave the country altogether.

In the year 898 in the Mohammedan calendar (1493), Boabdil fled to Morocco, carrying with him a bag of gold ducats from the Catholic king. There he came under the protection of his cousin, the King of Fez. For some thirty-six years he assumed an honored place in the Moroccan court, until he took the field of battle in some long-forgotten challenge to the throne of his kinsman and was killed. By all accounts, in this struggle of another, Boabdil the Unfortunate fought hard and valiantly.

"Such was the destiny prepared for him in the Book of Eternal Decrees," wrote an Arab scribe.

Meanwhile, in the decade after 1492, Jews continued to be scattered like chaff throughout the Old and, soon enough, the New World. In 1497, Portugal followed Spain with an expulsion order of its own, one that was in some respects harsher. Somewhere among the twice-expelled was Abraham Zacuto, who had been appointed the royal astronomer of the court, and upon whose maps and copper astrolabe Columbus had relied in his four voyages.

Don Isaac Abravanel, the intellectual mentor of the Spanish Jews, settled first in Naples, moved to Corfu, and ended his long, peripatetic life as a minister to the Doge of Venice. Once over his initial shock and bitterness, Abravanel's thinking about the tragedy of Sephardim began to change. So terrible a tragedy to his people could not stem from the machinations of mere mortals. A wider plan, surely a divine plan, must be at work here, a divine plan for the redemption of the people of Israel. Had not Maimonides said that the future is never bleak? That there would always be hope? That hope often emerged from the darkest hours? Abravanel moved toward an apocalyptic vision of this forced exodus.

He found his sanction in the book of Daniel, the one book of the ancient text that contained hidden messages about the schedule for the End Times. It was written in Daniel 12:6: "How long shall it be to the end of these wonders?" His role for his own diaspora began to come clear: "to comfort those who stumble in exile and remain of the multitude, to seek out in the Book of the Lord the good word as imparted to his prophets, and to inquire, 'how long will it be until the end of wonders?' "

The Jews were, he began to believe, on the cusp of salvation. They were in the last years of the last era of the world, the era of the Messiah. Only from strife, from contention, from suffering and testing could the golden age of David and Solomon come again, as had been prophesied. And then, as God had created the world more than four thousand years before, so he would end it. That end would come, Abravanel now predicted, in the year 1504 of the Christian calendar.

Italy, meanwhile, was no safe haven. On September 3, 1494, Charles VIII of France crossed the frontier between France and Savoy, and for the next four years, the Borgia pope, Alexander VI, was caught in a vise, largely of his own making, between the invader he had encouraged and the Spanish monarchs he was so eager to please. No less tormenting was the pope's personal battle with Savonarola. Without shame or hesitation, the Dominican friar from Florence continued his apocalyptic prophecies from the pulpit and his prediction of demise for wicked and wayward princes. In June 1495, he met with Charles VIII of France and threatened one last chance. "Most Christian Prince," he said, "you have incurred the wrath of God by neglecting that work of reforming the Church which, by my mouth, He had charged you to undertake, and to which He had called you by so many unmistakable signs. This time you will escape from the danger which threatens you. But if you again disregard the command which He now, through me, His unworthy slave, reiterates, and still refuse to take up the work which He commits to you, I warn you that He will punish you with far more terrible misfortunes, and will choose another man in your place."

A month later, Savonarola was summoned to Rome. "Come at once to Rome to give account of prophecies for which you claim divine inspiration," the papal Brief read. Savonarola excused himself from the summons. Then the pope demanded that the friar cease to preach, and instead, the friar carried on his jeremiad without interruption, denouncing Alexander's crimes with ever greater passion. After a terrible flood struck Rome in early December 1495, Savonarola expressed satisfaction and claimed credit as the Lord's herald. In 1497, Alexander could stand it no longer. In Florence Savonarola was excommunicated, arrested, tortured, tried, degraded, and then burned at the stake. At the burning place, two Dominicans, dogs now not of God but of the pope, threw a priestly robe over him and then stripped it off symbolically.

"I separate thee from the church militant and from the church triumphant," his executioner said.

"That is beyond thy powers," Savonarola replied softly.

In the martyrdom of Savonarola and the corruption of Alexander VI, the Spanish don of the House of Borgia, the meteorology for the deluge was created. In the martyr's words and writings could be found the inspiration for the concept of justification by faith alone, apart from Rome, which denied Rome's role as the mediator between God and man. It would be another twenty-five years before the actual deluge broke out in the person of Martin Luther and in the form of the Protestant revolt. Alexander died in 1504, a virtual prisoner of his malevolent son, Cesare Borgia.

Queen Isabella died in the same year. In her final days she wrote an extensive will. In it she defined her preparations for her Day of Judgment, chose her angelic protectors, confessed certain regrets about her exercise of absolute royal power, and sought to make peace with her maker. Her choice of saints was unsurprising. First among them was the Virgin Mary, "Queen of the Heavens and Lady of the Angels." Once again, she associated herself, as others had done repeatedly, with the Woman of the Apocalypse in chapter 13 of the book of Revelation. She threw herself on the mercy of St. Michael, the prince of the angelic cavalry, to "defend my soul from that cruel beast and old serpent who will want to devour me." She also invoked the spirit of St. James the Moorslayer, the patron saint of Spain, and of St. Dominic, the spiritual leader of the Inquisition and its hounds of God, who showed himself as an evening star to the eve of the end of the world. In her last hours, her passion as both Inquisitor and Crusader was undiminished. Her survivors, especially her husband, were not to cease their efforts to "conquer Africa, to fight for the Faith against the Infidel, and to honor the holy Inquisition against the depraved heretic."

She requested that she be buried in the Alhambra in Granada, her grave to be marked only with a plain stone.

The death of Isabella was a particular blow to Columbus, for he lost his most devoted supporter. In his second, third, and fourth voyages—in which Puerto Rico, the Antilles, Jamaica, Trinidad, Venezuela, and the isthmus of Central America were discovered—his reputation and standing with the Catholic monarchs, especially with King Ferdinand, had gradually declined, until he ended his life stripped of virtually all the honors and privileges that had been conferred upon him after the first voyage. Disease and a headlong plunge into slavery marred the second voyage. With its military expeditions into the heartland of Hispaniola, Columbus became the first conquistador of the New World, paving the way for the cruelties of Balboa, Cortés, Pizarro, and Coronado, who came later. To her credit, Queen Isabella called a halt to Columbus's slaving in 1495.

What great virtues Columbus had as visionary and explorer, he lacked as administrator and viceroy. The communities of the New World disintegrated into chaos and rebellion. His communications became increasingly incoherent, self-pitying, and grandiose. To the calculating Ferdinand, whose preoccupation was power and gold, these communications were particularly offputting. The situation reached its low point in the third voyage when the monarchs relieved Columbus of his command, and he was brought home in chains to be mocked once again in the royal court. On his fourth and last voyage, he was shipwrecked and marooned in Jamaica for a year, surrounded by hostile natives, contending with mutiny among his crew. From the cabin of his beached craft, with no prospect of immediate rescue, he wrote in despair to the monarchs:

"All that is left to me and to my brothers has been taken away and sold, even to the cloak that I wore, to my great dishonor. It is believed this was not done by your royal command. The restitution of my honors and losses, and the punishment of those who have inflicted them, of those who plundered me of my pearls, and who have disparaged my admiral's privileges, will redound to the honor of your royal dignity. The glorious memory will survive for Spain. I implore Your Highnesses' pardon. I am ruined. Hitherto I have wept for others. Now have pity upon me, Heaven, and weep for me, earth. Weep for me, whoever has charity, truth, and justice. I did not come on this voyage to navigate for gain, honor, or wealth. I came to Your Highnesses with honest purpose and sincere zeal, and I do not lie. . . ."

He was rescued. In the last year of his life he was to return to his role as supplicant to the royal court. But things had changed. With Isabella gone, the throne of Castile passed not to Ferdinand but to their daughter, Juana, and her husband, Philip of Austria.

The embittered Ferdinand receded into the role of mere regent, though he remained the King of Aragon. Once again (if temporarily) Castile and Aragon were separate domains. It was to this manipulative, marginalized, jealous, self-absorbed widower that Columbus appealed to restore his privileges and honors. But Ferdinand greeted the Admiral's requests with evasion, delay, and indifference, all clothed in flowery and comfortable words. His focus was on various schemes to have the crown of Castile restored to his head.

"It appears that his Majesty does not think fit to fulfill that which he, with the Queen who is now in glory, promised me by word and seal," Columbus wrote. "For me to contend for the contrary would be to contend with the wind. I have done all that I could do. I leave the rest to God, whom I have ever found propitious to me in my necessities." He died in Valladolid on May 20, 1506.

Only a few months later, in September 1506, Philip of Austria, known as "the Handsome," died abruptly and conveniently. Since Philip's wife, Juana, known as "the Mad," was insane, the Spanish nobles had no choice but to restore Ferdinand to the throne of Castile. For the next ten years, ruling in close association with his inquisitor, Jiménez de Cisneros, Ferdinand presided over the expansion of Spanish sovereignty in the Caribbean and the conquest of various provinces on the North African coast.

But these gains were peripheral to the prophecy that had been laid out for him. When in 1516 he was told he was dying, he protested that this could not possibly be. For, he muttered, he had not fulfilled his destiny as the Bat who would follow the conquest of Granada with the recapture of Jerusalem for Christ.

ACKNOWLEDGMENTS

I think of this book as the last of a quartet, a series of historical works which began with my biography of Galileo, published in 1994, and was followed by *The Last Apocalypse*, the story of Europe at the year A.D. 1000, and *Warriors of God*, my account of the Third Crusade of Richard the Lionheart and Saladin. All four books share some common themes and common methodology. All have focused on stories of ancient and medieval history which have great resonance for the present day, questions of science and faith, of millennial expectations and fears, of clashes between civilizations and faiths. All four books have peered into dark corners of Christian Church history in a time when Christians often divert attention from the history of their own faith by casting aspersions on other great world religions.

Once again I have shuttled between my offices at the Library of Congress and the Woodrow Wilson International Center for Scholars in Washington, D.C., and tapped the superb resources of both institutions. At the Library of Congress, I spent long periods in both the Hispanic and Middle East divisions. Reference librarians Levon Avdoyan, Mary Jane Deeb, Georgette Dorn, Michael Grunberger, David Kelly, Thomas Mann, and Carlos Oleve were, as always, eager to help. Phoebe Peacock did extensive Latin translation for me. Over the three years it has taken me to research and write this book, the Wilson Center, with the good offices of Lee Hamilton, Michael Van Dusen, and Rosemary Lyon, provided me with five diligent and whip-smart interns: Julia Choucair, Kirill Choulga, Courtney Nicolaisen, Morgan Ruthman, and Sarah Trice. Their help was crucial.

In the three research trips I made to Spain and Portugal, I held a number of important discussions with scholars. Especially useful were my talks and communications with Drs. Juan Gil and Consuela Valera in Seville, both experts on the Inquisition and Columbus, and with Dr. Francisco Domingues in Lisbon, an expert on the age of Portuguese discoveries. Their advice led me to new insights and new avenues of inquiry. For these trips I received assistance from Pilar Vico at the Tourist Office of Spain in New York; from the cultural attaché in the Embassy of Portugal in Washington, D.C., Manuel Pereira; and from cultural officers in the U.S. diplomatic service in Madrid and Barcelona: James Nealon, Edward Loo, and Carol Perez. At both the Archivo de las Indias and the Biblioteca Colombina in Seville I was graciously and efficiently received.

Lastly, to my editors at Doubleday: I thank Bill Thomas for his unwavering support and encouragement and Katie Hall for her literary skill and exquisite attention to the manuscript.

For the help of all these individuals and institutions, I am very grateful.

SELECTED BIBLIOGRAPHY

CONTEMPORANEOUS PRIMARY SOURCES

Alvarez Chanca, Diego. *Christopher Columbus's Discoveries in the Testimonials of Diego Alvarez Chanca and Andrés Bernáldes*, trans. Gioacchino Triolo. Rome: Istituto poligrafico e zecca dello stato, Libreria dello stato, 1992.

Anghiera, Pietro Martire d'. *De Orbe Novo, the Eight Decades of Peter Martyr d'Anghiera*, trans. Francis Augustus MacNutt. New York: B. Franklin, 1970.

———. *Selections from Peter Martyr*, ed. and trans. Geoffrey Eatough. Brussels: Brepols, 1998.

Baeza, Hernando de. *Relaciones de algunos sucesos de los últimos tiempos del reino de Granada, que publica la Sociedad de bibliófilos españoles*. Madrid: Impresora de M. Rivadeneyra, 1868.

Bernaldéz, Andrés. *Memorias del Reinado de los Reyes Católicos*. Madrid: Blass Tipográfica, 1962.

Burchard, Johannes. *Pope Alexander and His Court. Extracts from His Diary*, ed. F. L. Glaser. New York: Nicholas L. Brown, 1921.

Colón, Fernando. *The Life of Admiral Christopher Columbus by His Son Ferdinand*, trans. Benjamin Keen. New Brunswick, NJ: Rutgers University Press, 1959.

Columbus, Christopher. *The Voyages of Christopher Columbus, being the journals of his first and third, and the letters concerning his first and last voyages, to which is added the account of his second voyage written by Andrés Bernáldes*, trans. Cecil Jane. London: Argonaut Press, 1930.

———. *Christopher Columbus, his own book of privileges, 1502*, trans. George F. Barwick. London: B. F. Stevens, 1893.

Fita, Fidel. "El Proceso y Quema de Juce Franco," *Boletín de la Real Academia de la Historia*, XI (1887).

Las Casas, Fray Bartolomé. *The Diario of Christopher Columbus's First Voyage to America 1492–1493*. Oklahoma: University of Oklahoma Press, 1989.

Marchant, John. *A Review of the Bloody Tribunal*. London, 1770.

Navarrete, Don Martín Fernández. *Colección de los Viages y Descubrimientos, que Hicieron por Mar los Españoles desde fines del siglo XV*. 2 vols. Madrid: Imprenta Real, 1825.

Palencia, Alonso de. *Crónica de Enrique IV*. 3 vols. Madrid: Ediciones Atlas, 1975.

Pina, Ruy de. *Crónica de El Rei Dom João II*. Coimbra: Atlántida, 1950.

Polo, Marco. *The Travels of Marco Polo [The Venetian]*. New York: Horace Liveright, 1926.

Pulgar, Fernando del. *Crónica de los reyes católicos*. 2 vols. Madrid: Espasa-Colpe, 1943.

Puyol, Julio, ed. *Crónica incompleta de los Reyes Católicos (1469–1476)*. Madrid: Academia de Historia, 1934.

Raphael, David. *The Expulsion 1492 Chronicles: An anthology of medieval chronicles relating to the expulsion of the Jews of Spain and Portugal*. North Hollywood, CA: Carmi House Press, 1992.

Resende, Garcia de. *Chronica de El Rei D. João II*. Lisbon: Mello D'Azevedo, 1902.

Valera, Mosen Diego de. *Crónica de los Reyes Católicos*. Madrid: José Molina, 1927.

———. *Memorial de Diversas Hazañas; Crónica de Enrique IV*. Madrid: Espasa-Colpe, 1941.

Zurita, Jeronimo. *Historia del rey don Hernando el Católico*. Zaragoza: Diputación General de Aragón, Departamento de Cultura y Educación, 1994.

SECONDARY SOURCES

Ali, Syed Ameer. *A Short History of the Saracens*. London: Macmillan and Company, 1924.

Amador de Los Rios, José. *Historia Social, Política y Religiosa de los Judíos de España y Portugal*. 3 vols. Madrid: Ediciones Turner, 1984.

Arnold, Sir Thomas Walker. *The Legacy of Islam*. Oxford: Clarendon Press, 1931.

Axelson, Eric Victor. *Congo to Cape: Early Portuguese Explorers*. Johannesburg: Struik, 1973.

Baer, Yitzhak Fritz. *A History of the Jews in Christian Spain*. 2 vols. Philadelphia: Jewish Publication Society of America, 1961.

Baker, Rev. J. *The History of the Inquisition as it subsists in the Kingdoms of Spain, Portugal, etc, and in both the Indies to this day*. London, 1734.

Barba, Francisco Esteve. *Alfonso Carrillo de Acuña, Autor de la Unidad de España*. Barcelona: Editorial Amaltea, 1943.

Barreto, Mascarenhas. *The Portuguese Columbus: Secret Agent of King John II*. New York: St. Martin's Press, 1992.

Barros, João de. *Asia de João de Barros*. Vol. I. Coimbra, 1930.

Beazley, C. Raymond. *Prince Henry the Navigator: The Hero of Portugal and of Modern Discovery 1394–1460*. London: Frank Caas, 1901.

Bedini, Silvio A., ed. *The Christopher Columbus Encyclopedia*. New York: Simon & Schuster, 1992.

Bedoyere, Michael de la. *The Meddlesome Friar and the Wayward Pope*. Garden City, NY: Hanover House, 1958.

Beinart, Haim. *The Expulsion of the Jews from Spain*. Oxford: Littman Library of Jewish Civilization, 2002.

Brodey, Viviana. *Las Coplas de Mingo Revulgo*. Madison, WI: Hispanic Seminary of Medieval Studies, 1986.

Carillo, Jesús, ed. *Oviedo on Columbus*. Turnhout, Belgium: Brepols, 2000.

Charlevoix, Pierre François Xavier de. *Historia de la Isla Española o de Santo Domingo*. 2 vols. Santo Domingo: Editora de Santo Domingo, 1977.

Chiabrera, Gabriello. *Rime di Gabriello Chiabrera*. Milan: Societa tip. de Classici italiani, 1807.

Clemencín, Diego. *Elogio de la Reina Católica Doña Isabel*. Madrid: I. Sancha, 1821.

Collison-Morley, Lacy. *The Story of the Borgias*. New York: E. P. Dutton, 1933.

Condé, José Antonio. *History of the Dominion of the Arabs in Spain*. 3 vols. London: Henry G. Bohn, 1884.

Corvo, Frederick Baron. *A History of the Borgias*. New York: Modern Library, 1931.

Coulton, George G. *The Inquisition*. London: Ernest Benn, 1929.

Creighton, Mandell. *A History of the Papacy from the Great Schism to the Sack of Rome*. New York: AMS Press, 1969.

Cuartero y Heurta, Baltasar. *El Pacto de los Toros de Guisando y la Venta del Mismo Nombre*. Madrid: C. Bermejo, 1952.

Deagan, Kathleen, and José Maria Cruxent. *Columbus's Outpost Among the Tainos*. New Haven: Yale University Press, 2002.

Domingues, Francisco Contente. *Dicionario de historia dos descobrimentos portugueses*. Lisbon: Caminho, 1994.

Duff, Charles. *The Truth About Columbus and the Discovery of America*. New York: Random House, 1936.

Elliott, J. H. *The Spanish World: Civilization and Empire, Europe and the Americas, Past and Present*. New York: Harry N. Abrams, 1961.

Fernández-Armesto, Felipe. *Ferdinand and Isabella*. London: Weidenfeld & Nicolson, 1975.

Fernández de Oviedo y Valdés, Gonzalo. *The Conquest and Settlement of the Island of Borinquen or Puerto Rico*. Avon, CT: Printed for members of the Limited Edition Club, 1975.

Ford, Richard. *A Hand-Book for Travellers in Spain, and Readers at Home*. London: Centaur Press, 1966.

Frye, John. *Los Otros: Columbus and the Three Who Made His Enterprise of the Indies Succeed*. Lewiston, NY: Edwin Mellen Press, 1992.

Gerber, Jane. *The Jews of Spain*. New York: Free Press, 1992.

Gil, Juan. *Los Conversos y la Inquisición Sevillana*. 2 vols. Seville: Universidad de Sevilla, 2000.

Godrich, Aaron. *A History of the Character and Achievements of the So-Called Christopher Columbus*. New York: Appleton & Co., 1874.

Goldberg, Harriet. *Jardín de Nobles Donzellas, Fray Martín de Córdoba: A Critical Edition and Study*. Valencia: Artes Gráficas Soler, 1974.

Gottfried, Robert. *The Black Death and Human Disaster in Medieval Europe*. New York: Free Press, 1983.

Graetz, H. *History of the Jews*. Vol IV. Philadelphia: Jewish Publications Society of America, 1894.

Gregorovius, Ferdinand. *History of the City of Rome in the Middle Ages*. New York: Italica Press, 2000.

———. *Lucretia Borgia*. New York: D. Appleton & Co., 1903.

Harrington, M. R. *Cuba Before Columbus*. New York: Museum of the American Indian, Heye Foundation, 1921.

Hefele, Karl Joseph. *Life of Cardinal Ximenes*. London: Catholic Publishing and Bookselling Co., 1860.

Hillgarth, J. N. *The Spanish Kingdoms 1250–1516*. 2 vols. Oxford: Clarendon Press, 1978.

Hitti, Philip Khuri. *The Arabs: A Short History*. London: Macmillan, 1968.

Imamuddin, S. M. *A Political History of Muslim Spain*. Karachi, Pakistan: Najmahons, 1984.

Infessura, Stefano. *Diario della città di Roma de Stefano Infessura scribasenato*. Rome: Fonzani, 1890.

Irving, Washington. *The Alhambra*. New York: A.L. Burt Co., 1894.

———. *The Life and Voyages of Christopher Columbus, to which are Added Those of his Companions*. New York: George P. Putnam, 1851.

———. *Conquest of Granada*. New York: A. L. Burt Co., 1900.

Kamen, Henry. *The Spanish Inquisition*. London: Weidenfeld & Nicolson, 1965.

Lafuente Alcántara, Don Miguel. *Historia de Granada, Comprendiendo la de Sus Cuatro Provincias Almería, Jaén, Granada, y Málaga*. 3 vols. Granada: Imprenta y Libreria de Sans, 1843.

Lane-Poole, Stanley. *The Story of Moors in Spain*. New York: Putnam, 1886.

Las Casas, Fray Bartolomé de. *Historia de Las Indias*. 2 vols. Mexico City: Biblioteca Americana, 1951.

———. *History of the Indies*, trans. & ed. Andrée Collard. New York: Harper Torchbooks, 1971.

Lawee, Eric. *Isaac Abarbanel's Stance Toward Tradition*. Albany: State University of New York Press, 2001.

Lea, Henry Charles. *A History of the Inquisition of Spain*. 4 vols. New York: 1887–88, AMS Press, 1966.

———. *The Moriscos of Spain: Their Conversion and Expulsion*. Philadelphia: Lea Brothers & Co., 1901.

Lévi-Provençal, Evariste. *Histoire de l'Espagne musulmane*. Paris: G. P. Maisonneuve & Larose, 1950.

Liss, Peggy K. *Isabel the Queen: Life and Times*. Oxford: Oxford University Press, 1992.

Llorente, Juan Antonio. *A Critical History of the Inquisition of Spain*. Williamstown, MA: John Lilburne Co., 1967.

Longhurst, John B. *The Age of Torquemada*. Lawrence, KA: Coronado Press, 1964.

Lunenfeld, Marvin. *The Council of the Santa Hermandad*. Miami: University of Miami Press, 1970.

MacKay, Angus. *Spain in the Middle Ages: From Frontier to Empire, 1000–1500*. New York: St. Martin's Press, 1977.

Madriaga, Salvador de. *Christopher Columbus: Being the Life of the Very Magnificent Lord Don Cristóbal Colón*. New York: Frederick Ungar, 1940.

Manzano, Juan Manzano. *Cristóbal Colón. Siete años decisivos de su vida, 1485–1492*. Madrid: Ediciones de Cultura Hispánica, 1989.

———. *Los Pinzones y el Descubrimiento de América*. 3 vols. Madrid: Ediciones de Cultura Hispánica, 1988.

———. *Colón y su secreto: El predescubrimiento*. Madrid: Ediciones de Cultura Hispánica, 1989.

Maqqar-I, Ahmad ibn Muhammad. *The History of Mohammedan Dynasties in Spain*. Delhi, India: Idarah-I Adabiyat-I Delli, 1984.

Mariéjol, Jean Hippolyte. *The Spain of Ferdinand and Isabella*. New Brunswick, NJ: Rutgers University Press, 1961.

Mathew, Arnold H. *The Life and Times of Rodrigo Borgia, Pope Alexander VI*. London: Stanley Paul & Co., 1912.

McCabe, Joseph. *The Splendor of Moorish Spain*. London: Watts & Co., 1935.

McNeill, William H. *Plagues and Peoples*. New York: Doubleday, 1976.

Meredith, Robert K. *The Quest of Columbus: a detailed and exact account of the discovery of America, with the many difficulties, dangers, and triumphant return, being the history written by Ferdinand Columbus*. Boston: Little, Brown, 1966.

Merriman, Roger Bigelow. *The Rise of the Spanish Empire in the Old World and in the New.* 2 vols. New York: The Macmillan Company, 1918.

Miller, Townsend. *Henry IV of Castile 1425–1474.* New York: J. B. Lippincott Company, 1972.

Minkin, Jacob S. *Abarbanel and the Expulsion of the Jews from Spain.* New York: Behrman's Jewish Book House, 1938.

Morison, Samuel Eliot. *Admiral of the Ocean Sea: A Life of Christopher Columbus.* Boston: Northeastern University Press, 1983.

———. *Journals and Other Documents on the Life and Voyages of Christopher Columbus.* New York: Limited Edition Club, 1963.

Nader, Helen. *The Mendoza Family in the Spanish Renaissance, 1350–1550.* New Brunswick, NJ: Rutgers University Press, 1979.

Netanyahu, B. *Don Isaac Abravanel: Statesman and Philosopher.* Philadelphia: Jewish Publication Society of America, 1953.

———. *The Marranos of Spain from the Late 14th Century to the Early 16th Century, According to Contemporary Hebrew Sources.* Ithaca, NY: Cornell University Press, 1966.

———. *The Origins of the Inquisition in Fifteenth Century Spain.* New York: Random House, 1995.

Nicholson, Reynold Alleyne. *A Literary History of the Arabs.* New York: Kegan Paul International, 1998.

Ortega y Gasset, José. *Invertebrate Spain.* New York: W. W. Norton & Co., 1937.

Pastor, Ludwig. *The History of the Popes, from the Close of the Middle Ages.* Vol. 4. St. Louis: B. Herder, 1898.

Peréz de Hita, Ginés. *The Civil Wars of Granada.* London: Thomas Ostell, 1803.

Phillips, William D., Jr. *Enrique IV and the Crisis of Fifteenth Century Castile 1425–1480.* Cambridge, MA: Medieval Academy of America, 1978.

Pike, Ruth. *Enterprise and Adventure: The Genoese in Seville and the Opening of the New World.* Ithaca, NY: Cornell University Press, 1966.

Plaidy, Jean. *The Spanish Inquisition: Its Rise, Growth, and End.* New York: Citadel Press, 1967.

Prescott, William H. *The Art of War in Spain: The Conquest of Granada 1481–1492.* London: Greenhill Books, 1995.

———. *History of the Reign of Ferdinand and Isabella, the Catholic.* 3 vols. Philadelphia: J. B. Lippincott & Co., 1864.

Pulgar, Fernando del. *Claros Varones de Castilla.* Oxford: Oxford University Press, 1971.

Quesada, Miguel Angel Ladero. *La España de los Reyes Católicos.* Madrid: Alianza Editorial, 1999.

————. *La Guerra de Granada 1482–1491*. Granada: Diputación de Granada, 2001.

Rahferling, Meyer. *Juden in Portugal*. Leipzig: Ostar Liener, 1867.

Ramírez, Jerónimo. *De Raptv innocentis martyris guardiensi. Libri sex*. Madrid, 1592.

Randles, W. G. L. *The Unmaking of the Medieval Christian Cosmos, 1500–1760*. Brookfield, VT: Ashgate, 1999.

Ranke, Leopold. *The History of the Popes, the Church and State, and Especially of Their Conflicts with Protestantism in the Sixteenth and Seventeenth Centuries*. London: George Bell & Sons, 1886.

Rodd, Thomas, trans. *The Civil Wars of Granada and the History of the Factions of the Zegries and Abencerrages, two Noble Families of that City, to the Final Conquest by Ferdinand and Isabella*. London: Thomas Ostell, 1803.

Rogers, Col. H. C. B. *Artillery Through the Ages*. London: Seeley Service & Co., 1971.

Rolfe, Frederick. *Chronicles of the House of Borgia*. New York: Dover Publications, 1962.

Russell, P. E. *Portugal, Spain, and the African Atlantic, 1343–1490; Chivalry and Crusade from John of Gaunt to Henry the Navigator*. Brookfield, VT: Variorum, 1995.

————. *Prince Henry "the Navigator": A Life*. New Haven: Yale University Press, 2000.

Sanceau, Elaine. *The Perfect Prince: A Biography of the King Dom João II*. Porto: Companhia Editora do Minho, 1959.

Stannard, David. E. *American Holocaust: Columbus and the Conquest of the New World*. Oxford: Oxford University Press, 1992.

Thomson, Ahmad. *Blood on the Cross: Islam in Spain in the Light of Christian Persecution Through the Ages*. London: Tatla Publishers, 1989.

Tommasini, Oreste. *Diario della città di Roma di Stefano Inefessura Scribasenato*. Rome: Forzani E. E. Tiopgrafi del Senato, 1890.

Trachtenberg, Joshua. *The Devil and the Jews*. New York: Harper & Row, 1943.

Treen, María de Freitas. *The Admiral and His Lady: Columbus and Filipa of Portugal*. New York: Robert Speller & Sons, 1989.

Vigón, Jorge. *Historia de la Artillería Española*. Madrid: Instituto Jerónimo Zurita, 1947.

Villari, Pasquale. *Life and Times of Girolamo Savonarola*. 2 vols. London: T. Fisher Unwin, 1888.

Villon, François. *Complete Poems*, ed. Barbara N. Sargent-Baur. Toronto: University of Toronto Press, 1994.

Walsh, William Thomas. *Characters of the Inquisition*. Port Washington, NY: Kennikat Press, 1940.

Yerushalmi, Yosef Hayim. *The Lisbon Massacre of 1506 and the Royal Image in the Shebet Yehudah*. Cincinnati: Hebrew Union College, Annual Supplement, #1, 1976.

Ziegler, Philip. *The Black Death*. London: Collins, 1969.

INDEX

Printed in the United States
by Baker & Taylor Publisher Services